A Guide to
Vocational Assessment

A Guide to
Vocational
Assessment

FIFTH EDITION

Paul W. Power

An International Publisher

8700 Shoal Creek Boulevard
Austin, Texas 78757
800/897-3202   Fax: 800/397-7633
www.proedinc.com

An International Publisher

© 2013, 2006, 2000, 1991, 1984 by PRO-ED, Inc.
8700 Shoal Creek Boulevard
Austin, Texas 78757-6897
800/897-3202 Fax 800/397-7633
www.proedinc.com

Library of Congress Cataloging-in-Publication Data

Power, Paul W.
   A guide to vocational assessment / Paul W. Power—5th ed.
      p. cm.
   Includes bibliographical references and index.
   ISBN: 978-1-4164-0541-2
   1. Vocational rehabilitation. 2. Disability evaluation. 3. Vocational
evaluation. I. Title.
   HD7255.P68 2013
   362.4'0484—dc23

                                        2012010967

Art director: Jason Crosier
Designer: Lissa Hattersley
This book was designed in Minion and Myriad Pro.

Printed in the United States of America
5 6 7 8 9 10   21 20 19

This revised edition is dedicated to all professionals who are working to make a unique impact on the career journey of those with disabilities by also emphasizing positive-directed vocational assessment.

∾

Contents

# Preface

The revised fifth edition of *A Guide to Vocational Assessment* responds to the challenges of the 21st-century labor market offered to persons with significant mental or physical disabilities. This fifth edition strongly affirms the continuing efforts by rehabilitation professionals to change the traditional manner in which vocational assessment is conducted. It is my belief that several practices prevalent in evaluation badly underserve a significant group of those with physical and mental disabilities, and particularly those from diverse ethnic backgrounds. Many of these practices are delivered in an academic or institutional context and often offer a rather narrow view of human career potential. Though these environments have generally responded diligently to the assessment needs of those with disabilities, the evaluation programs frequently rely on the centrality of standardized paper-and-pencil measures. Consequently, often the assessment results offer an incomplete picture of the actual capabilities, strengths, and career opportunities of the consumer. A more embracing knowledge of those with disabilities that includes a comprehensive framework is needed to assist this population on their career journeys.

The question is asked: Will those with significant disabilities be able to compete successfully for appropriate jobs in this 21st century, which is characterized by global integration and rapid technological changes? They can, if the vocational evaluation process identifies a wider scope of career potential and suggests the possible development of marketable skills, even specialized abilities. Specifically, this volume contributes to a larger understanding of human potential by reexamining historical evaluation approaches and explaining newer strategies.

The sweeping arms of globalization and changes in social and economic systems are further contributory factors that make it decidedly difficult for adults, especially those with disabilities, to compete successfully today for long-term, stable employment. This edition of *A Guide to Vocational Assessment* acknowledges these modern phenomena, again presumes that many traditional assessment approaches are not appropriate for the modern job or career seeker, and suggests multiple evaluation approaches and insights that can be utilized to change the difficult to the possible and, eventually, to the probable. While many of this book's chapters underscore the utilization of traditional evaluation approaches, other chapters operationalize my added belief that vocational assessment is an individualized, creative, empowering, holistic process and experience of self-discovery. This edition's 15 chapters incorporate these issues, build on information explained in earlier editions, offer new material, and emphasize that the process of evaluation should identify the consumer's career-related strengths and potential to acquire specific skills. Today's worker with a disability must have these specialized skills to even be considered for productive employment.

Although 9 of the 15 chapter titles basically remain the same, the information in these chapters has been selectively revised from the fourth edition, with updated, expanded material, and, in some instances, reorganized for enhanced reader clarity. The other 6 chapters have been redesigned or redeveloped from the earlier edition. One of these chapters, Chapter 13, focuses exclusively on the transition-aged student, a topic receiving increased attention in vocational rehabilitation. Explained in this chapter is how more current research and practice have suggested newer, evaluation-related insights that can facilitate a more successful transition. Moreover, all of the chapters together contain more than 100 new references. All-new case examples have also been introduced for Chapter 3, and there are new case studies for each of the workbook's 15 chapters.

The workbook is intended, as it was in the fourth edition, for use with the text. Each chapter of the workbook provides discussion questions and exercises. This material has been selectively changed and reformulated to correspond to the respective chapter topic in the text. There are three new forms in the appendix that illustrate the information in Chapters 12 and 15. Of particular importance is the addition of a Suggested Format for the Vocational Assessment Report (see the Appendix and the forms located on the CD-ROM).

With these new features of the revised, fifth edition, this volume offers the perspective that rehabilitation agency expectations usually demand that assessment be conducted in a short period of time. The information explained in several chapters, highlighting self-assessment methods and many nonstandardized and standardized measures, responds to the briefer time period. Another perspective states that the process of vocational evaluation offers assessment options to both the professional and the consumer. If the evaluation process is going to be relevant and appropriate to the needs of diverse populations with disabilities, then various approaches to consumer self-understanding should be available. This edition continues and reemphasizes the substantive theme of earlier editions that assessment choice and different methods are necessary if the evaluation process is to be responsive to this population's employment or career demands, and the changing 21st-century employment realities. Adaptability of assessment approaches is a further consideration in several of this edition's chapters, highlighting the needs of ethnic minorities and those with disabilities.

Vocational assessment is the foundational step toward consumers' becoming aware that they possess many of the capabilities required to achieve job marketability. Today, workers are seeking personal meaning and satisfaction in employment and career pursuits. Providing an empowering experience for the consumer during career development opportunities contributes to this personal fulfillment. The different approaches included in the process of vocational assessment, and again emphasized in this revised, fifth edition, represent empowering activities. In turn, such involvement and assumption of responsibility help the consumer in the process of self-discovery and of acquiring skills for competing successfully in career areas of the 21st century.

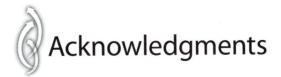# Acknowledgments

This new edition of *A Guide to Vocational Assessment* represents the generous efforts of several people who contributed their expertise and time to its development. First, I wish to thank my wife, Barbara, who not only assisted me in the preparation of the manuscript but also kept me on course during many life distractions. The book became an expression of her continued, accomplished assistance and of our editorial partnership. To Becky Shore of PRO-ED, Inc., who was a pleasure to work with, my gratitude. This revision is so much better because of her guidance, encouragement, and insightful changes through the manuscript phase. And my special acknowledgment and appreciation to Susan Emery and George Peterson, Vocational Evaluators in the state of New Hampshire, for their review and invaluable feedback during the development of Chapter 13. They are dedicated professionals who make a difference with their consumers with disabilities.

 Introduction

This book initially discusses the definition of disability, which, in turn, establishes a foundation for responding to the consumer's needs and developing the different approaches to be utilized in vocational assessment. This foundation consists of (a) a 21st-century concept of disability and the meaning of vocational rehabilitation, (b) historical themes and current trends in vocational rehabilitation assessment practice, (c) conceptualization and target areas of vocational evaluation, (d) a philosophy of assessment as a base for everyday practice, (e) the roles of the counselor during vocational assessment, and (f) expected evaluator competencies for vocational assessment. Each of these areas is discussed in this introduction.

Twenty-First-Century Concept of Disability and the Meaning of Vocational Rehabilitation

In the 21st century, an understanding of the current dynamics of vocational rehabilitation begins with a brief analysis of the term *disability* and its implications for service delivery. The conceptual meaning of disability has been shaped by historical intervention approaches, language, politics, institutions, and sociocultural practices (Thomas, Curtis, & Shippen, 2011). Until the past two decades, the concept of disability was heavily influenced by the medical model. This model affirms that disability is a personal aspect that can be evaluated and defined or diagnosed, and is the focus of health-care intervention.

Though this model is still influential in service delivery practices, since 1995 more attention has been given to the manifestation of disability or impairment within the environment. Emphasizing the concept of disability as an interactive factor, Maki and Riggar (1997) defined rehabilitation as "a holistic, comprehensive and integrated program of medical, physical, psycho-social, and vocational interventions that empower a person with a disability to achieve a personally fulfilling, socially meaningful and functionally effective intervention with the world" (p. 615).

It is now believed, consequently, that the environment is a major determinant of individual functioning as well as of one's rehabilitation (McCarthy, 2010; Mpofu & Oakland, 2010). Several sources (Hurst, 2003; Smart, 2005; World Health Organization [WHO], 2001) have proposed that disability is a social construct and is influenced by both personal and contextual factors. Personal factors include internal influences of functioning and disability, such as body structures and changes in functioning, individual activities and task participation, coping styles, education, lifestyle, health conditions, overall behavior patterns, gender, race, age, and past and current experience. Contextual factors embrace such external, environmental factors as prevailing attitudes toward disability, access to transportation, systems, policies, available services, support and relationships, products and technology, human-made changes to the environment, and other features of the physical, social, and attitudinal world (WHO, 2001).

If we accept that environment is a major determinant of individual functioning (Mpofu & Oakland, 2010), then we can understand rehabilitation as an intervention that integrates diagnostic information (medical and psychological) with psychosocial aspects of life (e.g., personality traits, coping abilities, stress, social support, environmental barriers), giving equal consideration to all factors impacting the person's vocational adjustment (Elliott, Kurylo, & Rivera, 2002). Rehabilitation planning identifies a person's strengths, builds on residual capacities, and is based on both productive output and productive living. Rehabilitation is no longer tied to manpower needs. As a result of this perspective, rehabilitation efforts are devoted to helping consumers with disabilities become more productive until they are able to function adequately in different settings. Although vocational goals are still most important in rehabilitation, other functional outcomes are also emphasized. These can be activities the consumer engages in on a regular basis and that require the use of time, strength, and mental or physical faculties. Such activities might be, for example, sheltered employment (transitional or long-term, homebound employment), self-employment, employment by others, volunteer work, or programmed day tasks.

The rehabilitation process is a form of social technology that assists consumers as they make the transition from patient to rehabilitant. The traditional rehabilitant was often characterized as being dependent and passive ("You do it for me"), whereas current rehabilitant behavior emphasizes initiating and participating, with a dominant focus on residual strengths and capabilities. If individuals with disabilities are to achieve functional outcomes, they must become rehabilitants. In other words, the rehabilitation process should help consumers to become empowered, as well as to assume more responsibility for achieving appropriate living goals. This task depends not only on the person's ego strength, the attitude of family members toward rehabilitation, and the degree to which rehabilitation programs meet specific needs, but also on the quality and extent of the assessment early in the rehabilitation process. An evaluation that reaches out to involve the consumer in rehabilitation planning, emphasizing what the person can do, rather than the extent of his or her limitations, will considerably facilitate the consumer's achievement of worthwhile rehabilitation goals. Assessment, then, is a dynamic of the rehabilitation process as well as an integral part of the consumer's rehabilitation.

In line with the current conceptualization of disability and rehabilitation, vocational assessment should include a multifactorial approach, which promotes the examination of a wide variety of consumer characteristics. Intervention decisions in rehabilitation should not be based on a single attribute, such as educational or work achievement. Other factors (e.g., family network, adjustment style to disability, social relationships) can be included to learn how an individual is going to adjust to work or similar productive situations. A more comprehensive exploration, then, demands both the broadening of the rehabilitation professional's knowledge of evaluation approaches and the integration of the consumer's interests, abilities, and other personality characteristics. Vocational evaluation information, consequently, should be verified by using different methods, tools, and approaches. Using alternative methods to validate findings can often be achieved by (a) observing an individual's demonstrated behaviors, (b) using an individual's self-report or expressed statements, and (c) administering some type of survey, inventory, structured interview, or test.

In summary, when identifying barriers to and facilitators of the consumer's overall life adjustment, professionals now recognize the environment as one of the key ingredients of vocational potential. An understanding of factors such as external support resources and attitudes, expectations, and demands from the family, neighborhood, and workplace is important for the consumer's rehabilitation adjustment. It may be not the individual's disability but the handicapping conditions in his or her environment that actually prevent career and employment adjustment. For the consumer's successful adjustment, environmental characteristics may have to be adapted to the person's unique abilities and limitations.

Historical Themes and Current Trends in Vocational Rehabilitation Assessment Practices

The history of vocational rehabilitation is characterized by recurring legislative mandates, the changing focus and expansion of eligible populations for rehabilitation service delivery, and the development of service methodologies fueled by labor market changes and technological advances. Added to these factors are the growth of professionalism within the rehabilitation and vocational evaluation fields, and philosophical changes emerging from the implementation of needs and labor market developments. Since 1920, federal legislation authorizing vocational and related educational services has grown from a small, temporary program for persons with physical disabilities to a broad army of programs serving persons with physical, mental, or emotional difficulties.

Pruitt (1986) explained that vocational evaluation emerged from the vocational rehabilitation field and borrowed heavily from many other fields, including education, clinical and industrial psychology, and counseling. But the directives of federal legislation authorized the expansion of rehabilitation facilities, thus facilitating the development of assessment approaches within, for example, sheltered workshops. Rehabilitation laws also focused attention on students with disabilities, those with severe disabilities, and other populations that had not been served.

Specific historical events, such as the expansion of supported work and the initiation of job coaching services, the development of commercial work samples, the growth of the private for-profit sector of vocational rehabilitation, the Rehabilitation Act of 1973, and the Americans with Disabilities Act of 1990, have influenced evaluation services. The numbers of sites where assessment practices could be implemented grew, and technology was incorporated into the evaluation process. These developments increased interest in vocational evaluation that is directed to environmental and situational factors, that is, the consumer's family situation, employer and co-worker attitudes, accessibility, and community issues, which include transportation, local economy, housing, and training opportunities. Specific trends emerged that influence the way vocational assessment is conducted. These trends, the implications of which will be discussed in the chapters of this book, are the following:

- A team approach to the vocational evaluation process is becoming increasingly prevalent. Input is invited from medical and allied health professionals regarding the functional abilities of the consumer. Physicians, nurses, physical and occupational therapists, social workers, and psychologists may provide valuable information that can be integrated into rehabilitation planning. An interdisciplinary team approach allows for the effective use of information that can be translated into effective planning, implementation activities (e.g., placements, support services), and vocational development for consumers (Interdisciplinary Council, 1994).
- A focus on discrimination practices, especially in the areas of pre-employment testing and screening, widens the scope of rehabilitation. The Americans with Disabilities Act of 1990 (ADA), and the reauthorization legislation of this act, have addressed potential areas of discrimination, mandated when employment testing should be done, and described how testing must relate to the essential functions of the job. Title I of the ADA organizes the types of testing accommodations under three broad categories: testing medium, time limits, and test content (Bruyere & O'Keefe, 1994). Special accommodations for those with the specific disabilities of visual, hearing, and orthopedic impairments are also mandated.
- Increased attention is given to the development of more appropriate assessment approaches for different ethnic and minority groups. These populations have been underserved, and most traditional evaluation methods involve standardization data that are not relevant to specific groups in a community. Furthermore, many

psychological tests contain selection bias—namely, the test may have different predictive validities across groups. The fact that a test predicts the achievement of one selected population does not mean that it predicts the achievement of another group, and assuming that it does so can result in content bias. In addition, the factor structure of a test may not be internally consistent (Walsh & Betz, 1995). Criterion-referenced measurement, consequently, is increasingly becoming the assessment of choice for many evaluators. A criterion-referenced test is one in which scores are expressed in terms of the behaviors or skills achieved, rather than in terms of a comparison with other people.

- To affirm the dignity and worth of all people, rehabilitation emphasizes consumer empowerment and the holistic nature of people. Consumer empowerment, which will be explained in Chapter 1, is an important focus when planning a vocational assessment approach. This holistic concept, moreover, includes nurturing the assumption that individuals with disabilities should be treated as persons with unique skills, residual capacities, functional limitations, and resources who interact with many life systems, with a particular emphasis on family and culture. Within these systems the mental and physical strengths of the person, and the resources of the environment, are emphasized. The focus is on accommodation and adaptation from an environmental perspective (Maki & Riggar, 2003).

- Assistive technology has been developed to help persons with disabilities in the areas of education, personal mobility, communication, recreation and leisure, and independent living. This technology has also helped to make the assessment process more available to those with severe disabilities. The use of adaptive devices should occur early in the assessment process to minimize consumer limitations.

- Shorter time periods are encouraged, when appropriate, for vocational assessment, to allow for achievement of goals in both the public and private sectors of rehabilitation agencies. Though a brief time span is not always desirable, especially for those with a severe disability, it may be necessary for efficient career planning.

- The rehabilitation process for most consumers is now being viewed as developmental (leading to a career) rather than static (completed once an entry-level job is secured). The medical course of certain disabilities, such as head injury and related neurological conditions, necessitates updated feedback on vocational planning, because conditions may change. Also, consumers move through different developmental stages, and consumer growth during these phases may demand more current information on the consumer's life adjustment and work-related capabilities.

- Within the field of appraisal there is a gradual shift from psychometric to edumetric models. These models concentrate on consumers' achievements relative to themselves rather than others, emphasize the professional and consumer working together to gather relevant information and examine it together, and do not isolate the consumer by scores and trait-and-factor analysis (Tymofienich & Leroux, 2000).

- Self-assessment strategies are becoming more commonplace in vocational rehabilitation practice. Due to the budget reductions that cause many states to eliminate central vocational assessment centers, rehabilitation counselors encourage consumers to take an active role in evaluating their interests, abilities, vocational options, and other aspects of themselves and the world of work. Self-administered interest inventories, values card sort, decision-making worksheets, career-information delivery systems, career-planning workbooks, and community-based assessment are slowly replacing standardized tests and inventories (Koch & Merz, 2001).

Conceptualization and Target Areas of Vocational Evaluation

The official definition of vocational evaluation was developed by the Vocational Evaluation and Work Adjustment Association (VEWAA):

> a comprehensive process that systemically uses work, either real or simulated, as the focal point for assessment and vocational exploration, the purpose of which is to assist individuals with vocational development. Vocational evaluation incorporates medical, psychological, social, vocational, educational, cultural, and economic data into the process to attain the goals of evaluation. (Dowd, 1993, p. 28)

This process refers to the data collection methods, usually formal assessment approaches and standardized testing, used to gather information about individual interests, abilities, and aptitudes in order to provide information to help these individuals gain insight about their vocational potential (Rojewski, 2002). Evaluation is a method of acquiring information and a process for helping individuals identify their functional competencies and disabilities. It evaluates factors such as vocational strengths and weaknesses, which can be assessed in the areas of personality, aptitude, interest, work habits, physical tolerance, and dexterity. Assessment is also prognostic because it attempts to answer questions such as whether a consumer will be able to work, or what kind of productive activity the individual will be able to do. An added evaluation goal is to identify the services needed to overcome functional disabilities that are barriers to successful performance.

Testing and *assessment* can be viewed as two, at times almost distinct, terms. Although both words convey the meaning that data are collected about persons, a test is a measuring device or procedure designed to identify specific variables about a consumer. Assessment is a more comprehensive process that typically extends beyond obtaining a number to reflect the strength or absence, for example, of a personality trait. The interview can be an assessment tool; the *Sixteen Personality Factor Questionnaire* (Cattell, 1986) is a career-related test. Psychometric tests usually just add up the number of correct answers or the number of certain types of responses or performances, whereas assessment is often more interested in how the individual functions, rather than simply the results of the functioning. If the counselor wishes to explore the consumer's ability to function in a work environment, the term *assessment* would be preferable to *testing* (Cohen, Swerdlik, & Phillips, 1996).

The process of rehabilitation assessment, therefore, is mainly one of diagnosis and prediction, helping both professionals and the consumer to gain information concerning promising directions for consumer development. Vocational evaluation can be conducted over varying lengths of time, depending on whether it is an itemized assessment, an exploratory assessment, a community-based assessment, or a comprehensive career assessment. Each direction determines the amount of time required for the evaluation process.

When planning an assessment approach for individuals with disabilities, Leconte, Castleberry, King, and West (1995) and Smith et al.

(1995) believed that three core principles should guide this planning process: humanistic, therapeutic, and holistic. A humanistic approach emphasizes both the individual's uniqueness and attention to personal needs and situations; a therapeutic evaluation aims to reduce anxiety and encourages growth by providing many opportunities for self-discovery and learning about the world of work; and a holistic approach targets an entire person in all relevant environments, such as home, community living, and social and interpersonal relationships (Rojewski, 2002). The process of vocational assessment can be understood from a systematic structure of six designated steps, as identified in the following table and discussed in various chapters of the text.

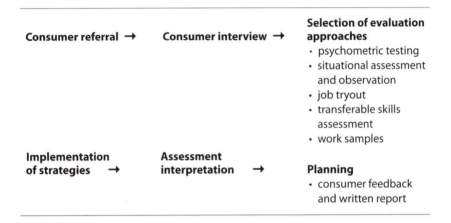

Consumer referral →	Consumer interview →	Selection of evaluation approaches • psychometric testing • situational assessment and observation • job tryout • transferable skills assessment • work samples
Implementation of strategies →	Assessment interpretation →	Planning • consumer feedback and written report

Evaluation can generate a course of action for individuals with disabilities that may range from competitive employment to effective, productive activity in their own homes. Evaluation and constructive feedback can also be the way to engage individuals in the rehabilitation process, as well as an effective approach for identifying needed services.

In this process of vocational assessment, the word *comprehensive* is emphasized, for evaluation incorporates medical, psychological, social, vocational, educational, cultural, and economic data. When exploring a person's capabilities, the helping professional seeks information on such broad consumer characteristics as work interest, general intelligence, values, needs, transferable skills, physical capacity, work tolerance, and special aptitudes. Obtaining this information often requires the involvement of professionals or experts in several disciplines.

The results of assessment approaches, moreover, should be considered as one piece of data that the consumer and the evaluator use as the consumer weighs vocational rehabilitation options. Many other sources of data should be used, including the consumer's self-knowledge and past educational and vocational experience. Credible predictions about employment opportunities must be further considered (Niles & Harris-Bowlsbey, 2005).

Information in rehabilitation assessment can be obtained both formally and informally. Informal assessment includes observing a person's behavior in a variety of situations, conversing with the consumer, or getting information about the consumer from other sources. Informal assessment is characterized by a lack of standardization and usually does not have validity or reliability data. Informal assessment would include reviews of social histories, checklists, forced-choice activities, card sorts, structured interviews, observations, and rating scales (Niles & Harris-Bowlsbey, 2005; Rojewski, 2002). Formal assessment includes such processes as the structured interview, mental testing (e.g., intelligence, aptitude, ability, personality, and interest tests), selected work samples, and job analyses. These formal assessments usually include standardized instruments and procedures that have been norm referenced, contain validity and reliability data, and provide detailed administrative and scoring information.

The choice of an approach depends on the objectives for the assessment. No single one of these methods can do everything because each deals with a specific, limited element of a multifaceted problem. Each approach provides optimal information for planning.

The interview approach is a person-to-person experience in which the professional obtains information relevant to rehabilitation goals. It can follow a structured or unstructured format and is a way for the consumer to learn about his or her own strengths and weaknesses as well as to recognize those abilities and aptitudes that may facilitate or mitigate against training demands. The interview is often the most useful way for many consumers with severe disabilities to learn the information needed for rehabilitation planning.

Psychometric tests have been used in assessment for many decades and are usually easy and relatively inexpensive to administer. Their validity with people with disabilities and handicaps, however, can be questioned. Testing accommodations may have to be made that can compromise the standardization data and the accuracy of measured results.

Psychological testing used as pre-employment screening is not permitted under ADA. Most tests were normed on populations other than people with disabilities, and in a rapidly changing labor force, future job applicants may have characteristics very different from those that typified the standardization sample. An additional concern is that tests may be overemphasized, overgeneralized, and erroneously viewed as evaluating the worth of people and their likelihood for future success (Cohen et al., 1996). It is also important to note that there are crucial differences between the demands of the test situation and the demands of the work or production situation (Neff, 1966). For example, in the test situation, attention, concentration, and motivation are maximized and under continuous control, while in the work situation these variables truly vary and are under limited control. Even with these caveats, tests are widely used and can provide some very useful information for rehabilitation assessment purposes.

Work samples are close simulations of actual industrial operations that are no different in their essentials from required operations on the job. Tentative predictions about future performance can be made based on performance on a work sample. This approach has a strong reality orientation and provides an opportunity to observe actual work behavior in a reasonably controlled situation. There are still unresolved problems of reliability and validity, however, and uncertainty as to the predictive efficiency of work samples.

The job analysis approach focuses on a description of the work to be performed, rather than on the worker's characteristics. The work or task is observed carefully, and detailed descriptions are written on what can be very complex activities. Although this method of assessment can be overanalytical, it is important to understand the detailed set of job requirements for a person whose potential for work is being evaluated. In the 1980s, job analysis techniques were used by rehabilitation personnel and employers to screen out applicants. The focus of the 1990s and beyond, however, has been a means to determine ways in which persons with disabilities can work.

In the situational assessment method, one of the most frequently used in vocational evaluation, an effort is made to simulate actual working conditions. The main orientation of the situation assessment is toward work behavior in general. It asks questions such as, "Can this person work? Can he or she get along with co-workers? How does this person work most effectively? What are his or her strengths and weaknesses as a worker?" The dual focus is on the exploration of consumer skills and consumer behavior in a work situation.

One of the oldest of the vocational assessment approaches, and the least popular among vocational evaluators, is job tryout. The individual is placed into an actual employment situation that includes pay on a fixed or variable scale, competition with other employees, the construction of the product, and environmental factors (noise, the attitudes of others, work pressures). The assessment is usually for a specific job or job segment, and if the individual performs satisfactorily, he or she is typically employed in the same job situation (Sankovsky, 1969).

A Philosophy of Assessment as a Base for Everyday Practice

Approaches to effective assessment must be developed not only from acquired knowledge and continued experience but also from a personal philosophy that embodies strong convictions about helping consumers with disabilities. These convictions provide a direction to evaluation and represent assumptions that, in turn, generate attitudes toward how assessment will be performed. Often, the professional's attitudes regarding the assessment situation and the consumer are more important than the content of the assessment. I have identified an assessment philosophy that has been formulated from working with consumers of varied disability conditions and from current trends in rehabilitation practice. The central issues of an individual philosophy of vocational assessment are as follows:

- Assessment should be integrated into the counseling process and the continuous interaction that takes place in rehabilitation between the professional and the consumer (Chope, 2008). In other words, vocational assessment should be part of larger service delivery systems. Often, consumers have the expectation that they must place themselves completely into the helping professional's hands to find answers to finding a job or obtaining suitable training. This belief is expressed in statements such as, "I will put all the responsibility on you, and when you are through, you will be better able to tell me what I should do." If consumers are to feel better about themselves, they have to feel some sense of autonomy and control over their futures. When vocational evaluation is integrated into the counseling process, consumers are helped to identify and understand the attitudes and feelings about themselves that militate against successful living and employment. Such involvement implies that the consumer is given more responsibility for developing rehabilitation goals. In counseling and vocational evaluation, limitations are recognized. More important, strengths that can be used for productive living can be discovered.

- Assessment occurs at many different levels in rehabilitation practice, and its results provide the foundation for overall vocational rehabilitation planning. At particular times during the rehabilitation process, these results can indicate specifically what action should be taken to meet a person's needs (Berven, 1997).

- During the vocational process, rehabilitation professionals must evaluate not only general employability factors (i.e., work habits, physical tolerance, intellectual and achievement levels of functioning, and the ability to learn) but also the consumer's socio-emotional competence. The current conceptualization of disability implies that the evaluator should identify the factors that enable the consumer to manage effectively his or her daily interactions with the environment, such as coping with prejudicial attitudes and utilizing community resources. An individual's constellation of attitudes and behaviors may be more influential in determining future success than other work-related factors. People lose jobs primarily because of deficiencies in work behavior and not because of skill deficits. For example, mental functioning should not be considered in isolation but must be weighed with the person's motivational and personality structure. Assessment should comprise the social and cultural factors that have an impact on either achievement functioning or training. The individual's likelihood of succeeding at future tasks is often based on personal attributes, such as coping style, motivation, relationship to others, understanding of self, manner of adjustment to disability, and ability to profit from experience, all of which have known predictive ability.

- Persons with disabilities frequently magnify partial inadequacy into a completely negative view of themselves. The helping professional should conscientiously use esteem-enhancing efforts during assessment, particularly in the initial interview. The goal of the assessment process is to diagnose and to seize opportunities for giving positive feedback to consumers. Such information can help individuals with disabilities achieve a renewed understanding of themselves as well as help them identify personal capabilities they can use to generate productive outcomes.

- As much as possible, the assessment process should be tailored to the consumer's individual needs and specific rehabilitation goals. As Cohen et al. (1996) pointed out, the evaluator should reflect on such questions as, "What information is needed? Does it seem likely that assessment can provide important information that is not available from other sources? What questions can be answered by assessment?" and "How will this consumer respond to or be affected by testing?"

- What is good for the agency is not necessarily beneficial for the consumer. The dimensions of vocational rehabilitation expanded in the 1990s and beyond to include goals that make up transitional employment or more productive use of leisure time. Often, the agency has the view that unless a consumer can meet traditional employment demands, assessment is not going to be valuable. Broader expectations for the consumer could possibly generate a more helpful attitude during assessment.

Roles of the Counselor During Vocational Assessment

This book is directed mainly at rehabilitation professionals and students in human services; its purpose is to help them develop basic vocational and rehabilitation skills or update their existing knowledge of consumer evaluation. Although many practitioners may believe that an early diagnosis of consumer strengths and work-related limitations is necessary, assessment does not make up a large part of their job duties unless they have been specifically trained as vocational evaluators. Fortunately, many allied health professionals are trained in diagnostic skills, which can be applied to exploring vocational goals.

For the rehabilitation counselor, the amount of time that can be devoted to this task of evaluation varies. Other case management functions are quite time-consuming. For professional and philosophical reasons that influence job responsibilities, counselors might hesitate to become involved in assessment tasks. Arguments about the role and function of the rehabilitation counselor have been going on for many years. Roessler and Rubin (2006) identified several studies that describe how rehabilitation counselors spend their time or view their jobs. The majority of time seems to be spent in recording, report writing, clerical work, counseling, and guidance (Rubin & Emener, 1979; Zadny & James, 1977). All the research reports suggest that the rehabilitation counselor has a diverse job role (Rubin & Emener, 1979; Wright & Fraser, 1976).

When rehabilitation professionals begin to evaluate either the consumer's eligibility for services or his or her capabilities for work-oriented productivity, they assume certain roles that will have an impact on the consumer. Each role conveys specific responsibilities. One of the primary responsibilities is to be a communicator, namely, someone who can establish a helping, interpersonal relationship with the consumer. This relationship should transmit empathy, trust, and the conviction that the rehabilitation professional is very willing to listen to the consumer's viewpoint and needs. If such a relationship is established, then, generally, the consumer will respond readily by providing needed information that relates to the building of a rehabilitation plan.

The rehabilitation professional is also a provider of information. Feedback to consumers should usually focus on what they *can* do, given the limitations of the disabilities, and not on what they *cannot* do. Each evaluation approach should be used to help consumers understand their remaining strengths and how these strengths can be used either in the work sector or in avocational activities.

Another necessary role of the rehabilitation professional is that of reinforcer. In attempting to cope with their disabilities, consumers face many frustrations and setbacks. The reality of perceived failure could be an everyday occurrence. These perceptions and disappointments lower consumers' self-concepts and contribute to their belief that there is probably not much opportunity to become a wage earner. The helping professional should take every chance during assessment to provide some needed feedback on the consumer's capabilities. For example, when a person with a disability reveals how a certain adaptation problem was handled, the professional should give needed support and, even if the adaptive attempt failed, should compliment consumers on the courage to discuss a disappointing experience.

Of course, one of the primary responsibilities during assessment is to be an evaluator—to know how to diagnose and then make predictive statements about rehabilitation outcomes. This role necessitates a comprehensive knowledge of diagnostic approaches and, more concisely, presumes that the helping professional understands human nature. The evaluator's role also demands knowledge of technology in such areas as adaptive devices. This knowledge includes the ability to select for each consumer the appropriate simulated experiences and specialized tests, as well as critical behaviors to be observed. Skills in rating and using observed behaviors to make recommendations for training and placement are also required (Vander Kolk, 1995). All of this information is acquired not only via standardized approaches to psychometric testing but also through the professional's intuition, willingness to listen to what consumers are saying, and understanding of what it means to experience a disability.

The National Seminar on Competency-Based Rehabilitation Education in Atlanta in July 1978 indicated that rehabilitation counselors, as well as vocational evaluators, must be capable of developing a systematic evaluation plan and writing useful evaluation reports (Rubin & Porter, 1979). Roessler and Rubin (2006) believed that counselors must be able to "manage" a comprehensive medical, psychological, and vocational evaluation of the consumer. The Interdisciplinary Council on Vocational Evaluation/Assessment reiterates the idea that assessment information should be verified by using different methods, tools, and approaches because the process requires a collaborative approach to data collection and decision making (McCarthy, 2010; Schuster & Smith, 1994). An implication of this management is that the counselor must be able to understand the process of obtaining assessment data, recognize the diagnostic instruments used, and organize all of this information for consumer planning purposes.

Current rehabilitation legislation and practice suggest a more active role for the rehabilitation counselor in evaluation functions. Although counseling is usually the only direct service provided in local rehabilitation offices, many assessment measures have been devised for use by rehabilitation professionals who work with persons with severe disabilities (Bolton, 1982). The *Functional Assessment Inventory* and the *Vocational Behavior Checklist* are two examples (Bolton, 1982). Boland and Alonso (1982) explained that in order to meet the demands of consumers in independent living, counselors must have the skills to develop and carry out highly individualized rehabilitation plans. Counselors also have to continually reassess their consumers to determine new areas of need and then change their rehabilitation plans accordingly. Rehabilitation professionals who work with individuals with severe disabilities often find even basic evaluations to be a challenge, in that their assessment must include determining functional limitations and capacities (Wright, 1980). Intake interviews with people with severe disabilities require identifying which specific independent available services are needed for the particular consumer. Such a task presumes an ability to understand consumer capabilities, a necessary step for actually evaluating rehabilitation potentials and goals.

Rehabilitation professionals should help their consumers acquire useful knowledge related to productive rehabilitation capabilities. For many years, the opportunity to do this has been given primarily to those specially trained in vocational assessment. Although psychologists or vocational evaluators are credibly performing very necessary jobs, still other rehabilitation professionals could perform many vocationally related diagnostic activities; but these assessment duties cannot be performed without adequate knowledge of basic evaluation situations, particular approaches, and developed methods. Even then, the extent of the professional's assessment tasks is limited. For example, many areas of personality functioning or disabilities that relate to brain impairment demand specialized training and should be evaluated only by professionals who have expertise in these areas.

It should be noted that different vocational evaluator roles have emerged from legislation and from recent developments in rehabilitation and technology fields. These roles include vocational assessment clinician, vocational and career expert, disability specialist, advocate, collaborator and coordinator, and educator. Although the functions of many roles have been extended in response to legislative mandates and technological advances, the basic roles themselves of evaluator, collaborator, and advocate have remained thematically consistent (Glisson, Iannucci-Waller, Johnson, & Thomas, 2004).

Expected Evaluator Competencies for Vocational Assessment

Recently, knowledge domains for the rehabilitation counselor were revisited and updated (Saunders & Leahy, 2010). These domains establish the foundation for the development of counselor competencies. Saunders and Leahy identified 3 general and 11 subdomain areas. For relevance to the vocational evaluator, the general area of vocational knowledge (i.e., pertaining to career counseling and assessment, job development and placement services, and vocational consultation and services for employers) is critical to assessment practice. Specifically, for example, the subdomain of career counseling and assessment includes

- theories of career development and work adjustment,
- tests and evaluation techniques for assessing consumers,
- psychometric concepts related to measurement (e.g., reliability, validity, standard error of measurement),
- interpretation of assessment results for rehabilitation planning purposes,
- computer- and Internet-based career resources (e.g., O*NET, OASYS),
- transferable skills analysis, and
- assistive technology (Saunders & Leahy, 2010).

Thus, there are different competencies that counselors should demonstrate when conducting rehabilitation assessment. As suggested by the Interdisciplinary Council (Schuster & Smith, 1994), these competencies include the following:

- the ability to select, adopt, and develop methods and approaches that are useful in determining an individual's attributes, abilities, and needs.
- the ability to use alternative methods and approaches that can be used to cross-validate information generated from other assessment sources.
- the ability to conduct formal and informal behavioral observation strategies that can be integrated in a variety of settings.
- the ability to collect and interpret ongoing data that can be used to promote successful transition through critical junctures of the individual's career development.
- the ability to interpret vocational evaluation and assessment data in a manner that contributes to the total service delivery system. Vocational evaluation and assessment team members must be capable of synthesizing and reporting formal and informal data in

a manner that promotes appropriate planning, appropriate goal setting, and coordination of needed support services.

- the ability to function as an effective participant on an interdisciplinary team.
- the ability to select, implement, and integrate evaluation and assessment approaches that are current, valid, reliable, and grounded in career, vocational, and work contexts.

Conclusion

The purpose of rehabilitation assessment is to plan a course of action. It involves exploring a person's strengths and weaknesses and discovering how the individual's potential for vocational adjustment can be enhanced. The scope of assessment is sufficiently broad to include the identification of specific problems relevant to achieving career goals, the development of goals, and the planning of strategies to resolve the problems and to attain the established objectives (Berven, 1997). Approaches in assessment are never used to measure people themselves but are used to measure people's characteristics, such as verbal skills, self-confidence, and intellectual capacities. Assessment today must be understood in a context of legislation, consumer advocacy and involvement, environmental demands and influences, professional collaboration, ethnically diverse consumer populations, and assistive technology.

In vocational rehabilitation, it is important for evaluation to have a comprehensive perspective, for it considers the physical, intellectual, and emotional components of personality as well as the influence of the environment on an individual with a disability. The interrelationships of feeling, mental functioning, and body capabilities must always be considered. The most useful assessment approaches take into account all three of these dimensions, and the consumer's participation in the evaluation process is crucial to the success of any assessment approach. Helping people with handicaps to become productive implies not only that there are various ways to gain information about potential functioning but also that consumers have the opportunity to understand diagnostic information in order to make educated decisions.

Questions that this book responds to are as follows: What are the varied assessment approaches that can tap the consumer's intellectual and emotional resources? How can persons with disabilities become integrally involved in the evaluation process? What reasonable accommodations need to be made to help individuals with severe disabilities to learn more about their career potential? How does the consumer's environment influence the identification of adaptive skills and motivation?

Chapter 1

Current Perspectives on Vocational Assessment

Consumer assessment is the first step and the most vital link to all successful rehabilitation activities. Many of the mistakes made in job placement can be avoided if an appropriate and accurate evaluation is performed. Assessment can also become a stimulus to the reluctant rehabilitation professional who considers job placement an undesirable task. Knowledge of what the consumer can do often encourages the professional to look for job possibilities that are in harmony with this awareness.

The rehabilitation professional usually sees the consumer some months after the occurrence of a chronic illness or disability. When the consumer is initially interviewed by the rehabilitation professional, he or she is customarily referred to an agency or rehabilitation resource, which performs the service of vocational assessment. The rehabilitation professional may be a rehabilitation counselor, a counseling psychologist, a social worker, or a related mental health worker. These professionals are usually not experts in vocational assessment methodology. They may lack the specialized training in the actual administration of certain paper-and-pencil tests or other well-developed approaches that explore employment or career potential. Also, an agency's policy may be that all consumers must receive a comprehensive evaluation at a specific assessment center. These centers can provide in-depth assessment opportunities, especially for consumers with specialized problems. When an assessment is conducted by another agency, the referring professional is a "purchaser of services."

The selection of evaluation measures is often based on the initial diagnosis, the time available to perform such an exploration, and the assessment knowledge of approaches and measures that can generate relevant information. The usual practice in most rehabilitation agencies is to purchase vocational diagnostic services. The waiting period for obtaining such information is often very long, which causes some consumers to lose interest in the rehabilitation process. Another possible problem is that other evaluation resources may not be available. Yet Roessler and Rubin (2006) explained that other assessment opportunities should be considered because many consumers have positive work histories that do not require intensive vocational evaluation. If a person is not returning to his or her previous job, a brief vocational analysis can be conducted to identify other employment options. Also, understanding the consumer's productive-related strengths early and providing him or her with this information can often strongly motivate the consumer to achieve rehabilitation goals.

In rehabilitation, particularly in state vocational rehabilitation agencies, many cases are reopened after services in the rehabilitation process have been interrupted. These consumers may not have to go through extended vocational evaluations again (depending on the circumstances), but updates of their employable strengths can be most useful. When the counselor has the ability to conduct such an exploration, this assessment can be used to expedite the achievement of rehabilitation goals.

This chapter discusses several issues that arise when the rehabilitation professional is referring the consumer to a vocational assessment resource. It also proposes a model of vocational functioning that identifies several factors for evaluating successful job placement, and suggests guidelines that can assist rehabilitation professionals in making good decisions when purchasing services. Selected topics that influence and are the basis of the assessment process complete this chapter, such as evaluating for appropriate job placement that includes the determination of work readiness, employability, and placeability, and the contributions of select prominent career theories.

Issues to Consider When Purchasing or Conducting Assessment Services

After a consumer is determined eligible to receive services from a particular agency, the professional begins the decision-making process to determine the most effective way to explore the individual's employment or career potential, when this goal is identified as a main priority for the consumer's return to overall life functioning. But an employment or career goal *may* not be in the consumer's immediate future if independent living goals have to be attained before beginning a job or a career. Regardless of the different goals for the consumer, this section will briefly discuss four issues that impact the individual's participation in vocational assessment: (a) understanding the employment market of the 21st century, including the work ethic today; (b) the timing of the actual assessment; (c) the opportunity for informed choice; and (d) formulating specific questions.

Understanding the Employment Market of the 21st Century and the Work Ethic

Employment is difficult to find for many people in the beginning decades of the 21st century. For those with disabilities, it's even more difficult. The unemployment rate for those with disabilities is at least 50% higher than it is for other workers (St. George, 2010). The job search can be a daunting and an elusive experience. Also, the decrease in labor demand has negative implications to those with a disability who are preparing to enter or re-enter the job market (Manthey, Jackson, & Evers-Brown, 2011).

Modern-day employers expect workers to embrace complementary and diverse skills (Duys, Ward, Maxwell, & Eaton-Comerford, 2008). The effects of globalization, technological and scientific advances, the reorganization and redesign of many jobs, the uncertainties that characterize the employment environment, the extensive use of part-time workers tied to production cycles—each has dramatically affected both the job search and the skills required for competitive employment (Power, 2011; Savickas, 2012; Zunker, 2006). Savickas believes that "the work world of the 21st century provokes feelings of anxiety and insecurity" (p. 13). He believes that temporary assignments and time-limited projects are replacing permanent jobs, and an employment career should be viewed as a recurrent selling of services and skills to employers who need projects completed. For those with disabilities who want to compete successfully in the 21st-century marketplace, they also must have specific skills such as

- interpersonal, social team skills;
- problem identification and problem-solving skills;

- education/academic skills; and
- the ability to grasp new knowledge technology, when possible.

Job adaptability is a key concept for those wishing to achieve appropriate employment. Adaptability is the ability to apply one's job-related skills to different work demands, the willingness to learn new skills, the capacity to develop coping skills to manage the work environment, and the ability to master career-related tasks associated with one's disability (Duys et al., 2008). This adaptability may also include, especially for those with young adult or later onset of disability, revisiting earlier job experiences and responding to changes psychosocially that occur subsequent to the onset of disability so that they can move beyond physical losses to value existing abilities and adjust to labor market demands (Ebener & Smedema, 2011).

Because of these phenomena in the 21st-century employment world, the work ethic may be better conceptualized as a kind of compromise, a concept that has evolved for several decades and one that continues to change. In the past, one's work ethic included the values of hard work and the personal qualities of honesty, industriousness, and integrity. These characteristics may still exist in many workers, but the appeal of the intrinsic value of work may have decreased. Economic turbulence and the factors of corporate downsizing may force many workers to withdraw from emotional involvement in work and to seek a number of external motivators from family and leisure activities. To labor in this modern day workforce may not be central to people's lives or at the core of a person's identity (Power, 2011).

For the professional, it may be a challenging task to operationalize the complexities and changes of the 21st-century labor market and their implications into vocational assessment practice. The following are suggestions to consider for this implementation.

1. Though paper-and-pencil testing, when conducted appropriately with consumers, can provide important information, the evaluator should also consider a more *hands-on* evaluation, such as situational assessment and work samples. These approaches could put the consumer in touch with the current dynamics of the labor market and workforce.

2. The evaluator should be aware that current workforce development policy has permanently linked the vocational rehabilitation system

to the broader workforce investment system. The state-sponsored workforce centers can be a valuable resource for current information of labor market trends (Power, 2011).

3. Vocational assessment planning should include a comprehensive, holistic evaluation approach that captures not only transferable skills but also the emotional characteristics the consumer brings to assessment. In their research, Hall and Parker (2010) found that low self-esteem is an ongoing and pervasive issue for people with disabilities who are looking for work. These consumers tend to be less assertive and less self-confident, and often show an inconsistency of social attitudes (Hall & Parker, 2010).

4. For those with especially adventitious disabilities, vocational and career interests may have to be redefined through different decision-making phases. The current culture of employment may not encourage the pursuit of long-time interests and vocational-related commitments may have to be updated with present-day demands.

5. The professional may have to consider the therapeutic dimensions of vocational evaluation. Consumers with disabilities could need assistance in developing personally fulfilling strategies for work.

The Timing of the Actual Assessment

In the rehabilitation process, assessment typically is performed soon after the consumer makes a request for vocational services. If the person with a disability is referred to an evaluation center, he or she may wait for a considerable length of time because most centers have long waiting lists. Therefore, to keep consumers motivated enough to pursue rehabilitation goals, rehabilitation professionals should conduct a beginning assessment that inhibits discouragement of continuing the process of vocational rehabilitation. An assessment performed soon after the initial consumer contact becomes the first step toward the development of an effective rehabilitation plan because the assessment gives the consumer a renewed awareness of productive strengths and capabilities. The initial consumer interview can become a useful approach for this evaluation, and this contact is also discussed in Chapter 6. This step often can become operationalized by also using self-assessment procedures (e.g., selected paper-and-pencil tests, card sorts). This approach to assessment is becoming popular with agencies that have consumers with the intellectual, physical, and emotional capacities to complete these evaluation tools.

Furthermore, a good time to use evaluation resources is when realistic information is needed to support the beginning awareness of a consumer's abilities or when the professional and consumer believe that a standardized, sophisticated assessment can help determine complex functioning. Such resources, however, should not be used primarily to keep the consumer "busy." Consumers may be referred for evaluation as a matter of routine, even when the evidence of the consumer's potential is already available and there is no need to further substantiate these data. In these situations, consumers often feel that pursuit of their perceived rehabilitation goals is being unnecessarily delayed. Because of these concerns, the initial interview meeting with the consumer should ascertain just what the consumer's goals are and how vocational evaluation can fit into the development of rehabilitation plans.

Timing also refers to determining with the consumer when assessment should be conducted after a disability-inducing trauma or after long-term institutionalization. For most consumers, the psychological adjustment to their mental and physical limitations may take weeks, months, or even longer. Some people never adapt to disability-related limitations and prefer a lifestyle that is characterized by overdependence or a decided reluctance to become work-productive. Whatever the length of time, a period of psychological adjustment is to be expected. As consumers go through this process of emotional adaptation, feelings of anxiety, depression (with its concomitant anger, confusion, and uncertainty about the future), and helplessness may dominate. When the professional perceives the strong influence of these feelings, he or she should give the consumer the option of delaying a planned evaluation. The presence of these emotions at the time of assessment can affect the reliability of the evaluation results.

On the other side of this timing issue, many rehabilitation professionals believe that assessment should not be delayed because the process itself may reduce negative emotions and thus facilitate the consumer's progress toward rehabilitation goals. These professionals believe that imparting assessment results that emphasize the consumers' residual strengths may alleviate their perceptions of helplessness. However, most persons with disabilities do need some emotional adaptation to the disability before formal assessment begins. Consumers who request rehabilitation services for themselves or who are eager to be employed again suggest a more positive attitude and psychological readiness that is conducive to involvement in vocational assessment.

The Opportunity for Informed Choice

The 1998 Rehabilitation Act Amendments stated the importance of consumer choice and self-determination, emphasizing that to empower a person is to provide him or her with the opportunity to make choices and decisions regarding his or her life (Kosciulek, 2004). Kosciulek believed that

> informed choice is a process during which a person sets goals, gathers information, considers a range of options, and then takes the responsibility for selecting the option that best meets his or her criteria. Informed choice refers to a person's ability to understand and use programs successfully. (p. 4)

The consumer then becomes the choice-maker in the vocational assessment process.

To facilitate the consumer's informed choice and to encourage appropriate consumer decision making, there is the assumption that the rehabilitation professional will use selected skills and knowledge to inform the consumer about the nature of vocational assessment, the available options for conducting the evaluation, and the potential outcomes. These skills include the following:

- listening to the consumer's family and learning about educational and work experience backgrounds
- identifying rehabilitation and vocational needs
- asking open-ended questions that encourage the consumer's further understanding of his or her background

Knowledge areas include the following:

- understanding the different approaches to vocational assessment
- communicating the perception of how these methods could be congruent to the consumer's disability-related needs, severity of disability, and work and educational experiences
- recognizing how assistive technology could enhance, when necessary, the consumer's performance during the assessment process

The way in which information about alternatives and options is presented must fit the consumer's needs and abilities (Kosciulek, 2004). When there is active consumer choice, frequently there is increased satisfaction with the assessment process. The consumer gains some control over the evaluation situation. Such control will vary, of course, from person to person and may be based on an individual's history (Houser, Hampton, & Carriker, 2000).

Although consumer empowerment and its resulting informed choice are relative newcomers in the vocational assessment process, this empowerment involves a partial transfer of responsibility and imparts a degree of control to the consumer. It also can facilitate and maximize training and employment opportunities for individuals with disabilities. In other words, the consumer becomes an active, informed participant who has an investment in a planning process to be used for short- and long-term career development. Vocational assessment, consequently, is an active process that functions in a context of empowerment. Importantly, during this shared decision process, the professional also gains an ongoing understanding of the most feasible way to pursue and achieve vocational evaluation goals. Figure 1.1 depicts a step-by-step procedure of the consumer empowerment process during vocational assessment.

Formulating Specific Questions

At the time of the referral of the consumer to an evaluation agency, questions should be directed to the agency that, in turn, will generate information feasible for the development of vocational assessment goals. These questions, from the referring source, may enhance the consumer's evaluation process:

- Is the evaluation agency aware of activities and situations that could aggravate the consumer's limitations or impair his or her general health?
- Can the vocational assessment include an appraisal of any aspects of emotional functioning that may be viewed as obstacles to appropriate job adjustment?
- Are there any assistive technology resources that could enhance the consumer's vocational capability?
- Is the referring agency able to share any previous assessment information that would identify or highlight the consumer's employment and career-related strengths?

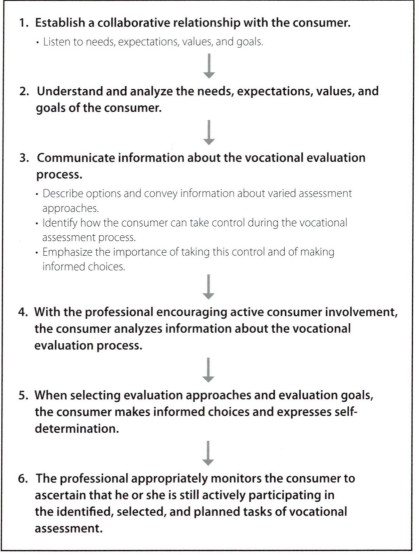

1. **Establish a collaborative relationship with the consumer.**
   - Listen to needs, expectations, values, and goals.

2. **Understand and analyze the needs, expectations, values, and goals of the consumer.**

3. **Communicate information about the vocational evaluation process.**
   - Describe options and convey information about varied assessment approaches.
   - Identify how the consumer can take control during the vocational assessment process.
   - Emphasize the importance of taking this control and of making informed choices.

4. **With the professional encouraging active consumer involvement, the consumer analyzes information about the vocational evaluation process.**

5. **When selecting evaluation approaches and evaluation goals, the consumer makes informed choices and expresses self-determination.**

6. **The professional appropriately monitors the consumer to ascertain that he or she is still actively participating in the identified, selected, and planned tasks of vocational assessment.**

Figure 1.1. Step-by-step procedure of the consumer empowerment process.

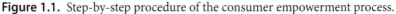

There are other questions, of course, that could solicit information about the consumer's career potential. The types of questions asked can decidedly influence the realistic outcomes of the vocational assessment process.

There is the added important consideration that there are many consumers for whom the traditional measures of assessment are not appropriate. For many consumers with severe disabilities or who represent ethnic minorities, for example, standard aptitude tests may provide little information that can be translated into suitable plans for education and training. Rehabilitation professionals, therefore, must look elsewhere for assessment resources for these populations. The professional should appraise carefully the available evaluation resources and determine which resources will provide the most usable information for rehabilitation purposes.

Model of Vocational Functioning

After addressing the issues when purchasing assessment services, the rehabilitation professional and the vocational evaluator should consider a model of vocational functioning that establishes a broad framework for vocational assessment.

Table 1.1 is a detailed model of vocational functioning and is an expression of both the current concept of disability and the meaning of vocational rehabilitation. This model identifies what needs to be assessed and embraces the humanistic and holistic principles identified in the introductory chapter. The model specifies the areas that need to be identified in evaluation. It depicts an individual's possible vocational functioning at a fixed point in time, usually at the time of the initial interview. The content of the model in Table 1.1 has been developed from various sources, including Farley, Little, Bolton, and Chunn (1993); Hershenson (1990); Knefelkamp and Slepitza (1976); Lofquist and Dawes (1969); Mpofu and Oakland (2010); Super (1957); and Thomas et al. (2011), as well as my own extensive professional experience in vocational evaluation. The model includes all people with disabilities: those who were born with disabilities and those who incurred disabilities because of accidents or illnesses. The model also includes women. Many women are part of the labor force outside of the home, and many of them who acquire a disability will want to return as wage earners (Belkin, 2009; Power, 2011).

Unfortunately, there are almost no specific assessment techniques available for the vocational evaluation of ethnic groups (Helms, 1992). Because different minority groups have various experiences and ways of presenting their attributes and abilities, it is not likely that a single

(text continues on p. 14)

Table 1.1
Model of Vocational Functioning

Vocational functioning	Vocational and independent living tasks and demands
Client's physical characteristics	
General appearance	• Work appropriateness • Employment interview

Stamina and endurance	• Work tolerance
	  Work full-time
	  Work part-time
	  Light physical activity
	  Sedentary work
	• Work pace

General health status	• Working conditions
	  Current level of response to work location
	  (hot, cold, humidity, noise, hazards, and other
	  atmospheric conditions)

Vision and hearing	• Work appropriateness and work conditions

Motor coordination
  Eye/hand/foot coordination
  Finger dexterity
  Mobility
	• Work demands
	  Transportation
	  Mobility in work space
	  Self-care

Personal hygiene	• Work appropriateness
Physical limitations	• Ability to meet work demands • Necessary job modifications
Client's intellectual characteristics	
General level of knowledge	• Self-knowledge • Knowledge of work demands • Awareness of entry requirements
Educational development	• Level of possible training • Language development and skills • Mathematics and computational skills • Level of reasoning

Aptitudes
  Verbal and speech
  Numerical
  Spatial perception
  Form perception
  Conceptual ability
	• Communication demands
	• Complete employment forms
	• Hold job interview
	• Ability to abstract and calculate
	• Measuring ability

(continues)

Table 1.1 *(continued)*

Vocational functioning	Vocational and independent living tasks and demands
Client's intellectual characteristics (continued)	
Work experience Homemaking Leisure time Avocational activities	• Skills and competencies developed • Safety consciousness • Ability of person to return to former job • Transferable abilities and skills to a work situation
Decision-making skills	• Initiative in work areas • Take opportunities for job and work development
Memory	• Ability to retain instructions • Training capability
Attention span	• Ability to follow work directions • Training capability
Work competencies	• Attendance • Promptness • Speed of production • Use of time
Interests	• Preferred types of jobs • Preference for certain types of work activities
Values	• Perception of work for life functioning • Work habits • Expectations for self in job situation
Disability-related knowledge	• Understanding of assets and disability limitations in relation to work
Adaptive behavior	• Ability to adjust to job requirements
Client's emotional characteristics	
Mood and temperament Indifferent Apathetic Cooperative Eager Self-assured Interested	• Relations to supervisors and other people • Frustration tolerance • Adjustment to strains and pressures of work environment
Needs[a] Responsibility Security Social status Variety	• Change orientation • Adaptability • Ability to take risks with self • Openness to alternatives

Table 1.1 *(continued)*

Vocational functioning	Vocational and independent living tasks and demands
Client's emotional characteristics *(continued)*	
Supervision/authority	
Recognition	
Creativity	
Independence	
Achievement	
Good working conditions	
Advancement	
Autonomy	

Attitudes
    Toward self
    Toward others
	• Sense of responsibility
	• Successful job performance
	• Relationship with others
	• Self-confidence in work situations

Motivation to work	• Seeks rehabilitation goals • Energy on job • Achievement level
Adjustment to disability	• Confidence in self as worker • Accepts limitations • Dependent or independent role
Personal and environmental coping skills	• Adjustment to the work environment
Environmental factors	
Family situation	• Family members supportive of rehabilitation goals • Family accepting of occupational choices • Family recognizes client capabilities

Available financial resources
    Workers' compensation
      benefits
    Supplemental Security
      Income
    Social Security Disability
      Insurance
    Primary source of support
	• Current finances are sufficient to meet client needs
	• Will occupation meet client financial needs?

Attitudes
    Employer
    Co-worker
	• Acceptance on job

Accessibility
    Work site
    Community
	• Availability of job opportunities

(continues)

Table 1.1 (continued)

Vocational functioning	Vocational and independent living tasks and demands
Environmental factors (continued)	
Community factors	• Availability and accessibility of job
Transportation	opportunities
Local economy	
Training opportunities	
Support network	
Housing	
Special considerations	
Medications	• Attention, concentration, stamina, and safety on job
Aids	• Transportation
	• Can drive own car
	• Can take public transportation
	• Needs assistance for transportation
Certificates, licenses, or union membership	• Job opportunity
Precautions	• Job and work flexibility
	• Job or work modification
Social skills	• Work demands
	• Relationship to others

[a]Lofquist and Dawes (1969).

assessment approach or measure can be equally valid for each ethnic group (Sedlacek, 1994). Vocational evaluation issues with these populations will be discussed in Chapter 4.

Any model, however, is developed from certain assumptions, and this model of vocational functioning is based on the following considerations:

- Work satisfaction depends on the extent to which individuals find adequate outlets for their abilities, interests, personality traits, and values (Super, 1990).
- Occupations are chosen to meet needs. The occupation that is chosen is that field or area that the person believes will best meet the needs that most concern him or her.

- An occupational choice is determined by the individual's socio-economic level, age, abilities, personality characteristics, education, and available opportunities. The choice is also determined by (a) inner limiting factors, such as limited physical abilities, limited mental capabilities, or scarce financial resources; (b) outer limiting factors, such as lack of availability of relevant training resources or poor employment outlook; or (c) outer directing factors, such as perceived prestige of occupations and positive family and employee expectations for return to work.
- A person's vocational preference, living situation, work environment, and self-concept change with time and experience, making occupational choice and adjustment a continuous process.
- The experience of disability represents a transitional period in the sense that many behaviors common to the pre-disability state are gradually replaced.
- The changes that the onset of disability precipitates frequently have traumatic implications for the family, organization, or work system in which an individual is embedded.
- Work itself may not be central to the lifestyle or aspirations of some persons, and, for many, it has connotations that repel rather than attract (Zytowski, 1965).
- Prevalent career choices, which are primarily based on research studies using samples of boys and men, may not be applicable for girls and women. Although research that is more longitudinal in scope is needed regarding girls and women, current vocational practices should recognize the distinctive needs of women as well as minimize gender-role bias.
- Assessment can be a proactive tool to initiate change, rather than one that is used in a more passive, defensive way to ensure that someone is not being "categorized" inappropriately (Sedlacek, 1994).

Evaluating for Appropriate Job Placement

This model of vocational functioning is particularly useful for eventual job placement activities. The goal of helping consumers obtain gainful employment should influence each step in the rehabilitation process, from the referral and first interview through every step taken with the consumer, including the last follow-up contact. Assessment, training, and vocational or adjustmental counseling can be carefully viewed through the perspective of placement. Over the years, job placement has maintained the viability and growth of vocational rehabilitation. At the same time, this activity in rehabilitation has created the most concerns for the rehabilitation professional and potential employers.

Many rehabilitation professionals view their job responsibilities as being mainly counseling or case coordination. Performing job development tasks and generating employer awareness about hiring persons with disabilities are considered by many to be unwelcome activities. In turn, many employers today claim that consumers referred to them for possible jobs are, in reality, not "job ready." Yet, one of the continuing facts in rehabilitation is that when a rehabilitation professional competently engages in job and employer development activities, including vocational assessment, and refers consumers who have the appropriate attitudes, behaviors, and skills to hold particular jobs, the consumer can be competitive for available jobs, even in a tight labor market.

Traditionally, placement was a cluster of professional activities as part of workforce development that, until 1995, was separate from public and nonprofit vocational rehabilitation (Maki & Riggar, 2003). In the mid-1990s, policy debate over block grants and one-stop shopping, from which emerged vouchers and service integration, led to a general consideration regarding the manner in which public vocational rehabilitation services were delivered. Although models of placement were originally derived from federal legislation, and included counselor-provided services and placement-professional-provided services, new models have developed that include marketing, team networking or mentoring, and demand-side placement (Stensrud, Millington, & Gilbride, 1997). Communication technology fuels the team networking or mentoring approach, and demand-side placement implies that "employers are the people most directly responsible for employing people with disabilities" (Stensrud et al., 1997, p. 206).

Assuming that consumer assessment, however, is an indispensable initial step for job placement, this evaluation should be perceptively, efficiently, and comprehensively conducted. This approach may frequently be performed by the rehabilitation professional whose primary job task is not work evaluation. Issues related to the assessment responsibility are discussed in Chapter 2.

The assessment exploration for job placement can also be developed to allow the rehabilitation professional the opportunity to gain necessary information in an expeditious manner. This assessment can be based on operationalizing the general concepts of work readiness, employability, and placeability. There has been much confusion, however, regarding the definition and application of *work readiness* (Vandergoot, 1982). Bitter (1968) believed that it is a general term relating to an individual's personal attributes in the world of work and suggested the specific term *job readiness*. Such readiness is the extent to which an individual's qualifications fit the skill requirements of a particular job. Sinick (1969) distinguished employability from placeability. *Employability* refers to someone who possesses the requisite skills and work personality; *placeability* refers to the perceived attractiveness of an applicant to an employer.

The concepts of work readiness, employability, and placeability are useful in understanding the process of vocational assessment as a beginning step for eventual consumer placement. Employability and placeability are components of work readiness. These concepts also provide a perspective for exploring those consumer characteristics needed to respond to labor market demands.

Work Readiness

Farley et al. (1993) defined readiness as the

> level of self-knowledge (interests, aptitudes, abilities, strengths, limitations, work values, needs, etc.) and knowledge of the work world or amount of occupational information (the nature of work involved in specific jobs, duties and requirements, education and training needed, where jobs are to be found, salary levels, outlook for the future, etc.) the individual possesses. (p. 9)

There are different methods for determining work readiness. The general approaches, which are explained in greater detail later in this book, include the following:

- Analysis of work history
- Analysis of educational and social data
- Interviews with consumer and family

- Medical and psychiatric consultation
- Psychological testing
- Work samples evaluation
- Analysis of part-time or temporary work experience
- Analysis of on-the-job training experience

Any one or a combination of these eight approaches can be used when determining either employability or placeability. There is also a useful measure, the *Work Readiness Profile* (Rowe, 2003), which is a tool designed to assist in the initial assessment of individuals with disabilities. It seeks to identify what people can do in terms of abilities, supports, and empowerment, rather than on the level of disability. Focusing on older adolescents and adults with disabilities, it can be self-administered in 15 to 20 minutes. It is available from the Australian Council for Educational Research Limited (ACER), 19 Prospect Hill Rd., Camberwell, VIC 3124, Australia, sales@acer.edu.au.

Employability

During the initial interview, an assessment has to be made as to whether the consumer is ready for work. Although the model of vocational functioning presented earlier in this chapter provides a broad structure for assessment activities, more specific questions must be asked in order to ascertain whether an individual has the ability to meet the varied requirements of jobs and occupations. Walls, Zane, and Werner (1979) developed the *Vocational Behavior Checklist,* which identifies eight areas of employment-related capabilities. Bolton (1982) clarified these areas as described below, and they are quite useful for understanding employability issues.

- *Prevocational skills*—The consumer's vocational interests and potential; knowledge about his or her need for work and what a job is
- *Job-seeking skills*—Behaviors needed for locating and applying for employment, such as understanding ads and completing applications
- *Interviewing skills*—Behaviors needed to conduct an effective interview with a prospective employer, including understanding

the interview situation, responding, and asking appropriate
questions

- *Job-related skills*—Skills one should bring to a job situation, such
  as following rules and adjusting to the work environment
- *Work performance skills*—Behaviors of arriving at work on time,
  following instructions, working safely, using and caring for tools,
  and so forth
- *On-the-job social skills*—Getting along with others and
  constructively handling criticism
- *Union and financial security skills*—Understanding and following
  company policies, such as obtaining pay, overtime, union
  functions, insurance, and benefits
- *Decision-making skills*—Ability to make choices for job
  opportunities and engage in vocational planning

Upon understanding these work-related skill areas, questions can
be developed for assessing a person's potential for employment.

Physical Questions

Is the consumer at the maximum level of physical capacity?

Can the consumer travel to and from a job? Use public
transportation?

Can the consumer work a full workday? A full workweek?

Can the consumer meet the physical demands of the kind
of work sought (current level of performance in strength,
climbing, stooping, reaching, talking, and seeing)?

Does the consumer understand the nature of his or her
disability?

Is the consumer aware of activities and situations that would
tend to aggravate the disability or impair general health, such
as cold, heat, work location, humidity, noise, hazards, and
atmospheric conditions?

Does the consumer recognize danger signs, like fatigue or
coughing, that can be warnings that rest or treatment may be
necessary?

Is the consumer aware of the need for periodic examinations
or further treatment?

Is the consumer capable of living independently?

Would the consumer's personal appearance be acceptable to employers and co-workers? Poor personal grooming, dirty clothes, or inappropriate clothing are three major problem areas.

Does the consumer have a number of unfortunate personal mannerisms (tics, failure to maintain eye contact, etc.)?

Psychological Questions

Do the consumer and family accept the consumer's limitations?

Do the consumer and family recognize the consumer's capabilities?

Is the consumer sincerely motivated toward employment?

Can the consumer adjust to the strains and pressures of a work environment?

Does the consumer react appropriately to supervision?

Can the consumer get along with others, such as co-workers and supervisors?

Is the consumer a dependable worker in terms of attendance, promptness, and appropriate use of time?

Are the consumer's personality traits suitable for performing the usual job tasks?

Are there personal or social problems that might affect the consumer's performance on the job?

Does the consumer regularly engage in any antisocial or seriously maladaptive behaviors?

Occupational Questions

Are the consumer's aptitudes, skills, knowledge, and experience commensurate with current and future job requirements?

Can the consumer do the job; namely, what is the consumer's capability for productivity, speed of learning, and ability to do accurate and efficient work?

Is the consumer aware of wages and hours?

Do the nonmonetary, psychological rewards of working complement the consumer's needs, values, and long-range goals?

Does the consumer have an occupational goal; namely, is he or she oriented toward employment?

How does the consumer feel about work?

What jobs has the consumer held, for how long were they held, when did the consumer leave, and what were the reasons given by the consumer for leaving?

What aspects of the job were most satisfying to the consumer and why was this so?

Socio-environmental Questions

Do the important people in the consumer's life accept the consumer as a worker?

Would the consumer's family be supportive of the consumer as a worker?

Is the consumer presently receiving monetary benefits because of the disability?

In defining vocational evaluation as "a comprehensive process that systematically uses work, either real or simulated, as the focal point for assessment and vocational exploration" (p. 1), Farley et al. (1993) also developed an approach that focuses on vocational choice assessment and planning as integral to employability and identifies the following attributes as targets for employability evaluation strategies:

- Vocational readiness
- Aptitudes
- Interests
- Vocationally relevant personality factors
- Work temperament
- Strengths and limitations
- Work values and needs

Important to the approach for developing employability is for the consumer to select an appropriate and suitable occupational goal, and then devise a plan to achieve that goal. The consumer's involvement in this planning process is necessary, because the more knowledge the individual has about his or her personal traits, the more effectively the individual can participate in developing realistic goals (Farley et al., 1993). Furthermore, although traditional approaches focus on person variables, environmental factors are not ignored and should be considered in the consumer's assessment. The environmental variables include such factors as personal (finances and family support); community (transportation, housing, service delivery programs, support network, local economy, accessible community, and training opportunities); workplace (employer attitude, co-worker attitude, accessible work site, and technology); and general (legislation, economy, benefits, and labor market trends; Farley & Bolton, 1994).

The amount of exploration into employability-related concerns depends on the consumer's problems and needs, as well as the barriers that hinder productivity. Yet, it is not only the physical, psychological, occupational, and socio-environmental areas that make the difference between readiness and lack of readiness for most types of employment. The attitudes and feelings of the consumer, as well as the attitudes of prospective employers and the expectations of family members, are also important determinants of employability. An evaluation of job employability should include an assessment of consumers' fundamental systems of values and their basic feelings and perceptions about themselves, especially as these feelings and perceptions relate to work. From this information, the professional can gain a beginning idea of the consumer's motivation. All in all, personality factors take on tremendous importance insofar as employability is concerned. During the evaluation, attempts must be made to assess how these attitudes affect performance and what, if anything, can be done about them.

The determination of employability, consequently, can be identified largely during the initial consumer interview. The Arkansas Research and Training Center in Vocational Rehabilitation has developed a useful readiness instrument titled the *Employability Maturity Interview* (EMI; Roessler & Bolton, 1987). The EMI is a 10-item structured interview developed to assess readiness for the vocational rehabilitation planning process. The EMI's main purpose is to identify those consumers needing additional vocational exploration and employability services. Additionally, Marrone, Horgan, Scripture, and Grossman (1984) provided a practical list of positive and negative indicators of consumer job readiness, especially employability, which can be used during the assessment interview. These indicators are modified and summarized below.

Positive Indicators

The consumer has a work history that is recent, consistent, or both.

Work has a value to the consumer that he or she can express.

The consumer has a course of illness that is relatively predictable.

There is evidence that the consumer has cooperated in a physical or mental health treatment program.

The consumer appears to communicate a good impression of himself or herself physically, verbally, or both.

The consumer states that significant persons contribute life support to his or her vocational rehabilitation process.

Negative Indicators

The consumer consistently misses appointments without a good excuse.

The consumer does not express interest in vocational rehabilitation with work as a goal.

The consumer has no stable living situation or steady source of income.

Contingencies exist that interfere with vocational planning (e.g., court cases, child custody proceedings).

The family or significant others are heavily invested in the status quo. For example, they are satisfied with their current income or are insistent that the family member with a disability not return to paid employment.

The consumer is persistent in maintaining a strong, rigid interest in an unrealistic vocational goal.

Placeability

Placeability is the ability of the individual to meet the hiring requirements of employers, particularly as defined by personnel officers. An individual can be employable without being placeable—for example, a consumer who possesses many job-related skills but is not able to obtain a job in a particular geographical area. Criteria for placement readiness include the following:

- To what extent can the consumer participate in the job-finding process?
- Does the consumer know and use sources of job leads?
- Can the consumer develop a resume or a personal information packet?
- Can the consumer satisfactorily complete a job application?

- Can the consumer present himself or herself adequately in a job interview?
  - ❖ *Can the consumer make his or her capabilities clear to employ- ers, and can the consumer account for problems, such as periods of unemployment?* Most chronically unemployed people fail to seek work with sufficient frequency. Interviewing the consumer should reveal the reasons for this failure, such as fear, lack of financial need to work, and lack of a job goal. Job frequency probably depends on job opportunities to some extent. Most consumers are handicapped in an employment interview by an inability to explain some of their problems in a manner that induces a prospective employer to overlook or accept such prob- lems. Typical problems are age, history of institutionalization, history of lengthy unemployment, physical disability, and poor work history. An evaluation of whether the consumer can ex- plain his or her skills to an employer is needed, because employ- ers basically hire job applicants for skills that they are known to have. During the job interview, consumers need to explain their skills, usually in a very brief period of time.
  - ❖ *Is the consumer reasonably free of mannerisms that annoy the em- ployer?* This area can be easily evaluated by simply looking at the consumer and deciding whether his or her personal appearance would be acceptable to employers and co-workers.
- Would the consumer continue a job search if met with some rejections?
- Would the consumer conduct himself or herself appropriately if starting work tomorrow?

An explanation of placeability also includes such job market fac- tors as (a) unemployment rate in the consumer's skill area, (b) availabil- ity of jobs in the geographic area, (c) union requirements, and (d) wage requirements. During the evaluation process, the rehabilitation profes- sional should always keep these factors in mind.

Selected Career Theories as Relevant to Vocational Assessment

Traditionally, established theories of career development have stimu- lated research into vocational choice and decision making. Yet selected theories can not only respond to the challenges of the modern worker in a turbulent economy but also provide a useful framework for understanding specific areas that should be targeted in vocational assessment. Furthermore, they can suggest insights into consumer adaptability, an essential part of the job-seeking process in the 21st century. The following theories are very briefly explained, and then their implications for vocational evaluation are identified.

Super's Life-Span Theory

In his widely recognized approach to career development, one that continues to stimulate research (Niles & Harris-Bowlesby, 2005), Super posited that career choice is a developmental, lifelong process influenced by one's self-concept. Self-concept is the core of Super's theoretical contribution and it covers a person's entire life span (Sharf, 2002). The theory does not directly and necessarily describe the vocational development of individuals with disabilities; it has relevance for vocational assessment both in the evaluation process and objectives.

In assessment, relevant information about the consumer is collected. During this directive and nondirective exploratory process, the consumer can be given the opportunity to put into words his or her understanding of self-concept. This meaning establishes a guideline to consider career options and suggests how one's self-concept needs to be clarified or modified, if necessary, to respond to opportunities in the current labor market. Frequently, moreover, consumer feedback gained by learning assessment results may enhance the consumer's self-concept. Vocational evaluation then becomes a source of consumer motivation.

Holland's Work Personality Theory

In his highly influential and researched career theory, John Holland proposed a link between an individual's personality characteristics and corresponding job titles. Organizing the massive data about people and jobs into six different types (Realistic, Investigative, Artistic, Social, Enterprising, and Conventional) was a significant contribution to vocational counseling practice. Added to this contribution was his belief that it is necessary to explore the degree of fit or congruence between the personality type and current or prospective work environments.

Exploring this congruence, especially with the instruments that have been developed, such as *My Vocational Situation* and the *Self-Directed*

Search, may be a first step in the assessment process. The data gathered from the *Self-Directed Search*, for example, provide a useful framework for the consumer to identify occupational environments that allow the person to express the diverse aspects of his/her personality (Niles & Harris-Bowlesby, 2005). Such diversity promotes adaptability, which, in turn, facilitates the widening of vocational options. Adaptability is a hallmark of 21st-century job searches.

John Tiedeman's Decision-Making Theory

John Tiedeman believed that challenges are essential for human growth and the consumer should be an active participant in the career counseling process (Duys et al., 2008). He asserts that choice is at the threshold of change and adaptability and that people continually redefine their career interests and commitments. In understanding the phases of his proposed decision-making model, which include the anticipatory and implementation phases, there are the concepts of exploration, crystallization, choice, and specification.

The exploration stage is more relevant to vocational assessment, yet Tiedeman's theory actually provides a context for the vocational assessment process. This context includes three areas: (a) building an awareness of career options, (b) reconsidering and re-evaluating vocational options, and (c) revisiting planned employment goals or previous job or training experiences (which is not a personal setback but is actually part of the normal recycling process; Duys et al., 2008). This belief of recycling, a core belief in his theory, is a good fit for consumers with a disability and important to consumer feedback during the vocational assessment process.

Social-Cognitive Career Theory

Based on social cognitive theory, this approach emphasizes how expectations, career self-efficacy, and goals influence vocational choices. These three key concepts are identified in the context of people and their environments, including economic variables and the consumer's culture. They are also important target areas of vocational assessment.

In the perspectives of this theory, the assessment interview should include an exploration of which skills the consumer has achieved that facilitate his or her vocational performance, and what is the consumer's level of persistence at overcoming obstacles to personal self-efficacy, and outcome expectations and goals (Niles & Harris-Bowlesby, 2005). Also, inaccurate beliefs and outcome expectations should be identified. Such inaccuracy may cause foreclosure on the attainment of realistic work options.

Situational Career Theory

This theory includes several career exploration approaches that relate to social systems, such as career choices by accident, status attainment, resources, and prevailing economics. Environmental factors, moreover, that are beyond the individual's control can exert a major influence on the vocational/career course of a consumer's life. The theory also embraces the validity of chance opportunities.

During vocational assessment, this approach re-emphasizes the importance of exploring ethnic and family factors and the impact of discrimination and stereotyping on vocational choices. The theory highlights the premise that employment and career decisions are subject to the demands of society and available opportunities. In evaluation it suggests that the professional focus on other relevant socio-economic factors, such as the perceived status of a career occupation, community influences on job seeking, and the availability of training and/or other educational opportunities.

Conclusion

There are several perspectives to consider when planning rehabilitation assessment. Although the principal focus of any vocational evaluation should be the determination of job readiness, this focus is developed through the understanding of consumer characteristics, the concepts of employability and placeability, and those consumer and environmental factors that may be positive or negative factors in the consumer's eventual job placement. An awareness of all of these indicators lays the groundwork for the selection of appropriate assessment goals and the information needed to accomplish these objectives.

Chapter 2

Issues for Developing an Effective Vocational Assessment Process

Three areas are discussed in this chapter that represent the foundation of an effective assessment. First, an identification of the various ethical and legal standards related to vocational assessment provides a professional environment conducive to credible, productive outcomes. Second, from the evaluator's perspective, establishing guidelines when preparing the consumer for the assessment process lays the groundwork for empowering the consumer. Third, there are several additional factors to consider during the beginning phases of the evaluation process, such as pinpointing the purpose of assessment, understanding the impact of the disability on the evaluation process, and undertaking the selection and administration of assessment measures that provide a necessary perspective for the consumer's involvement. These additional factors bring into sharper focus the necessity of appropriate measures during the assessment process.

Legal and Ethical Issues in Vocational Assessment

The Code of Professional Ethics, developed by the Commission on Rehabilitation Counselor Certification in June 2001, was revised in January 2010 (Tarvydas, Cottone, & Saunders, 2010). Anticipating emerging problems and key changes in the ethical obligations of rehabilitation counselors, specific, selected standards were redefined, revisited, or added in such areas as multicultural and diversity challenges, professional disclosure, roles and relationships with consumers, the use of technology, advocacy and accessibility issues, and forensic ethics. This new or revised information evolved from empirically based definitions of specific competencies (Tarydas et al., 2010), as well as from research identifying the requirements, for example, of cultural competence, or job analysis, or critical incidents. The new Code offers guidance to the rehabilitation counselor and is consistent with the provisions in other, relevant professional codes (Tarvydas et al., 2010).

Cottone and Tarvydas (1998) defined ethics as "an attempt to assess and to judge human decisions and behavior against an accepted standard primarily in a non-religious context" (p. 6). The evaluator is often confronted by ethical dilemmas and may need to access the Code of Professional Ethics for guidance. For more detailed information the reader is directed to the Code of Professional Ethics associated with the specific professional organizations. There are six legal and ethical areas to consider when providing evaluation services: (a) test development and selection; (b) test fairness, including an identification of the types of testing accommodations; (c) test interpretation; (d) test-taker rights in assessment; (e) test privacy; and (f) evaluator competencies.

Test Development and Selection

Caution must be exercised when depending on test instruments to provide information about consumer needs and traits. The consumer's evaluation program should be carefully planned to avoid the overuse or indiscriminate use of testing. Instrument selection should be tailored to the consumer's needs, and tests designed specifically for certain disability groups should be used to ensure the accuracy of outcome scores. It is important that the purpose of the assessment and the intended use of its results be made known to the consumer prior to evaluation. An orientation must also be provided to the consumer prior to and following test administration so that the results of the assessment can be placed in proper perspective with other relevant factors. The professional should ensure that instrument limitations are not exceeded and should conduct periodic review and retesting to prevent consumer stereotyping (Rayman, 1990). In schools, for example, caution should be used when interpreting results. Decisions must be based on people's abilities and behavior rather than on a diagnosis or label.

Vocational assessment can be used as both a descriptive measure of consumer functioning and an indicator of potential. When exploring consumer capability, the rehabilitation professional must examine the appropriateness of the testing instrument with regard to reliability, validity, and norming populations. Sensitivity must be used when working with people from different cultural and linguistic backgrounds and with young people who have different types of disabling conditions.

Testing should be used only when necessary, and the rehabilitation professional should be aware of the proper use of testing and the specific instruments from which to choose. Each test should be defined according to what it measures and its use, and populations for which the test is appropriate should be described. The process of test development should also be described, and any specialized skills needed to administer the test and to interpret scores should be identified. When selecting a test battery, adequate interpretive strategies should be available (Bolton, 1982).

Test Fairness

The evaluator must proceed with caution when attempting to evaluate the performance of minority group members or other persons who are not represented in the norm group on which the instrument was standardized (Rayman, 1990). Matkin (1980) wrote, "The vocational evaluator is ethically obliged when reporting outcomes to indicate the reason why consumers fail to perform at average or above levels and ways for remediating the deficiency" (p. 59).

The consumers' needs and their reactions to the assessment process should be carefully considered. Environmental influences (e.g., room temperature, ventilation, restricted movement, inappropriate language in the instructions) and consumer traits (e.g., sensory defects, inability to read, motivation level, lighting, test-taking strategies) demand consideration to ensure that "outcome measures reflect an accurate assessment of the evaluated traits" (Rayman, 1990, p. 60).

Tests should be of proven quality and appropriate for the consumer, given the manner in which the test results will be used. Tests should be administered under the same conditions that were established in their standardization. When tests are not administered under standard conditions or when unusual behavior or irregularities occur during the testing session, this must be noted and the results designated as invalid or of questionable validity. When there is a need to modify tests to accommodate certain disability groups, attention should be given to assessment methods that do not compromise the validity and reliability of the test. Scores obtained from tests that are not reliable or valid do not reflect the effects of the individual's disability. As the issue of test modification becomes more important, it becomes necessary to consider whether and how tests can be modified (Gordon, Stump, & Glaser, 1996). The Americans with Disabilities Act of 1990 (ADA) reemphasizes the requirement for reasonable accommodations to the physical or mental limitations of persons with disabilities, including modifications to examinations (Nester, 1994). The types of testing accommodations for individuals with disabilities usually fall into the following three categories.

Testing Medium

This refers to the use of a different method to present the same information, for example, large print, a reader, or audiotape. (It should be noted that changing a test from a printed version into a sign language version is a translation into another language, rather than simply a change of medium [Nester, 1994].)

Time Limits

For many individuals with disabilities, it is necessary to change a test's time limits. There is often the difficult problem of determining exactly how much extra time should be allotted so that the person with a disability is neither helped nor hindered. Possible accommodations include eliminating (in some circumstances) the use of timed power tests, exploring the opportunity to conduct empirical studies to determine appropriate time limits, or reporting two time scores: one that recognizes the test's published guidelines, and one that allows for any modification due to the individual's physical or mental limitations (Holzbauer & Berven, 1999).

Very little is known, however, about the effects of deviations from standard test administration procedures (Gordon et al., 1996). Guidelines regarding accommodations typically are developed to accompany standardized tests or are ordered separately (Ziezula, 1986). Further investigation into appropriate assessment accommodations, as well as into the effects of test modification, is urgently needed.

Test Content

Although any change in test content needs to be consistent with the validity data on which the test was based, changes in test content can be divided into the following categories: (a) change in individual test questions; (b) change in the question type; and (c) change in the knowledge, skill, or ability that is being measured (Nester, 1994). Accommodations can be implemented according to these changes if another type of question exists to measure the same ability and if the skill to be tested can be evaluated in another manner (e.g., through an interview, through work experience requirements; Nester, 1994). Note, however, that changing or deleting a skill or ability is justified only if the helping professional has no appropriate way to measure these factors and he or she believes that the specific skill or knowledge area is not a job requirement for the person with a disability.

Test Interpretation

The interpretation of scores should take into account any major differences between the norms or comparison groups and the actual test takers. Using tests for purposes not specifically recommended by the test developer should be avoided unless there is evidence to support the intended use. Proper interpretation requires knowledge about the test that can be obtained by studying its manual and other materials, along with current research literature with respect to its use. Particular attention should be directed to issues of reliability (which is a prerequisite to validity), validity, norms, and administration and scoring variation (RUST Statement, 1990).

How the passing score was determined should be explained, and evidence discussed to support the appropriateness of the scores. Test interpretation should include all other relevant information about the consumer (e.g., educational background, motivation, adjustment to disability; Bolton, 1982). Important decisions about consumers should not be based on the results of one test or a single testing session. Only when two or more instruments or sources of information suggest the same conclusion should crucial decisions be considered with a consumer (Bolton, 1982).

Test-Taker Rights in Assessment

Test takers have the right to know in advance of testing why they are being tested, how the testing will benefit them, how the test data will be used, and how much time and money the testing will cost them. They also have the right to participate in planning and scheduling of the testing.

Test takers have the right to refuse unnecessary and outdated tests and to be tested in an atmosphere that is free from distractions and conducive to positive test performance. Also, they have the right to be assessed via the most appropriate instruments and techniques available.

Test takers have the right to complete, comprehensive, clear, and honest explanations, analyses, and applications of their test results. They have the right to discuss their test results with people competent at interpreting test protocols, relating test data to other available data, and answering questions. Finally, they have the right to have their confidentiality protected and to have further counseling or assessment, if indicated.

Test Privacy

The privacy of the consumer must be respected, and all information and materials obtained during the assessment process should be safeguarded. Policy standards developed by the American Counseling Association (ACA) concerning the responsibility of users of standardized tests state that confidentiality of information and materials should be maintained (RUST Statement, 1990). The policy also states that the consumer should be informed about who will receive the assessment information and under what circumstances it will be released. Test scores, moreover, should be released only to persons qualified to interpret them. When making any statements to the public about tests and testing, the evaluator must give accurate information and avoid false claims or misstatements. Special efforts are often required to avoid unwarranted connotations of such terms as *IQ* and *grade equivalent scores* or other technical scale names (Rayman, 1990).

The confidentiality of test instruments and test data is paramount in maintaining the integrity of tests and the validity of test results (Blackwell, Autry, & Guglielmo, 2001), and therefore testing materials should be stored in a secure place.

Evaluator Competencies

A relatively long period of intensive training and supervised experience is required for the proper use of individual intelligence tests and most personality measures, and a minimum of specialized psychological training is needed for educational or vocational proficiency tests. Different tests demand different levels of competence for administration, scoring, and interpretation. The helping professional must recognize the limits of professional competence and perform only those functions for which he or she is prepared. If the evaluator, for example, is using computer-based test interpretations, he or she should be trained in the construct being measured and the specific instrument prior to using the computer application (Rayman, 1990). Testing should be conducted only when necessary, and the rehabilitation professional should be aware of the proper use of testing and the specific instruments from which to choose.

Vocational evaluators should demonstrate competencies not only in the areas surveyed during the assessment and rehabilitation process but also in the world of work, the study of human behavior, and understanding the limitations of test interpretation. Vocational evaluators or related professionals should periodically reexamine their own competencies, as well as keep abreast of current labor market trends, employment requirements for various occupations, and work modification techniques.

It is important to note that cultural diversity themes are addressed throughout the revised Code, which establishes a foundation of understanding for the culturally competent counselor. These themes include expanding the importance of considering diversity issues in evaluation, assessment, and test interpretation; providing for informed consent in consultation; and clarifying cultural meanings of confidentiality and privacy (Cartwright & Fleming, 2010).

Consumer Preparation in Assessment: The Evaluator Perspective

Once the decision is mutually made to obtain a certain type of vocational evaluation and the facility or agency to conduct this assessment is selected, the consumer must be carefully prepared. This is the one area often neglected during the entire rehabilitation process. Assumptions are often made either that the referring agency will perform this task or that consumers do not need any preparation apart from the name and address of the evaluation facility and the types of tests or assessment procedures that will be used. However, the professional can ensure the reliability of the entire assessment experience by explaining the purpose of evaluation and the ways the results can aid the consumer in achieving realistic rehabilitation goals.

Imparting information and responding to the consumer's questions and related concerns should be the focus of this preparation. Professionals should discuss with their consumers the purpose of assessment, its part in the rehabilitation process, and the ways in which evaluation information can help to identify the consumer's strengths and indicate obstacles to reaching rehabilitation goals. Procedures that will be used in the assessment can be explained, after which advice can be given to the consumer about the best way to prepare mentally and physically for the evaluation. For example, consumers may need to be told that getting a good night's sleep the night before and eating a good breakfast can contribute to better performance during the evaluation. Additional information that should be communicated includes the starting time, the amount of time the assessment usually takes, and directions to the facility. Finally, the professional should mention that he or she will receive a report from the evaluation resource and will discuss it with the consumer. This can often alleviate consumer concerns about learning the assessment results. If it is the policy of the particular agency or other evaluation resource to carefully explain test results to the consumer, then this practice should be mentioned.

When the professional decides to use standardized measures to gain information for rehabilitation planning, he or she should prepare the consumer for this opportunity. The professional should create a relaxed, nonthreatening atmosphere and solicit the consumer's input for the particular goals of assessment. In other words, explaining the purpose of assessment and how it fits into the development of effective rehabilitation planning frequently helps the consumer to identify personal goals for evaluation. For consumers representing different minority groups, it is important to understand the individual's worldview, which can include attitudes toward the assessment experience and self-knowledge. Certain cultures have definite attitudes or inhibitions about being tested. The importance of learning more about, and, especially, becoming aware of, personal strengths should also be stressed. Such questions as, "How do you feel about identifying your capabilities and interests?" and "What particular information about yourself would you like to have?" can encourage the consumer's input. It is necessary to be aware of the consumer's level of understanding and the obstacles that might block his or her comprehension of these questions and the assessment process itself. Speech and hearing limitations, intellectual deficits, and the side effects of medication can present barriers to effective communication.

It is further suggested that the professional be alert to any signs of consumer hesitancy or ambiguity about being involved in evaluation. The possible source of this resistance should be identified. For example, many consumers know from past experience that they test poorly. The thought of another possible failure experience arouses tremendous anxiety. Information about vocational evaluation opportunities, how the assessment results will be used, and the relationships between assessment and the world of work can all reduce some of this fear. When the consumer is told that the actual purpose of vocational evaluation is to identify strengths or capabilities that can be used for potentially satisfying, work-related goals, some of the threatening aspects of an upcoming assessment experience are minimized. Consumers may still remain anxious, but at least they realize that the professional is supportive and understand why the evaluation is going to be conducted.

Consumers bring much of their past, particularly in the areas of vocational functioning, to the initial interview. They then look ahead to possible directions for a satisfying future. Consumers with a disability often present themselves as persons who have been functioning in some kind of vocational environment. Such pre-disability, work-related characteristics are not completely extinguished by the disability experience; rather, they serve as both guidelines for current functioning and foundation areas for renewed or further vocational development.

Persons who were born with disabilities may have a slower vocational development, but they still have the same potential vocational behaviors as persons who have disabilities as the result of traumatic experiences. Such experiences disrupt the behavioral adjustment patterns that have been formed during one's life. In contrast to the latter population, the life of the individual with a congenital disability has not been suddenly upset by a traumatic, disabling event, although some persons disabled at birth never do adapt to their limitations.

An important aspect of consumer preparation is the consumer's degree of readiness for the assessment process. Readiness for involvement in vocational and employment diagnosis should be identified during the initial interview. Several criteria that can be used to determine readiness are the following:

1. *Motivation*—A consumer's motivation regarding participation in the assessment process is a determination that can be assisted by exploring the nature of the consumer's disability and the consumer's employment history, individual strengths according to self-report, and current interview behavior.

2. *Stability*—This criterion refers to the consumer's physical and emotional condition, including endurance for evaluation involvement. Disabilities such as head injury and other neurological traumas frequently necessitate long periods of recovery and should be reasonably stable before the consumer's participation in the career assessment process is considered.

3. *Availability for assessment*—This criterion implies that accessible transportation is available for the consumer and that sufficient time during the consumer's rehabilitation will be allotted to assessment.

4. *Expectations*—This presumes that significant others in the consumer's environment have positive attitudes concerning the consumer's participation in vocational assessment. Negative attitudes toward the consumer's involvement from persons who have a decided influence on the consumer's life can undermine the evaluative process.

5. *Medication management*—When consumers present themselves for vocational assessment, most are taking some form of medication, which may have an effect on the consumer's attention, concentration, and stamina. The helping professional should identify the consumer's medications and ascertain their effect on the assessment process.

6. *Consumer awareness*—This awareness includes an understanding of the goals of the evaluation process and the demands implied in different assessment tasks. Such awareness must also consider cultural factors that relate to rehabilitation services, as well as attitudes toward the disability itself. Many individuals representing cultural minorities have definite ideas about sharing personal information with helping professionals who are not members of the

same ethnic group, or they may view the assessment process as another failure experience designed by the dominant culture. These perceptions should be identified and discussed as part of the consumer's evaluation preparation.

After acquiring consumer input and making a determination of consumer readiness, the vocational professional must make a decision about the sequence of tests that should be administered. This choice should not be made, however, until the rehabilitation worker decides what further information must be obtained after the initial interview, if the chosen test will be used for diagnostic purposes. My priority in the sequence of standardized measures is for the formal evaluation process to begin with interest tests. Frequently, the consumer can take home an interest test after the initial interview, but the professional must be very careful about reliability and related test-taking issues, as discussed in Chapter 5.

Regardless of the sequence in which tests are administered, certain general precautions should be taken. During testing, all possible distractions should be reduced and consumer fatigue minimized. Also, the consumer should realize that every effort must be exerted to do as well as possible. Of course, most consumers experience anxiety and apprehension when taking a test. However, when the nature of the test, background information concerning the norm group, and relationship of the particular measure to the assessment goals are all communicated, this tension can be reduced. Questions about an assessment measure should be solicited. When consumers are informed of the confidentiality issues of assessment and are told that when taking an interest or personality measure, they are actually describing themselves to themselves, they often feel better about the evaluation.

Consumer preparation is based on timely and knowledgeable communication from the rehabilitation professional. Understanding consumer needs and disability-related limitations, the uses of a test, and the factors that enhance the reliability of the consumer's involvement (e.g., rest, minimal distractions, control of anxiety, best possible effort) can contribute to developing a relaxed, nonthreatening atmosphere that can help to make the assessment experience a valuable one for the consumer.

The experience can also facilitate the consumer's sense of empowerment. Instilling consumer empowerment is now integral to the rehabilitation process, and how this is frequently achieved is discussed in Chapter 1.

Additional Factors to Consider During the Beginning Phases of the Evaluation Process

Even with careful preparation of the consumer, additional issues must be taken into consideration when developing assessment plans. There is the ever-present possibility that evaluation, especially psychometric testing, will do more harm than good. Unless particular attention is directed to the choice of an appropriate test, the prudent use of administration procedures, and the enlightened interpretation of assessment results, the consumer and rehabilitation professional will have a decidedly negative experience.

Consumers bring a variety of individual traits, competencies, and limitations to rehabilitation opportunities. They also bring a distinctive cultural background and individual expectations, attitudes, and values that emerge from their ethnicity. Frequently, factors such as motivation, interests, ethnicity, and work tolerance may be just as important to reaching rehabilitation goals as the qualities of intelligence and learning-related aptitudes. Using standardized test instruments is not always the best way for evaluating many of these consumer characteristics. Observation of the consumer in different settings and evaluation of trial periods in a job situation can be better methods for understanding rehabilitation potential. For example, a consumer with a congenital disability may have had different life experiences than populations on whom the standardized tests were normed. If this disability is present in someone who is African American, Hispanic, or Asian, then there is an added range of varied life experiences. The use of standardized, psychological measures, therefore, may not be appropriate in certain cases, and other assessment approaches should be explored.

The inappropriateness of standardized tests is especially true when such measures are used only for exploring the person's potential for learning. The test performances of persons with severe disabilities are often affected by emotional issues and sensory and motor limitations.

Comparing the performance on a particular test of a person with a disability to that of the norm group used to standardize the measure (when the norm group did not have comparable limitations) is discriminatory.

The issue of learning capability stimulates the following question: How do people learn? Frequently, the selection of assessment approaches and the choice of specific psychometric tests depend on a person's learning style. Learning-style models are based on the assumption that individuals have learning differences that are unique and need to be accommodated (Griggs, 1985). Each individual has a learning style and has been taught tasks in a different manner. Some people are more verbal and learn best through the spoken word; others are more visual and need to see charts, pictures, or demonstrations. Still others do not master a task until they experience doing it. To evaluate the learning-style preference of the consumer with a disability requires identifying specific strategies that will assist him or her in learning more about personal strengths and employment-related assets. A person's learning style may have to be assessed through a nonstandardized screening battery, which can generate specific remediation information.

When the purpose of evaluation is to understand the consumer's level of current functioning, the use of standardized measures may be justified. The rehabilitation professional wants to know how the consumer scores on the measure and how this compares to the scores of persons without disabilities. The careful use of tests, particularly aptitude and achievement measures, is warranted because specific knowledge of how a consumer's abilities or competencies compare with those of persons without disabilities may be necessary for rehabilitation planning to be relevant. After all, the consumer may work with people who do not have disabilities, and he or she has to meet their work demands. Information regarding both how the consumer will meet these demands and what will be needed in order to compete in a training or work situation is crucial when developing rehabilitation plans.

If the rehabilitation professional pays particular attention to disability effects and their impact on the vocational assessment process, then evaluation can become a valuable opportunity for the consumer. This attention presumes that the evaluator is knowledgeable about the nature of the disability and particular tests or approaches to be used in this process. This knowledge is especially important in the two areas of selection and administration.

Assessment Selection

There are many factors to consider when selecting either an assessment approach or a particular evaluation measure. Several of these factors follow.

> Age of disability onset
> Nature of physical and emotional limitations
> Medication effects
> Relationship of the consumer's life experiences to the content
>   of the proposed evaluation measures
> Learning-style preferences
> Educational experiences
> Whether verbal level of the assessment is appropriate to
>   consumer's reading ability
> Difficulty of the concepts expressed in the measure
> Extent of impaired manual ability
> Length of attention span
> Whether a person with visual impairment has enough sight
>   to handle large objects, locate test pieces in a work space, or
>   follow the hand movements of the rehabilitation professional

Furthermore, when the goals of either employability or placeability are being studied, an important consideration is the appropriate selection of an assessment approach. Although the evaluation agency and the consumer will largely determine the approach, the referring professional should consider relevant criteria. Seligman (1994) has identified several criteria to be used when planning career evaluation; these have been adapted for vocational rehabilitation: What are the goals of rehabilitation assessment? Although vocational behavior is multifaceted and involves many areas of human functioning, the evaluator should focus on areas that are relevant to vocational goals. Such a focus does not imply the necessity of exploring the ways in which interests, abilities, and personality interact to influence life adjustment, career choice, and vocational goals. In rehabilitation assessment, relevant information about the consumer should include vocational interests, possible transferable skills, needs, values, abilities, other personality characteristics, assistive technology, and characteristics of the current labor market.

How is the consumer likely to respond to and be affected by assessment? Chapter 3 of this book identifies different types of consumers who present themselves for vocational evaluation. Many of these consumers can harbor anxieties about the assessment experience, and these anxieties should be addressed during the initial consumer interview. Issues such as motivation, alertness, length of the assessment, the evaluator's ability to establish rapport, and the consumer's cognitive skills are to be considered, along with the consumer's ability to respond. Also, the interactions among setting, consumer, evaluator, and assessment materials are dynamic ones that are subject to a variety of influences.

Are there additional resources that may provide information that would otherwise be collected by vocational evaluation approaches? School or job records can be quite useful, as they provide information about the consumer's academic and work history. During the consumer interview, information may be disclosed honestly that provides sufficient data about the consumer's functioning, thereby frequently alleviating the need for further assessment.

Assessment Administration

To minimize consumer anxiety, the less involved and performance-based tests should be administered first. When possible, tests should be administered individually and in small blocks of time rather than in concentrated periods. Also, many persons with physical disabilities, especially those with severe impairments, tire easily. Fatigue can be lessened when tests are given in short intervals. Moreover, if rapport is established between the professional and consumer, the consumer should feel free to tell the professional that he or she is tiring, and time limits will be adjusted as necessary.

For many persons with severe disabilities, the manner of recording answers may have to be changed. For example, a consumer may not have use of either hand or, even with use of one hand, have great difficulty in correctly marking the answer space. The use of another person to record the answers or a specifically designed answer sheet may be required.

Particular attention should be paid to whether the consumer understands the directions for taking a particular measure. It is helpful for the professional to ask the consumer to explain directions after they have been given.

Conclusion

If the professional acknowledges the opportunity to learn needed information about a consumer's vocational capabilities and understands how disability limitations affect the evaluation process, a timely, relevant diagnostic experience for the person with a disability can be facilitated. Vocational assessment, of course, is conducted to obtain needed information. It is part of the overall rehabilitation process and, as an integral factor in the consumer's development toward rehabilitation goals, it presents an invaluable opportunity for self-awareness and effective decision making. To achieve this effectiveness, the professional and consumer must work together. When the person with a disability is involved in vocational evaluation, and the professional is knowledgeable about the different ways to gain information about a consumer, the process will be meaningful. The following chapters of this book discuss how this evaluation experience becomes an important first step for the consumer to achieve rehabilitation goals.

Chapter 3

Understanding the Consumer With a Disability

There are a number of vital considerations when preparing vocational rehabilitation plans for consumers. One of the most important ingredients in effective assessment and eventual rehabilitation planning, however, is the evaluator's understanding of the meaning of disability and an awareness of the differences between the terms *impairment, disability,* and *handicap.* The helping professional's perception of what these terms mean can influence the selection of assessment approaches and the achievement of rehabilitation goals.

The International Classification of Functioning, Disability, and Health (de Kleijn-deVrankrijker, 2003; Peterson, Mpofu, & Oakland, 2010; World Health Organization [WHO], 1980) defined *impairment* as "a problem in body function and structure due to a significant deviation or loss" (Peterson et al., 2010, p. 5). *Handicap* was defined as a barrier in the environment. Later, these terms were redefined. *Impairment* was considered an activity limitation; handicap was replaced with the term *participation restriction*; and *disability* was meant to focus on the individual, societal, and body-related aspects of impairments, activity limitations, and participation restrictions in the environment (Peterson et al., 2010).

The perception of disability, however, is still evolving. It is now increasingly focusing on the complex interrelationships of the consumer and the environment, as stated in the introduction of this volume. Environmental assessment approaches and multifaceted evaluation plans can respond to this expanded meaning of disability. With this environmental focus, and taking into consideration the different perceptions of the meaning of disability, the development of assessment planning and selection of evaluator approaches could vary.

Consumer dynamics can facilitate or impede the achievement of both assessment and rehabilitation goals. Consumers with mental or physical disabilities begin the assessment process with a wide variety of distinctive vocational assets and problems, including personality difficulties that can represent barriers to their own career productivity. Thematic to all these difficulties with the selected, diverse consumers described in this chapter is the current or eventual reality of bias in the workplace. People with disabilities are subject to discrimination in this environment, in the form of labeling, stereotyping, and status loss (Draper, Reid, & McMahon, 2011). A stigmatizing experience should be recognized during the vocational rehabilitation process. If the consumer perceives it as an obstacle to exploring career opportunities, then it should be addressed by the evaluator, especially during the assessment interviews.

Recognizing both current assets and difficulties is important in the identification of vocational approaches that can be discussed with the consumer for possible use during the assessment process. This chapter identifies different types of consumers and some stereotypical characteristics pertaining to needs, strengths, and emotional issues in the rehabilitation assessment process. These types are not descriptions of actual consumers.

To be noted is that the different categories of consumers with a disability who are described in this chapter do not include those with significant visual or hearing impairments. For these consumer populations an assessment specialist is usually desirable (Gallagher & Wiener, 2008; Saladin, 2008). Apart from very specialized tests for these specific populations (e.g., the *Cognitive Test for the Blind,* the *Hearing Measurement Scale*), many of the informal and formal assessment approaches discussed in this book can be adapted for individuals with visual and hearing impairments, and this is identified in the specific exploration of these measures.

The Restorer–Achiever

Typically, restorer–achievers either have been born with a physical disability or have incurred a disability after years of satisfying work. Generally, they are between the ages of 30 and 45, have a strong work ethic, and, through working, have gained a sense of both stability and identity in their lives. Importantly, these individuals believe they possess many work-related skills. Although they harbor feelings of loss because of disability-related limitations, they are anxious to return to work and are usually open to many job alternatives. They perceive their disabilities as a fact of life, an inconvenience, a cause of frustration, or a combination of these.

These consumers can manage their own affairs and typically come to a state or private rehabilitation agency for training or other remedial help (e.g., prosthetics, job leads). Unfamiliar with the different resources that can assist them in their rehabilitation efforts, they seek information on how to reenter the job market. Although they are often suspicious about the kind of help the agency can offer, they are task oriented, show much energy and motivation, and possess a positive attitude shaped by past experiences. They need and want the help that rehabilitation agencies can provide. These consumers have many of the employable traits that are necessary to hold a job (e.g., psychological readiness, a work personality previously shaped by conscientiousness and competitiveness, transferable job skills). What they particularly need from assessment is to be shown that they have transferable skills and abilities that can help them to regain employment, as well as support from the helping professional when planning rehabilitation goals.

Case Example: Curtis

Curtis, age 34, unmarried, and born with a medical diagnosis of "moderate cerebral palsy," has recently lost his job because of a company takeover. He has a college degree in accounting and worked successfully since graduation for a manufacturing firm as an accountant before a conglomerate bought the business and brought in their own managerial staff. Curtis has his own apartment and has lived independently since leaving school. He has several physical limitations but with assistive technology has been able to perform the physical and cognitive demands of business accounting. He has won several awards for his work. Despite some physical limitations, and with remediated speech therapy during college, Curtis has further participated in many community-based activities and assumed leadership responsibilities in selected organizations.

He presents himself for vocational rehabilitation services. Though he is eager, if necessary, to learn new tasks, he is still sad about leaving his company of many years. Curtis views evaluation as an opportunity to possibly re-tool many of his work-related skills or develop newer ones that would help him to be more competitive in today's labor market.

Issues to Consider

- Present challenging assessment approaches to explore optimal capabilities.
- Solicit Curtis's input frequently during the evaluation, especially with regard to personal feelings about performance on evaluative tasks and to encourage an increased sense of control.
- Solicit input, with Curtis's permission, from his previous employer about work behaviors and skills.
- Suggest assessment approaches that take into account previous work experience and that provide detailed information about capabilities, available support, and Curtis's medical condition.
- Consider transferable skills information an important aid in identifying consumer work-related strengths.
- An attempt should be made to identify the consumer's perception of any medication effects on his past work performance.
- Consider any update of how newer developments in assistive technology can enhance work performance.

Evaluation Approaches to Consider

- The consumer-oriented interview
- Self-assessment tools that explore transferable skills, self-esteem, interests, and any anger resulting from the loss of employment
- Formal assessment approaches, using appropriate accommodations, such as the *Tennessee Self-Concept Scale* (Fitts & Warren, 1996) and the *Sixteen Personality Factor Questionnaire* (16 PF; Cattell, 1986)

The Secondary Gainer

Secondary gainers are consumers who usually either are ambivalent about returning to work or make no pretense about desiring to seek paid employment. They usually attempt an assessment experience because they are required to do so to receive continued disability-related benefits. Long periods of medical recuperation for many consumers may have created the strong suspicion that it is not going to be possible to enter the competitive labor market. Often, paid employment provides these consumers with little increase over compensation payments, and rehabilitation may offer little incentive for renouncing these secure and steady payments.

These consumers frequently have attitudinal problems, including a pessimistic view about their occupational future. Surprisingly, during the assessment process they may be cooperative and anxious to learn about the evaluation results. At the same time, their actual career or job outlook is characterized by extreme caution, suspicion, and a reluctance to learn about their own capabilities. They may be more concerned with life adjustment demands and their own identity as people with disabilities than with worker identities. Importantly, they may associate assessment primarily with testing, and they feel reluctant about going into situations in which they might look bad or feel inadequate.

The concept of secondary gain proves to be of particular concern with regard to consumers who receive insurance payments. They generally have had little confidence in themselves as workers and now view their dependent roles as the preferred style of living. Disability strengthens the dependency. Family members may also encourage this dependence because they may unwittingly contribute to helplessness and an inactive lifestyle. Both lowered family expectations regarding the performance of household responsibilities and exaggerated attention to the person's needs may further contribute to this dependence. The family attempts to make the person's life easier and less burdensome, and in doing so not only meets the person's needs but also removes responsibilities related to home and family goals. Dependency becomes a way of life, and the person with a disability is very comfortable in an existence wherein needs are easily met and demands are minimal.

In interview sessions during vocational evaluation, secondary gainers are often manipulative. They try to present their current life situations in such a way as to solicit sympathy for their disabilities. There are difficulties in establishing plans of action to meet life responsibilities. These individuals convey a lack of foresight regarding future plans and little willingness to meet scheduling demands for medical, training, and counselor appointments during the rehabilitation process. They focus more on the negative aspects of their lives. The secondary gainer may have had many negative experiences associated with work. Employment that is personally fulfilling has never been found, and now the disability provides an excuse for not working.

Many consumers who have found a secondary gain in dependency also have continued physical pain related to their disabilities. This is particularly true of workers who have injured their lower backs. These workers often display unusual postures, limps, patterns of inactivity, or a reliance on medication and prosthetic appliances to help control the pain. Ironically, reliance upon such methods often serves to maintain dependency and, in turn, reduces the probability of successful vocational rehabilitation (Lynch, 1979). Pain becomes a dominant reality in their lives and precipitates fear, chronic complaining, and depression.

Surprisingly, the person's self-esteem is often not affected because of the continued gratification of dependency needs. The role becomes satisfying because it may force others to care for the consumer. Compensation benefits accruing from an injury also increase the reinforcement value of the sick role. These consumers, consequently, have work-readiness problems.

Consumers who want to maintain the status quo of an inactive lifestyle express another form of secondary gain. Frequently originally middle-aged people with good work histories, secondary gainers become injured and then resist any efforts to return to the work sector. They are basically very angry at having disabilities, but the anger is suppressed and takes the form of reluctance. The disability is perceived as a burdensome and unwelcome disruption in what was a stable, conservative lifestyle, and they claim, "I've done my work already … I can't do anything more." They resist attempts to plan rehabilitation goals, and they are reluctant to follow through with any vocational plan. During work evaluation, they often cannot organize effectively, and because of slowness and hesitancy, their assessment productivity is below competitive standards. These consumers often claim they lack the physical energy to meet the job expectations of others.

Case Example: Rebecca

Rebecca is a 28-year-old White woman. She is married with one son, age 5 years, and her husband is self-employed, specializing in carving birds and then selling them at county and state fairs, through a website, and at a local retail store specializing in fine arts and crafts. Rebecca, a high school graduate with 2 years of community college, worked for 7 years in the retail field and described her work as "unfulfilling and unsatisfying." She reports that to bring some excitement into her life she joined the National Guard, regularly attended to her military responsibilities, and was deployed to Iraq 8 months ago.

As a member of the military security force in Iraq, she was riding in a truck during a convoy assignment when her truck detonated an improvised explosive device (IED), causing two of the personnel their lives and leaving four others with debilitating injuries. Rebecca was severely wounded, with facial and leg injuries. Her right leg was amputated to stabilize her medical condition. After triage at a field hospital and, later, surgery at a military hospital in Germany, she was transferred to a military hospital in the United States, near her home and family. A counselor from the Veteran's Administration (VA) approached Rebecca about beginning the steps in career counseling, and this was her response:

We never had much money while I was growing up, and I had to struggle to complete high school and community college. And my memories of working retail are not pleasant ones. I believe that right now I have no marketable skills, and I will get good money from my compensation because of my injuries. My husband has been a decent provider, and why do I want that stress from working? Right now I am well cared for, and though my rehab will take a long time, my goal now is to adjust to my disability and not worry about anything else.

Issues to Consider

- Seek detailed information about physical, mental, and cognitive capabilities; available support network for facing the unknown; and medical condition
- Present clear and cogent alternatives to a life of dependency on disability-related benefits
- Identify family issues and expectations for seeking a vocational career
- Plan brief assessments that give immediate, positive feedback
- The professional should communicate concern and reflect Rebecca's feelings, and explain that her reluctance or resistance may actually be a fear of losing compensation

- During assessment and further rehabilitation planning, Rebecca should be involved in any decisions and given appropriate responsibility. Continued feedback on career-related strengths and attempts at consumer empowerment may help raise the consumer's level of career expectations

Evaluation Approaches to Consider

- Self-assessment approaches that would explore Rebecca's perceptions of her loss and her cognitive, aptitude, and interest functioning. The consumer-oriented interview could facilitate this exploration.
- Such standardized measures as the *Quick-Test; Shipley; Wide Range Achievement Test–Fourth Edition*; appropriate work samples; *Sixteen Personality Factor Questionnaire* (16 PF), Form E; *Tennessee Self-Concept Scale*; the *Self-Directed Search; Kuder DD*
- When feasible and with appropriate accommodations, situational assessment

The Angry Resister

Many consumers who begin rehabilitation assessment with good work histories, motivation to work, and confidence in themselves as workers also display a "you-owe-me-something" attitude or say, "I will go back to work, but only on my terms." Often, they bring a history of personality disturbances (Lynch, 1979). Pre-disability life situations were often troubled, and their personalities hindered their ability to cope with their problems. The occurrence of disability adds another source for inadequate coping. These consumers believe that life owes them a lot, including topflight rehabilitation services, the helping professional's total time and attention, or perhaps an exceptional compensation package. Frequently, in response to efforts aimed at helping them, angry resisters state, "Yes, but ..." or they do not follow through with anything that has been suggested or agreed to (Pickman, 1994).

Overall, the main source of these consumers' anger is their disability, which has caused the disruption of a stable lifestyle. They usually want to return to their former place of employment, but they may have had a job-related disabling accident, and the employer views the injured worker as "incapable of functioning productively not only in that person's former capacity but in any capacity involved in the employer's business or operations" (Eaton, 1979, p. 61). Such rejection affects the consumer's self-concept, and with this deterioration in self-esteem comes hostility.

Another source of anger may be the perceived losses accruing from the disability situation. Because the onset of accidents is sudden, many consumers with disabilities are unprepared to handle the physical, social, psychological, vocational, and financial implications of their injuries. They may no longer have control of their life situations and thus have lost their self-determination (Lynch, 1979). For many people with disabilities, lingering anger is a sign of unresolved grief; perhaps they have never been given the chance to come to terms with their losses. These feelings of loss stimulate individuals to question their self-worth, and, in turn, they develop grandiose plans in order to counteract self-doubts. For example, these consumers may want money to begin their own businesses, and they often feel that this money is owed them because of their disabilities.

Other consumers who can be typified as angry resisters are critical of rehabilitation possibilities, rigid in their own work expectations, and resistant to counselor suggestions. They express behavioral patterns that tend to turn people off, such as appearing late for counseling appointments or demanding too much of the counselor's time. During vocational assessment, they may ask for detailed reasons for every request that is made of them and are hesitant to cooperate with the counselor in reaching evaluation objectives unless such goals are in complete harmony with their own wishes. Consequently, what occurs during assessment is a conflict between the expectations of the consumer and those of the rehabilitation professional. Although this conflict may also occur with secondary gainers or those who are ambivalent about their own rehabilitation gain, angry consumers are determined to have their vocational wishes followed.

Case Example: Robin

Robin is a 35-year-old woman who lost her job 6 months ago. She is talking to the vocational counselor about being fired, and the time immediately following that.

Two months ago I was talking with one of the telephone solicitors when my boss storms in and begins raking me over the coals for a sudden drop in sales I really had nothing to do with. I sat there in shock. I was so angry that I wanted to yell back at her, but I kept my cool. But for the rest for the day I couldn't get it out of my mind. No matter what I was doing, it haunted me. I finally got so angry that I burst into her office and told her just what I thought of her. I even let her have it for a few lousy things she's done in the past. I am still pretty angry, and during the past 2 months I've been trying to figure out where I can get a new job or maybe how I can get my old job back.

Robin is unmarried and was diagnosed with multiple sclerosis (MS) 5 years ago. Upon learning of the diagnosis, her boyfriend of 2 years immediately terminated the relationship, and she reports that she still feels hurt and angry about that. "My MS has been a real burden in my life. I had an AA degree in business, worked as a legal secretary for several years. But with the unpredictable remissions and exacerbations, and with other limitations associated with my illness, I couldn't continue to handle the stress of that job. Telephone soliciting allowed me to control my work hours, and I thought I was good at it." Robin further reports that she lives independently and that money from her parents' estate contributes significantly to her income. Six years ago, both of her parents were killed in an automobile crash. There are no siblings, and her deceased mother's sister lives about an hour's drive away. Robin states that she has short bouts of depression, becomes at times very upset over her limitations, and enjoys a small circle of friends who are in a book club with her and meet for dinner twice a month.

Issues to Consider

- The consumer's anger must be addressed before any assessment can provide a reliable estimate of job-related capabilities.
- The consumer should have an opportunity to air his or her feelings during the assessment planning interview. An understanding of the consumer's feelings surrounding being fired may facilitate her involvement in evaluation tasks.
- The consumer's medical condition in the perspective of vocational capabilities should be clarified, with an emphasis on information about career-related strengths and support in facing an uncertain progression of the illness.

- Assessment should provide an opportunity for short-term realistic experiences that provide immediate feedback about work potential.
- Assistive technology resources should be explored that could possibly enhance work performance during both evaluation and employment acquisition.
- Career or work expectations should not be raised to an unrealistic level, since false hopes only provoke anger and resentment.
- An attempt should be made to identify the consumer's perception of her illness or disability experience and its impact on daily life. Such exploration could include any regular medications Robin takes and their effect on her behavior.

Evaluation Approaches to Consider

- The use of the consumer interview to not only collect necessary information but also establish a working relationship built on trust
- Self-assessment measures that include the emotional and interest areas of consumer functioning. These measures could include the *Interest Check List* (U.S. Department of Labor, 1981) and the *Self-Directed Search* (Holland, 1994).
- The *O*NET* (Hanson, Matheson, & Borman, 2001), the *Sixteen Personality Factor Questionnaire* (16 PF; Cattell, 1986), and the *California Psychological Inventory* (CPI; Gough & Bradley, 1996), to identify acquired work skills, vocational interest patterns, and emotional functioning. With appropriate accommodations, select work samples might further identify work-related strengths.

The Consumer With Developmental Disabilities

Many consumers who present themselves for rehabilitation are functioning at a borderline or lower level of intelligence, that is, a measured IQ of 70 to 79 (Wechsler, 1997). They may have been in special education classes in school, and when schooling formally concluded, they remained at home. Overprotective parents or underdeveloped social skills become inhibiting factors when faced with choosing opportunities that bring job possibilities. There has been no transition to the world of work.

Because these consumers have never learned about the behavioral demands of working, they usually approach the assessment situation

cautiously and anxiously. These behaviors typically are caused by igno-
rance, rather than by rejection of work itself. With little self-confidence
and little knowledge of their employment-related assets, they are passive
at the beginning of the rehabilitation process. At the same time, however,
people with developmental disabilities want to work. When initially presenting themselves for vocational rehabilitation, they are cooperative but
hesitant because of the unknown.

Inexperience with work and the many years under close supervision by others have created dependency patterns that rarely include self-
initiating behavior. Although their energy level and motivation may be
high, consumers with developmental disabilities have limited capacity
to solve their own problems. These consumers are almost exclusively
outer-directed, and they look to rehabilitation as a resource that will lead
them by the hand to job opportunities.

The assessment situation becomes an important beginning for individuals who are developmentally disabled because it can provide them
with necessary feedback about job-related capabilities. They have been
tested many times, and their perception of assessment might be that it
presents another failure situation. Also, these individuals have difficulty
reaching their maximum skill levels because of behavioral limitations,
most of which derive from a lack of awareness about what is expected in
a work situation.

Case Example: Maurice

At birth Maurice was diagnosed with Down syndrome. Currently 19 years
old and living at home with his parents and one sibling (a sister, 4 years
older), he recently completed high school special education classes.
Many years ago, just before beginning school, test results showed below-
average intelligence. Yet, with tutoring and other educational interventions,
he was able to accomplish the required course work and received a special
certificate upon high school graduation. Though his reading and arithmetic
levels are significantly below those of his age group, he is able to follow
simple instructions for most independent living tasks, is very personable,
and has participated for several years in the Special Olympics, specializing
in track events. He is also well known around a popular local health club
and assists the gym manager on a part-time basis in many chores.

Maurice's parents are now both retired as educators; his father was a college professor and his mother a high school English teacher. The family has traveled extensively during the last 5 years, and now they are particularly concerned about their son's future living arrangements and a vocational career. Maurice's mother was 45 years old when he was born, and because both parents have no siblings, they are worried about his future living arrangements. Maurice's current part-time job is temporary, as it is based on a friendship and not a stable position at the health center. Maurice agrees with his parents that he needs to identify his work capabilities, which was not done during high school because of the school's severe budget cuts and consequent lack of resources. He now presents himself for vocational counseling.

Issues to Consider

- An exploration of realistic job-related abilities and cognitive and behavioral limitations and a discussion of the situational approach could all be considered. Placement in an actual work environment provides an opportunity for feedback on job-keeping behaviors and usually offers a more feasible diagnostic picture than what could be learned from paper-and-pencil measures.
- Selected work samples and other "hands-on" evaluation activities may help the consumer better understand his abilities and the demands of the working environment. Acknowledging important job-keeping behaviors is a decided step toward employability.
- With Maurice's permission, a family meeting could facilitate the building of trust between the professional and the entire family group. During this meeting, future housing possibilities could be explored, referrals suggested, and transportation and any assistive technology arrangements discussed.

Evaluation Approaches to Consider

- The consumer interview
- Before work sample and situational assessment approaches are considered, the evaluator might wish to explore and/or administer:
  - Reviewing educational records
  - *Vineland Adaptive Behavior Scales–Second Edition* (Sparrow, Cicchetti, & Balla, 2005)

- *Reading-Free Vocational Interest Inventory–Second Edition* (R-FVII-2; Becker, 2000)
- Interest Card Sorts
- *Geist Picture Interest Inventory–Revised* (Geist, 1988)
- *Peabody Picture Vocabulary Test–Fourth Edition* (PPVT-IV; Dunn & Dunn, 2007)

The Consumer With Chronic Mental Illness

Many consumers referred to vocational rehabilitation have been institutionalized for years. Included in this population are individuals with diagnosed severe mental illnesses. The deinstitutionalization movement in mental health has facilitated the return to community living of thousands of persons with mental illness who otherwise would have remained in state hospitals. However, this movement brings distinct problems to rehabilitation. Usually, people with mental illness have not been taught the skills necessary to function appropriately in the community. Years of institutionalization have created behaviors that inhibit the assessment process. Often combined with this passivity are minimal amounts of formal education, a feeling that opportunities for the future are quite bleak, and a lingering sense of inferiority. When confronted with an assessment situation, these consumers usually do not say very much, often giving the impression that they have no demonstrated commitment to change and find it uncomfortable to take the risk of learning more about themselves and their abilities for work. During assessment, they generally give the impression of being bored. Many isolated individuals want to work but are hesitant to take that first step to learn about themselves or understand realistic work demands. The assessment opportunity can be a valuable time to provide positive feedback about themselves.

Consumers with psychiatric impairments have a degree of disability that is usually much greater than is typically encountered in current vocational evaluation systems. The impairment manifests itself in pervasive and aberrant behaviors, feelings, and cognitions. When a person has a psychiatric disability, his or her deficits in psychobiological processes, such as memory, attention, perception, and concept formation, hinder social interaction. The socially limited person faces problems different from those faced by individuals who have physical disabilities (Murray, 1990). The disability itself may not be understood readily and may exhibit a broad range of variability in terms of the impact on the individual's functioning at any given time (Beley & Felker, 1981). Although the consumer may possess work-related assets, these may be masked by passive–dependent behaviors or extrapyramidal motor effects associated with long-term use of psychotropic medication (Beley & Felker, 1981). Also, there is rarely a permanent cure for mental illness. Higher levels of functioning may improve, but mental patients have a common tendency to regress (Anthony, Howell, & Danley, 1984). Vocational evaluation conclusions that represent one point in time can be misleading. Yet an effective vocational evaluation for those with mental illnesses builds on existing psychological information and incorporates the socio-environmental demands of an employment situation.

Case Example: James

This 38-year-old African American man is single with a high school degree and reports that he has job-related skills. James has been hospitalized seven times in 11 years. His usual symptoms are thoughts of suicide, severe depression, anxiety, difficulty sleeping, and feelings of sinfulness, worthlessness, and hopelessness. Precipitating causes of hospitalization have varied. Mainly, they involved loss of a therapist, stress from a job situation, too much interpersonal contact, increased exposure to heterosexual situations, and raised tension resulting from conflict between guilt feelings and sexual feelings. The diagnosis has ranged from chronic schizophrenia to obsessive-compulsive personality with depressive, hysterical, and paranoid factors.

Currently, James is seeing a therapist, is living alone in a furnished apartment, and is regularly taking prescribed medication. He is an active member of a community social club and attends two or three of their activities each month. His therapist reports that he is making progress in therapy and, though he has not been employed now for several months, is preparing himself for employment. His work history includes jobs as a forklift operator, bricklayer, and plumber's assistant. James's mother and father are still living, but James reports that he sees them infrequently and has lost contact with his brothers and sisters.

Issues to Consider

- The vocational evaluation approach used with consumers who have psychiatric disabilities is only slightly different from the vocational intervention approach used with other persons with disabilities. The important differences are in emphasis. More time is needed, for example, for those with mental illness to go through the process. More alternative vocational environments are needed to allow these consumers the opportunity for reality testing and exploration. Social and emotional difficulties may be subtler and more easily overlooked (Anthony et al., 1984), and approaches should be used to identify these problems. Murray (1990) noted that emerging developments in the vocational evaluation of persons with psychiatric disabilities, such as psycho-education (combining educational objectives with assessment) and supported employment (providing consumers with weekly feedback from a supervisor and a job coach in the form of functional assessment), are generating approaches that are being used to compensate for consumer deficits and ease the stress associated with assessment.
- Though employment intervention is viewed as one of the most effective interventions for the recovery and rehabilitation of people with psychiatric disabilities, numerous barriers contribute to the high unemployment rates of this population. Negative social attitudes and stigma, Social Security disincentives, lack of transportation, career development issues, poor motivation, and the high cost of accommodations, along with discrimination displayed by employers and co-workers, have all been reported as significant barriers to employment (An, Roessler, & McMahon, 2011; Bruyere, 2000; Grove, Leslie, & Scott, 1999; Roessler, 2002). Fear of disability disclosure and making appropriate requests for legal protection are two of the many issues that should be brought to the attention of rehabilitation counselors.
- An in-depth assessment of the consumer's psychological dysfunction, with an additional focus on the vocational implications of the consumer's disability, should be conducted.
- Although existing psychometric instruments rarely provide normative data for this population, a multiple-perspective approach to evaluation could be considered. This approach should focus on assessing the environment in which a consumer wishes to function,

including the skills and supports necessary to function in that environment.
- During the evaluation process, much support should be provided because of the consumer's anxiety about the new situation.
- A comprehensive assessment of the consumer's functioning in life, learning, and work should be included in a multiple-perspective evaluative approach. A consumer often needs to address basic social living skills before his or her employability can be explored.
- The planned evaluation activities should be coordinated with the consumer's therapist. Both professionals must work together, especially if the assessment process becomes too stressful. Information from the therapist about the consumer's current medication and how it could affect evaluation performance needs to be obtained.
- The interview should be used to ascertain motivation, energy level, affect, residual capabilities, and the ability to focus on goals.
- When drugs were last taken should be identified, along with what they were and how they have affected the consumer. If drugs have been consumed recently and a behavioral change is noted, then the reliability of the assessment can be seriously compromised.

Evaluation Approaches to Consider

- MacDonald-Wilson and Nimec (2008) emphasized that a rehabilitation assessment and a traditional psychiatric diagnosis are very different, in both process and the use of evaluative tools. Rehabilitation assessment "identifies both existing and needed skills and resources, which are selected based on their likely impact on goal achievement … and on objective evaluation of skill performance and resource accessibility" (p. 529). These professionals further believe that this assessment contains three components: an overall rehabilitation goal, a functional assessment, and a resource assessment (MacDonald-Wilson & Nimec, 2008).
- Because a vocational evaluation should be designed somewhat differently for those with psychiatric disabilities, Murray (1990) offered the following suggestions:
  - The evaluation should be administered in a patient and flexible manner that links procedures to the particular stress-tolerance level of the consumer, who needs continued encouragement.

- The evaluator should have high expectations, because many people with psychiatric difficulties are able to achieve a higher level of functioning than has previously been expected.
- Functional skills should be evaluated, namely, those generic work-related qualities such as dependability, attention span, work tolerance, speed, production, and attention to detail. Independent living capabilities are also important.
- Evaluate social skills. To accomplish this evaluation, structured simulated-work sites are suggested. In these evaluations, the focus on social skills is on such behaviors "as the ability to get along with co-workers and supervisors, to communicate effectively, to behave in socially appropriate ways, to take instructions, and to be punctual, dependable, and flexible" (MacDonald-Wilson & Nimec, 2008, p. 152).
- Emphasize situational assessment. This approach to evaluation can explore consumers' on-the-job attitudes and behaviors because observation, which is the main technique for situational assessment, is necessary to gather information regarding attitudes, motivation, perseverance, and self-confidence.
- A number of instruments that measure both learning and working environments have been developed (MacDonald-Wilson & Nimec, 2008), such as the following:
  a. *Learning and Study Strategies Inventory* (Proctor, Prevatt, Adams, Hurst, & Petscher, 2006)
  b. *Standardized Assessment of Work Behavior* (Griffths, 1977)
  c. *Situational Assessment: Scales to Assess Work Adjustment and Interpersonal Skills* (Rogers, Hursh, Kielhofner, & Spaniol, 1990)
  d. *The Work Behavior Inventory* (WBI; Lysaker, Bell, Bryson, & Zito, 1993)

The Consumer With Traumatic Brain Injury

For several decades brain injury has been recognized as a distinct disability category. The significance of the number of motor vehicle accidents causing head injuries and the publicity around the large group of military service personnel incurring traumatic head injuries severe enough to preclude returning to a normal lifestyle have aroused the attention of rehabilitation professionals. They are continuing to explore the most feasible, effective approaches to evaluate and then address the injury's effect on daily life and career functioning.

Between 400,000 and 600,000 Americans sustain head injuries each year, and between 30,000 and 100,000 persons incur traumatic head injuries that result in disabilities severe enough to prevent a return to a normal lifestyle (Fayne, 1989). Of all age groups, 15- to 24-year-olds have the highest rate of head injuries, and the chief cause of head injuries is motor vehicle accidents (Zeigler, 1987).

Traumatic brain injury often results in myriad cognitive, behavioral, and physical disabilities. Cognitive disabilities can include varying degrees of short-term memory loss, difficulty in concentrating, problems in processing abstract information, decreased self-awareness and insight, poor retrieval of stored information, impairment of abstract reasoning, and impaired processing in planning, initiating, and carrying out actions. Physical and sensory disabilities can include impairments in speech, vision, hearing, fine- and gross-motor skills, and balance. Behavioral and emotional difficulties can result from a combination of specific neurological damage and feelings of frustration that come from having to cope with the overwhelming effects of the traumatic brain injury (Ruff & Schraa, 2008; Virginia Commonwealth University, 1989). These difficulties can include changes in mood and affect, feelings of vulnerability, lack of inhibitions, and inappropriate social behavior. Goal-formulation and problem-solving difficulties, as well as vocational–educational problems, also occur.

Musante (1983) believed that the approach to vocational evaluation and rehabilitation of this population is basically different—for several reasons—from other populations who may exhibit similar behaviors. Although psychological factors cannot be ignored, it has been suggested that an underlying organic component affects behavior, cognition, and emotions. Psychological testing alone may not reveal all of the deficits that will be seen in a work setting. Musante, in citing relevant research studies, explained that a major difficulty in evaluating persons with head injury is estimating their ability to function in view of present inconsistencies.

The following are other factors that rehabilitation counseling professionals evaluating persons with traumatic injury need to address:

- Expression of anger is a frequent reaction to the evaluation process, compounded by emotional lability and impulsivity.

- Inherent problems exist in using standardized tests and work samples with this population.
- Nonstatic evaluations are needed over longer periods of time. In other words, techniques should be used within evaluation and work adjustment training programs to improve reading ability and abstract thinking. This can be approached in terms of generalized reading ability, as well as in reading and following instructions for specific task completion (Musante, 1983).
- Baxter, Cohen, and Ylvisaker (1985) believed that the appropriateness of formal assessment is based chiefly on three considerations. First, the consumer must not be seriously confused. If the individual is unable to orient to the task and remain so oriented, interpretation of results will be virtually impossible. Second, the consumer should have an attention span of 30 minutes or more to allow for meaningful testing sessions. Third, if the consumer is in a period of rapid recovery, extensive testing is usually not indicated. Brief screening instruments can be used to establish levels of functioning for program planning.

To enhance one's role as a professional working with those who are traumatically brain injured, the vocational evaluator should function as a member of the rehabilitation team. Both neurocognitive testing and vocational assessment itself must be communicated at a level that will allow the consumer to slowly adjust and understand his or her strengths or weaknesses (Ruff & Schraa, 2008). Interactions among team professionals can facilitate the identification, documentation, and gradual remediation of the consumer's medical symptoms. To benefit optimally from vocational assessment, moreover, the evaluator should communicate with the personnel associated with the consumer's medical treatment to ascertain whether this consumer is medically stable, functioning at an appropriate communication level, and emotionally ready for the demands of vocational assessment. An individual who is referred prior to vocational exploration and has significant difficulties in areas such as memory, concentration, judgment, learning, and perception may become easily frustrated in a vocational evaluation setting (Fayne, 1989).

The role of the vocational evaluator with this consumer population is complex and demanding. One must be able to understand the information from a neurocognitive assessment in the following domains:

(1) attention and concentration, (2) memory and learning, and (3) executive functioning/problem-solving ability (Ruff & Schraa, 2008). Knowledge of these evaluation results will help the evaluator design a realistic, comprehensive assessment plan that can operationalize vocational rehabilitation potential.

The following case example describes some of the factors that contribute to the challenges emerging from consumers with a traumatic brain injury.

Case Example: Leonard

Leonard is a 25-year-old Hispanic unmarried Marine sergeant who had been on duty in Afghanistan for 11 months. Prior to this tour he had been in the Marines since high school graduation and reportedly thoroughly enjoyed his military service and was highly regarded by his peers. However, while leading his squadron patrol in a village supposedly occupied by the Taliban, he was accidently severely wounded by a drone attack. The apparent misplaced bomb killed three civilians and two of Leonard's Marine squad members.

Leonard was immediately evacuated to a field hospital in a coma and was diagnosed with a traumatic brain injury, broken leg, and shoulder and chest injuries. He was taken from this evacuation center to a hospital in Germany and later transferred to a Veteran's Hospital near his family home in Texas. Leonard came out of his coma while being transferred to the United States.

Upon arrival at the Veteran's Hospital, he continued treatment for his leg, shoulder, and chest wounds, and reportedly this was progressing nicely. Treatment was also begun on Leonard's brain injury, and he received periodic neurocognitive assessments. They indicated significant limitations in memory, speech, attention and concentration, and learning capacity.

During Leonard's lengthy hospitalization, his physical injuries healed and there was noticeable progress because of intensive physical, occupational, and speech therapies. His latest neurocognitive assessment indicated predictors for outcome, namely, where and how Leonard will live following discharge and how much functional independence is possible (Ruff & Schraa, 2008). During this period of discharge planning, a vocational counselor was introduced to Leonard. A positive appraisal of an available support network and a stable emotional status for Leonard facilitated the beginning intervention of the vocational counselor.

Issues to Consider

- The evaluator should receive an updated progress report from health professionals. Identification of the specific recovery stage in this consumer's overall rehabilitation is necessary.
- Assessment may have to be repeated during vocational rehabilitation, since those with traumatic head injury can have differential behavior and cognitive effects throughout the course of rehabilitation.
- Specific emotional issues should be explored, such as anger and depression. In Leonard's case, anger over the cause of the injury may need attention and possible further mental health intervention.
- Pre-injury vocational strengths, and possible pre-existing learning disabilities, should be explored. Possibly the results of neuropsychological testing and pre-existing school records and work history could be integrated (Ruff & Schraa, 2008).
- Assessment should be planned so that it validates the consumer's strengths.

Evaluation Approaches to Consider

- The structured consumer interview
- Interviews with family members to help them establish a constructive working relationship with Leonard during the performance of rehabilitation tasks. The family can also be helped in identifying how to more effectively utilize their resources to support Leonard (Ruff & Schraa, 2008).
- The appropriate use of selected work samples and standardized tests, with necessary assistive technology and/or accommodations, should be considered. Emphasis should be on interest exploration and cognitive/aptitude assessment of residual abilities.
- Self-assessment approaches can also be used as an effective intervention.

The Consumer With a Learning Disability

For the past 30 years, adults with learning disabilities have been identified in greater numbers and are the fastest growing group with disabilities in the United States (Feldman, 2006). Diagnosis of specific learning disabilities is a complex and controversial issue due to the extreme heterogeneity of persons with learning disabilities and the lack of a clear consensus on a single definition of learning disabilities (McCue, 1989). Learning disabilities are characterized by specific and severe underachievement (a discrepancy between learning potential as evaluated by intelligence tests and academic performance) in language (aphasia), reading (dyslexia), writing (dysgraphia), mathematics (dyscalculia), spelling, and/or reasoning (Feldman, 2006).

Learning disabilities are lifelong conditions, but the manifestation of a learning disability varies over time based on the individual's age, developmental stage, and specific settings (Vogel, 1989). According to McCue (1989), it is more likely that a person will experience a type of learning disability characterized by a subgroup of symptoms. For example, an individual might have a variety of perceptual and spatial difficulties but have intact phonetic language skills. Assessment procedures vary accordingly and should not be exclusively limited to available formal, standardized measures or to academic settings.

Although specific learning disabilities have been viewed primarily as academic or special education problems, the disabling aspects of a learning disability appear to be magnified as the individual is confronted by increasing and more complex demands of work, home, social situations, and community living (Hursh, 1989). Learning disabilities interfere with a range of activities important to getting and keeping a job. Individuals with these problems may have difficulties making decisions about appropriate and realistic career choices or completing job applications, or they may show cognitive and perceptual characteristics that result in accidents, errors, inefficiency, attention problems, poor judgment, trouble being on time, or difficulty learning new tasks or task sequences (Feldman, 2006; Kroll, 1984). A learning disability is an invisible disability often misunderstood by employers or friends and always confusing to the individuals themselves. On the job, the worker may appear unable to concentrate and be forgetful, disorganized, insolent, rude, or "spaced out" (Hursh, 1989).

Regarding a definition of learning disabilities, regulations adopted by the Rehabilitation Services Administration (RSA) state that

a specific learning disability is a disorder in one or more of the central nervous system processes involved in perceiving, understanding, and/

or in using concepts through verbal (spoken) or written language or nonverbal means. This disorder manifests itself with a deficit in one or more of the following areas: attention, reasoning, processing, memory, communication, reading, spelling, writing, calculation, coordination, social competence, and emotional maturity. (McCue, 1989, p. 19)

There are many important considerations concerning vocational assessment of those who have learning disabilities. Two questions that should be addressed are (1) what, if any, is the functional limitation in employment that results from deficits in language, reading, writing, mathematics, spelling, or reasoning and (2) what kind of assessment should be conducted?

McCue (1989) believed that this assessment should include the following:

- Psychoeducational assessment, which focuses on the intellectual and academic manifestations of specific learning disabilities
- Psychological and neuropsychological assessment, which address the cognitive, language, perceptual motor, and emotional manifestations of specific learning disabilities
- Medical and neurological evaluations, which focus on the medical and etiological considerations of the importance of assessment and treatment of specific learning disabilities
- Vocational assessment, which addresses the functional manifestations of specific learning disabilities with respect to work

If possible, consequently, a comprehensive assessment should be conducted to identify all potential areas of deficit. Because individuals with learning disabilities can show a broad range of cognitive, behavioral, and emotional problems, relying on one specific battery might fail to identify an individual's specific disorder. The comprehensive assessment is accomplished through a combination of clinical and psychometric tools, which include (a) the clinical interview; (b) collection of historical data, such as developmental milestones or school records; (c) direct behavioral observation; and (d) norm-referenced tests. Because no established battery of tests exists that sufficiently addresses all of the cognitive, behavioral, and emotional domains required for a comprehensive assessment, assessment must be accomplished by combining a variety of instruments to cover areas of functioning (McCue, 1989).

Because many adults, moreover, especially those with above-average cognitive abilities, have experienced difficulties in employment due to learning problems, these individuals will have spent much energy either hiding these difficulties or developing compensatory strategies that allow them to minimize the effects of the disability on academic or job performance. Examples of compensatory strategies include using a dictionary to improve spelling or using a word processor to alleviate handwriting difficulties (Simpson & Umbach, 1989). Consequently, when consumers are involved in evaluation tasks and do not have access to these aids, they may become quite anxious or even resistant to difficult tasks because of the fear of painful disclosure (Vogel, 1989). Also, an individual often hides learning-disability–related limitations or receives sympathetic treatment from others that can inhibit eventual appropriate work adjustment.

Case Example: Alice

Alice is a 21-year-old single White woman who comes to you for vocational counseling. With a degree from a rural high school, she reports that she has had difficulty with language, spelling, and reading tasks for many years. This was brought to her attention during grammar school and she had to repeat a grade. She claims that this repetition did not really help her, and because her small rural high school had no funds for learning assessment and consequent remediation, she experienced continued difficulties while in school and graduated with barely a C average. Both of her parents left school after the second year of high school, took care of the family farm, and were more comfortable ignoring the requests of Alice's teachers for assessment than making any effort to address their daughter's problems. There are no siblings.

Following Alice's graduation from high school, her parents asked Alice to stay at home for a while to take care of the mother's elderly parents so that her mother could obtain employment in a retail store to supplement the family income. Alice did so until the grandparents passed away, within 3 months of each other, when she was almost 20 years old. She then found employment in a small assembly factory near her home, but had continued difficulty grasping some of the complexities of the required tasks, which had to be done quickly. Alice states that she was always "on edge" in her work environment and had problems getting along with her few co-workers because of her impatience and frustration. She believed she was going to be terminated, and then the company did suddenly furlough several workers, including Alice, because of an unexpected drop in work orders. Someone then recommended that she see a rehabilitation counselor for possible identification of her work-related problems and possible re-training.

Issues to Consider

- Explore the consumer's understanding of her work problems and what information has been given to her about their impact on daily functioning.
- A comprehensive vocational evaluation should be conducted, to be preceded by a neuropsychological evaluation. The evaluations and their results should be integrated with any educational history.
- Assistive technology resources should be considered when exploring employment opportunities appropriate to assessment results and consumer expectations.
- Emotional difficulties that emerge supposedly from learning disabilities should be addressed and specific interventions planned.

Evaluation Approaches to Consider

- The structured consumer interview, to collect family and educational histories and consumer's perception of learning and work-adjustment problem areas
- A selected battery of neuropsychological measures, to be arranged by a professional
- Administer the *Learning and Study Strategies Inventory* (Proctor et al., 2006).

The Consumer Recovering From Substance Abuse

Because of the continuing, significant incidence of chemical and alcohol abuse in this country, as well as the increasing recovery rate due to the large number of available substance abuse programs, a large number of recovering addicts are presenting themselves for vocational rehabilitation services. Evaluators are highly likely to encounter individuals with substance abuse or dependency. Persons with disabilities, according to Ebener and Smedema (2011), are at a disproportionately greater risk for substance abuse problems than are members of the general population. While currently there is no widely standardized screening practice in use in vocational rehabilitation to identify persons who may benefit from rehabilitation, existing evidence suggests that it can often be a hidden condition that the evaluator may not become aware of until later in the vocational rehabilitation process (Moore & Keferl, 2008).

As specified by the Americans with Disabilities Act of 1990, these individuals are not eligible for vocational services unless they are actively in treatment. But those consumers who are in treatment present a variety of problems and provide a daunting challenge to the vocational rehabilitation professional. This challenge is illustrated in the following case example, and the example offers both a stimulus and a structure for discussing specific evaluation issues.

Case Example: Beverly

Beverly is a 29-year-old woman, married, with two children ages 8 and 6 years. Currently separated from her husband of 9 years, she characterizes her marriage as one of extensive drinking and many violent fights. Recently Beverly attacked her husband, Luke, with a knife, claiming self-defense from the beating he gave her. She was arrested for this, and Luke pressed charges, which he later dropped. Luke has been diagnosed by a community mental health agency as a severe alcoholic and is currently involved in an extramarital affair with his secretary. He operates a window installation business. Luke also has an 8-year-old daughter by a previous marriage who lives with him.

At the time of the birth of her 6-year-old son, Beverly was addicted to PCP and was under the influence during delivery. The hospital took the boy away from her, had her arrested, and gave custody of both children to the father. Six months after the birth Beverly was arrested for shoplifting. She spent a few days in jail after both of these arrests but never served any time for the offenses beyond that. Her husband lives nearby and still maintains custody of their two children. Beverly is afraid for her children and is working to prove child abuse in order to increase her chances of regaining custody.

Beverly dropped out of high school in the 10th grade. After two attempts to pass the GED, she finally passed and enrolled in beautician school. Currently she does beautician work from her own home, which she has rented for 4 years. She earned her beautician's license 4 years ago, and with periodic financial help from her mother she has managed to stay out of heavy debt. Beverly claims that she was attacked by her father when she was a child in an attempted rape. Her father is now deceased; her mother has been a drug addict and an off-and-on drug dealer over the years.

Beverly reports that she became a crack addict when she received her beautician's license several years ago, but when her sister, also a drug addict and a prostitute, died of AIDS 2 years ago, Beverly turned herself in to a community health center and sought drug rehabilitation. She wants her children back and mainly for this reason is attending abuse classes and is voluntarily being tested weekly for any drugs in her system. Beverly claims that she is serious about her drug rehabilitation and would like to improve her quality of life by getting a better job through training, especially in the health field. Also, she feels that her current work as a beautician could induce drug relapse because of the pressures arising from trying to please others. Beverly asserts that she has a low level of tolerance for stress.

Issues to Consider

- Beverly's emotional reaction to the death of her sister and the temporary loss of her children
- Influence of her mother on her drug rehabilitation
- What does Beverly mean by "improved quality of life"?
- Placeability issues regarding job availability and Beverly's vocational marketable skills
- Continued motivation for drug rehabilitation
- Attitude toward current rehabilitation and how she is handling pressure from current job-coping behaviors
- Level of self-esteem

Evaluation Approaches to Consider

- When planning a vocational evaluation with those who are recovering from or in treatment for substance abuse, the professional should consider his or her role as a rehabilitation counselor or evaluator. For example, a trusting relationship with the recovering addict should be established so that this individual will be more willing to express feelings and relate a more accurate history of substance abuse behavior.

- Communication about social history, a reconstruction of the presenting problems, and identification of any life-style issues that are associated with relapse (Gorski, 1990) might all be identified during the initial interview. Self-defeating behaviors could also be identified, as well as mistaken core beliefs that might suppress painful feelings and encourage rational thinking. The ways in which the consumer responsibly manages feelings and emotions without relying on the use of harmful substances could also be explored during the interview.
- A structured consumer interview can be utilized to explore both expectations for future employment and anger management skills.
- Explore using the *Tennessee Self-Concept Scale* (Fitts & Warren, 1996), *Minnesota Multiphasic Personality Inventory* (Hathaway, McKinley, & Butcher, 1990), and *Wide Range Achievement Test–Fourth Edition* (Wilkinson & Robertson, 2006).
- A formal measure may be needed to explore the effect of continued drug abuse on the individual's cognitive functioning and emotional strengths.
- Because these specific consumers are in recovery, the initial interview does not necessarily have to explore what they may need to do to successfully manage their drug rehabilitation. The vocational evaluation does not actually focus on whether the consumer is currently drinking or taking drugs, as eligibility for vocational services to those who are addicted precludes these behaviors.

Conclusion

These types of consumers represent the varieties of people who present themselves for rehabilitation. Categorizing is one way to identify the many work-related behaviors that consumers show; such behaviors can either facilitate or deter progress toward rehabilitation goals. Categories often overlap because many persons with disabilities display, for example, both angry resister and secondary gainer traits. Regardless of the way the professional understands these behaviors, however, most individuals with disabilities have strong inhibitions about going into an assessment situation in which they might look bad. They believe that assessment might portray them as being more inadequate than they really are. Many people also have negative expectations of the counselor because they perceive that their counselor has negative expectations of them. Professionals may have corresponding low expectations for the rehabilitation success of their consumers, and although such feelings may be quite warranted, this attitude breeds distrust and apprehension.

For consumers who have histories of physical or mental disabilities, the most difficult part of the assessment phase of rehabilitation is not necessarily its content but the very fact that they must be evaluated. Fear of a strange situation, poor test-taking skills, feelings of inferiority, discouragement attributable to past failures relating to the disability, and perhaps a hostile attitude from the counselor can cause conflict and anxiety. Vocational evaluation can even be seen as a humiliation: a method for proving and exposing the consumer's limitations.

Consumer assessment, then, becomes an opportunity for professionals to ask themselves the following questions:

1. *Will my characteristics as a helping professional make a difference in the person's assessment performance?* The assessment process involves a complex interaction between the professional, the consumer, and situational variables. The manner in which rapport is established and maintained and the way in which the evaluator responds to the person's attitudes and feelings have a bearing on how successful the professional is in attempting to elicit the consumer's best efforts.

2. *How can I, as a professional, recognize and accept the individual's fears, apprehensions, distrust, and skepticism?* By recognizing and accepting these perceived behaviors, professionals can begin to acknowledge the emotional rewards needed to give stimulus or meaning to the rehabilitation experience. Support, approval, and encouragement are important professional responses that become more meaningful to persons as they progress through the steps in the rehabilitation program. These responses also can help to increase self-confidence.

3. *What can I, as a professional, do to enhance the reliability of the assessment situation?* In other words, what can be done to reduce

anxiety and to generate mutual respect? The professional's expectations of the person with a disability can be the key to trust and confidence. If the professional possesses high, positive expectations for consumers, usually consumers will respond accordingly and attempt to be open and provide as much energy as possible in the assessment situation. Paying attention to emotional needs and listening intently are tools that can help build mutual respect.

The answers to these questions influence the effectiveness of assessment. Such questions pervade the assessment process and demand attention as professionals attempt to learn more information about their consumers. Ways to respond to these issues in assessment, as well as ways to formulate a comprehensive assessment approach toward varied consumer behaviors, are discussed in the next chapters.

Multicultural Dynamics and Practices in Vocational Assessment

With the increasing cultural diversity in our society, broad-based multi-cultural issues receive more attention in the delivery of services to those with disabilities. Moreover, the career development of racial and ethnic minorities has particularly gained increased attention (Grier-Reed & Ganuza, 2011). A shift in population demographics also may be partially responsible for the recent emphasis on cultural issues in rehabilitation counselor training and practice (Dana, 2008). Four ethnic groups constitute nearly 35% of the population of the United States (U.S. Census Bureau, 2010). The U.S. Bureau of the Census reported that in 2010 the Hispanic population became the largest minority in the United States, making up 16.3% of the U.S. population. The Black population made up 12.6% of the total population, while Asians and Pacific Islanders constituted 5% of the population. Native Americans and Native Alaskans together make up 1% of the population, and 2.9% of the population are identified as belonging to more than one race. It is a fact that minority growth will steadily increase, and, consequently, the number of minority individuals with disabilities will also increase (Campbell, 1991). It seems also that there is a documented linkage between race/ethnicity and disability (Maki & Riggar, 2003).

All phases of vocational evaluation from assessment of work performance to the results of standardized testing are affected by culture (Glisson et al., 2004). In fact, an exploration of both the counselor's and the consumer's culture is essential to the process of assessment (Donnell, Robertson, & Tansey, 2010). Fortunately, a small but distinct body of empirical literature has emerged that examines issues in the development se of career assessment instruments across cultures (Leong & Harng, 2000). In fact, even with the relatively small volume of published literature, notable contributions in career assessment with culturally diverse groups have been reported since 1995 (Flores, Spanierman, & Obasi, 2003). Unfortunately, the culturally relevant literature published during the 1990s has not become part and parcel of the vocational assessment delivery system of rehabilitation services (Dana, 2001). It is only quite recently that more focused attention has been given to assessment services for rehabilitation consumers from different cultures. While there has been a recent emphasis on the integration of ethnicity, race, and culture in comprehensive assessment (Dana, 2008), the specific emphasis has been on the assumption that, whenever possible, evaluation approaches should still be psychometrically sound, and scores and scales should be free from cultural bias and have the same vocational and career meaning for consumers from all racial and ethnic groups (Dana, 2001).

When culture has been discussed, it has usually been limited to such groups as African Americans, Native Americans, Asians, and Hispanics/Latin Americans. The meaning of *culture* is comprehensive and includes thoughts, customs, values, and beliefs of racial, ethnic, and religious groups (Dana, 2001). Culture is a learned behavior shaped by human experience and imposed upon individuals by their families, friends, and neighborhoods (Pekerti, 2008).

This chapter will discuss many of the issues confronting vocational evaluators when working with consumers from ethnic groups. In addition, suggestions will be provided for such areas as appropriate administration and the interpretation of assessment data with regard to their use with rehabilitation consumers representing ethnic minorities.

There is a tendency to understand broad racial groups as single, homogeneous entities. But individuals from racial minority cultures have within each minority group differences that affect the way they function. There are many cultural factors that may differentially impact individuals with disabilities and the way they react to vocational evaluation (Glisson et al., 2004).

Specific Issues

Vocational assessment involves the collection of information in order to help consumers make choices about career or work options. Evaluation includes the identification of a person's beliefs, skills, abilities, academic achievement, interests, personality type, and values (Flores et al., 2003). The assessment process leads to the development of choices, and there are many internal and external influences on this decision-making step. For ethnic minority consumers, these influences not only shape what happens during the vocational evaluation but also impact the direction a career choice is going to take. Cultural variables such as identity development, worldview, acculturation, socioeconomic status, primary language, family expectations, value orientation, communication and decision-making styles, time, and language all influence the career decision process (Flowers, Griffon-Dixon, & Trevino, 1997).

Members of ethnic minorities with disabilities present a distinct cultural challenge to the vocational evaluation process (Alston & McCowan, 1994; Dana, 2008). All of the variables previously stated come into play during the selection, administration, and interpretation phases of assessment. A traditional approach to these necessary phases may be in direct conflict with the values and worldviews held by minority group members. It is important, consequently, when working with consumers representing different ethnic minorities to focus on an understanding of what culturally competent vocational assessment is. Such knowledge should harmonize with recognition of a cultural definition of disability. Some contend that disability is a construction of culture, and that the causes and qualifying conditions of disability and the behavioral expectations for those with disabilities and responses by others are culturally determined (Dana, 2001).

Skiba, Knesting, and Bush (2002) believed that culturally competent assessment is "a comprehensive process that uses the results of assessment to identify and remedy educational conditions that systematically disadvantage certain groups of students. . . . It uses both individual and system-wide data" (p. 72). Although this definition concerns special education students, it has an action focus, directing the professional to use those evaluation approaches that are not discriminatory toward ethnic minority groups. Flores et al. (2003) reported that culturally appropriate career assessment requires information gathering that is culturally encompassing. Collection of information occurs throughout the assessment process and is used to guide the selection and administration of assessment tools, interpret the assessment information, and develop career and job interventions. This information should suggest cultural variables that may be related to the consumer's career or job problem, which in turn should influence the selection of methods and tools that are culturally sensitive.

For the counselor to develop a relevant perspective when conducting assessment with consumers from ethnic minority groups, it is helpful to understand some of the traditional flaws said to be inherent in assessment measures related to diversity groups:

- Anxiety in the assessment situation
- Unfair content
- Improper interpretation of scores
- Lack of relevance
- Impaired communication; namely, when the counselor and the individual use a different language, complications can range from different interpretations of body language and gestures to the obvious spoken differences
- Poor modifications of the environment—the counselor is not aware of available technology and techniques for test and environmental modifications, nor of the implications of these in the individual's life

For the rehabilitation professional to develop and ensure culturally competent assessment demands recognition, moreover, of the issues of bias (including institutional racism), the criteria for cultural competence, and the unique considerations that are integral to ethnic minority consumers when they present themselves for vocational evaluation. An understanding of these issues can facilitate an approach to assessment that will respond to consumer needs and perhaps assure plausibility when career or job decisions are made.

Bias

Historically, bias has occurred in (a) applications of standard assessment instruments with populations from different cultures (e.g., bias can be expressed by a counselor's attitudes and beliefs that generate prejudicial judgments based primarily on a single attribute, such as color, socioeconomic status, and race; Dana, 2001); (b) a counselor's taking shortcuts by selectively processing information based on previously entrenched stereotypes and misconceptions, half-truths, and exaggerations, and consequently selecting evaluation approaches that are perceived as supporting the stereotypes (Pichette, Accordino, Hamilton, Rosenthal, & Wilson, 2002); and (c) selecting measures that have not been validated for the specific consumer group that is the target for evaluation. Dana (2008) asserted that "assessor bias typically occurs as a consequence of stereotyping and ethnocentrism or minimizing differences among members of different racial/ethnic groups and European origin Americans, but it also can exist because of prejudice and racism" (p. 575). Whiston (2000) believed that "instruments may be biased in terms of the content being more familiar or appropriate for one group as compared to another group" (p. 316). The population of a particular subgroup may not have been exposed to the necessary experiences that generate a sense of familiarity with the test items (Zurcher, 1998). Tangential to this bias is the concept of cultural equivalence, namely, whether the constructs used in test items have similar meanings within and across cultures. Assessment items could have one meaning in one culture but have a different meaning for persons from another culture (Whiston, 2000). Measures of intelligence, for example, may lack construct validity when used with minorities because the measures may be evaluating not inherent aptitude but rather the extent to which test takers share middle class knowledge and values (Skiba et al., 2002).

While bias can occur with test selection, test interpretation, and translation challenges, especially for persons who do not speak English as their first language, it can be accentuated by differences in communication styles and patterns. Significantly, cultural attitudes and beliefs about disability and illness are basic to the administration of assessments (Donnell, Robertson, & Tansey, 2010). Moreover, because of the technical limitations in traditional vocational assessment, evaluation of consumers who are culturally and linguistically diverse, as well as those with severe disabilities, presents difficult problems (Parker, Hansmann, & Schaller, 2010). Parker, Hansmann, and Schaller provided two frameworks for identifying the limitations of traditional vocational evaluation for ethnic minority consumers.

1. *Vocational tests and work evaluation systems that typically present inadequate reliability and validity for the measures used during the assessment processes.* Relevant to this concern is the question whether tests accurately predict outcomes for ethnic minority group

members in comparison to White, middle class individuals. The latter persons predominantly represent the national norms, and consequently test results may be inappropriately applied to minorities. If not enough individuals from diverse backgrounds are included in the standardization sample or reference group on which a test is normed, score interpretations for minority consumers may not accurately reflect their true abilities as compared to the types of persons who made up the standardization sample (Overton, 1996). Minority populations are undersampled, and test results when used with minorities are questionable (Parker et al., 2010).

2. *Instruments and test items that require reading and comprehension levels that exceed examinees' abilities.* This is another bias-related limitation related specifically to the traditional use of standardized tests. Measures that use language to assess psychological, social, or cognitive functioning may frequently evaluate knowledge of standard English rather than aptitude or achievement. There also may be offensive stereotypical use of language and pictures in test items and materials (Zurcher, 1998). Items may contain cultural representations unfair to particular subgroups within a culture.

As noted earlier, the examiner may be a source of bias during evaluation. One's ethnic and social class prejudices may interfere with assessment practices. Evaluators who are unfamiliar with consumers' culture and language may inadvertently stereotype, misjudge, or intimidate their consumers because of difficulties in verbal and nonverbal communications. Skiba et al. (2002) reported that the possibility of examiner effects in evaluation must be considered. The degree of evaluator familiarity appears to influence to some extent the outcomes of standardized assessment, especially for consumers of a lower socioeconomic status.

In summary, tests may be biased against a person or groups of persons by containing items that favor one group over another, by having criteria used for selection and prediction that vary greatly among different groups, and by not considering such test-related factors as motivation, anxiety, and the test sophistication of those taking the assessment (Hood & Johnson, 2007).

One cannot conclusively rule out, therefore, the possibility of bias affecting the vocational evaluation process, but is this bias sufficient to explain lower minority test performance (Skiba et al., 2002)? Other factors, of course, come into play. For example, many consumers who undergo vocational assessment may have suffered over the years from inadequate educational facilities and the lack of education resources in general. Teacher and instructor expectations, curricula, and quality of instruction may be unequal in educational environments for those from a lower socioeconomic class. When vocational evaluation is conducted, therefore, for ethnic minority groups with disabilities seeking appropriate school-to-work transition, such institutional racism may have a decided impact on performance.

Cultural Competence

Because of the increasing reality of the culture–disability interaction, vocational evaluators require training to gain knowledge about the beliefs concerning disability in their consumers' cultures and how assessment approaches can be developed that have more accurate predictive validity. This training could include the following:

- Determining the acculturation status of consumers prior to the administration and interpretation of standard assessment approaches (Dana, 2001)
- Applying methodology and research findings to the choice, use, or adaptation of standard assessment instruments
- Developing an awareness of attitudes, beliefs, knowledge, and skills in working with culturally diverse groups (Flores et al., 2003)

There is the accurate perception that rehabilitation counselors are perhaps not adequately trained to provide responsible and ethical vocational evaluation services for people unlike themselves. On-the-job training usually has to suffice for most evaluators, who are guided by the statement of the Code of Professional Ethics (F6) that the professional "will be cautious when selecting tests for disability or culturally diverse populations to avoid inappropriateness of testing" (Marshall, Leung, Johnson, & Busby, 2003, p. 60). Becoming a culturally skilled evaluator, however, is not easy, and it can be characterized as an active process that is ongoing and never reaches a conclusion (Sue & Sue, 1999). Flowers et al. (1997) identified five approaches that are minimally necessary for the professional to achieve cultural sensitivity:

1. Being sensitive to one's own cultural heritage and valuing and respecting differences
2. Having an awareness of one's own values and biases and how these biases can affect persons with disabilities who are culturally diverse
3. Developing a comfort level with differences that exist between oneself and persons being served who represent ethnic minorities
4. Developing a sensitivity to circumstances, such as an awareness of personal bias, that may dictate the referral of an ethnic minority consumer with a disability to a member of his or her own race or culture
5. An acknowledgment of beliefs and attitudes concerning disability and minority consumers

Donnell et al. (2010) added to these approaches with the suggestions that the counselor be aware of the consumer's cultural viewpoint and values as they relate to the consumer's group identity, and that the counselor have the ability to build a relationship with the consumer, given his or her awareness and knowledge.

Sensitivity and awareness of values, attitudes, and beliefs appear to be essential components of cultural competence. The acquisition of multicultural skills to be used during the assessment process is a continuous career journey. Research and insightful practice approaches are identifying the changes necessary to bring more relevance to the evaluation process for those who are both disabled and from a minority culture. Some of these approaches are discussed later in this chapter.

Multicultural Consumer Considerations

Many ethnic minority consumers who also have significant disabilities have a poor success rate with regard to achieving goals initiated for their vocational evaluation process (Alston & McCowan, 1994; Pichette et al., 2002). The realities of bias, institutional racism, and the lack of appropriate training for culturally competent skills in career assessment are all contributing factors. Added to this list of suggested reasons for poor or questionable consumer outcomes in evaluation are specific consumer issues that have received attention in the literature (Alston & McCowan, 1994; Dana, 2001; Parker et al., 2010; Prince, Uemura, Chao, & Gonzales,

1992). There are four issues—response style, performance motivation, language, and acculturation—and each can affect assessment results and contribute to the lessened usefulness of those results.

Response Style

Consumers from different cultures may approach vocational evaluation with different assessment styles. Sue and Sue (1977) reported how the response sets of certain ethnic groups may invalidate the results of some inventories. There may be a mind-set among particular ethnic minorities to respond to an interest measure, for example, with certain expectations in mind. A consumer may not endorse interests that reflect a separation from parents or that conflict with the values of his or her culture.

Alston and McCowan (1994) believed that the response style of African Americans may contribute to a poor perception of their abilities. They tend not to attempt a complete response when given a question. Scores may be lowered, consequently, because partially completed responses are treated as incorrect responses in the final score tally. Most African American consumers also have a somewhat different concept of time (Tien, 2007; West-Olatunji, 2009). Their perspective of time is not necessarily defined by clocks or calendars but measured by significant events. When vocational tasks require their subscales to be administered on a timed basis, and further demand that the examinee work as quickly as possible, the African American consumer may work at an individual pace with little regard for time restrictions. If the score is even partly determined by the total items answered correctly, African American consumers will likely have lower scores, although an analysis of score sheets may reveal high accuracy for those items attempted. Overall, because of the response-style factor, actual results on an assessment measure may not be a true reflection of the potential of the minority consumers (Prince et al., 1992).

Performance Motivation

Most consumers with disabilities and from ethnic minority cultures bring to their vocational evaluation experience a history of oppression, being stereotyped about their race and disability, and perhaps inequitable social consequences, namely, differential educational and vocational opportunities due to discrimination. All of these factors can result in systemic deficits that influence the accuracy of evaluation results. Minority consumers may mistrust the entire assessment process because of past discrimination—a bias that also could influence career or employment choices (Parker et al., 2010). Low expectations for success because of these negative factors could influence motivation for expending high energy during evaluation.

A related consideration is the emphasis on self-analysis and introspection required during much of the assessment process. Hispanics, for example, may be uncomfortable and unfamiliar with this demand (Smart & Smart, 1992).

Previous life experiences, consequently, can be an important motivational variable for many ethnic minority consumers with disabilities (Atkins, 1988). Life experiences can shape one's view of the world (Alston & McCowan, 1994) and contribute to feelings of distrust and the perception that vocational assessment may highlight one's deficits in a final evaluation report. All in all, evaluation can be viewed as a possible "failure experience." "Fear of embarrassment to perform because one may fail is an example of the need to avoid failure," stated Alston and McCowan (1994, p. 43).

Language

Cultural language barriers are present when English is not the consumer's first or preferred language (Dana, 2001). There may be disparities in the consumer's language skills, the language used in assessment measures, and the evaluator's language. Even when the particular measure is available in the consumer's preferred language, the technical adequacy of the translated version should be considered (Prince et al., 1992). Furthermore, many consumers, because of their low economic status or long-standing immigrant status, may have had only limited exposure to the usage of Standard English. Unfortunately, inferences about intelligence and personality, especially in the workplace, are often made on the basis of how well one speaks Standard English (Heath, 1989). The language differences, if they are not taken into account in the evaluation process, may lead to a serious misrepresentation of the consumer's career or job potential (Alston & McCowan, 1994).

Acculturation

The consumer's culture can affect the behavioral expression of a disability, and acculturation becomes a significant component of the vocational evaluation process. Acculturation is a psychological and sociological adaptive process and refers to the degree to which a consumer assimilates the beliefs, customs, and values of the dominant culture and the individual changes that occur as a result of the interaction with a new culture (Dana, 2001; Donnell, Robertson, & Tansey, 2010). Many ethnic minority consumers, for example, who also have disabilities may live lifestyles that are indistinguishable from those of the mainstream. They also may have the ability to function comfortably in multiple cultural settings, and they may be more resistant to discrimination and occupational stereotyping (Dana, 2001). Other ethnic minority consumers, however, may be assimilated into the dominant culture but maintain a separatist identity and cling strongly to the values of their ethnic backgrounds. Many Latin and Asian American women, for example, when exploring career options after the early onset of a chronic illness or disability, may believe they face strong pressures to select more traditional, career-oriented directions.

The more acculturated a consumer is in terms of middle class, mainstream American values, perhaps the more comfortable that person will be with a vocational evaluation process that emphasizes long-term goals and rational problem solving (Dana, 2001). In the beginning of assessment it may be important for the evaluator to determine the adequacy of specific, standard approaches that will be used in the career or job exploration process. Such a determination may minimize the level of consumer distrust.

In summary, the specific issues of bias, an evaluator's cultural competence, and multicultural consumer considerations provide a framework for reshaping the vocational assessment process so that it becomes more relevant for the ethnic minority consumer with a disability. Traditionally, approaches in evaluation originate from a Eurocentric bias (Dana, 2001). A knowledge gap exists for assisting culturally diverse consumers with disabilities to undertake career exploration. It is imperative for evaluators to explore how the customary components of the vocational evaluation process can be modified to achieve useful information for ethnic minority consumers with disabilities. With the emergence of laws and research showing inequities due to the use of particular measures (Zurcher, 1998), approaches must be designed that accurately reflect the strengths and potential of consumers with disabilities from a variety of cultural backgrounds.

There are a number of factors, moreover, that can enhance the assessment experience for consumers with a disability representing an ethnic minority culture:

- The counselor should convey cultural self-awareness and knowledge of his or her own limitations regarding an understanding of the consumer's culture-related vocational needs.
- The potential effects of the counselor/evaluator differences should be anticipated.
- The consumer's cultural belief system should be validated.
- The career- and disability-related problem that becomes a focus for the evaluation should be articulated from the consumer's cultural perspective. An exploration of the origins of the consumer's identity, acculturation, and worldview may facilitate this expression. For example, if the main problem related to the consumer's assessment is undecidedness about career direction, then an understanding of identity and acculturation factors that have contributed to this problem could be acquired.
- Resistance from a culturally different consumer should be anticipated and dealt with early in the assessment process.
- As much as possible, the consumer should be actively involved in the assessment process. This implies knowledge of how to develop a collaborative relationship with a consumer from a different culture, and then an understanding of what aspects of the assessment process are more opportune for this involvement.

The Assessment Interview for Varied Ethnic or Minority Consumers

The process of vocational assessment with consumers from varied ethnic or minority groups should be comprehensive, using different methods, tools, and approaches to collect information. If there is reluctance to use standardized tools with persons who have severe disabilities and represent ethnic minorities, an evaluator can use the beginning interview as a screening, diagnostic, and career-planning tool. The question is often asked, however, "Why is this interview any different from an assessment interview with the majority of consumers with disabilities who are at the initial phase of the rehabilitation process?" The difference resides in the agenda that is introduced by ethnic minority persons, their histories, and frequently the influences that may impact the evaluation process itself. The interview serves as an introduction to career planning or job retraining development.

Prior to beginning the interview, a decision should be made about whether this session should be structured or unstructured. A structured interview, in which questions have been planned prior to the interview, is standardized and less susceptible to bias. The unstructured interview allows for more flexibility as the interviewer encourages the consumer to discuss problems, interests, and behaviors relevant to the goals of the interview (Pichette et al., 2002). Selecting the type of interview depends on interview goals. For consumers who are seeking information about their capabilities, values, and interests relevant to job or career planning, and for the evaluator who must have specific information in order to plan a tailored assessment process and identify those obstacles that might impede the achievement of vocational rehabilitation goals, a semistructured interview might be a more appropriate choice.

There are varying degrees of structure among intake interviews, but in vocational assessment there are specific topics that should be covered. Such a necessity might demand an established order in which questions are asked and initial responses are further explored (Pichette et al., 2002). The amount of structure for the interview, especially during its initial phase, can vary. The consumer may have issues that need to be addressed, and it could be very helpful for the consumer to share these concerns before responding to other relevant areas of rehabilitation planning. To be noted is that Chapter 6 provides a more detailed discussion of this "structured versus nonstructured" topic.

Interview goals, the skills needed by the rehabilitation professional to effectively conduct the interview, the specific areas to explore during the interaction between the evaluator and consumer, and selected issues that arise during the interview exchange are all topics that must be addressed if this diagnostic tool is to be relevant to the needs of the consumer.

Interview Goals

For ethnic minority consumers with disabilities, the interview goals are basically the same as those identified in Chapter 6, "The Consumer

Interview as an Effective Assessment Tool," but two of these goals may have further implications for these persons.

1. *Develop rapport between the professional and the consumer* (Farley & Rubin, 2006). When interviewing an ethnic minority consumer, the person's cultural belief system should be validated. Sharing one's own beliefs and expectations, being aware of personal biases and prejudices, and developing an atmosphere of comfort and trust through a willingness to listen to the consumer's story and affirm one's own concerns might facilitate the development of rapport. Usually the consumer will not willingly engage in the sharing of information unless this rapport has been established.

2. *Give the consumer necessary information about the role and function of the agency, available services, and consumer responsibilities* (Farley & Rubin, 2006). Added to this communication should be attempts to ensure confidentiality about the assessment process and its outcome. This information depends on agency guidelines, but these guidelines should be carefully explained to the consumer, as should the procedures for managing the assessment results. Although ensuring confidentiality is important for all consumers, for those representing cultural minorities it may be a heightened issue because of past failure experiences or perceptions of an unfriendly rehabilitation system.

Interview Skills

There are specific competencies that the interviewer should possess if there is going to be an open exchange of information. Several of these competencies are ones needed by all vocational rehabilitation professionals, but they receive particular emphasis when working with consumers from ethnic minority backgrounds. The important skills are as follows:

- *The ability to listen nonjudgmentally, extend empathy, ask open-ended questions, and closely observe demonstrated behaviors.* Initial impressions acquired in the interview may be susceptible to bias and may negatively affect the interviewer's attitude and selection of interview topics. Information to revise these beginning impressions may be obtained by carefully observing the consumer's nonverbal behavior and listening closely to his or her communication (Pichette et al., 2002).

- *The ability to be aware of biases, stereotypes, and prejudices.* The awareness itself may prompt a reduction of negative attitudes and facilitate a sharing of information. Because of past learning experiences, it may be difficult for many interviewers to manage negative attitudes, but such control and openness is vital if the evaluation is not going to be significantly compromised.
- *The ability to understand that there are cultural differences and that the consumer is a cultural entity* (Feist-Price, Harley, & Alston, 1996). Acknowledgment of this fact is an initial step to listening about the consumer's cultural background and determining how the assessment process may have to be shaped to accommodate the strengths, needs, and any perceived career-related limitations of the consumer.
- *An ability to understand empirical findings that may affect usage of approaches traditionally used in vocational assessment.* Such knowledge includes any revisions or re-standardization of accepted procedures. Because a more comprehensive approach is appropriate for those with especially severe disabilities who are ethnic minorities, other state-of-the-art practices should be identified and accommodated without compromising their measurement value.

Interview Areas to Explore

Chapter 6 suggests a structure for organizing interview facts. Topics related to consumer functioning are highlighted as necessary areas to explore to acquire adequate diagnostic information. Of these topics, the consumer's interests, values, and aptitudes are particularly important (Flores et al., 2003), but there are several factors that should be added in order for the evaluation to have sufficient information for career planning.

- *The consumer's worldview.* The worldview establishes a frame of reference through which one experiences life. It can be defined as assumptions people are socialized to hold about the makeup of the world (Sarason, 1984). It is the foundation for values, beliefs, and attitudes and encompasses all the cultural norms and most family expectations of the particular ethnic group (Ponterotto, Casas, Suzuki, & Alexander, 1995). Hood and Johnson (2007) believed that the worldview includes "the individual's perceptions of human nature (good or evil); focus on the past, present or future; the emphasis given to individual or group goals; and locus of responsibility" (p. 299). For example, a person's perspective might focus more on the expectations and needs of the group, such as family, rather than individual needs and wishes. When the consumer is in the process of making career decisions, the values, expectations, and interests of the family may be viewed as more important than his or her own personal choices. The consumer's frame of reference, or worldview, can be explored by asking the following question: "When you are going to make choices for the selection of a job or career, what are your beliefs that may influence those decisions?"

- *The consumer's acculturation.* This construct can be defined as the emotional and behavioral changes that occur as the consumer interacts with a new or dominant culture (Ponterotto et al., 1995, p. 359). Acculturation can refer to the degree of integration with the host country's cultural patterns (Hood & Johnson, 2007). It relates to ethnic identity development and refers to how much the consumer absorbs the values, beliefs, and language of the dominant culture. Some consumers may view their host culture negatively and their own culture positively, or may have assimilated the values, beliefs, customs, and language of the host culture to such a degree that their behavior suggests a positive view of the host culture and a negative view of their own. The consumer may understand and approach the assessment process no differently than a consumer whose entire life has been entwined with the values and beliefs of the host culture. The evaluator should explore the consumer's racial identity, since an understanding of this dimension can influence the approaches and modifications to be used during the assessment. To explore the level of a consumer's acculturation, the evaluator may consider the consumer's age, number of generations of his or her family living in the dominant culture, the language generally preferred, and the extent of activities and relationships within and beyond the consumer's own cultural group (Paniagua, 1994). A question that could also determine the consumer's acculturation is, "What is your understanding of and expectations for the assessment process as it prepares you to make job or career decisions?"

- *The consumer's primary language.* This information may be documented before the interview. The interviewer, however, upon understanding that the consumer's familiarity with the host culture's language is not well developed, will have to identify how any language limitations will affect vocational assessment planning.

- *Barriers and consumer problem areas.* Though the identification of obstacles to pursuing vocational evaluation and limitations to the development of relevant career plans is not limited to ethnic minority consumers with disabilities, the nature and context of these barriers or problems might be quite different for different ethnic populations. The social context of these problems needs to be explored. The quality of previous academic and training experiences, family attitudes, and possible negative attitudes in employment and career sectors should be discussed. Perceived discrimination and negative stereotypes may influence whether the consumer will enthusiastically endorse and participate in career exploration. The ethnic minority consumer's previous school or vocational training experiences should be discussed. A lack of community resources and the quality of instruction may have affected the value of previous training. Questions can solicit feedback in these areas: "Can you tell me something about what you learned from your school training?" "Do you think that what happened in school or your previous employment has prepared you to explore other jobs or careers?"

Donnell et al. (2010) added to the above interview questions by identifying the following culturally appropriate questions:

- Tell me a little about your background (current residence, place of origin, family network, past health issues, previous education).
- Tell me what your interests are (hobbies, career and educational goals).
- When in trouble, where do you find strength or help (social networks, family relationships, health and other community resources)?
- How do you deal with difficult times (cognitive resilience, coping styles, community or family resources)?
- How would you describe your health (disability status, perception and description of disability, understanding of disability-related issues)?
- What have you been told is affecting you (explores health status and perception of health-related issues)?

Selected Issues That Arise
During the Interview Exchange

Consumers begin vocational evaluation with their own sets of beliefs, attitudes, values, and goals in place. Ethnic minority consumers usually differ from the majority culture in a variety of ways. The combination of sociopolitical factors, minority status, and discrimination presents unique concerns that should be explored during the interview (Whitehead, 2003). Encouraging consumers to share their life histories can help the interviewer identify the areas of worldview, acculturation, primary language, and potential barriers—all of which can provide a framework for planning evaluation strategies.

The interview is usually the first contact between the consumer and evaluator, and inferences about the consumer's career or job potential are usually drawn from the information that emerges during this session (Pichette et al., 2002). Interviewer bias is a constant threat during evaluation, but bias can be reduced during the intake interview with increased self-awareness, especially if the professional watches the tendency to assign problems to minority consumers while excluding the influence of situational factors. The professional should seek interview information to disconfirm initial negative inferences, and wait to review a consumer's file or information received from a referral source until after the initial session (Pichette et al., 2002).

The practice of some professionals is to begin the evaluation process with as little information as possible regarding the consumer. If problems do not arise because of the initial disregard of vital information, and if anecdotal records are considered not important for an effective interview, then perhaps all of this information can be put aside until after the opening interview. Many evaluators believe they can be more open with the consumer with as little information as possible before their initial contact.

Based upon the information gained from the interview, as well as attention paid to the referral question, a decision is made regarding what evaluation approaches are to be used to explore the consumer's vocational potential and career or job readiness. The consumer should participate as much as possible in this decision making. This process involves selecting appropriate measures and approaches, administering the measures or approaches, and interpreting the results. Although a description of each one of these steps is in different chapters of this book, there are particular considerations that should be addressed when evaluating the ethnic minority consumer with a disability.

Selecting Appropriate Measures and Approaches

Information gained from the interview is needed when the evaluator and consumer begin to select the feasible approaches for continuing the assessment process. For example, acculturation information is needed to make a decision on the adequacy of standard tests for multicultural consumers, with or without various corrections for culture (Dana, 2001). If interview data suggest that the consumer with a disability has assimilated the behaviors and values of the host culture, or has a bicultural orientation—namely, an equal knowledge of both an original culture and mainstream European American culture, and the ability to function in either cultural setting with comfort (Dana, 2001)—then this information will greatly influence the choice of evaluation approaches and particular test selection.

The American Psychological Association has provided ethical standards (APA Ethical Standard 2.04) for the selection of measures, emphasizing familiarity with reliability, validity, a review of the scale's development, normative data, and proper applications of assessment techniques (Flores et al., 2003). No evaluation instrument is culture free, and perhaps what evaluators should be seeking are culturally fair approaches, since assessment outcomes will be influenced by cultural factors.

When considering assessment approach outcomes, there is the feasible option of identifying checklists and rating scales, though these measures may not possess the reliability and validity credibility of standardized tests. But for ethnic minority consumers who may perceive vocational assessment as a threatening, anxiety-producing experience, those tools can represent less of a threat and can generate useful information. This is particularly true for personality assessment instruments, since their construct validity can be challenged when used with consumers from minority cultures in the host environment.

Consequently, to achieve fairness for individuals from different races, genders, disabilities, or ethnic backgrounds when selecting evaluation approaches and instruments, the professional needs to carefully examine the standardization and norming procedures for relevance to the consumers. At the same time, caution must be used in this selection, for people from very similar backgrounds may categorize themselves in very different manners (Whiston, 2000, p. 321). Whiston provided three guidelines for this assessment selection:

1. Evaluate the documented evidence related to the instrument's appropriateness, that is, reliability and validity.
2. Review the data provided by the publisher on the performance of individuals from different races.
3. Consider whether the sample sizes are sufficient for the different groups.

Inventories that are normed on the dominant culture "raise significant questions for counselors whose consumers may not identify themselves with that dominant group" (Prince et al., 1992, p. 28). The use of translated measures is an assessment modification employed by many evaluators, but translations warrant such considerations as the following:

• Has the test followed appropriate translation procedures, so that cultural equivalence is assured? Items may have different meanings in varied cultural contexts.
• Does the translation instrument maintain the same response format so that the scores can be interpreted accurately?
• Do the constructs used in the instrument, such as interest and personality inventories, exist in the consumer's culture?

All of these guidelines can help the evaluator at the selection phase of the assessment process. Added to this framework is the necessity to explore whether the consumer has the ability to understand the assessment instructions and how many approaches may be required for an appropriate evaluation. Although there are definite limitations when using standardized tests with ethnic minority consumers with disabilities, there are other effective approaches that have been traditionally used in vocational evaluation that can be applied to this consumer population.

These are discussed in other chapters of this book and include situational assessment, supported employment, and work samples. With work samples, for example, the evaluator must attend to many of the same issues as with standardized paper-and-pencil tests, such as the norm sample, validity, reliability, and item content. But one of these approaches may provide sufficient information about the consumer's job potential, as well as identify the person's employment- or career-related strengths and residual abilities.

For ethnic minority consumers for whom vocational evaluation is an unfamiliar experience, this author recommends that situational assessment or supported employment be conducted soon after the interview and before any paper-and-pencil testing. Both of these approaches, when handled appropriately, can be less threatening and solicit information about what the person can do, instead of having a sweeping focus on limitations and career-related deficits. The identification of the latter is important, of course, but an initial affirming experience in evaluation can help the consumer gain confidence in the assessment process. Such confidence may enhance the value of another part of the evaluation process, namely, the paper-and-pencil testing. When used with attention to cultural factors, standardized assessment can solicit important information for vocational rehabilitation planning.

Hood and Johnson (2007) noted that "attempting to remove all cultural differences from a test is likely to compromise its validity as a measure of behavior" (p. 300). But if the evaluator uses caution and knowledge of the consumer's culture, then intelligence, aptitude, personality, and interest assessment can help the consumer identify personal capabilities and the evaluator to acquire comprehensive information for employment or career planning.

Suggestions for paper-and-pencil tests are made in the following areas.

Intelligence

Chapter 8 in this book discusses the nature of intelligence and its measurement implications for those with disabilities. Recommendations for selected tests are provided, but when the assessment of intelligence is applied to those who also represent an ethnic minority, there are serious controversies. Not only is the relationship between IQ scores and occupational success quite complex (Anastasi, 1988) but also it has been reported that as a group, Black Americans score approximately 1 standard deviation below White Americans on most standardized tests of cognitive ability (Hood & Johnson, 2007). Although this differential may be decreasing, the test results of consumers who have experienced racial discrimination may have an impact on their career opportunities. Also, many of the test items have a cultural bias against those who are not members of the majority culture. But test developers have now become extremely sensitive to this issue, and they also attend to the realities that within each culture there is a wide range of differences, and that a very small number of ethnic minorities have been included in the norming samples (Hood & Johnson, 2007).

To achieve more equitable assessments, it is perhaps more feasible to consider the concept of intelligence in a variety of ways, and not solely as a cognitive construct that includes verbal and abstract abilities. Sedlacek (1994) suggested the term used previously by Sternberg (1985), "experiential intelligence, which involves the ability to interpret information in changing contexts, to be creative. … Standardized tests do not measure this type of intelligence" (p. 550). This definition embraces the notions of dealing effectively with reality and the art of adjusting. Unfortunately, there are no available paper-and-pencil tests that directly explore these concepts, though there are culture-fair measures that attempt to minimize bias. Racial or ethnic minorities may not score higher on culture-fair tests in comparison to traditional measures of intelligence (Sattler, 1993), but these are specific tools that may provide the evaluator with information that can be useful in career planning. These instruments are recommended because they provide information on certain aspects of intellectual functioning while being relatively user-friendly to those populations who may find paper-and-pencil testing particularly challenging. Three of these specific tools, namely, the *Beta III, Raven's Progressive Matrices,* and the *Kaufman Brief Intelligence Test,* are described in Chapter 8, "Intelligence Assessment in Vocational Rehabilitation"; and three others are identified below.

Naglieri Nonverbal Ability Test–Second Edition (NNAT-2; Naglieri, 2009). This measure uses figural matrices to assess the general cognitive ability of persons from a variety of cultural backgrounds. The test does not use words or language in any of the items, and the figures that make up the individual items are not specific to any particular culture. While the instrument was being standardized on English-speaking individuals from around the United States, it was also being standardized on a similarly sized Spanish-speaking sample of Hispanic American students. This test is available from the Psychological Corporation, San Antonio, Texas.

The *Comprehensive Test of Nonverbal Intelligence–Second Edition* (CTONI-2; Hammill, Pearson, & Wiederholt, 2009). This measure is a battery of six subtests that identify different but interrelated nonverbal intellectual abilities. It offers oral or pantomime instructions, and a review of the mean standard scores for the school-age sample on the CTONI showed that Whites, African Americans, Hispanic Americans, Native Americans, and Asian Americans all scored well within the normal range (Hammill et al., 2009). The test is available from PRO-ED, Austin, Texas.

The *Culture Fair Intelligence Test*. Developed by R. B. Cattell, this measure is available in three levels, with Level Three applicable to adults. This level has four culture-fair tests, each with its own separate norms. Giving the instructions in a foreign language or in pantomime will not affect the difficulty of the test. The test has been administered in several European countries and in selected African and Asian cultures. The measure is available from the Institute for Personality and Ability Testing (IPAT; Anastasi, 1988).

The selection of tools measuring a concept of intelligence implies that "there is a need to think of measures differentially in order to achieve equitable assessments for all" (Sedlacek, 1994, p. 550). As mentioned several times in this book, the evaluator should identify the purpose of assessment and how the results are going to be used. The exploration of experiential intelligence can be quite useful when assisting a consumer in the choice of training and employment opportunities, and nonverbal and creative approaches may have to be used to identify the degree to which a consumer who is ethnic minority and disabled possesses this intelligence.

Aptitude and Achievement

Chapter 10 identifies several approaches to this aspect of assessment and provides recommendations for useful tools. Frequently, however, for ethnic minorities, work samples and situational assessment methods could be the more feasible ways to explore aptitude- and achievement-related abilities. When the evaluator selects standardized measures in this area, time constraints become an important concern. It is recommended that tests be selected that allow for practice trials. Also, since most of the aptitude measures have time limits, it is suggested that in order to maintain the integrity of the assessment the testing of limits technique should be used only after the entire test has been administered using standard procedures (Sattler, 1993), and items that are obtained during testing of limits are not credited to the person's score (Alston & McCowan, 1994). If a consumer does not complete the test because of time limits, moreover, the evaluator could re-administer the test without reference to time constraints or speed when giving the directions (Sattler, 1993). The consumer may perform better with the removal of time pressure.

Personality

The concept of personality has many dimensions, and because there are recurring questions of "over-pathologizing" racial groups because of results on personality measures, as well as the fact that these groups usually have not been included in norming samples, it is important to have a clear, useful definition of personality when it is explored in vocational evaluation for minority consumers with disabilities. Assessment is conducted with a training or employment focus, and consequently, such personality traits as motivation, needs, values, attitudes, mood, and temperament assume relevance as targets for exploration. Chapter 9 in this book discusses the varied approaches to evaluating these factors and identifies many of the precautionary steps to be taken when administering personality tests to the general adult population of those with disabilities. But there are added cautions for minority consumers who are undergoing the evaluation process.

Lonner and Sundberg (1985) believed that when selecting personality measures, a rule of thumb may be "to select from a small number of the older and more widely used tests" (p. 201). Although there is safety in tradition and the existence of extensive norms, the rehabilitation professional must still be concerned about concept equivalence (explained earlier in this chapter), the current influences of language and acculturation on the consumer's test-taking behavior, and whether many of the traditional, widely used instruments included ethnic groups in the norming samples of recent revisions. For example, the *Minnesota Multiphasic Personality Inventory–Second Edition* (MMPI-2; Hathaway, McKinley, & Butcher, 1990) was apparently developed incorporating representatives of only two racial or ethnic minority groups, namely, Black and Native American. It has been reported that MMPI-2 profiles indicate no substantial mean differences between these ethnic group samples and the general normative sample on the MMPI-2 validity and standard scales (Graham, 1993). Yet Graham wrote, "Only small MMPI-2 differences have been reported between African Americans and Caucasians in the normative sample, and these differences could be accounted for by socio-economic differences between African Americans and Caucasians" (p. 199).

For all the personality tests identified in Chapter 9 of this book, there are manuals available that should provide information on norming samples and studies on various ethnic groups. The evaluator could read this information closely before selecting a personality measure to use with ethnic or racial minority consumers with disabilities. This author recommends, however, that informal approaches, such as observation, analysis of the consumer's disability and vocational history, and checklists, be used whenever possible when exploring the factors of motivation, values, needs, and attitudes. If a clinical dimension must be added to the assessment process, then a careful examination of all the current information on the proven, traditional tests is strongly recommended.

Added to the instruments discussed in Chapter 9 are three approaches that can supplement information initially gained from the interview or situational assessment. They are particularly useful for providing a beginning understanding of a consumer's motivation, values, needs, and attitudes.

Rotter Incomplete Sentences Blank–Second Edition (RISB-2; Rotter, Lah, & Rafferty, 1992). For this test, consisting of 40 sentence items, the test taker is asked to complete the sentences to express "your real feelings." This measure has fairly objective scoring. The response content can reveal many of the consumer's needs, values, and attitudes related to his or her career future, although in verbal feedback the evaluator may at times identify the relationship between the particular response and the consumer's training and employment expectations. In contrast to using a more clinical, diagnostic format, the evaluator uses a template that is more career focused. The author has frequently employed this method, especially with multicultural consumers, and obtained significant information related to rehabilitation planning.

Mooney Problem Checklist (Mooney & Gordon, 1950). This measure is available in an adult form; the problems addressed include health and physical development, living conditions, employment, social and recreational activities, personal–psychological relations, and the future, both vocational and educational. Emphasis is on individual items and self-reported problems or sources of difficulty. Considerable evidence has accumulated regarding this measure's effectiveness (Anastasi, 1988).

State-Trait Anxiety Inventory. This was designed to measure anxiety in adults, and it distinguishes feelings of anxiety from depression. Developed by Spizlberger, Gorsuch, and Lushens (1970), the instrument has high concurrent validity with other scales utilized to assess anxiety, and has also high relevance for culturally responsive assessment. It has been adapted into 48 languages (Donnell et al., 2010).

In vocational assessment, personality testing is primarily used not for diagnostic purposes or to probe deeply into a consumer's psyche but to support observations or hypotheses gained from the interview or consumer records. The goal is to identify those factors, both positive and negative, that will maximize the consumer's vocational potential. When this perspective is kept in mind, and the evaluator understands what is needed for appropriate training or job adjustment, then personality assessment can be quite beneficial for all consumers.

Interests

Evaluators often depend on inventories to explore a consumer's interests or to predict future success and satisfaction. In other popular intelligence, aptitude, and personality instruments, the rehabilitation professional should be aware of any potential biases that may result in the dissemination of misleading information. There are particular concerns to address when using interest measures with consumers who have disabilities and who represent ethnic minorities. The consumer's socialization and acculturation in the minority culture can affect career choices. The minority consumer may frequently embrace values that differ from those of the dominant culture. The family, for example, may be valued more highly than one's career. Asian American women and Latinas may face pressures toward more traditionally feminine career directions.

Because many persons from different ethnic cultures lack role models during the formative years of elementary and high school, interest assessment may not actually identify the range of possible career choices.

The usefulness of a particular inventory for a given minority population, consequently, must be questioned. Because a number of the most frequently used inventories organize interests around Holland's hexagonal model, the evaluator should explore whether the six-factor structure remains accurate and meaningful across cultures (Prince et al., 1992). Also, interest inventories that are normed on the dominant culture provoke necessary questions for helping professionals whose consumers may not identify themselves with that dominant group. Prince et al. offered the following suggestions for using interest measures with consumers representing a minority culture:

- If the consumer's primary language is not English, the evaluator should explore administering a version of the inventory that corresponds to the person's language.
- The consumer's test-taking attitude and response style need to be explored. Consumers from different minority backgrounds may have certain expectations in mind when responding to an inventory. A minority consumer with a disability, for example, may not wish to endorse interests that reflect a deviation from the interests of his or her parents.
- When interpreting interest test results, the evaluator should be sensitive to the consumer's response, which may reflect cultural values and reinforce cultural stereotypes. It is also possible that the consumer has a restricted range of interests. The helping professional, consequently, should encourage the consumer to broaden his or her career considerations to reach beyond those reflected by the measured interests.

Because these multicultural issues may inhibit a comprehensive exploration of the consumer's interests when using standardized inventories, it can be appropriate to place more emphasis on the interview as an effective approach for identifying interests. Chapter 7, "Interest Assessment in Vocational Rehabilitation," outlines a specialized approach to interest evaluation that may elicit more useful and reliable information. Included in this evaluation exploration is an identification of the consumer's career and education aspirations. These expectations can shape the career outlook of consumers with disabilities, but relatively little is known when it comes to the aspirations and expectations of ethnic minority consumers (Bowman, 1995). There has been some reported research, however, on gender differences among these populations (Bronzaft, 1991; Grevious, 1985; Payton, 1985). Also, considerable research is being conducted on the cultural validity of career assessment instruments, much of it aimed at evaluating the cross-cultural validity of John Holland's model of assessment of career interests (Leong & Hartung, 2000). But more research is needed, and in the absence of reported studies, the evaluator should rely on the creative use of the consumer interview to obtain information about specific career aspirations, expectations, and interests. Some of the methods for soliciting this information were discussed earlier in this chapter and also are covered in Chapter 6.

Administration of Assessment Approaches

To reduce the potential bias perceived by the evaluator in the available assessment instruments, various forms of evaluation approaches—that is, the interview, situational assessment, and selected work samples—should be considered for administration. When administering evaluation approaches to consumers who have disabilities and who represent cultural minorities, the same general guidelines are usually followed as are applied to all consumers in vocational assessment, but there are specific cautions to be followed. Most of the assessment manuals provide information on how to orient consumers to the selected tests or evaluation areas. With these directions, a trusting environment should be established that, in turn, helps considerably to reduce the consumer's anxiety and frustration. What can further reduce apprehension is empathic gestures, careful listening to the consumer's concerns, and a careful explanation of what approaches are going to be used, what the instruments measure, and how they are connected to the suggested training objectives and career goals that emerged from the comprehensive interview.

The degree of rapport between the administrator and consumer can vary according to the cultural background of the consumer (Whiston, 2000). Eye contact and leaning forward toward the individual, for example, may not be appropriate for certain Asian consumers. But many difficulties with the administration of assessment instruments can be avoided if the evaluator familiarizes him- or herself with the test instructions, the boundaries of what is acceptable for assessment administration, and the consumer's culture (Whiston, 2000). Unfamiliarity with the nature and purpose of specific assessment approaches and with the consumer's ethnic background can penalize someone from the outset (Lonner & Sundberg, 1985).

Prior to beginning the administration of the assessment measures, the evaluator should explore the consumer's prior experience with assessment. The consumer's reading level should be determined and response style to test items, particularly in the personality and interest areas, pinpointed. Certain instruments allow for a brief practice session, and feedback from this exercise could provide information on customary ways of responding. To avoid embarrassing themselves, and in harmony with their own cultural and family expectations, consumers from minority ethnic backgrounds might tend to agree with nearly everything on the evaluation measure. Trial sessions give the evaluator an opportunity to provide reinforcement. Such affirmation can further reduce the consumer's anxiety over the testing situation.

Research reports have suggested that the relationship between the examiner and examinee has some influence on the assessment outcome, though race itself may not have that much of an impact (Whiston, 2000). Certain evaluator characteristics are vitally important in establishing an open, trusting relationship with a consumer who may have genuine misgivings about the value of the entire assessment experience. A willingness to take the time before test administration to listen to the consumer's concerns, and administering the instruments with clarity and impartiality, are beginning steps to developing a satisfactory rapport. Rapport enhances evaluation outcomes.

Interpretation of Assessment Outcomes

Chapter 14 discusses quite comprehensively the issues emerging from the opportunity to discuss evaluation results with the consumer. The suggestions and guidelines offered in this chapter would also apply to consumers who represent ethnic minorities and with significant disabilities. But there are added guidelines that should be considered at the "interpreting" phase:

- Because of the lingering presence of institutional bias in some rehabilitation agencies, or the existence of career assumptions about various cultural groups, the evaluator should use caution when interpreting test results with culturally diverse consumers. For example, the assumption may still exist that only certain careers or jobs are available for specific minority persons, even though this has been shown to be untrue.

- Information gained from the assessment interview, such as facts pertaining to the consumer's acculturation, worldview, and racial identity, should be integrated into the interpretation process (Flores et al., 2003).

- Consideration should be carefully given as to how the evaluation results will impact the consumer's family members. The family can become either a facilitator or a barrier to the realistic incorporation of the results into the development of rehabilitation plans.

- The evaluator should understand any differences between the normative or comparison group used to validate the measure and the consumer's population group. As often stated in this chapter, there is the possibility that particular assessment tools have limited value for consumers from certain reference groups.

- As it is true for test interpretation for all consumers, the evaluator should look for consistencies in data across assessment tools and methods before making definite conclusions for the development of the rehabilitation plan.

Apart from these suggestions, it is important to note that the consumer's socioeconomic status may have more influence on the assessment results than ethnicity or instrument bias (Whiston, 2000). More research is needed to support this theory, and yet the evaluator should explore the individual's SES and what may be its influence on assessment performance. Unfamiliarity with any assessment process, lack of education opportunities and available resources, and a distinctive value system are all factors associated with a low SES level. A working partnership with the consumer and an understanding of the consumer's cultural background will assist the evaluator considerably in communicating the assessment results.

Conclusion

Because of the increased racial and cultural transformation of the demography of the United States (Pack-Brown, Thomas, & Seymour, 2008), rehabilitation counselors must examine carefully the available assessment tools for bias and other discriminatory content. These perceptions must be weighed with those factors that can enhance accuracy and the productivity of assessment. During the evaluation process, information should be obtained that eventually will lead to appropriate rehabilitation planning. This goal necessitates counselor competency and an evaluation environment that encourages consumer fairness and offers adaptive guidelines and other related opportunities for alternative methods of ensuring consumer understanding.

Understanding Selected Concepts in Vocational Assessment

For many years, procedures for testing people with disabilities have left much to be desired (Parker, Hansmann, & Schaller, 2010; Sherman & Robinson, 1982). To date there is little information regarding the practical value of most assessment measures for this population (Gysbers, Heppner, & Johnston, 2009). Even when assessment measures are appropriately modified, the meaning of the scores is uncertain. Unfortunately, fully developed test modifications that are suitable for all individuals with disabilities do not currently exist. Also, there is little information about the way available tests compare for those who have disabilities and those who do not (Sherman & Robinson, 1982). Vocational evaluation for people with disabilities, women, and people from minority backgrounds has raised such questions as, What kind of norms should be used when testing persons with disabilities? For those with severe disabilities, what types of assessment approaches are preferable? Are evaluation measures that are developed on nondisabled populations reliable and valid for individuals with disabilities (Parker et al., 2010)?

Two important functions of tests are selection and diagnosis. This book focuses on the use of selected tests to explore and identify the consumer's independent living skills, as well as his or her career- and work-related strengths and limitations. However, test results that reflect a person's disability do not provide an unbiased estimate of his or her potential. The issue of which tests and other evaluation approaches are appropriate for individuals with disabilities is a crucial one in rehabilitation assessment.

Paper-and-pencil tests and many work sample systems are classified in several ways, including (a) individual or group, (b) verbal or erbal, (c) highly structured or unstructured, (d) closed-choice or n-ended, (e) objective or subjective, and (f) machine-scored or scored y judgment. Psychometric tests and work samples may also vary a great deal in the degree of standardization quality and amount of interpretive information they furnish. Consequently, when using these measures for vocational evaluation, the helping professional has to determine the measures' appropriateness for consumers. The different social and cultural histories and experiences for those with disabilities should be recognized (Gysbers et al., 2009). Certain standards for evaluating these methods should be employed to choose the most appropriate and available measure. This chapter discusses these standards and other relevant issues and explains the guidelines for interpreting test scores.

Appropriate Norms and the Criteria Problem

A *norm* refers to the group of people on whom an assessment procedure has been standardized and from whom the scores on a particular measure have been obtained to determine level of performance. There are a wide variety of possible types of norms—local, regional, national, competitive, and disability group norms—that could be used in vocational evaluation. All are possibilities, but evaluators seem to place an emphasis on competitive or industrial norms. Yet there are problems in the development of industrial norms, such as those pertaining to cost benefits, accessing of occupational areas, and specific jobs. Even if information could be collected for this development, could the traditional definition of "norm" based on consumer performance be extended to include the "norming" of the expectations held by evaluators, trainers, and employers? Because norms are value laden and are used for predictive purposes, can they actually contribute to the better understanding of consumers? These are important questions that are not completely answerable and should prompt the evaluator to use norms cautiously when working with those with severe disabilities and who are not included in the norm group. Norms are usually interpreted in a process that also involves the evaluator's skills. But the issue of identifying appropriate norms still remains a challenge for vocational rehabilitation. A measure's normative group, of course, should be comparable to the individual taking the test.

Fundamentally, it is important to know about the population used to norm the particular instrument. The norm groups used for such testing need to be large enough to include a wide range of diversity, or it needs to be stated that the instrument has been tested only with a selected population (Niles & Harris-Bowlsbey, 2005).

In rehabilitation, a test's normative group should be appropriate for the individual taking the test, but the problem is that many assessment procedures have not been standardized on a representative sample. This is true, for example, of most paper-and-pencil tests. Also, vocational evaluation involves prediction. A predictive assessment measure that cannot be used in exactly the same surroundings as the behavior that is to be predicted is definitely limited. For this reason, assessment procedures other than paper-and-pencil tests are frequently used in vocational evaluation. The best prediction of what persons will do in a given situation is usually what they did the last time in that situation. Consequently, the approaches of work samples or situational assessment (which are explained in a later chapter) are frequently used for predictive purposes because they can tap into a person's previous experience.

Rehabilitation agencies have conducted a great deal of research and development on assessment procedures. However, norms are available on only some of the tests used by rehabilitation agencies, and rarely is there an interest in comparing the test scores of those who have disabilities with the scores of those who do not (Sherman & Robinson, 1982).

Approximately 30 years ago, a practice that was adopted to make the results of selection tests minimally prejudicial was *race norming*, in which a consumer's test scores are compared only with those of his or her own ethnic group. Race norming was used by the federal government, but because of the charge of reverse discrimination and because the Civil Rights Act of 1991 bans any form of "score adjustment" on the basis of race, color, religion, gender, or national origin, the use of separate subgroup norms for employment purposes is now illegal (Aiken, 1997). The issue of general versus special norms, as applied to the vocational evaluation of those with disabilities, is both confusing and controversial. On the one hand, general norms may discriminate unfairly against people with disabilities. The evaluator must consider the purpose of the assessment—is it to compare an individual's performance with that of members of another group, or to estimate the person's future performance? Parker et al. (2010) believed that the major cause for the confusion is that "rehabilitation personnel frequently fail to make a conceptual separation between descriptions and predictions" (p. 144).

Because of these norm-referenced difficulties, many of the measures used in rehabilitation assessment should determine what a consumer can do, rather than how he or she stands in comparison to others. Initially, the rehabilitation professional needs to determine the skills necessary to accomplish tasks satisfactorily in an employment situation (sometimes by consulting manuals that identify these tasks). Then the assessment will provide an estimate of whether or not a consumer has the capability to perform, with training, the necessary tasks.

With norm-referenced tests, there are domain- and criterion-referenced measures that also establish a basis for test interpretation (Bolton, Parker, & Brookings, 2008). Criterion-referenced approaches, moreover, are gaining widespread acceptance in the rehabilitation field. This assessment method is more applicable to those with severe disabilities and can be used to determine if consumers have developed employability and independent living skills. In rehabilitation practice, it has been discovered that the best prediction of a person's performance on a particular job is the person's actual performance on that job for an adequate period of time. In other words, the best predictor is the criterion behavior (Parker et al., 2010).

Norm-referenced tests yield information about a test taker's relative standing, while criterion-referenced measures yield information about a consumer's mastery of a particular skill. "Has this consumer mastered the skills necessary to be employable in a certain occupation?" is a type of question that a criterion-referenced test may seek to answer (Cohen et al., 1996). When a consumer's performance is compared to a standard of mastery called a criterion, the criterion-referenced assessment "uses as its interpretive frame of reference a specified content domain rather than a specified population of persons" (Anastasi, 1988, p. 101; Bolton et al., 2008). Examples of criterion-referenced measures include many behavior assessment tools, which may also use rating performance measures that target single or multiple skills. The criterion can be a specific behavior or behaviors, a test score, an amount of time, a rating, a psychiatric diagnosis, an index of absenteeism, and so on.

Anastasi (1988) believed that "the most distinguishing factor of criterion-referenced testing is its interpretation of test performance in terms of content meaning. The focus is clearly on what test takers can do and what they know, not on how they compare with others" (p. 103). A criterion-referenced measure, consequently, has a clearly defined domain, rather than a specified population of persons. The criterion in criterion-referenced assessments usually derives from the values or standards of an individual or organization (Cohen et al., 1996). An agency determines, for example, a reasonable level of proficiency, regardless of how well other consumers perform. Criterion-referenced interpretations provide information about what individuals with disabilities can do, whereas norm-referenced interpretations provide information that compares one person's performance to that of other people (Cohen et al., 1996). For a job-related criterion to be adequate, it should be quantitative, should parallel the actual job requirements, and should be measurable with some degree of consistency (Owings & Siefker, 1991).

The most basic scores used in criterion-referenced assessment are pass–fail or right–wrong, with single skill scores ranging from completely correct to completely incorrect. When multiple skill scores (scores resulting from multiple observations) are used, then percentages and rates are used.

In vocational assessment a continued question for the evaluator is what qualifies as a "good" test or evaluation procedure. The criteria for a good test should include clear instructions for administration, scoring, and interpretation. A good evaluation approach measures what it purports to measure, is reliable, and yields assessment results that are based on appropriate norms for the population being evaluated. The following sections on validity and reliability explain the issues that need to be addressed with these factors.

Validity

Although Section 504 of the Rehabilitation Act of 1973 and the Americans with Disabilities Act of 1990 (ADA) specify many requirements, one in the ADA has important relevance for rehabilitation assessment:

> An organization covered by these regulations shall assure itself that tests are selected and administered so as to best ensure that the test results reflect the applicant's aptitude, achievement level, or whatever other factor the test purports to measure, rather than reflecting the applicant's impaired sensory, manual, or speaking skills, except when those skills are the factors that the test purports to measure. (ADA, Sec 104.42 (b)37)

In other words, the concept of validity can be considered the most important test property (Gysbers, Heppner, & Johnston, 2009) and is particularly important when determining the appropriateness of any use of a test. Validity provides an estimate of how well a test measures what it purports to measure, and this concept is central to both rehabilitation legislation and the vocational assessment process.

Rehabilitation professionals should always refer to the validity of a particular use of a test. It is the use, and not the test itself, that has validity (Cohen et al., 1996; Sherman & Robinson, 1982). Validity is not an either/or attribute of the use of a test; it exists in varying degrees in various situations. Conducting validity studies by no means ensures that a particular application of a test is appropriate (Sherman & Robinson, 1982). In fact, validation of tests for populations of people with disabilities has been rare. Few, if any, validation studies have given attention to the applicability of the test producer's validation to local conditions. Differential validation research on testing people with disabilities is virtually nonexistent in the private sector. Such studies are considered infeasible because of the small numbers of employees with disabilities in similar jobs (Parker et al., 2010; Sherman & Robinson, 1982). The ADA implies that a handicapping condition should have no effect whatsoever on test scores unless the test is explicitly designed to measure an ability directly related to the handicap. However, such an implication raises the question of whether a modified test or the test administration procedure is sufficient to maintain the validity of the test content and the credibility of the testing medium. It may be too ideal to modify assessment measures to the degree that they are unaffected by a consumer's disability. Most test developers believe that this ideal is largely unattainable.

Predictive validity, however, offers the greatest promise for comparability of test results between the population of those who have disabilities and those who do not. Predictive validity also gives an estimate of the strength of the association between test scores and a measure of performance on the criterion to be predicted (Sherman & Robinson, 1982). Consequently, it has been recommended that

> sponsors of large testing programs ... modify tests to accommodate most kinds of sensory and motor handicaps and ... conduct predictive validity studies in order to ascertain whether the modified tests have a predictive power near that of the standard test used with the general population. (p. 126)

It is believed that this is an achievable form of comparability, although empirical studies would have to be conducted in order to determine the actual feasibility of the approach (Sherman & Robinson, 1982). At the end of the research, it should be possible to determine whether modified and standard forms of a test actually have comparable predictive power.

The validity of a test may be evaluated by (a) scrutinizing its content, (b) relating scores obtained on the test to other test scores or other measures, and (c) performing a comprehensive analysis of "not only how scores on the test relate to other test scores and measures but also how they can be understood within some theoretical framework for understanding the construct the test was designed to measure" (Cohen et al., 1996, p. 175). Betz and Weiss (2008) believed that there are three major types of validity: content, criterion-related, and construct validity. Three other types of validity will also be explained, namely, predictive, face, and incremental validity.

Content Validity

Content validity refers to how representative the test items are in terms of assessing the behavior and skill the test was designed to sample. One way to estimate the design sample is to determine carefully what items make up the domain or content of some specific behavior. A sample of items is then pooled to represent different levels of the behavior. When the items are pooled, it is thought that the resulting test will discriminate among individuals at different levels of mastery. A statistical procedure called factor analysis is sometimes used to assess content validity. This procedure groups test items into different factors, suggesting that the items in a factor relate to some specific content or knowledge base. Content validity is most likely to be reported for achievement tests. Also, content validity for work evaluation procedures exists when the duties and tasks of the work sample or situational assessment are highly similar to those of the job itself.

Content validity is an important issue when considering test fairness. Although test fairness is not a fixed concept, and experts disagree on its meaning, it is particularly relevant for evaluators and employers when evaluation approaches are developed and results are used for employment decisions. The ADA implies that when decisions are going to be made from test scores, the items on a particular test must be relevant to the specific job or jobs to which the applicant is applying. Employers must demonstrate that the skills measured by their selection tests and other hiring procedures are job related (Aiken, 1997).

Criterion-Related Validity

This type of validity refers to the extent to which a measure of a trait is related to some external behavior or measure of interest. The external measure represents a behavior that is important to focus on during, for example, the evaluation of employability or placeability, and the evaluator expects the measure to predict performance on the established criterion in the work sector. To determine the value of the criterion-related validity, there should be a strong relationship between the trait or behavior being measured and the criterion itself. Also, the instrument should not measure other variables that do not correlate with the designated criterion. In other words, criterion-related validity focuses on a relationship between two variables (Betz & Weiss, 2008).

Construct Validity

Construct validity, which is more theoretical than the other types of validity, refers to the degree to which a test measures any hypothetical construct. It is most likely to be used in measuring psychological traits and characteristics. For example, anger is a hypothetical construct that can exist in different forms. What anger is, as well as where and when it is likely to be experienced, is linked to psychological theory. In construct validity, it is suggested that something like anger exists; next, the anger is related to a theory concerning the phenomenon; and finally, a test, in measuring the construct of anger, attempts to predict the way anger differentiates people in terms of the construct. In vocational rehabilitation, a convenient starting place in determining construct validity of evaluation procedures is to examine the worker functions required in successful performance of the job. These functions are identified very clearly through job analysis techniques. Construct validation emphasizes the analysis of the job in terms of standard definitions of the constructs underlying successful performance of job duties and tasks. Examples of such constructs are speed in performing the task, eye–hand coordination, and finger dexterity.

Predictive Validity

Predictive validity refers to the relationship between a test and some criterion. It can be established by giving a test to a group of persons and then assessing the eventual outcomes for the group. Most commonly in determining predictive validity, a test is administered to a group of persons who are then placed into a training program or job. At some later time, data are collected on training or job success criteria, and these are correlated with the initial scores. These predictive validity procedures have an advantage in that they can show the particular instrument's ability to differentiate between persons who are successful on the job and those who are not.

Face Validity

Face validity is a subjective appraisal of what a test seems to measure. Face validity is a judgment based more on a test's measurement design than on its content. It is concerned with the extent to which the instrument measures, or "looks like" it measures, what it is intended to measure. It is not the same as content validity. Face validity is about a judgment about a test after it has been constructed. Content validity focuses on the issue that while the test is being constructed, the test items are an adequate sample of a specific domain of content that defines what is being measured (Betz & Weiss, 2008).

A test that measures anger, for example, should have items that seem to measure anger. Although face validity is a very crude technique, it is often necessary in order to ensure that a test is acceptable to potential users or test takers. For example, if a test used to predict job performance has no obvious relationship to the job, rehabilitation professionals may be less likely to use it. Importantly, face validity can establish rapport between the test taker and the test administrator.

Incremental Validity

Many vocational evaluators are interested in using multiple predictors, because an additional predictor can explain something about the criterion measure not explained by predictors already in use. For example, a consumer's score on an aptitude test, such as the *Bennett Mechanical Comprehension Test* (Bennett, 1992), may be used as one indicator of training and future employment success. High scores on behavioral rating scales that have been validated may also predict training and employment success. An aptitude or work sample test may not be the most efficient way to predict successful training and employment productivity. An evaluator may find that another measure has good incremental validity because it reflects a different aspect of preparation for successful training outcomes. So, predictor measures are included only if they demonstrate that they can explain something about the criterion measure that was not already known from the other predictors (Cohen et al., 1996).

Issues pertaining to validity are particularly important to the rehabilitation professional when conducting vocational assessment. For example, if a written test is employed to make decisions about individuals or groups, all the available evidence should be studied before any attempt is made to interpret the scores. Also, a test that is going to be used for prediction or selection should be validated in the specific situation in which it is going to be used. Validity awareness further implies that the professional will be up to date, not only on new knowledge about assessment procedures but also about the qualities or individual traits they measure.

Another issue with validity revolves around the term *validity coefficient*. This is a correlation between a test score and a criterion measure and is expressed by a number. A measure may be used, for example, to select personnel for long-term training or to predict success in school. Anastasi (1988) explained that the validity coefficient "provides a single numerical index of test validity, and is commonly used in test manuals to report the validity of a test against each criterion for which data are available" (p. 163). However, validity coefficients may change over time because of changing selection standards. But the interpretation of a validity coefficient must take into account a number of concomitant circumstances (Anastasi, 1988). Although the correlation should be high enough to be statistically significant at some acceptable level, such as at the 0.01 or 0.05 level, the rehabilitation professional needs to evaluate the size of the correlation in light of the uses to be made of the test.

As an example of the use of the validity coefficient, Bolton (1979) reported that the validity coefficients for the *Workshop Scale of Employability* (with 500 consumers of the Chicago Workshop; Bolton, 1982) were 0.23, 0.23, and 0.26 for the three criteria of early placement, long-term placement, and maintenance, respectively. He continued to say that the corresponding validity coefficients for a sample of 100 consumers of the Indianapolis Goodwill Workshop were 0.43, 0.43, and 0.31. Consequently, Bolton concluded correctly that placement in employment was clearly more predictable using the *Workshop Scale* in Indianapolis than in Chicago. The rehabilitation professional can then attempt to identify the factors that may have accounted for the difference, such as economic conditions or differences among the sample groups. But the question remains, "How good is a coefficient of 0.43?" (Bolton, 1979).

An answer can be obtained by asking, "What is the use of a particular measurement?" Is the measurement being used for prediction (i.e., employment), for selection of consumers, or to support the validity of the instrument? Bolton (1979) believed, however, that a validity coefficient of 0.43 is about average, and seldom do coefficients exceed 0.60.

Validity concerns are also important when the rehabilitation professional refers a consumer to an evaluation resource or agency to determine vocational potential. Questions pertaining to validity include the following:

> Does the vocational evaluation program have competently
> trained personnel?
> Are there clearly specified objectives to the assessment
> program, and does the program have the particular resources
> to accomplish the vocational evaluation?
> Can the consumer, despite physical and emotional limitations,
> meet the demands of the particular vocational evaluation
> experience?

Thoughtful consideration of these questions can enhance the credibility of the assessment phase of the rehabilitation process.

Reliability

Reliability refers to the dependability, consistency, and precision of an assessment procedure. A reliable procedure is one that produces similar results when repeated. An assessment task is reliable when consumers who are involved in the evaluation process receive the same or similar score results if the evaluation measures are repeated.

Reliability is usually expressed by the coefficient r. It is a convenient statistical index for estimating indexes of the relationship between distributions of test scores when a test (or some equivalent form) is administered to a single representative sample of subjects or consumers on two or more occasions. The coefficient is expressed as a ratio, of which both numbers range from 0 to 1, and represents the degree to which a group's test scores fluctuate from test to retest. If test scores are reliable, the test–retest correlation coefficient should be high. For example, high scores on one occasion should be matched by high scores on a second, and low scores should relate to low scores. The following is an identification of some correlation coefficients:

0.80–1.00 *Very high correlation*

0.60–0.79 *Substantial correlation*

0.40–0.59 *Moderate correlation*

0.20–0.39 *Little correlation*

0.01–0.19 *Practically no correlation*

The following are three traditional ways of estimating the correlation coefficient:

1. *Test–retest*—The test or other assessment procedure is re-administered to the same people after a 1- or 2-week interval. The scores on the first administration are correlated with the scores on the second administration, and a correlation coefficient is obtained. Consumers, however, do not usually retake tests, so accuracy is quite important in this particular approach in estimating the correlation coefficient. If a consumer is given unreliable information, then he or she may act upon it (Gysbers et al., 2009).

2. *Alternate or parallel forms*—Although not employed as frequently as the test–retest method, the use of two or more parallel forms of the same assessment instrument can provide the best estimate of reliability. These parallel forms are administered to the same subjects within a 1- to 2-week interval.

3. *Split–half*—In this approach, the items in a written test, for example, are assigned arbitrarily to two forms. For example, even-numbered items may constitute one set and odd-numbered items the other set. Item pairs, or test halves, must be equal in terms of difficulty and content, and individuals taking the particular measure must have the opportunity to complete the entire test. Then, each consumer receives two scores on the same instrument, and the two sets of scores are intercorrelated. Both halves, of course, are administered at the same time.

Unfortunately, the reliability data provided for most tests are incomplete (Aiken, 1997; Shertzer & Linden, 1979). Both the labor required and the cost involved prohibit the evaluation of the reliability of any measure for all people on whom the measure may be used. Rehabilitation professionals are then faced with the problem of searching among reliability data provided for a particular test or another appraisal measure in order to find the population that corresponds as closely as possible to the consumers with whom they intend to work.

One question frequently raised is, "What constitutes practical, acceptable reliability?" The answer depends on the type of measurement instrument used (i.e., intelligence, personality, aptitude, or interest), the purpose for using the instrument, and the degree of accepted reliability. Different types of published tests show different ranges of reliability. Personality inventories, for example, tend to be less reliable than achievement tests. It is important to note that the purpose of using a measurement instrument influences what is considered an acceptable level of reliability. If an instrument is used to make diagnostic decisions, such as determining the level of academic training at which the consumer should begin, then the test should have a reliability coefficient from 0.80 to 1.00.

Another question that should be asked when discussing the reliability of an instrument or other assessment approach is, What are the sources of variation among test score differences between consumers engaged in the assessment? Thorndike and Thorndike-Christ (2008) identified many such factors, including the following.

1. *Lasting specific characteristics.* These are characteristics, such as ability or knowledge, that are unique to a particular test and that make it possible to respond to an unusually difficult item correctly. One's educational experience may provide knowledge on particular test items or demands that allows one to do well on certain areas of the measure or evaluation approach.

2. *Temporary general characteristics.* A temporary health condition, fatigue, motivation, and emotional strain are considered relatively short-term deviations. These factors may also cause fluctuations in attention.

3. *Administration and appraisal of test performance.* This would also comprise characteristics of the testing situation, which include how

one perceives the assessment situation, the different ways evaluators explain the assessment approach, or the attention they provide
to sustain a standardized environment.

All of these sources of variation should be kept in mind when preparing consumers for the vocational assessment experience. Awareness
can facilitate careful preparation of consumers, as well as particular attention to one's own style of conducting assessment. To enhance the reliability of the assessment situation, the rehabilitation professional should
explore not only the consumers' history in taking tests or other evaluation procedures but also (a) their motivation for the vocational assessment process, (b) any emotional pressure they might be experiencing,
(c) the possible effects of their disability on test-taking performance, and
(d) the appropriateness of the difficulty level of assessment tasks in relation to the consumers' current capabilities. Furthermore, the rehabilitation professional should be familiar with the environment in which the
vocational assessment will take place. The situational variables mentioned previously can have a decided effect on a consumer's performance.

Reliability issues are also important when tests are considered for
persons who have severe disabilities. Such factors as test instructions,
item content and format, and methods for answering the test items are
designed to make a particular test useful for a specific population. When
a different population with different characteristics is introduced, the
test procedures might have to be changed.

Test Modifications

Bolton, Parker, and Brookings (2008) explained that there are usually
three types of test modifications: changing the way the test is presented,
making accommodations in the response format, and changing the environment in which tests are administered. Importantly, when persons
with disabling conditions are not able "to clearly formulate or articulate answers to some type of test items, examiners may need to incorporate the 'acculturation' of applicants into their interpretation of test
responses" (p. 24). More specifically, Enright, Conyers, and Szymanski
(1996) identified the most common test modifications, such as administration in oral, large print, or Braille format; individualized versus
group administration; provision of extra time; use of an interpreter; use

of word processors or nonwritten methods to record responses; and use of adjustable desks to accommodate wheelchairs.

Salvia and Ysseldyke (1995) conceptualized testing accommodations and adaptations in terms of presentation and response formats, as well as the setting and timing of the assessment measure. They suggested examples of accommodations or adaptations, such as in presentations using large-print editions of tests, oral reading of directions, and the use of magnifying equipment, and in the response format, such as using a template typewriter or computer for responding or giving a response in sign language. The setting of a test could be modified for a small group or for taking the test at home, and timing could be adapted to include more breaks during testing, if appropriate, or extending the testing sessions over several days.

However, unlimited time may be inappropriate. Pure speed tests are used in the employment context to test such skills as perceptual speed and clerical accuracy. The time limit usually cannot be adjusted on these tests because speed is the factor that is being tested. In addition to the issues raised by the modifications of selected measures, there have been other approaches to test accommodations used when feasible during evaluation practice. Two examples are *within-group norming,* which entails the conversion of all raw scores into percentile or standard scores based on the test performance of the consumer's own group (basically, an individual with a disability is being compared only with other members of his or her own group) and *differential cut-offs,* whereby, for example, a passing score for one group may be 65 but a passing score for members of another group is 70. Both modification approaches must be cautiously used so as not to compromise the integrity and credibility of the results that may be used for planning purposes.

Vocational evaluators must be aware of the responsibilities for users of standardized tests (Cottone & Tarvydas, 1998). These standards state that evaluators should seek the expertise of professionals experienced with disability issues when considering test modification. This preparation is necessary because evaluators need to familiarize themselves with alternative test forms and special norms, and to report any modifications when drawing conclusions (Enright et al., 1996). Because modified tests raise several complex issues, consumers with disabilities undergoing vocational assessment should learn as much as possible about the specific evaluation measures. It is important that these consumers receive, as appropriately as possible, individualized guidance before taking any standardized test. When adapting or modifying tests or evaluation measures, the rehabilitation professional must be very careful, however, not to make changes that can alter the nature of the task.

Another area of test modification that must be carefully considered is individual versus group administration.

Individual or Group Administration

Tests are often administered in group sessions, and many persons seem to perform better with this format. Group-administered tests are more economical and usually provide data of acceptable reliability and validity (Bolton et al., 2008). People with severe disabilities can also experience vocational evaluation in small groups, such as three or four persons. In this case, the test needs to be appropriate for each person in the group. A test should be individually administered when a consumer is extremely anxious or fearful of the testing situation or has a severe sensory impairment or motor disability that requires the adaptation of testing procedures. Other reasons for individual test administration include the absence of a convenient and practical way to use group administration; the desire not to interfere with others in a group taking a test; and further consideration for consumers with disabilities, such as wanting to reduce their anxiety over the test (Sherman & Robinson, 1982). For example, a Braille version of an assessment procedure should be individually administered to consumers who are blind.

When considering individual administration over group test taking, the rehabilitation professional should be cautious of the effects of interaction between himself or herself and the consumer. Such interaction might negatively influence the consumer's assessment experience. For example, the professional might be uncomfortable with a particular disability or inexperienced in the administration of a specific measure. These problems can cause him or her to become irritated or impatient, which, in turn, may deflate the consumer's test score.

There are instances, of course, in which a disabling condition has almost no effect on test performance, and, consequently, modifications are not needed. Furthermore, some modifications will have no effect on the test results. Yet, very severe disabling conditions can have a great impact on test performance, and their influence on test results can be considerable. Generally, when a disability imposes a language obstacle;

interferes with the understanding of test items, problems, or materials; or prevents a person from making the responses required for indicating test answers (such as using a pencil or marking responses on answer sheets), then the evaluation measure falls considerably short of evaluating the factors it is intended to assess. Also, many people with disabilities must take drugs that are antispasmodic, anxiety reducing, or anticonvulsant. Many of these medications can easily lower the credibility of the assessment results. The rehabilitation professional should match the evaluation procedure to the particular limitations of the disability that affect assessment performance.

Specific Criteria for Assessment Selection

There are specific criteria to use, consequently, when choosing a particular instrument or assessment approach, such as the following:

- *The nature and stability of the consumer's disability.* Physical and cognitive implications of the disability should be considered.
- *The validity and reliability of the instrument.* For standardized assessments, this information is usually found in the test manual.
- *Time required for administration.* Time provisions may necessitate test modifications or assistive devices.
- *The training needed for scoring and perceived scoring difficulties*
- *The consumer's performance motivation for the particular instrument or assessment approach.* Motivation to perform in a testing situation may vary for consumers from culturally diverse backgrounds with disabilities (Parker et al., 2010). The disclosure of information in a process that requires self-analysis and introspection may lower the motivation level of specific consumers. A sense of distrust toward the rehabilitation system and the results of vocational assessment may also inhibit one's positive attitude toward participation in this process. These attitudes can be explored prior to actual assessment and a determination made as to how they compromise one's involvement in the appraisal process.
- *Level of consumer acculturation as it relates to language and performance demands during assessment.* Does this process adequately tap the expectations and strengths emerging from the consumer's culture? An assessment situation, moreover, that only is directed

to planning long-term goals and does not consider the person's short-term, immediate needs may not be in harmony with the consumer's real world. Frequently, a combination of approaches that address both long- and short-term issues may be more suitable for the person with a disability (Smart & Smart, 1992).

- *Training needed for the interpretation of assessment results.* Knowledge and experiences of utilizing vocational assessment approaches may prompt the counselor to be aware that many tools used traditionally in vocational assessment may reinforce, for example, existing segregation of men and women into traditional male and female occupational groups. But does the instrument use same-sex norms, comparing an individual's scores on selected tools to those of people of the same sex? The use of combined-sex normative scores may restrict women's choices by failing to suggest occupational alternatives that are nontraditional (Parker et al., 2010). Fortunately, the separate measurement of vocational interests for men and women has been largely eliminated (Parker et al., 2010). But test interpretation requires not only interpersonal skills but also the skills to effectively communicate the relationship between the characteristics and purpose of a specific appraisal approach, assessment results, and the consumer's expectations for a productive career.

- *The assessment instrument's usefulness to the consumer.* The consumer's initial interview should provide some information about his or her expectations, values, and needs. When preparing the consumer for the assessment process, this information can be used to show further how particular assessment approaches can respond to these consumer factors.

Selecting the appropriate assessment measure or approach requires the counselor to make decisions. While there are hundreds of assessment instruments, those appraisal tools relevant to the vocational needs and values of disability populations are much smaller in number. Choosing which ones to use depends not only on the aforementioned criteria but also on the counselor's background, place of employment, and understanding of measurement principles.

As stated earlier in this chapter, the application of traditional assessment measures to those with severe disabilities presents problems because of technical limitations. After evaluation, persons with disabilities seek advice regarding their future employment and career. To provide appropriate guidance in this important area, rehabilitation professionals should be aware that there are also cultural and gender considerations that influence the assessment process. Parker, Hansmann, and Schaller (2010) explained that these factors include "performance motivation, response style, level of acculturation, inappropriate norms, and gender restrictiveness" (p. 135). Individuals from certain ethnic backgrounds, for example, may be uncomfortable with disclosing information. Performance on language-based measures, moreover, may be influenced by the level of acculturation of the test taker. Also, the evaluator should ensure that the assessment process does not reinforce the existing segregation of men and women into traditional masculine and feminine occupations.

To prevent many of these problems, before beginning the actual assessment process the rehabilitation professional should explore the test taker's level of acculturation and his or her past experience with testing. Such an exploration can alert the evaluator to specific consumer needs and help the professional to become more sensitive to cultural characteristics (Parker et al., 2010).

Interpreting Test Scores

When reading assessment reports from an evaluation resource or explaining test scores to a consumer, the rehabilitation professional should understand how to interpret various types of test scores. Raw scores derived from psychological tests and inventories are converted to some form of standard score that indicates a relative position in a distribution of scores obtained by the norm group. Norms are the bridge for converting raw scores into standard scores and percentiles. Test norms, usually found in the particular test manual, enable the rehabilitation practitioner to compare a consumer's performance to those of an appropriate reference group. Comparison must frequently be made to obtain specific information for predicting a consumer's performance level in various educational and vocational areas.

Some examples of scores that appear in consumer evaluation reports are as follows:

1. *Stanine scores*—range from 1 to 9.
2. *T scores*—transformed standard scores with a mean of 50 and a standard deviation (*SD*) of 10.

3. *Percentiles*—not to be confused with percentage scores; express the proportion of the group that falls below the score obtained by the consumer. For example, a percentile rank of 55 means that 54 out of 100 of the scores in the normative sample were lower than the consumer's.

Figure 5.1 shows the relationships among different types of test scores in a normal distribution. It identifies, for example, that a *T* score of 60 is 1 *SD* unit above the mean, corresponds to a stanine score of 7, and is approximately equivalent to the 84th percentile. The figure is a useful guide when interpreting test scores, especially when explaining *T* scores and stanine scores in terms of the corresponding percentile score. Frequently, percentiles are more readily understood by consumers.

It is important for the evaluator to be aware that any test or assessment modifications can affect the results, making interpretation problematic. Scores may reflect the effects of a modification. Certain types of

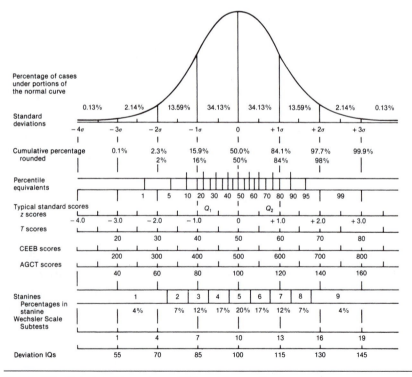

Figure 5.1. Relationships among different types of test scores.

modifications may actually alter the constructs the tests were developed to measure (Enright et al., 1996).

Critical Analysis of Selected Assessment Approaches

Although it is possible for the rehabilitation professional to rely mainly on the opinions expressed in published reviews or manuals of a specific assessment approach, the evaluator should also conduct a personal review of the particular test or assessment approach to make a decision on its applicability to a designated consumer with a disability. The following criteria can provide some guidelines to the evaluator for making judgments on the usefulness of an assessment approach for persons with disabilities.

- *Clarity*—Clarity of purpose and recommended use
- *Dimensions*—Dimensions that the assessment approach purports to measure
- *Availability of particular test forms*—If the forms are not essentially the same, major differences should be mentioned.
- *Clarity of administration*—If parts of the test are timed separately, how many starting points are necessary? Do the directions appear easy, both for the administrator and the test taker? What is the total time needed to complete the test?
- *Norm groups*—How many subjects were involved? Are they representative and appropriate for your setting? Are there norms for each group with which you might wish to compare a person's score?
- *Interpretation of scores*—How are the scores expressed?
- *Item criteria*—What criteria were used for item selection?
- *Item analysis*—Was an item analysis done to determine item discrimination and difficulty?
- *Method of validation*—Validity as determined by the author and others
- *Reliability*—How was reliability determined? Is it adequate for using the instrument with confidence?
- *Test characteristics*—In your opinion, what are the desirable and distinguishing characteristics of the tests?

- *Test problems*—In your opinion, what are the problems you see in the test? (Betz & Weiss, 2008; Bolton, Parker, & Brookings, 2008; Gysbers et al., 2009; Niles & Harris-Bowlsbey, 2005)

Conclusion

When a consumer attempts to carry out a task during rehabilitation assessment, whether a paper-and-pencil test, work sample, or job tryout situation, his or her performance will be a complex function of several elements. These elements are the consumer's (a) capacity to carry out the task, (b) effort level, and (c) appropriate direction of efforts. For consumers with disabilities, the factor of capacity must be cautiously measured. This factor must take into account the issues of appropriate norms, the testing environment, and the possible mental and physical limitations of the consumer. Motivation and energy present particular concerns because there are no specialized techniques for measuring them. A careful exploration of the consumer's capacity, motivation, and energy can lead to more accurate predictions in rehabilitation assessment.

Prediction is an integral part of rehabilitation evaluation. It involves finding out what the consumer can do. His or her capacities can be evaluated by many approaches, assuming that the rehabilitation professional is aware of validity and reliability issues. However, evaluating available drive and energy resources, as well as the appropriateness of the direction in which that energy is applied, calls for assessment strategies that go beyond psychometric measures. Exploring other assessment approaches might, for certain populations of those with disabilities and who represent ethnic minorities, reduce the factor of test bias. Such bias is particularly true of ability and achievement tests. Content bias has been a problem in the past, though now these tests are typically reviewed for bias by panels of individuals representing the full range of racial, ethnic, gender, and socioeconomic groups (Betz & Weiss, 2008). Furthermore, the vocational evaluator may not be interested only in the consumer's actual performance on the selected assessment measures, but may be more concerned about the adequacy of the interaction between proposed jobs and the consumer and the employer's and employee's satisfaction. Both adequacy and satisfaction embrace the factor of acceptability, namely, whether the consumer is trainable for proposed jobs, and what the job situation is like. These issues highlight the importance of situational assessment that includes studying the situation in which the person will be functioning. Such a direction for assessment can alleviate many concerns arising from the problem of norms. Many evaluators respond to this challenge of exploring the most appropriate way to identify career-related capabilities by using job analysis and feedback from potential employers. Situational assessment also includes a variety of evaluation paths and approaches. These methods are explained in the following chapters.

Chapter 6

The Consumer Interview as an Effective Assessment Tool

Just as effective rehabilitation planning begins with a thorough evaluation of the person's residual capacities, an assessment approach also should provide useful and reliable information for the rehabilitation professional. Traditional evaluation approaches are still frequently used in vocational assessment, and this can be unfair to the consumer. (Some of these issues are discussed in Chapters 1, 4, and 5.) Many of the assessment instruments traditionally used were developed from theories that assume that certain consumer traits are unalterable. However, many aptitudes, abilities, and other so-called traits are not static; rather, they are influenced by the situational variables that surround a person's evaluation or learning experiences. The pattern of failure in the lives of many persons with disabilities, perhaps the negative influence of family members, or the stereotypic expectation from many rehabilitation professionals that certain consumers cannot do well in evaluation can decidedly influence a consumer's response to evaluation. These attitudes can also inhibit the consumer's motivation or performance.

Since 1999, there has been a renewed emphasis on consumer empowerment, self-determination, satisfaction, and informed choice, as well as on consumer-driven employment outcomes. These concepts are providing both a foundation and a context for the development of new approaches in vocational evaluation. They have been fueled by rehabilitation legislation, entrepreneurship in assessment practice, and attention to consumer needs. Vocational evaluation should be offered, consequently, as an empowering event for the consumer. What facilitates the reality of empowerment is not only the evaluator's attitude but also the communication of appropriate, sufficient information to the consumer. With information, the consumer may expand his or her choices, even to choosing vocational services and employment goals. But informed choices, consumer self-determination, and satisfaction, all emerging from empowerment, begin with the consumer interview conducted at the beginning of the vocational rehabilitation and evaluation processes.

The interview is one approach among many assessment techniques that can provide meaningful information related to planning effective training programs for persons with severe disabilities. The interview can be used to identify the specific training needs of persons with disabilities (Menchetti & Rusch, 1988). These programs usually focus on developing work-related skills and behaviors. Training variables can play an important role in evaluating the employability of persons with disabilities. These variables, such as motivation, the ability to get along with others, the capacity to learn from previous experience, and attention to task, are not taken into account by traditional evaluation techniques. Assessment strategies that emphasize prediction and predominantly measure general abilities, achievement, and aptitudes may be of little use for many individuals with severe disabilities.

Because of the difficulty in using much of the standardized data to develop interventions that can make a significant difference in the individual's ability to reach rehabilitation goals, the interview can be used as an evaluation tool and as a vehicle to convey relevant information that can help the consumer choose approaches to assessment and reflect on satisfying employment goals. An intake interview, of course, is required in all rehabilitation agencies. Farley and Rubin (2006) defined this interview as "a conversation between a counselor and a consumer with a definite mutually acceptable purpose" (p. 39). The interview is a technique for gathering information by means of discussion.

Saladin, Parker, and Bolton (2012) and Berven (2008) distinguished between *intake interviews* and *initial interviews*. Intake interviews usually focus on completing consumer information forms and providing information about the agency and services available. Initial interviews, on the other hand, focus on building relationships and developing a beginning understanding of the consumer's culture, needs, aspirations, and goals (Saladin et al., 2012). Both of these interview approaches can be structured or unstructured. Structured interviews consist of prescribed questions that are asked in an established sequence, while unstructured interviews offer more flexibility and the interview format is left to the judgment of the interviewer (Berven, 2008). In vocational rehabilitation, the initial interview can be semistructured. The professional has definite information expectations for the encounter with the consumer but is flexible in how the questions are asked and the information to be obtained. Each of these forms is discussed more at length later in this chapter.

The purpose of the initial interview may differ according to the agency's and professional's expectations, but usually it serves to accomplish the following objectives:

1. Develop rapport between the professional and consumer (Farley & Rubin, 2006)
2. Help consumers identify their own strengths and weaknesses as well as recognize and become aware of personality traits, abilities, and aptitudes that may facilitate achieving rehabilitation goals. Through nondirective problem exploration, reflection, and clarification of feelings for self-acceptance and insight, the consumer may gain self-understanding, which is a necessary goal for the rehabilitation process. This is particularly important for persons with disabilities, who need to appreciate their residual physical, intellectual, and emotional assets. During medical treatment, attention usually focuses on the impairment or illness. Patients grow accustomed to focusing on what they cannot do. Interview feedback can help consumers alleviate these perceptions and focus on more helpful knowledge about themselves.
3. Help the consumer feel more comfortable about the rehabilitation process, and help the consumer gain a feeling of self-confidence. As mentioned in the previous chapter, many persons with disabilities harbor anxiety or tension about the possibility of reaching rehabilitation goals. Dependency patterns may already have been developed, or an assessment situation during vocational rehabilitation might revive memories of previous failures in testing. This memory only stimulates added anxiety. The interview creates an opportunity for the professional to begin to ease that anxiety and provides a chance for the consumer to discuss particular fears about the rehabilitation experience. It also provides a context for responding to consumer questions, a chance to verify known information, and an opportunity to identify consumer preferences.

4. Provide the counselor with beginning information for vocational assessment planning and eventual rehabilitation training. This information is acquired through direct exploration of factual data from the consumer's work history, academic records, family history, and any available test data. The acquisition of this information is integral to the interview process. Such information also includes which modifications the consumer needs to engage appropriately in the vocational evaluation process and what has previously been used to assist the consumer to adapt to particular assessment demands.

In addition to building relationships and providing information, the initial interview can be a valuable opportunity to generate necessary facts for rehabilitation planning and, with the consumer's involvement, to determine the best possible employment or career direction. It is also a chance for the interviewer to help consumers become aware of their own responsibility for making decisions when they learn additional information about themselves. Such a realization can help the person gain some control over the rehabilitation outcome, as well as gain a sense of empowerment. What is needed, however, is an interview framework to organize this information and facilitate this awareness for rehabilitation purposes. This framework should consider the interpersonal and environmental setting in which the interview takes place, the content of the interview, the format selected by the interviewer for the meeting, and the professional's interview style for conducting the interview.

There are occasions, moreover, when more than one interview meeting is needed in order to obtain the information necessary for planning purposes. Time considerations or a consumer's initial reticence about disclosing information can extend the interview beyond one session. Regardless of the time it takes to learn more about the consumer, the interview can be more evaluation based. When using the initial interview as a diagnostic resource, there are two general steps, each of which depends on the other: (a) conducting the interview itself and (b) using a structure to collect the information gained from this interview. Certain dynamics generate an effective interview. Also, if the interview is to be a valuable opportunity for a beginning evaluation of the consumer, a framework for organizing the facts must be identified. All of these issues are discussed in this chapter.

Prior to beginning the consumer interview, a review of the consumer's case file may be necessary. During this brief review, the professional must be careful not to become biased from the information, since any bias toward the consumer can undermine the integrity of the vocational evaluation process. For example, a case file might identify a previous diagnosis. This diagnosis might influence the interviewer or even lead to misinterpretation or misunderstanding. Each evaluator should have a personal belief about how to deal with such information. Areas to review in the case file include (a) medical history and prognosis, (b) educational and employment experiences, (c) previous vocational evaluation or rehabilitation technology services, (d) any current adaptive equipment used, and (e) functional limitations that may require accommodations in order for the consumer to participate in the evaluation or eventual education or employment settings.

Beginning the Interview

Berven (2008) explained that "clinical judgment is basic to the entire interview assessment process" (p. 256). When responding to both the consumer's statements and his or her nonverbal behaviors, the interviewer makes judgments about this information. The method chosen to obtain this information depends on what type of consumer information is to be acquired, the circumstances in which it is to be obtained, and the individual conducting the interview. It is important to note that interviewers learn about consumers not only from what the consumers say but also from how they say it, including how, in general, they present themselves during the interview (Cohen et al., 1996). Unless the rehabilitation professional develops a relationship with consumers, the counselor cannot help these people with disabilities feel better about themselves, recognize their productive capabilities, or control their own fears about future training or other rehabilitation opportunities. Experienced interviewers attempt to create a positive, accepting climate in which to conduct the interview. The process for developing this relationship at the beginning of the interview includes two components: (a) contextual interviewing and (b) personal interviewing. Both of these concepts, described at length by Carkhuff (1969) and Anthony (1979), apply to this evaluation process.

Contextual Interviewing

Contextual interviewing is concerned with both the environment in which the interview is conducted and the way the rehabilitation professional physically relates to the consumer. For example, it considers (a) the location of the professional's office, (b) privacy and confidentiality factors, (c) where the professional sits while interviewing, and (d) the number of distractions that are present in an office. For example, many interviews are conducted with the professional sitting behind a desk and the consumer sitting in front of it. The desk represents a barrier to communication, acting as a distancing factor between two people. Consumers usually feel very strange with this arrangement and often feel more comfortable if the professional moves away from the desk. If this is not possible, then having the consumer sit beside the desk reduces some of this communication difficulty.

Also, having too many posters hanging in the professional's office can be very distracting. A few posters, if appropriately placed, can have a calming effect on the consumer and convey a personal dimension of the professional. However, if the office is a mini-museum (even if there is an interesting assortment of collectibles), the consumer may feel overwhelmed.

Another facet of contextual interviewing involves whether the rehabilitation professional takes notes or uses an agency's standard interview form to write comments while talking with the consumer. If possible, the consumer should complete this form before the interview itself. If this is not possible because of some functional limitation, the agency should assist the consumer. Before the interview begins, the professional should scan the form to discover any needed information that might be missing, while learning basic demographic facts about the individual. The professional should tell the consumer in advance if notes are to be taken during the interview. Consumers often become cautious about revealing information if they do not understand how it is going to be used by the interviewer.

Contextual interviewing establishes a mood by creating an atmosphere in which people feel more comfortable and are reassured that they are receiving direct attention. The rehabilitation professional's office can be a form of communication that helps both to reduce the consumer's anxiety and to develop a good relationship during the interview. The warmth that is expressed by the office decor, the professional's placement in relation to the consumer, and the maintenance of privacy and confidentiality can promote communication between the interviewer and the person with a disability. Good interviewing is the result of not only the complex interplay of the rehabilitation professional, the consumer, and the purpose of the interview but also the setting in which it is conducted. Overall, as Berven (2008) stated, "a well-organized physical environment may convey the perception of care, organization, and responsibility that will also be followed in dealing with the consumer" (p. 259).

Personal Interviewing: Structured Versus Nonstructured

This section expands the information provided on this topic in Chapter 4. Deciding whether to follow a structured or nonstructured approach to gain information from a consumer is related to the process of contextual and personal interviewing and flows from the type of questions the professional would like to ask during the interview. The amount of structure in an interview, however, may be affected by evaluator, consumer, and agency variables.

Structured Interviewing

Many evaluators feel more comfortable asking planned questions that represent agency expectations and what is directly needed for rehabilitation planning. Those questions can be replicated from consumer to consumer, and, especially when the evaluator has poorly developed interview experience, preplanned questions may provide necessary guidelines for obtaining necessary information. The structure can contribute to interview efficiency.

Many consumers, moreover, bring to the initial interview a considerable amount of anxiety, or they may have difficulty expressing themselves. A structured interview usually solicits specific, brief answers. The consumer is not encouraged to elaborate or talk extensively about responses. When the time allotted for the consumer interview is limited, a structured interview does save time, as the entire assessment may take place in 1 or 2 days. Unfortunately, in some instances, this type of interview may miss important information.

Nonstructured Interviewing

A nonstructured interview does not rely on lists of prepared questions. The specific questions asked may differ significantly from consumer to consumer, and the exploration prompted by an open-ended question may identify the uniqueness of the consumer's disability situation (Wiger & Huntley, 2002). The level of rapport, moreover, can be higher than in a structured interview (Groth-Marnat, 2003).

When time allows, what is recommended in vocational evaluation is an interview that is not solely structured or nonstructured in its entirety. The first part of the consumer interview can use a more nonstructured, nondirective approach that will help to establish rapport, will allow more for the consumer's interpretation of the question, and will encourage consumers to express themselves more openly, rather than only responding with "yes" or "no" or brief, factual responses (Morrison, 1993; Power, 2011; Scissions, 1993; Wiger & Huntley, 2002). Examples of some open-ended questions follow.

- What brings you here today?
- Tell me about yourself.
- What positive things do people tell you about yourself?
- Do you have any questions about this assessment process?
- How do you think your disability has affected your possible career choice?
- Ideally, how would you like this vocational assessment process to turn out for you?
- What do you think vocational assessment can accomplish for you?

The interviewer's questions should relate as closely as possible to the topic being discussed and flow from the immediate dialogue between the consumer and professional. Too often, questions are asked to change the subject when the helping professional becomes uncomfortable with the consumer's responses. Timing is also vitally important because questions can inhibit a consumer from pursuing a subject further, especially when discussing the more negative aspects of work history or disability experience. Also, comments such as, "That sounds very interesting" or "It does take a lot of courage to look honestly at a person's background" are usually more conducive to soliciting information than questions, which can be limiting.

Key questions during the consumer interview are usually open ended, and they help to establish a more productive relationship at the beginning of the evaluation process. When it is possible, the evaluator, instead of telling consumers what they must do, explores what they plan to do (Miller & Rollnick, 2002). Of course, the evaluator's own style of relating will influence both the type of questions asked and what emphasis will be placed on a structured or nonstructured format. But broader responsiveness should be encouraged in order to gather needed information, especially the information related to understanding the psychosocial aspects of one's disability.

The professional may receive several responses that contribute to understanding the applicant's motivation and interests. When probing for information, the counselor can use such beginning words as *how* or *why* to provide the consumer with a chance to be more flexible in his or her response. A tactful use of the word *what* can also solicit information, but the professional must then try to employ a reassuring manner and tone. An abrasive tone of voice immediately inhibits consumers from talking. Many questions are asked too directly, causing the consumer to feel reluctant to reveal needed information. For example, "Why did you leave that job?" might be too direct. Instead, a more appropriate inquiry may be, "How did you happen to leave that job?"

During the interview the individual with a disability usually has a story to tell—a story with problems, conflicts, and perhaps unhappiness. This story may be wide ranging in subject matter or narrowly focused on a particular area, depending on variables such as the nature of the referral question, the nature and quantity of available background information, the demands (with respect to time and the willingness or ability of the consumer to respond) of the particular situation, and the judgment of the interviewer (Cohen et al., 1996). The content of the interview, consequently, can vary from one situation to the next, and the tone of the interview as set by the interviewer may also vary. Interviews that are used as assessment tools in vocational evaluation are more exploratory, covering areas such as those identified in Table 6.1 later in this chapter. The interview should include the consumer's disability history and his or her current problems with life adjustment. Many rehabilitation agencies may require, however, more of a structured interview, in which all the questions that will be asked have been prepared in advance. For individuals with disabilities, there are several issues, such as relationships to helping professionals, family expectations for return to work, and personal feelings related to the onset of the disability, that may only emerge from an open-ended, wide-ranging interview format (Power, 2011).

Enhancing Interview Effectiveness

If the interview is to be used as an assessment approach, the rehabilitation professional must not only establish and maintain a good relationship with the consumer but also stimulate the person with a disability to participate productively in the interview. Such productivity is frequently encouraged by an interviewer who is warm and accepting, conveys understanding to the consumer by verbal or nonverbal means, and prefers to ask open-ended questions (Cohen et al., 1996). Also, the conversation must keep moving productively to achieve needed information. This entails communication, flexibility, control of the interview situation, organization of the information embedded in much of the interview conversation, and the processing of data according to interview goals.

Carkhuff and Anthony (1979) identified four communicative skills that, when used by the rehabilitation professional, can considerably enhance the effectiveness of the interview situation. These skills—attending, observing, listening, and responding—are fundamental and should be used throughout the entire interview session to help the consumer become involved.

Attending

Attending refers to the physical positioning of rehabilitation professionals as they talk with consumers. It requires the counselor to establish eye contact and sit in such a way that both interest and attention are communicated to the consumer. Eye contact should be natural, direct without constituting a stare, and generally constant because frequent breaks in eye contact suggest inattention.

Observing

Observing means that the interviewer first watches for specific aspects of the consumer's appearance and behavior and then uses this information to draw some careful inferences concerning the consumer's functioning (Carkhuff & Anthony, 1979). For example, when observing the consumer's use of eyes, grooming, changes in posture, and, in particular, changes in the positioning of the head and shoulders during the interview, the rehabilitation professional gains a first, tentative understanding of the consumer's interest and motivation in the assessment situation.

Listening

Like observing, listening can promote the consumer's participation in the interview and facilitate the disclosure of information important for rehabilitation planning. Listening implies attention not only to the consumer's verbal expression but also to the accompanying tone of voice, such as loudness, softness, and rapidity of speech. Listening also requires that possible judgments about the consumer's behavior be suspended. It is very easy to formulate attitudes about the consumer as the interview proceeds. At this stage of rehabilitation involvement, these perceptions can become obstacles to a genuine and reliable understanding of the consumer's functioning. By actively listening to what the consumer is saying, the professional communicates continued concern that, in turn, often prompts the consumer to discuss valuable information needed for rehabilitation planning.

Responding

In responding to the consumer's verbal messages during the interview, the rehabilitation professional is attempting to help the consumer become aware of his or her feelings, especially those regarding the disability situation. The professional initially responds to verbal content as the consumer expresses specifics relating to his or her immediate situation. The professional then responds to the meaning that is inherent in the consumer's statements and nonverbal behavior. Finally, as consumers express the immediate feelings that each aspect of the disability arouses in them, the professional promotes continued exploration of those feelings by responding to them (Carkhuff & Anthony, 1979). The following is a suggested format for this development of responding:

[*Responding to the content of the consumer's expression ("So you're saying . . ." or "You're saying that . . .")*]:

CONSUMER:	My family ignores me most of the time.
INTERVIEWER:	You're saying that members of your family leave you alone.

[*Responding to the immediate meaning* ("*You mean . . .*")]:

CONSUMER: I am very upset because my disability prevents me from enjoying life.

INTERVIEWER: You mean that you don't understand all your disability still allows you to do.

[*Responding to the immediate feelings* ("*You feel . . .*" *or* "*That can really make you feel . . .*")]:

CONSUMER: I have tried many times to return to work, but I just can't bring myself to face my employer again.

INTERVIEWER: You feel anxious about what the employer might say to you.

The interviewer's responses during the interview should be frequently interspersed with words that express feelings. The most direct way to introduce a response to feeling is to use the opening, "You feel . . . ." The rehabilitation professional can vary the form of the response, as long as he or she includes a specific feeling, word, or phrase that the consumer recognizes as interchangeable with the feeling expressed in his or her own statements.

To promote a positive relationship between the consumer and interviewer, and to convey to consumers that they are respected as persons, other techniques may have to be used. One approach is for the professional to immediately introduce himself or herself and then briefly explain the job of a rehabilitation professional. (Many persons are confused about job functions of rehabilitation counselors or vocational evaluators. They may believe that the professional's only responsibility is to get the person a job.) To help the consumer feel initially comfortable about the interview situation, the professional can ask, "Could you tell me why you feel you are here at this agency today?" Consumers usually respond to this question, and a small exchange helps both the professional and the consumer understand the purposes of the interview. During the beginning of the interview, therefore, there should be time for relationship building and clarification.

With an awareness of these interpersonal skills and approaches, the rehabilitation professional also needs to determine at the beginning of the interview what topics should be emphasized and which areas are most critical to explore for eventual rehabilitation planning. Again, before the interview, the professional should scan the agency application form to identify these areas. At times, however, the interview as an assessment resource might have to be conducted over several sessions. Such consumer disability factors as poor attention span or poorly developed communication skills may dictate a slower interviewing pace. Some topics, such as a criminal record or sporadic employment history, may be too sensitive for the consumer to introduce immediately. The professional may want to proceed cautiously, helping the consumer to discuss initially those topics about which he or she seems to be most comfortable. When the consumer believes that the interviewer can be trusted, he or she becomes more willing to reveal the sensitive, but necessary, areas for rehabilitation assessment. Often, this takes more than one session.

Continuing the Interview

Many other dynamics should be addressed during the interview if this dialogue is to be successful in providing the necessary information for rehabilitation planning. The following dynamics are particularly important: (a) the timing of reinforcement, (b) the effective use of confrontations, (c) the client's use of silence, (d) the establishment of interview control, (e) the avoidance of hostility, (f) the awareness of certain processes that reveal information, and (g) specific ethical considerations relevant to the interview.

Timing of Reinforcement

One of the purposes of the interview is to facilitate responsiveness from the consumer. There are several ways to accomplish this goal, some of which concern relationship building through effective communication skills. Other approaches focus on helping the consumer to talk more readily about the negative aspects of his or her background. Persons with disabilities usually have encountered many personal failures or rejecting attitudes. Their self-concepts are often low, and they are understandably hesitant to talk about areas that might convey a negative impression. Low marks in school, the inability to hold a permanent job, and low motivation in exploring productive opportunities are frequently difficult to reveal in an interview situation. At the same time, these issues need to be discussed in order for the professional to identify possible obstacles for reaching rehabilitation goals.

The professional can attempt to make it as easy as possible for consumers to talk about negative aspects of their backgrounds by playing down the importance of that information via some casual, sympathetic remark. For example, when the consumer begins to mention that he or she received low marks in school, the professional can compliment the person for having been able to recognize this difficulty and then face up to it. Rehabilitation professionals who give the slightest indication that their judgments are adversely influenced by unfavorable information will get no further information of this kind.

A skillful professional gives frequent "pats on the back," or verbal reinforcement, and never openly disagrees with a consumer on any point or gives the impression of a cross-examination. The technique of expressing agreement places heavy demands on facial expressions and general interviewing manners, including avoiding words that convey a negative meaning. For example, words like *weakness, fault,* or *liability* can be replaced by *shortcoming.*

Spontaneous comments by the professional create a favorable climate for conversation. These remarks provide some continuity to the consumer's verbal expression as well as help the consumer in revealing negative information. In fact, comments can often be used in the place of questions. For example, the comment "I can imagine there were some really tough problems in a job like that one" can be used instead of the question "What were some of the most difficult problems you faced on that job?"

Also, by using such words or expressions as *and then, mm-hmm,* and *right,* the interviewer provides some small encouragement and at the same time helps the consumer feel more at ease during the interview.

Effective Confrontation

During the interview, the rehabilitation worker should identify contradictions in what the consumer is saying. The consumer might be setting very unrealistic goals in relation to his or her abilities or past experiences. He or she might also be employing defensive strategies that may block appropriate rehabilitation planning, such as denial or the projection onto others of his or her own anger. The professional wants to help the consumer identify and resolve these discrepancies.

Confrontation should be used only after a good consumer relationship has been established. There are many ways to confront a consumer.

Comments should not include accusations, judgments, or solutions to problems. Carkhuff and Anthony (1979) suggested that using a format such as "On the one hand you say (feel, do) …, and on the other hand you say (feel, do) …" is only minimally threatening to the consumer because it focuses on an element of contrast that comes entirely from the consumer's own frame of reference.

Consumer's Use of Silence

Silences often occur during the interview, perhaps because consumers are nervous, shy, or anxious about revealing information relevant to their disabilities. Silence is also a form of reluctance, which is discussed later in this chapter. However, silences are often a positive form of communication, telling the professional that a certain subject is probably quite difficult to discuss. Or, a consumer simply may have exhausted a particular subject and is waiting for the professional to suggest another topic area. Silences should not be maintained for too long without an interviewer response. The following are some examples of responses in a silent situation:

> "You feel uncomfortable about discussing this subject further."
> "Perhaps we should change the subject."
> "It is difficult to talk about those areas of your life that remind you of failure and pain."

Many consumers are silent during the interview because they have limited verbal skills, the result of functional limitations. In these instances, the interviewer has to be more directive in the interview situation, providing reinforcing statements like, "This is your first time in this agency and I can understand that it would be difficult to talk about yourself." The low-verbal consumer frequently finds it hard to elaborate on any topic suggested by the professional. The Interview Guide for Consumers With Functional Limitations (see the Appendix and the forms located on the CD-ROM) suggests a form for facilitating both interview conversation and the disclosure of needed information.

Controlling the Interview

Control of the interview means simply that the interviewer guides the consumer to talk about the topics necessary to explore vocational circumstances appropriately. Time is limited, and important information must be obtained in a relatively short period of time. The consumer, however, may want to talk about nonpertinent information or evade pertinent facts. But there are approaches that can help the interviewer to control this specific diagnostic session, without severely inhibiting the consumer's verbal expression.

1. *The helping professional must plan the interview carefully.* He or she needs to identify what information should be collected while remaining cognizant of the consumer's limitations and thresholds.

2. *The rehabilitation counselor should initiate the interview in a positive way.* Listening intently to the consumer's responses, asking open-ended questions, and providing information that indicates the counselor's understanding of what the consumer is saying can help to create a positive experience for the interviewee.

3. *The rehabilitation counselor must direct the focus of the interview.* Although many consumers may be somewhat fearful of the interview situation, and their anxiety may interfere with their ability to communicate, the interviewer should keep the interviewee talking, staying on the topic about which the interviewer needs information. Repeating a critical word, phrase, or sentence that the consumer has just used, asking a related question that cannot be answered "yes" or "no," stating an area that you as an interviewer would like to hear about, and defining specifically what it is you want to know are all ways to help the consumer to remain focused.

4. *The helping professional should structure the interview situation but also make it meaningful and personal.* The professional can keep the conversation rewarding for the consumer by moving to a new, relevant topic at the moment the interviewee mentions it; providing a statement that allows a natural transition to take place when a change of topic is needed; attempting to refocus the consumer by alluding to an area that was previously discussed; and making a personal remark about something the consumer may have said or done.

Avoiding Hostility

Hostility may occur during the interview because of the interviewer's or the consumer's chronic stress; a conflict within the consumer because he or she faces two mutually exclusive choices; or a clash of opinions, viewpoints, or ethnic backgrounds. If the interviewer, however, accepts the consumer and allows him to appropriately vent some feelings, then the interviewer can often minimize the hostility. By acknowledging that the perceived conflict is a problem—without attempting to solve it for the interviewee—the interviewer can assure the consumer that this problem will be considered in the vocational plans and that through this planning the consumer can hope to decrease his or her stress. Each of these approaches may alleviate the consumer's hostility or anger.

In addition, during the interview, certain dynamics occur between the rehabilitation professional and consumer that can reveal information about the consumer's mental and emotional functioning. There are four areas that the professional should especially look for.

1. *Association of ideas*—A consumer may be discussing some of the difficulties in finding a job and then switch suddenly to talking about his or her disability benefits and how they have alleviated many adjustment problems. Thus, the consumer has probably indicated that the problem in finding a job is not isolated but is actually connected to receiving entitlement payments.

2. *Shifts in conversation*—A sudden shift in conversation can indicate that consumers feel that they are telling too much and do not want to reveal more information about that particular subject. Perhaps a consumer begins to talk about material that becomes too painful to pursue and decides to avoid further discussion. A sudden shift in topics during the interview should be responded to by the rehabilitation professional. Statements such as, "On the one hand, you were talking about ... and now you are discussing .... This is confusing to me and I wonder if you would clarify it," can encourage a response from the consumer.

3. *Recurrent references*—A consumer may repeatedly return to a certain subject. Such repetition often indicates a main focus of reference or the consumer's true feelings about a disability situation. Someone who continually mentions that her family is pleased that more time is spent now with family members than before the onset of the disability can be suggesting that it is really more rewarding to be at home than to return to employment. The professional should explore frequent references, because they usually contain valuable information related to the consumer's motivation and expectations for rehabilitation evaluation involvement.

4. *Inconsistencies or gaps*—A consumer may tell a story that is primarily straightforward but has unexpected gaps. For example, the person with a disability may carefully neglect to give any reasons for leaving the last job. Being alert to such gaps, the professional can mildly confront the consumer with a statement exploring the reason for such inconsistency—for example, "As you were talking, I noticed that something seemed to be left out. Could you give me some idea of what this is?"

Specialized Interview Topics and Approaches

Interview Issues With Selected Populations

Although the interview material explained in this chapter can usually apply to all populations with disabilities, specific concerns and issues arise with consumers who are experiencing circumstances that require extra attention. These special circumstances, arising from the consumer's race, ethnicity, or disability, may occasionally stimulate the interviewer's bias. Such bias may be expressed by stereotypical expectations or selectively processing information based on misconceptions. These attitudes could be diminished by using a semi-structured interview format, obtaining further information, and increasing one's self-awareness of possible bias (Power, 2011).

Many of the issues discussed in this section, moreover, emerge from the interview guidelines (beginning, continuing, and conclusion) discussed in previous sections of this chapter and have implications for selected populations. Examples of these populations are those who (a) have chronic mental illness, learning disabilities, or the residuals of a head trauma; (b) represent varied ethnic backgrounds; (c) are injured workers who are not motivated to explore return-to-work options; (d) are classified as "older workers"; (e) are adolescents involved in school-to-work or adult life transition; or (f) have been diagnosed with AIDS. As the rehabilitation process progresses, consumers can become increasingly aware of cultural differences, negative attitudes toward returning to work, and their own physical, emotional, and intellectual limitations. These consumers can show anxiety, irritability, and even agitation—all problems apparently born of frustration. Such problems may also be reactions to many experiences of failure, and vocational evaluation may highlight failure. Whatever symptoms the consumer shows, the rehabilitation worker must keep in mind certain guidelines for conducting the interview.

Consumer's Perceptions of Inadequacy

The skillful interviewer should try to shift the consumer's own perceptions of inadequacy (e.g., "I'm going to look bad during the rehabilitation process") to a mode of information seeking, discovery, and problem solving. To accomplish this goal, the rehabilitation worker should attempt to create a positive consumer–interviewer partnership during the assessment process. For example, the purpose of the interview, as well as the different steps to follow in the rehabilitation process, can be carefully explained. The consumer can be asked to explain the perceived difficulties he or she anticipates during this process, and to describe possible strategies for responding to or solving these problems. In this way, the evaluator may gain valuable insights while the consumer may realize that the interview and the succeeding steps in the rehabilitation process are significant (Vogel, 1989).

Consumer's Expectations

When consumers begin the assessment process, they usually have a specific set of expectations. Koch (1998) believed that these initial expectations tend to be self-fulfilling and that discrepancies between expectations and what actually occurs in assessment can result in premature termination of evaluation. Expectations can be categorized as preferences (what one wants to occur) and anticipations (what one thinks will occur). Expectations should be discussed at different times during assessment, because the discussion can both clarify the roles of the evaluator and consumer and suggest the type of assessment outcome.

Using Specific Examples

The interviewer should be quite literal and explicit when talking with a consumer who has brain injury or chronic mental illness. Specific examples can be used to illustrate a question. For example, when asking the consumer, "Whom did you like best in your last job?" the evaluator could also describe what "like best" means.

Encouraging the Consumer

The interviewer should be encouraging to the consumer during the interview, calling attention to the person's assets and success. Consumers who are aware of their own cognitive deficits frequently have problems with self-esteem. Identifying the consumer's specific strengths may facilitate the building of self-worth.

Exploring Family Relationships

With consumers with learning disabilities or cognitive, emotional, and perceptual deficits, family background should be explored during the interview, with attention given to how the consumer perceives the family reaction to the disability. The interview might explore the consumer's interpersonal relationships with family members. When this information can be obtained, it can suggest possible areas of difficulty in a training or work situation. Also, such information may indicate possible obstacles to or resources for the consumer's vocational rehabilitation.

Examining Records

An examination of previous records, when available, may be particularly helpful when collecting all the assessment information for rehabilitation planning. Such records include neurological exam results and school and employment records.

Discussing Assessments

Especially for those with learning disabilities or head injuries, specific problems are created in vocational assessment. Some of these problems can be administrative procedures requiring reading, multiple-step individual tasks, and the lack of opportunity to explore or fully understand performance expectations (Hursh & Kerns, 1988). With an awareness of these potential difficulties, the evaluator can inform the consumer of what further vocational assessment may involve and how the difficulties can be minimized.

Being Specific

With consumers who are experiencing mental illness, it is especially important for the evaluator to include specific information. Interview data must include such topics as type and frequency of medication, as well as involvement with a counselor, therapist, or community mental health agency.

Considering Racial and Cultural Backgrounds

When interviewing persons with disabilities who are from ethnic backgrounds different from their own, helping professionals need to be aware of their consumers' culture. Language capability, work roles, cultural and religious beliefs, and available support systems should be considered. Racial and identity development should also be identified. Obstacles to career advancement can be explored, such as the attitudes of significant others, discrimination in the workplace, and other barriers posed by the social, political, and economic system. Further areas that need to be explored are the consumer's level of acculturation and the way he or she identifies with his or her culture. The consumer's attitude toward seeking help about disability-related issues can also be important for rehabilitation planning. Among minority cultures, there are critical inter- and intragroup differences. Understanding these topics can be a starting point for understanding a consumer who represents a minority culture and who has a disability. Race and ethnicity are fundamental concerns in the delivery of rehabilitation services. Further issues related to these consumers and the interview are discussed in Chapter 4.

Recognizing Evasiveness

Because many injured workers show behaviors such as unwarranted dependency, passivity, and a reluctance to take any initiative for employment planning, the interviewer should be alert to consumer evasiveness. Evasiveness can take such forms as changing the topic as soon as employment goals are mentioned, answering questions with questions, or using meaningless statements. The interviewer may have a better chance of soliciting needed information by using nondirective techniques, as well as stating that he or she really is interested in knowing about specific areas that affect the consumer's vocational plans.

Providing a Comprehensive Interview

When the rehabilitation professional is working with students with significant disabilities, specific factors should be addressed during the screening interview. Vocational evaluation procedures that have been integrated into educational settings typically involve a variety of personnel. In addition, school-based vocational programs primarily target disadvantaged students and students with mild and moderate disabilities for services (Levinson, 1994).

These school-based programs are usually multilevel programs that use a variety of techniques to gather information. The content of the interview should include an exploration of needs, values, behavioral tendencies, work habits as shown in past employment, temperament, and social–interpersonal skills. This information should not be identified in isolation, but should be combined with psychological, educational, social, medical, and other data to provide a comprehensive picture of the student (Levinson, 1994).

Specific Ethical Considerations Relevant to the Interview

Chapter 2 identifies and discusses selected ethical principles relevant to the vocational evaluation process. There are five domains of ethics that are particularly applicable to the initial consumer interview: confidentiality, informed consent, interviewer–consumer relationship, competencies, and sharing interview results.

Confidentiality

Policies, laws, and procedures have been developed pertaining to (a) the professional duty to warn and protect, (b) professional misconduct, and (c) the perceived abuse of children and vulnerable adults. Apart from these issues, the information shared between the interviewer and the consumer is confidential. It is important for the interviewer to be aware of agency policies regarding interview information and how these data will be stored.

Informed Consent

In Chapter 2, there is a brief discussion on the issue of consumers having the right to participate in the decision-making process concerning assessment approaches, to be informed about how the evaluation results are going to be used, and to receive as much information as possible about the evaluation process itself. This communication begins during the interview, with the interviewer using language that the consumer can understand. There may be some consumers who do not have the mental capacity to make informed choices, but all consumers should be treated as if they are capable until there is evidence to the contrary (Wiger & Huntley, 2002).

Interviewer–Consumer Relationship

It is important that the professional keep an open mind with regard to the consumer's vocational expectations identified during the interview. While the evaluator might mentally formulate the best vocational plans for the consumer, later in the interview it may become apparent that such ideas are opposite of what the consumer wants from both the evaluation process and vocational rehabilitation. There should be some negotiation near the end of the interview in which the professional makes clear his or her concerns for the consumer (Miller & Rollnick, 2002). Occasionally negotiations become somewhat conflicted, but it is ethically inappropriate for the interviewer to urge his or her own personal agenda that is clearly not in harmony with the consumer's own best interests.

Competencies

The interviewer must decide whether to follow a structured or unstructured consumer interaction, or a combination thereof, and know what to look for relevant to assessment planning. Training in the use of different interviewing techniques is also necessary.

Sharing Interview Results

"Consumers are entitled to the results of the interview unless it may prove harmful," stated Wiger and Huntley (2002, p. 23). Feedback to the consumer at the conclusion of the interview must be carefully and, at times, delicately communicated. Because the evaluator may be communicating mainly hunches and speculation, to be verified later in the assessment process, many interviewers restrict this feedback session to positive information learned about the consumer, what may be needed for adaptive or accommodation purposes, and what are perceived obstacles that may confront the consumer during the evaluation process.

Career Style Interview

A valuable interview technique has been developed that uses easily recognizable topics for understanding consumers, and can be especially appropriate for those with disabilities. This strategy solicits a verbal narrative of the consumer's life story, and thus offers a comprehensive and personally meaningful understanding of the consumer. Refined during the last 20 years (Savickas, 1995, 1998; Savickas, Nota, Rossier,

Davwalder, Duarte, Guichard, Sorese, Esbroeck, & Van Vianon, 2009), in its most recent version this approach, called the *Career Style Interview* (CSI), utilizes the narration of the consumer's story, a story that is prompted during this narration by the interviewer's questions seeking information about the consumer's role models, favorite magazines, television shows, books, movies, hobbies, leisure activities, and school subjects. Early recollections are further explored (Taber, Haltung, Briddick, Briddick, & Rehfuss, 2011). By both asking clarifying questions and making reflective statements during the interview, the interviewer may identify the consumer's central life goal, role models, preferred work and social environments, manifest interest, dominant preoccupations, and perhaps viable solutions to the basic life problems (Taber et al., 2011).

The interviewer's clarifying questions and interpretive reflections are the core of this Career Style Interview approach. However, while maintaining the basic integrity of the CSI's interview areas and questions, this author adds a time frame to a few of the established questions to capture the "before and after" of disability onset for those who are seeking career options. The responses to these questions will yield results similar to the goals of the CSI, namely, facilitating greater self-knowledge, highlighting a person's uniqueness, and identifying specific behaviors and expectations relevant to the person's search for an appropriate career (Taber et al., 2011). Overall, the CSI is an easy to use tool that can yield significant information about the consumer's viewpoints on activities and goals that can be relevant to the assessment process. The following are modified Career Style Interview questions (Taber et al., 2011).

1. How can I be useful to you in developing your career options?
2. Before your disability, whom did you admire and now whom would you like to pattern your life after?
   ◆ What do you admire about these role models?
   ◆ How are you now like each of these role models, and how are you different from them?
3. What magazines do you read regularly? What do you like about them? What TV shows do you really enjoy? Why?
4. Tell me about your favorite book/movie.
5. What do you like to do with your free time? What are your hobbies?

6. Do you have a favorite saying or motto? Can you tell me a saying you remember hearing?

7. What were your favorite subjects in school? What subjects did you really dislike? Why?

8. Before the onset of your disability, what were your earliest recollections? Since your disability, can you recall any stories happening to you?

Contributions From Solution-Focused Counseling

Apart from interview-process dynamics, there is the overriding issue of the interviewer's philosophy, beliefs, or perceptions of not only what the interview should accomplish, but also what should be achieved during vocational assessment. Solution-focused counseling, as proposed by Araoz and Carrese (1996), has several contributions that should be considered during the interview. These factors have implications for the consumer's motivation, self-determination, and planning.

1. Assessment goals should focus on what is possible and changeable.

2. The interviewer should emphasize how the assessment process will address vocational challenges and difficulties.

3. During the interview it is not necessary to pursue a lengthy detailed history of vocational adjustment difficulties. An explanation of the process of assessment may be more relevant.

4. During the interview, the interviewer should place further emphasis on the consumer taking responsibility, as much as appropriately possible, for his or her involvement during the assessment process.

5. The interviewer should comment on what is working well for the consumer, rather than what is not, discuss the consumer's revealed strengths and resources, and encourage the consumer to have high but realistic and appropriate expectations for the assessment process.

Motivational Interviewing

Since 1993 motivational interviewing has been used to address consumers' motivational concerns. Manthey, Jackson, and Evans-Brown (2011) stated that "a large volume of research indicates that motivation is a key element in returning to work" (p. 4). Originally developed in the addictions field, but now also used in the treatment of consumers with mental illness (Arkowitz, Westra, Miller, & Rollnick, 2007), motivational interviewing provides direct feedback, emphasizes the consumer's personal responsibility for change, offers advice, and reinforces the consumer's hope and optimism (Miller & deShazar, 1998). This style of interviewing supports self-determination. It also focuses on goals and values exploration, increasing confidence for change and readiness for change, and places an emphasis on providing a variety of options and empowering personal choice (Manthey et al., 2011).

Motivational interviewing avoids argument and supports self-efficacy (Wagner & McMahon, 2004). It attempts to reduce a reluctance to make changes involving work adjustment. This could be initially achieved by intentionally focusing on a collaborative relationship with the consumer, soliciting the consumer's own ideas and solutions regarding this adjustment, and openly supporting the consumer's autonomy and choice (Moyers, Martin, Manuel, Miller, & Ernst, 2007).

When the vocational evaluator decides toward the beginning of the interview that a motivational interviewing style might address the consumer's problems, the following steps could be followed, many of which are suggested by Lewis and Osborn (2004), Miller and Rollnick (2002), Wagner and McMahon (2004), and Manthey et al. (2011).

1. Maintain a calm, supportive discussion, expressing empathy as often as possible.
2. Explore discrepancies between the consumer's current behavior and perceptions and projected rehabilitation outcomes.
3. Provide information and open-ended questions that identify the disadvantages of the status quo and the advantages of enthusiastically participating in the evaluation process.
4. Offer new perspectives and identify consumer strengths and resources in ways that can contribute to positive change.
5. Help the consumer make a commitment to mutually agreed-upon goals for vocational assessment, and express optimism about this commitment as an important step to change.

Motivational interviewing, consequently, presents an opportunity for consumers to discover their capabilities and to emphasize their career-related strengths in a context of support from the evaluator. Information is communicated in response to consumer statements and feelings. The consumer realizes through relevant information sharing that there are choices and that changes are possible.

Concluding the Interview

As the consumer talks about personal history, the disability, and the disability's implications for his or her immediate life, the information that is generated is most important for rehabilitation planning. The key to using this information effectively is to have a structure for organizing interview facts. The structure of the interview can be an interview guide that the rehabilitation professional completes immediately following the interview, or a mental outline that the professional follows while talking with the consumer. After gathering the interview information in this framework, the professional can then begin to make rehabilitation plans.

Table 6.1 provides a format for organizing the information emerging from the interview. This table also provides questions that may be used to solicit information relevant to a particular interview topic. Each item should be explored during the interview. The way each item relates to training or employment is listed in the right-hand column. Further, Bordin (1943) developed an additional interview structure that can accommodate these items or topics. Though identified over 50 years ago, the basic structural concepts still have remarkable relevance for rehabilitation professionals who need guidelines during the assessment interview. The following is a brief explanation of Bordin's approach.

1. *Problem appraisal*—identification of the person's problem, as well as motivation to change or assume responsibility for problem solution. Included in this appraisal is an identification of the factors related to the career problem, such as the part that is played by the family in problem development and resolution, financial resources, marriage plans, and academic achievement.
2. *Personal appraisal*—a picture of the consumer is obtained from a variety of demographic, psychometric, and social data, and should include an assessment of strengths as well as weaknesses, present

(text continues on p. 163)

Table 6.1
A Structure for Organizing Interview Facts

Items of client functioning	Approaches for gaining information about areas of client functioning	Relationship to training or employment

1. General appearance and behavior	*Observe*	• Personal habits
		• Appropriateness
		• Work behaviors:
		  ◆ Neatness
		  ◆ Relationship to co-workers
		  ◆ Dependency
		  ◆ Relationship to evaluator and future supervisors

2. Principal way of communicating	*Listen* to the way client talks about problems and himself or herself.	• Attention • Comprehension and retention of instructions • Reality contact
3. Mental processes and content	*Observe* the way the individual verbally constructs his or her life experiences; *listen* to the association of ideas, shifts in conversation, and inconsistencies and gaps in the conversation.	• Realistic expectations • Judgment and problem-solving ability • Reality contact • Potential to learn work demands
4. Mood and affect	*Observe* nonverbal behaviors; *listen* to the client's affect as he or she talks; *ask:* How are you feeling now?	• Response to pressure • Adaptability • Emotional reaction to disability
5. Coping resources	*Ask:* What do you think you do best? What are the most difficult problems you have faced? How were they handled? Have you experienced recent stress? How did you manage? How do you handle pressure on the job or at home? What is your present living situation?	• Independent functioning • Frustration tolerance • Handling failure or setbacks • Response to pressure • Confidence/self-concept • Adjustment and maturity
6. Orientation toward other people	*Ask* the client to describe the relationship with his or her co-workers. *Ask:* How do you feel when you are in social situations? Whose opinion do you see as valuable to you in your life planning?	• Interpersonal skills • Job-keeping behaviors • Relationship with supervisor and co-workers • Social acceptability
7. Capacity for facing problems	*Explore:* What are the most difficult problems you have faced? How were they handled? What is your reaction to your disability? How do you handle unpleasant situations?	• Job-getting behaviors • Seeking of training opportunities • Adjustment and maturity

Table 6.1 *(continued)* 161

Items of client functioning	Approaches for gaining information about areas of client functioning	Relationship to training or employment
8. Education and training experience	*Ask:* Tell me about what you have done best in school or any other training.	• Skills and competence • Job alternatives
9. Social factors	*Ask:* Who is available to help you during vocational rehabilitation? Who does not support you?	• Available support services • Assistance in problem solving • Identification of external barriers
10. Energy level	*Ask:* How do you think things can be different for you? What can you do about it? Are you willing to take risks to make changes? I would like to hear how you spend your time each day. *Watch* for recurrent references in the interview.	• Motivation • Identification with productive role • Job-seeking behaviors • Job-keeping behaviors • Regular work attendance • Promptness • Work production • Lack of time wasted

11. Goal-directedness	*Ask:* What type of work do you see yourself doing 5 years from now? What are you looking for in a career? What are you looking for in a job?	• Growth and development
		• Job-objective behaviors:
		  • Seeks a vocational goal
		  • Has an appropriate work objective

12. Strengths of client	*Ask:* What do you do well? What do you like about yourself? What do you feel are your strong points? What have you learned from your work experience?	• Compensatory skills • Confidence • Job-keeping behaviors • Relevance for work • Sufficiency of work

13. Interests of client	*Explore* educational experience:
	  • Competencies
	  • Particular difficulties
	  • What was liked best
	Explore work experience:
	  • Special areas of interest
	  • Special areas of competence
	  • Major duties and responsibilities
	Explore leisure time and general interests.
	Ask: What would be the ideal job for you?
		• Training goals
		• Job objective behaviors
		• Job alternatives
		• Readiness for work

14. Work history	*Ask:* What kind of work have you performed in the past?	• Skills and competence • Adaptability and adjustment • Stability

(continues)

Table 6.1 *(continued)*

Items of client functioning	Approaches for gaining information about areas of client functioning	Relationship to training or employment
15. Disability factors	*Ask:* Describe your present disability. How does it limit you? Are there any medications? What are the effects?	• Performance • Training selection and disability • Transfer of skills
16. Outer-directing factors	*Explore:* family and peer expectations; perceived prestige of certain occupations; economic job market opportunities; available support services	• Motivation
17. Outer-limiting factors	*Explore:* presence of prejudicial attitudes; geographical opportunity; accessibility of training and work sites; family expectations; financial resources and current job market opportunities; available transportation; other external barriers	• Opportunity for training and employment • Motivation
18. Expectations	*Ask:* What would you like to accomplish as a result of participating in assessment? What do you think will happen during the assessment process? What kind of assessment services do you think you will receive?	• Congruence between assessment process and client • Motivation • Possible remediation of incongruencies
19. Return to available family and outpatient status	*Explore:* lingering guilt; hope; anxiety; coping strategies; gradual realization; reorientation. *Ask:* What are the family's expectations for you? How have you managed your return to the family?	• Information • Manage stress • Time and energy for self • Enlarge scope of values • Role redefinition and reclaim family life • Gradual realization • Support • Maintain family boundaries

status and functioning, and developmental history. This history includes information about the onset of physical or mental disability, family background, early interests and abilities, and perhaps early vocational choices and plans.

3. *Prognostic appraisal*—an evaluation of such factors as motivation for vocational assessment and the follow-through of vocational planning. This appraisal can also include an assessment of whether the evaluation should focus only on an identified problem or could be extended to the identification of the consumer's potential to learn skills that solve other career problems.

Another approach to organizing interview information is the following suggested format of directing and limiting factors:

1. Inner-directing factors
   - Recognized values
   - Strong motivation
   - Developed coping styles
   - Learned skills from educational and work experiences
2. Outer-directing factors
   - Family influences
   - Educational level
   - Available resources
3. Inner-limiting factors
   - Mental disability
   - Low education level
   - Unrealistic career expectations
   - Personality disorders
4. Outer-limiting factors
   - Lack of family and peer support
   - Inaccessibility to necessary resources
   - Discrimination

An additional way to organize the interview information gathered from the consumer is a theme analysis approach. The information obtained from such content domains as educational and work experiences, social and vocational factors and goals, and disability-related issues is organized according to themes, such as the following:

1. The consumer's career-related strengths
2. Consumer characteristics, i.e., values, interests, general appearance and behavior
3. Interaction with environmental contexts, i.e., family, peers, and specific culture
4. Personal and career goals
5. Disability factors, i.e., current emotional reaction, medications, perceived meaning of disability (Power, 2011)

When the interview concludes, either because of time considerations or the rehabilitation professional's realization that needed information has been obtained, the consumer should be asked to indicate what has been learned during the interview session. Because the consumer may have difficulty reviewing this information, pointing out one or more strengths that have been observed should stimulate the discussion, for example, "Well, I have learned that you seem to get along unusually well with people, and this, of course, is a tremendous asset in any job situation."

It is important for the consumer to leave the interview feeling positive about the experience and understanding what is needed for successful achievement of rehabilitation goals. This feeling can be achieved through summarizing information that has been gained from the session. Again, the review focus should be on the consumer's identified strengths. The ideal interview represents a beginning for the consumer, providing a new awareness of identified strengths and knowledge of the opportunities that rehabilitation offers. Also, the end of the interview is an important time to clarify any questions and discuss vocational evaluation arrangements.

Frequently, consumers begin the initial interview with mixed feelings about their involvement in the vocational evaluation and rehabilitation processes. Many realize that they are beginning a path that may bring change, and there could be a reluctance to learn new skills or embark upon vocational training. Many consumers are aware of the need for change but may have limited confidence that they can successfully make the transition to employment or training. Others may have established expectations for their career future and do not want the evaluation results to modify their perceived plans. The professional often realizes during the interview that there are motivational issues that should be addressed.

Figure 6.1 shows the form that I use during the consumer intake interview. Some of the items listed follow those already identified in Table 6.1. I complete this form after the intake interview or other needed sessions with the consumer for use when rehabilitation plans are developed. Relevant planning necessitates the use of this information, and it becomes an important step in rehabilitation planning.

Consumer Information Items	Comments	Training Goals
Work history and experience		
Education and training experience		
Social factors		
Disability factors		
Principal way of communicating		
General appearance and behavior		
Mental processes and content		
Mood and affect		
Coping resources		
Orientation toward other people		
Capacity for facing problems		
Energy level		
Goal-directedness		
Strengths of client		
Interests of client		
Outer-directing factors		
Outer-limiting factors		
Expectations		

Figure 6.1. Consumer intake interview form.

Conclusion

This chapter suggests ways for the interviewer to gain information about a consumer, especially when traditional assessment approaches are perceived as quite limited in providing the necessary data. Using the interview as an effective diagnostic tool requires the establishment of a positive, helping relationship between the consumer and interviewer.

It also demands the counselor's understanding of those interview dynamics, including what to look for and how, that will generate information useful for vocational assessment. When all of these dynamics are achieved, both the interviewer and the consumer can begin to gain feedback that is crucial for eventual rehabilitation planning.

Chapter 7

Interest Assessment in Vocational Rehabilitation

In vocational rehabilitation assessment, the exploration of a consumer's interests frequently becomes the beginning focus for both vocational evaluation and planning. Interest assessment is a key component of career interventions (Tracey, 2010). It can also be a type of shortcut in career decision making, helping consumers to make choices by affirming their likes and dislikes and by identifying activities that are integral to their lifestyles (Athanasov & Van Esbroek, 2007). Interest exploration is particularly important in the 21st century, with its constant labor market changes, its wide diversity of career opportunities, and the continued advances in assistive technology (Fouad, Smothers, Kantamneni, & Guillen, 2008).

An awareness of the consumer's interests is useful in identifying and documenting a vocational goal and intermediate objectives in arriving at that goal. Interest exploration can provide a major focus for much of assessment. If understanding the consumer's interests is achieved during the initial interview, the rehabilitation professional can begin to delineate (a) the objectives of assessment, (b) needed services, and (c) the possibilities of appropriate outcomes for the consumer.

When administering a battery of assessment instruments, it is often helpful to begin with interest measures. Because they are less threatening than intelligence, personality, and aptitude tests, they can facilitate rapport between the evaluator and consumer. Such instruments can also provide a foundational direction for further vocational assessment, especially in the personality and aptitude areas. For example, if a consumer's interest profile shows a dominant interest in the mechanical or technology area, then additional evaluation instruments may be selected to explore the harmony between aptitude and personality areas with mechanics and technology.

Interest exploration can also stimulate counseling by suggesting occupations that had not been previously considered by the consumer or rehabilitation professional. While, originally, interest evaluation was directed primarily to consumers with professional expectations and goals, interest assessment approaches have also been developed for consumers who are considering non-professional occupations or who may not possess the intelligence or reading ability to complete the more traditional or commonly used instruments. Furthermore, for some consumers who are older and can no longer participate in their former occupations because of a physical disability or chronic illness, and who now must change their career lifestyle, interest measures may identify new possibilities (Fouad et al., 2008).

In other words, a comprehensive interest exploration for the consumer can increase considerably the person's employment options. In order to assist the professional in using interest assessment effectively, this chapter describes the types of consumer interests, the issues in interest exploration, and the measurement of interests. This chapter includes a specialized approach to interest assessment and discusses unique concerns in interpreting interest measures.

What Are the Consumer's Interests?

The term *interest* can be used to mean degree of interest, strength of motivation and drive, or need (Shertzer & Linden, 1979). Super (1957), who pioneered interest measurement, identified three types of interest:

1. *Expressed interest*—The verbal statement of liking for any stimulus, such as an object, activity, task, or occupation. Research has suggested that expressed interests are not as good a predictor of occupational choice as interest inventories (Whiston, 2000).
2. *Manifest interest*—The evidence of participation in an activity, occupation, or task that can be observed by others.
3. *Tested interest*—Interests measured by such objective approaches as free-association measures.

Salomone (1996) believed that "counselors may be inclined to rely more on the results of inventoried than on expressed or manifest interests" (p. 379). When predicting a future occupational choice, early research favors the verbal expression of interest or aspiration (Salomone, 1996). But later research suggests that interest inventories are still the most sought-after and effective intervention strategies (Spokane, 1991). When assisting consumers for interest assessment, perhaps rehabilitation professionals will need to explore the implications of consumers' verbal statements of preference (expressed interests) and the results of both standardized and nonstandardized interest inventories. Whiston (2000) believed that expressed and measured interests are equally good at predicting occupational choice.

Holland (1959) expanded the notion of interests when he stated that people project their views of themselves and the world of work onto occupational titles. He believed that interests reflect personality and that a career choice depends on a person's orientation to the environment. Holland identified six occupational environments: realistic, investigative, social, conventional, enterprising, and artistic. Each orientation expresses a somewhat distinctive lifestyle, which is characterized by an individual's values, interests, interpersonal skills, and ways of dealing with daily problems. A person's major lifestyle determines his or her main direction of occupational choice.

The focus of interest assessment, moreover, usually includes two populations: young adults with disabilities who may have little or no vocational experience, and adults who are engaged in a career transition because of a disability event or diagnosis of a chronic illness. Career goals are usually different between these two groups. Youths with a disability, for example, who are pursuing employment opportunities after completing their formal education may have had little or no exposure to the occupational world. Their knowledge of job requirements or a variety of choice may be quite limited (Fouad et al., 2008).

Selected Issues in Interest Assessment

One of the most important generalizations in several decades of research is that interest assessment suggests the *direction,* rather than the strength, of a person's interests. However, many persons show wide discrepancies between interest and achievement. Interests and abilities are not highly correlated (Sundberg, 1977). A consumer may have a high degree of ability to do something but not be interested in it. Strong interests do not guarantee occupational success. Interests identify a domain of preference, and abilities point to the potential level of skill or attainment. Yet, abilities and interests interact, and there is a small but significant relationship between them (Lent, Brown, & Hackett, 1994). A person's interest in a certain occupational area can often motivate him or her to develop skills to become proficient in that line of work, and interest inventories have been found to be good predictors of future academic and career choices (Whiston, 2000).

Vocational Aspiration Versus Realism

Frequently, the interests that are identified by paper-and-pencil inventories conflict with a consumer's verbalized interests; or consumers express an interest in an area in which they have no measured aptitude or ability. It is not unusual for a consumer to "fix" on one vocational objective. This might indicate parental, family, or other environmental influences. Various approaches can be used to resolve this discrepancy, including the identification and analysis of different levels of jobs in the consumer's interest area. In service-related occupations, for instance, there are differences both in the education and time of training required for the jobs of physician and policeman. Both occupations serve people and require a consumer's commitment to and interest in other persons. A description of the duties involved in the performance and training required in each employment area may assist consumers in realigning their own career or job expectations.

Selection of Interest Measures

The "choice of interest" inventories should be based on the kind of information provided and not simply on availability, low cost, or time required for administration. Fouad et al. (2008) added that the interest assessment measures should show evidence of adequate reliability and validity and, when appropriate, cross-cultural validity. These measures should also be developed from appropriate norms. Available guidelines of interest measures should identify both the readability level of the specific instrument and whether it is suitable for persons with cognitive and severe physical disabilities. Hood and Johnson (2007) offered many guidelines for the selection of the type of interest inventory—namely, whether the evaluator should choose a more lengthy measure, or whether the item content is the most appropriate for the consumer's expressed vocational goals. Several of these guidelines follow:

1. The evaluator should determine how motivated the person with a disability is to participate in the assessment process. A clear understanding and acceptance of the purpose for testing, and an expression of an interest in the results beforehand, will facilitate an individual's motivation.

2. For consumers who wish to make fine distinctions within a general occupational area—for example, inhalation therapist and physical therapist—many interest inventories are of limited value. Before a decision is made, interest inventories must be supplemented with other information (e.g., abilities, values, previous work experiences, job availability) about the person and the situation.

3. For those consumers with significant emotional problems, interest inventories may not be the most appropriate measures. A reason for this is that these consumers tend to make negative responses and endorse more passive interests than do people who are not emotionally disturbed. Before interest assessment can begin, the emotional issues should be addressed.

4. The evaluator should identify how long it has been since the consumer participated in formal interest assessment. For persons under age 20, interests are more likely to change, though adults who are experiencing an eventful life transition might begin to express a latent interest that has never been revealed by measurement. Hood and Johnson (1997) believed that evaluators should consider re-administering an interest inventory if it has been longer than 6 months since the consumer last completed one.

5. The test manual should clearly state what the instrument was designed to measure and whether the instrument possesses adequate reliability.

6. Rehabilitation counselors should use vocational measures that have norms that are appropriate for their consumers.

7. The language and items of the inventory should be carefully reviewed.

8. Familiarity with the consumer's response style will assist in generating credible test-taking behavior. The consumer's ethnic culture will affect response style.

9. Interest inventories in use today place an emphasis on self-exploration. They expand career opportunities and attempt to achieve a degree of sex fairness. The inventory's available manual should explain sex-balanced items that characterize male and female gender role socialization, with the desired result of both men and women obtaining similar raw scores and having equivalent score distributions across, for example, the six Holland themes.

10. The appropriateness of the interest measure to the consumer's reading level, the consumer's cultural background, and his or her readiness to take interest inventories are important factors in instrument selection.

Gender Differences

Traditionally, interest measures have provided different result patterns for men and women, provoking continued stereotyping of occupations. This stereotyping can influence gender differences during career exploration. Although many inventories are eliminating sexist language and using same-sex normative scores, the evaluator should still explore the consumer's level of gender role specialization and perceived sociopolitical barriers (Whiston, 2000).

The Measurement of Interests

Various approaches for measuring interest include self-estimation, interviews, checklists, questionnaires, and tests, known as inventories. Interest inventories were initially developed in the mid-1920s as "a facilitative response to an established premise which linked occupational interest with job satisfaction" (Phillips, 1978, p. 10). They were developed to assess individual areas of interest and compare subsequent subjective interest scores with the measured interest of successful professionals in a wide variety of occupations. Inventories have been used principally in vocational and education guidance (Shertzer & Linden, 1979). The inventory is the result of its interaction with the individual and cannot be considered separately in any way.

These measures attempt to quantify interests by providing a score to describe a consumer's feelings of like or dislike. They elaborate acceptance–rejection propositions. Individuals are asked to provide answers such as "most liked" and "least liked" to the content of items, which forces them to make a choice. Their choices are self-estimates of their feelings, emotions, and attitudes toward those items. Their responses yield scores of general interest from which, directly or by comparison, interest in particular occupations or fields of activity can be estimated. Shertzer and Linden (1979) believed that this approach assumes that each group of people "under investigation have a pattern of interest in common that is different from that of some other group" (p. 178).

If interest measures are used properly, they can be a helpful gauge for evaluating future job satisfaction. However, they should be used to complement other methods of assessment, and the test items should be carefully checked for age- and disability-related appropriateness. Interest evaluations may not be appropriate for every consumer. A person who has incurred a disabling on-the-job injury may be quite satisfied with previous employment but seek another occupation in a similar interest area. This individual may not feel the need for occupational interest assessment.

When exploring a consumer's interest areas, the rehabilitation professional should associate this information with results from aptitude tests, a review of previous work experience, knowledge gained from the assessment interview, and medical reports. Harmony must be achieved between the person's interests and his or her capabilities. For example, if a consumer shows a dominant interest and willingness to work in data-related occupations, rather than people- or idea-related careers, then information is needed about the person's clerical skills; perceptual speed and accuracy; numerical computation; and, in many instances, spatial relations and eye, hand, and finger coordination abilities. In contrast, if interest evaluation results indicate a very strong preference for idea-related occupations, then information should be obtained about the individual's aptitudes in reading comprehension, language usage, math reasoning, and artistic and creative endeavors.

Interest inventories can be classified in a variety of ways, such as by age, occupational level, or type of item. Two types of interest scales predominate. One type measures the strength of a person's interests in broad fields of activity, such as outdoors, health-related activities, or technology. These scales are usually described as *general* or *basic scales*.

They refer to one type of activity. The other type of scale assesses the similarity of a person's interest patterns to those of people in specific occupations. These scales are called *occupational scales* and are heterogeneous in terms of item content. Scales of this type are based on items that differentiate between the interests of people in an occupation and people in general.

To facilitate interest exploration, the rehabilitation professional should be aware of the advantages of computer scoring. Such interest measures as the *Strong Interest Inventory* (Strong, Hansen, & Campbell, 1994) and the *Career Assessment Inventory–Enhanced Version* (Johansson, 1986) have forms that can be completed, mailed to the nearest computer scoring service, and returned within 10 days. The computer processing provides consumer profiles that can be easily read and interpreted. They may include narrative-style interpretations, which individualize the interest scores and explain in detail the meaning, significance, and limitations of interest measurement.

Furthermore, these interactive systems allow consumers who have the ability to use them to become more actively involved in the assessment process. These systems also provide individualized, immediate feedback and can be linked to large databases that offer up-to-date information about career opportunities that may be in harmony with the consumer's reported interests. There are concerns about cost and confidentiality, but these issues should be balanced with the advantages of using these systems (Fouad et al., 2008). Sampson, Dozier, and Colvin (2011) believed that one singular advantage for those persons with a disability is the opportunity to access career guidance resources by using the Internet to interact with a professional and to obtain, for example, assessment information that requires specialized expertise.

The following are some recommended interest measures that can be used to generate useful information in rehabilitation assessment. They are grouped into two categories: (a) inventories appropriate for consumers with low reading skills and (b) measures for persons with a higher reading capability.

Tests Appropriate for Persons With Low Reading Skills

Geist Picture Interest Inventory–Revised

This measure (Geist, 1988) quantitatively assesses 11 male and 12 female general interest areas: persuasive, clerical, mechanical, musical, scientific, outdoor, literary, computational, artistic, social service, dramatic, and personnel service. The Geist can facilitate interest exploration of individuals with verbal disabilities. The test booklet contains 44 triads of drawings, representing major vocations and avocations, with 130 drawings in all. Only occupations that are recognizable in most parts of the United States are included.

With most consumers, the Geist is self-administering. It can be used with individuals or groups and has no time limit. When a consumer has a severe reading disability, the directions and questions under the pictures are read aloud to the consumer, who circles the drawings of his or her choice. The test can be scored by the examiner, and the manual contains easily understood directions. The Geist also contains a motivation questionnaire for both males and females. This booklet includes the motivational analysis of occupational choices, which, in turn, suggests reasons or motivations behind each choice of drawings.

The *Geist Picture Interest Inventory–Revised* is available from Western Psychological Services, 625 Alaska Ave., Torrance, CA 90503, 800/ 648-8857.

Reading-Free Vocational Interest Inventory– Second Edition

The *Reading-Free Vocational Interest Inventory–Second Edition* (R-FVII-2), which was revised in 2000, is a non-reading vocational preference test for use with those 13 years and older who have mental retardation, a learning disability, or other disadvantage. The inventory consists of pictorial depictions of occupations in a forced-choice format presented in 55 triads in a non-reusable booklet. All items in the measure depict the type of occupations in which, for example, consumers who have mental retardation or a learning disability have traditionally been productive and proficient (Becker, 2000). These occupations include automotive, building trades, clerical, animal care, food service, patient care, horticulture, housekeeping, personal service, laundry service, and materials handling. The R-FVII-2 is suitable for both individual and group administration and has no time limits (the publisher's catalog indicates that the test takes about 20 minutes to administer). The inventory has been normed on a nationwide basis to samples of boys and girls, Grades 7 through 12, with educable mental retardation (EMR), learning disabilities (LD), and trainable mental retardation (TMR). These sample groups generally consisted of approximately 1,000 individuals (Siefker, 1996). It is important to note that this revised tool complies with Title IX's prohibition of sex discrimination in education and reflects 25 years of work and research with individuals with physical and mental disabilities around the world.

Although the consumer must be able to visually perceive line drawings and mark responses with a paper and pencil, no reading is required. This inventory can be quite useful for a beginning interest exploration after a determination of employability has been made. The R-FVII-2 is available from Elbern Publications, Columbus, OH.

Picture Interest Career Survey

Developed by Brady (2007), this tool is a quick way to identify interest areas. The survey consists of 36 items, each containing three pictures. The consumer decides which one of the three pictures is most interesting and circles that picture. The result is an occupational code that suggests occupational themes that best suit the consumer's personality (2011). The test is available from JIST Publishing, 875 Montreal Way, St. Paul, MN 55102, 800/328-1452.

Tests More Appropriate for Those With Higher Reading Abilities

Strong Interest Inventory

The *Strong Interest Inventory* (SII; Strong, Hansen, & Campbell, 1994) is one of the oldest and most scientifically developed interest surveys. The inventory is easy to administer, requires at least a sixth-grade reading level, and requires a computer for scoring. Because the test authors have integrated Holland's (1959) theory of career development with the empirical approach traditionally used in scoring and interpreting, consumers receive scores displayed on scales based on the Holland typology (Fouad et al., 2008). The Holland theme scale contributes a conceptual framework within which to organize and interpret the data reported on the total Strong profile for both men and women.

There are 25 basic Occupational Scales in the Strong. Four new Personal Style Scales (work style, learning environment, leadership style, and risk taking and adventure) have been added to the profile sheet from the 1984 edition. This inventory produces scores on five sets of scales: the Administrative Indexes, General Occupational Theme Scales, Basic Interest Scales, Occupational Scales, and Personal Style Scales. In its current form, the Strong consists of 317 items and can be completed in 25 to 35 minutes (Hood & Johnson, 2007). This test is mainly applicable for use with persons who are oriented toward professional, semiprofessional, or managerial occupations that attract college graduates. For others, the relevance of the instrument is questionable. Also, the Strong should be interpreted only by persons who have had supervised experience in evaluating consumers' objective interests.

The Strong is available from CPP, 1150 Hamilton Court, Menlo Park, CA 94025, 800/624-1765.

Kuder Occupational Interest Survey–Form DD

This inventory (Kuder, Diamond, & Zytowski, 1985) includes such occupational areas as outdoors, mechanical, computational, scientific, persuasive, artistic, literary, musical, social service, and clerical. Seven personal-oriented areas are also included: Group Activity, Stable Situations, Working with Ideas, Avoiding Conflict, Directing Others, Working Independently, and Acting Spontaneously. This measure employs a forced-choice, three-item response format. Consumers select the item they prefer or would like most, and the one they least prefer.

The test is administered easily; its directions are explicit and may be understood readily. No time limit is specified, and most consumers can complete the form in approximately 30 minutes. Scores are given on a profile covering 10 occupational areas. At least a sixth-grade reading level is required, and the inventory can be applicable for persons who are college bound or who seek shorter training. The inventory can be used with consumers who are deaf if their reading level is adequate. Because the test is not timed, it can be orally administered to consumers who are blind.

The *Kuder Occupational Interest Survey–Form DD* is available from Kuder, Inc., 302 Visions Pkwy., Adel, IA 50003, 800/314-8972.

The Self-Directed Search

The result of more than 20 years of research by Holland (1959), the *Self-Directed Search* (SDS; Holland, 1994) is a self-administered, self-scored, and self-interpreted vocational counseling tool. This measure has two main purposes: (a) to provide a vocational counseling experience for people who do not have access to professional counselors or who cannot afford their services and (b) to multiply the number of people a counselor can serve (Fouad et al., 2008). Cutts (1977) explained that persons who have vocational questions such as, "What career shall I follow? Is my tentative choice reasonable?" or "What alternatives do I have in career choice?" and adults who are wondering about their current job status should be aided by this inventory.

Fouad et al. (2008) explained that the Form R (1994) revision of the SDS is intended for use with high school and college students and other adults at a reading level of seventh or eighth grade. The Form E (1990) version is intended for junior high school students and adults with limited reading skills who are at a fourth-grade reading level. The measure can be used as a framework for organizing personal and occupational information. Consumers can usually complete the SDS booklet in approximately 40 minutes.

The SDS is considered self-interpreting, but the manual states that the counselor is expected to aid in the interpretation. Consumers might need help in understanding the five profiles in the assessment booklet. Each contains the estimate, on each of the five scales, of a person's resemblance to each of the six personality types (i.e., Realistic, Investigative, Artistic, Social, Enterprising, or Conventional). Each type was briefly described, as follows, by Hood and Johnson (2007).

> *Realistic*—People who enjoy or do well in technical, physical, mechanical, or outdoor activities.
> *Conventional*—People with interests or skills in keeping records, organizing data, attending to detail, or following through on others' instructions.
> *Enterprising*—People with interests or skills in business, management, sales, public speaking, or leading others.
> *Social*—People interested or skilled in working with or helping others (e.g., teaching, counseling, nursing).
> *Artistic*—People who like or do well in music, art, writing, drama, or other creative activities.
> *Investigative*—People with scientific, mathematical, analytical, or scholarly interests or skills.

Cutts (1977) stated that because the order of the six types is always the same, the five profiles should have the same general shape. The professional should be aware that the implications of a well-defined, highly differentiated profile (showing high scores in some areas and low in others) versus a flat profile, which is undifferentiated, reflect consumer confusion and present a variety of consumer problems and counselor questions.

The SDS scales have a moderate degree of internal consistency. Samples of 2,000 to 6,000 first-year college students show a range from 0.67 to 0.94. Retest reliabilities show that the SDS summary codes have the highest degree of reliability, as compared to the subscales, which reflect a lower degree of reliability. Also, the item content and format reflect clear content validity. Items are stated in direct ways that require minimal interpretation and are related to the scale. Content is consistent with well-established vocational knowledge.

The SDS includes an assessment booklet and an occupational classification booklet. To use this inventory, the consumer fills out the assessment booklet and obtains a three-letter occupational code. The code is then used to locate suitable occupations in the occupational classification booklet *The Occupational Finder*. Through a series of questions related to occupational daydreams, competencies, and preferences for activities and occupations, the assessment booklet provides an estimate of the consumer's interests in a number of occupational areas. In summary, the SDS can serve as a beginning measure for interest exploration, and it can be used periodically throughout a person's entire career. The SDS offers many alternative occupations.

The SDS is available from PAR, Inc., 16204 North Florida Ave., Lutz, FL 33594, 800/727-9329.

Career Assessment Inventory–Enhanced Version

Developed to cover the vocational areas of occupations requiring less than a 4-year college degree, the *Career Assessment Inventory–Enhanced Version* (CAI; Johansson, 2003) overlaps to some extent with the more "nonprofessional" occupations covered by the earlier (1985) CAI (Johansson, 1986). The majority of items developed for the CAI were based on an understanding of job descriptions of various occupations and related activities detailed in the *Dictionary of Occupational Titles* (DOT; U.S. Department of Labor, 1977) and the *Occupational Outlook Handbook* (U.S. Department of Labor, 1990). A determined effort was made to avoid items that would imply a career or interest that would be applicable more to one gender than the other. The professional reviews of the test items and the field-testing with sixth and eighth graders provided the necessary data for the final wording of the CAI. The first 151 items are activity-type items, the next 43 relate to school subjects, and the remaining 101 include occupational titles.

Both versions of the CAI (i.e., regular and enhanced) are patterned after the *Strong Interest Inventory*. They both include the same types of scales: administrative indexes, non-occupational scales, general theme scales, basic interest scales, and occupational scales. The CAI occupational scales have been coded according to Holland's classification system. The two systems produce similar results in most cases (Hood & Johnson, 2007).

The measure is written at a sixth-grade reading level and requires between 20 and 40 minutes to complete. The interpretive profile measures the consumer's interest on three separate scales:

> *Scale 1*—Gives a graphic representation of the way the consumer's individual orientation to work relates to the six basic occupational themes: realistic, artistic, conventional, enterprising, social, and investigative.
>
> *Scale 2*—Reveals the strength or weakness of the consumer's interest in approximately 23 academic areas, such as mathematics, social science, and teaching.
>
> *Scale 3*—Compares the consumer's interest with people already employed in 75 occupations on the CAI.

Reliability studies indicated that test and retest scores for the various samples showed very stable patterns for the groups. Also, the concurrent validity data presented for both the student samples and adult samples were of the same magnitude as data evidenced by similar scales on the *Strong Interest Inventory* and the *Strong Vocational Interest Blanks* (Strong et al., 1994).

There is an enhanced version of the CAI, written for the eighth-grade reading level, that focuses on careers requiring up to 4 years of college and includes many of the most rapidly growing professional occupations. This version consists of 370 items divided into three major categories: activities, school subjects, and occupations. Completion time is approximately 40 minutes. The scale scores provide information in such areas as the six general occupational themes and 25 basic interest scales, broken down into several specific areas of interest (i.e., animal service, mathematics, creative arts, community service, law and politics, and clerical service). A narrative report provides scale descriptions, score interpretations, and comparisons, and a profile report graphically presents scores on each scale.

This inventory is computer scored, and the information obtained from the measure can be very useful to both the consumer and the professional for rehabilitation planning purposes. The CAI covers a wide range of occupations and offers many suggestions for associations between the consumer's interest and particular occupations.

The CAI is available from Pearson, 19500 Bulverde Rd., San Antonio, TX 78259, 800/627-7271.

Interest Check List

Developed by the U.S. Department of Labor (1981), this inventory's primary purpose is to serve as an interviewing aid when the rehabilitation professional believes that further information on a consumer's interest is desired. There are 115 activities on the checklist, and they are divided into 23 job clusters. This inventory requires at least a sixth-grade reading level and 20 to 30 minutes to complete. The items and job categories were taken from the DOT and are related to occupations requiring limited postsecondary education. It can be hand scored by the examiner, and the inventory is especially valuable in facilitating interest exploration with the consumer during the initial phase of the rehabilitation process.

Occupational Aptitude Survey and Interest Schedule–Third Edition

Developed by Randall Parker (2001), the *Occupational Aptitude Survey and Interest Schedule–Third Edition* (OASIS-3) consists of two related submeasures: the OASIS-3 Aptitude Survey and the OASIS-3 Interest Schedule. The instrument is intended to assist in the career development of students in Grades 8 through 12 who are disabled, nondisabled, or disadvantaged. It can be administered individually or in groups and takes from 30 to 45 minutes to administer. The Interest Schedule measures such qualities as Artistic, Scientific, Nature, Protective, Mechanical, Industrial, Business Detail, Selling, Accommodating, Humanitarian, Leading–Influencing, and Physical Performing. This schedule contains 240 items scored as *like*, *neutral*, or *dislike*. Both schedules have median reliabilities ranging from .78 to .98. The OASIS-3 is available from PRO-ED, Inc., 8700 Shoal Creek Blvd., Austin, TX 78757-6897, 800/897-3202.

Ohio Vocational Interest Survey–Second Edition

The *Ohio Vocational Interest Survey–Second Edition* (OVIS-II; microcomputer version) was developed in 1986 to assist consumers from Grade 7 through college age, as well as adults, with their vocational plans. This inventory has no time limit, though it usually requires about 45 minutes to administer.

This inventory has an acceptable reliability (from the .70s to the low .80s), and the norms were developed from a sample of occupations drawn from a pool of 2,700 occupations that represent 99% of the workforce. The appealing aspects of this measure include the wide range of persons for whom it is appropriate, the availability of computer scoring, and the test's similarity to the *Strong Interest Inventory* (Strong et al., 1994) and the *Career Assessment Inventory* (Johansson, 1986).

The test is available from The Psychological Corporation, 555 Academic Court, San Antonio, TX 78204, 800/211-8378.

Career Exploration Inventory

Developed by John Liptak (2007), this not only is an interest measure but also offers the opportunity for the consumer to explore one's leisure and learning worlds. The consumer responds to 96 items and scores the responses in relation to 16 interest clusters. The instrument helps the individual to begin the career exploration process and is available from JIST Publishing, 7321 Shadeland Station, Suite 200, Indianapolis, IN 46256 (Power, 2011).

Career Decision-Making System–Revised

The *Career Decision-Making System–Revised* (CDM-R), developed by Harrington and O'Shea (2008), asks consumers to rate themselves in terms of career fields, school subjects, school plans, job values, abilities, and interests. Each of the six Holland interest categories is represented by 20 of the 120 items. The measure has two levels (Grades 7 through 10 and high school students and adults), and consumers score their own answer sheets by counting the number of responses in each category. The results are used to suggest career clusters that consumers may wish to investigate (Hood & Johnson, 2007). The inventory promotes an exploration of values, abilities, interests, and training options.

The test is available from Pearson, 19500 Bulverde Rd., San Antonio, TX 78259, 800/627-7271.

O*NET Interest Profiler

This is a self-scored instrument designed to measure interests by Holland's six personality types for persons in middle school through adulthood. It may be printed out, copied, and distributed along with the score report and an interpretive booklet (Niles & Harris-Bowlsbey, 2005). It is available from the United States Employment Service.

Campbell Interest and Skill Survey

This instrument combines the self-assessment of skills with an exploration of interest. There are 320 items resulting in scores on seven orientation scales (corresponding to Holland's six themes), 29 Basic Interest and Skill Scales (5 to 6 categories of the orientation scales and representing various occupational activities), and 58 Occupational Scales. The profile provides four categories: *Pursue*—high interest and high skills; *Develop*—high interest and lower skills; *Explore*—lower interest and high skills; and *Avoid*—lower interest and lower skills (Whiston, 2000). On the interest scales, the individual scores indicate strength of attraction for each occupational area, while the skill scales represent an estimate of self-confidence in performing well in the specified area (Walsh & Betz, 1995).

Overall, this instrument is similar to the Strong in that it includes both general and occupational interest scales; it differs in its inclusion of a set of self-report skill scales to match each of the interest scales (Hood & Johnson, 2007). It is a user-friendly instrument with an Internet version available. The reading level of the instrument is sixth grade, it can be administered to individuals 15 years and older, and the completion time is approximately 25 minutes. This survey is available from Pearson (800/627-7271).

Counseling Helps in Interest Exploration

Table 7.1 relates the usefulness of the different inventories that measure interests to varied levels of formal preparation required by occupations. Because interest exploration can facilitate vocational or life planning when it is begun early in the rehabilitation process, professionals find it

Table 7.1

Usefulness of Inventories for Occupational Preparation:
Formal Preparation Required by Occupation

Inventory	No high school degree	High school degree	2 years' preparation beyond high school	3 or more years' preparation beyond high school
Kuder (DD)	U	U	U	U
CAI	U	U	U	NU
Geist-R	U	U	LU	NU
OASIS-3	U	U	LU	NU
SII	U	U	U	U
SDS	U	U	U	U
Interest Check List (U.S. Dept. of Labor, 1981)	U	U	U	NU
Campbell Interest and Skill Survey	U	U	U	U
R-FVII-2	U	U	LU	NU
OVIS-II	U	U	U	U
Career Exploration Inventory	U	U	U	NU
Picture Interest Career Survey	U	U	LU	NU
*O*NET Interest Career Survey*	U	U	U	U

Note. U = useful; LU = limited usefulness; NU = not useful. Kuder (DD) = *Kuder Occupational Interest Survey* (Form DD; Kuder, Diamond, & Zytowski, 1985); CAI = *Career Assessment Inventory–Enhanced Version* (Johansson, 1986); Geist-R = *Geist Picture Interest Inventory–Revised* (Geist, 1988); SII = *Strong Interest Inventory*; SDS = *Self-Directed Search* (Holland, 1994); R-FVII-2 = *Reading-Free Vocational Interest Inventory–Second Edition* (Becker, 2000); OVIS-II = *Ohio Vocational Interest Survey–Second Edition* (Hoyt, 1986).

helpful to structure this area of evaluation. The following guidelines are suggested when developing this assessment.

Interest Exploration With Consumers Who Have at Least a Seventh-Grade Reading Ability

Step 1. To particularize one's interests, consumers can take the *Interest Check List*, the *Ohio Vocational Interest Survey*, or the *Career Exploration Inventory*.

Step 2. To particularize interest areas for occupations requiring preparation of at least 3 years beyond high school, consumers can take the *Strong Interest Inventory* (computer scored), the *Self-Directed Search* (hand scored), the *Career Decision-Making System–Revised,* or the *Campbell Interest and Skill Survey.* To particularize interest areas for occupations not requiring preparation beyond high school or that require 2 years' maximum training after high school, consumers can take the *Career Assessment Inventory* (computer scored).

Interest Exploration With Consumers Who Have Below a Seventh-Grade Reading Ability

Step 1. Consumers can take the *Interest Check List*, though many of the items may have to be read aloud, or the *Picture Interest Career Survey.*

Step 2. Consumers can take the Geist (hand scored) or the R-FVII-2.

Step 3. For all reading groups, identification of consumers' interests should be explored in business sales and management (Enterprising); business operations (Conventional); technologies and trades (Realistic); natural, social, and medical sciences (Investigative); creative and applied arts (Artistic); or social, health, and personal services (Social).

With a beginning knowledge of the consumer's interests in these job clusters (which relate to Holland's 1959 typology), the rehabilitation professional can then consult resources that provide detailed descriptions of a wide variety of occupations. One volume that is particularly valuable is the *Guide to Occupational Exploration* (Harrington & O'Shea, 1984). The data in this publication are organized into 12 interest areas with 66 work groups and 348 subgroups. Each subgroup has its own six-digit unique code and title, taken from the DOT. Within each subgroup, related occupations are identified. For the 66 work groups, descriptions of kinds of job activities, work requirements, clues for relating individuals to the type of work, preparation for entry into jobs, and other pertinent items are included. One of the appendixes in this publication has information regarding how to organize career and occupational information resources. It contains techniques and procedures for cataloging and filing occupational information according to the structure in the *Guide to Occupational Exploration.*

When using the guide and when a consumer's assessment suggests interest in different work groups, each work group can be explored. This exploration determines whether the consumer still wants to consider each area and whether the training requirements are in harmony with the individual's capabilities. Subgroups that identify many occupations should be examined to assess whether one or more of them seems to suit the consumer's interests and qualifications better than the others.

When exploration of all the relevant groups has been completed, along with identification of possible occupations of particular interest, then the collected information is organized. This information can then be used, with other data and facts, for rehabilitation planning. The *Guide to Occupational Exploration* provides a convenient crossover from information about the person with a disability to potentially suitable fields of work or other areas of productivity.

A Specialized Approach to Interest Assessment

Within the past 15 years, more interest measures have been devised for nonprofessional occupations and for persons planning to enter the workforce after high school. However, more effective assessment instruments for those with physical and mental disabilities need to be designed. Other methods for interest exploration must also be used for consumers who have very low reading abilities or very limited knowledge about jobs and activities. During the interview with the consumer, direct questions can be used to gain information about existing interest areas. This information may be unreliable, superficial, and unrealistic, in part because questions can elicit responses that are susceptible to a consumer's tendency to respond by giving socially approved answers.

However, even apart from the difficulties of using direct questions, the interview can still be employed effectively to solicit information about a consumer's interests. Friel and Carkhuff (1974) devised a model to assist in identifying interests as well as expanding interest options. It involves understanding the consumer's total functioning in physical, emotional, and intellectual areas. This approach can be modified for use in an interview situation. It implies that the rehabilitation professional must become very active when assisting the consumer in exploring interest areas. The six steps to this approach have been modified by the author for application to the interview.

Step 1. Assist the consumer in exploring interests by asking questions such as the following:

- From the jobs that you have had, what did you particularly like or dislike? For example, did you like working on your own, and was your supervisor friendly to you?
- In these jobs, what did you feel you could do especially well?
- When you were in school, what subjects did you particularly like and dislike? Why?
- From the people that you know in your life, what jobs do they have that are of particular interest to you?
- When you watch television and see people doing various jobs, are there any that are of special interest to you?
- What do you enjoy doing in your spare time?

It is important for the rehabilitation professional to understand the reasons behind an identified interest. Is the interest caused by some external pressure (e.g., what parents or friends told the consumer that he or she would like)? An added resource that can at least facilitate the consumer's exploration of interests is newspaper want ads, especially those in the Sunday edition. The professional can read these ads to the consumer and then encourage a response, or the consumer can carefully read them, check any openings that have an interest for him or her, and then discuss them with the rehabilitation professional.

Step 2. Assist the consumer in exploring his or her values by asking questions such as the following:

- When you were working, what do you feel was important to you?
- What is the reason that it was important to you? For example,

was it important to work with your hands, or not to have close supervision? Did you like the particular job, or know it was something you could do well?

The goal in these questions is to develop an understanding of what a consumer means by a particular value.

Step 3. Categorize the information that has been generated about the consumer's values. Friel and Carkhuff (1974) suggested organizing these values into the physical, emotional–interpersonal, and intellectual categories. For example:

- *Physical*—dressing well on the job; working in a comfortable office atmosphere
- *Emotional–interpersonal*—having job security; having people close by when working; interacting frequently with people
- *Intellectual*—liking the opportunity to make decisions

Step 4. Further categorize the information into:

- *"People" occupations.* Includes the areas of service (nurse or social worker), education (teacher), business (salesperson), providing goods and services, and recreation (coach and artist).
- *"Things" occupations.* Includes business (accountant or secretary), technology (providing mechanical services, e.g., mechanic or electronic technician), outdoors (forest ranger or landscaper), and science (developing research and methods, e.g., biologist).

Step 5. Now, help the consumer identify which of the interest categories best fits his or her values.

For example, if the consumer mentions that the most important work value is job security, then an interest area appropriate to that dominant value should be chosen. It could be helpful to the consumer to display his or her values in the physical, intellectual, and interest areas in one column and then match these values to the occupational information gathered under "people" and "things." The specific occupations identified by the professional must be in harmony with the consumer's stated values. The more occupations that are suggested, the more extensive will be the consumer's own exploration.

Step 6. Finally, identify the educational and occupational requirements demanded of particular employment areas that are congruent with the consumer's values.

Some jobs require less than a high school diploma; others may require a high school diploma or its equivalent—namely, apprenticeship training after high school, 2 years of junior or community college, or 4 or more years of college. Consumers should also decide how much education they want. The professional should gauge the consumer's educational capability by studying school records or previous paper-and-pencil testing. Of particular value during this interest exploration are the DOT and the O*NET Occupational Information System (Hanson, Matheson, & Borman, 2001). If the professional knows how to use those valuable resources, the number of occupational alternatives can be greatly expanded. Once a main interest area is identified and consumers are aware that it is in harmony with their dominant values, then these resources provide a large amount of information about the particular occupations relevant to this interest area.

Taking these six steps sequentially is often a lengthy exploration process, but it is a very legitimate use of the rehabilitation professional's time because it encourages the consumer's involvement in both interest exploration and rehabilitation programming. Most of the steps are designed to elicit the consumer's thoughts and feelings about past, present, and future career activities.

Conclusion

In summary, there are several ways to learn about the consumer's interests, such as self-estimation, interviews, checklists, questionnaires, and standardized assessment tests. Many of these tests, for example, the *Self-Directed Search* and the *Strong Interest Inventory*, are the most frequently used tests in all of vocational assessment. Several interest assessments, however, rely on self-ratings, and there is considerable disagreement, as reported in the literature, over whether self-ratings provide as much information as psychometrically determined measures of the same interest constructs (Parker, Hansmann, & Schaller, 2010). While counselors can avoid the expense of formal vocational testing by having the consumers do simple self-ratings, and also by providing consumers with more involvement and control over the assessment process, rehabilitation counselors are taking a risk when they make decisions based solely on their consumers' rating of their interests (Parker et al., 2010).

For both the counselor and the consumer, a more feasible arrangement would be to administer at least one or two self-rating measures, and one or two standardized interest tests. Comparing the results among the interest measures may facilitate some agreement or harmony among the consumer's interest traits. This procedure also generates a lower risk factor. When collecting information about the consumers, it is also important to note the following considerations, some of which have been mentioned earlier in this chapter.

1. A strong motivation toward certain types of occupational behavior is expressed by a wide number of responses to an extremely wide range of stimuli.
2. Interest inventories suggest the direction, not intensity, of the consumer's interests. They respond to the question "What kind?" and not "How much?"
3. A legitimate interest in a vocational area often has little effect on grades earned in the curriculum leading to that area.
4. Individuals' interests tend to be less varied with increasing age.
5. Dominant themes running through standardized interest inventories are as follows:
   a. Trait factors: Human behavior may be ordered and measured along dimensions of defined traits.
   b. Interest inventories have an overall positive direction.
   c. Interests and abilities, as previously stated, are not highly correlated.
6. The scores or results of interest inventories, whether standardized or non-standardized, are
   a. reflective occasionally of fakeability.
   b. able to suggest that interests change over time. As explained earlier in this chapter, for individuals with a disability, especially of an onset in early or middle adulthood, preferences change because of perceived limitations or the influences of environmental factors (e.g., family members, peers, educational and medical personnel).

    c. influenced by the individual's socialization, familiarity with a wide range of vocational opportunities, and occupational stereotyping. A consumer's interests may have been restricted due to societal attitudes, including occupational stereotyping still prevalent in many cultures.

    d. not able to suggest that a high measured interest alone can predict successful work-related skill acquisition or success in a specific job.

The reliability of interest measures, consequently, is a continuing issue in vocational assessment. The professional should, of course, attempt to enhance the reliability of the interest assessment with careful attention to factors that affect credibility, such as the consumer desiring to meet family expectations and not his or her own, the need to please the rehabilitation counselor, the desire to support an unrealistic career expectation/goal, low motivation, and coping with emotions associated with the occurrence of one's disability. This author has found it helpful to explain to the consumer, "When taking this inventory, you are describing yourself to only yourself, and an open and honest response will help you make more satisfying career choices following assessment. Assessment is mainly for you."

When the consumer has completed the interest inventory, the evaluator should make sure that the consumer has answered a sufficient number of items. Providing the interest profile results to the consumer just before the interpretation session will help him or her understand the information. This information may suggest what alternative courses of action are really feasible or satisfying for a consumer, and the effective use of the interview can further help to identify different paths to rehabilitation goals. But the question remains: Which one of these possible alternatives should the consumer take?

Chapter 8

Intelligence Assessment in Vocational Rehabilitation

An important area of rehabilitation assessment is the exploration of a consumer's ability to solve problems, adapt to new situations, and show competence when confronted with new learning demands. Competence itself is both ability oriented, emphasizing positive coping skills, and situation oriented, emphasizing a person's ability to function during environmental interactions (Sundberg, 1977). One of the approaches to measuring competence is the assessment of intelligence. Intelligence tests represent a highly specialized field with a vast body of literature and research surrounding their use. But this area of vocational assessment can be easily misunderstood by counselors. Unfortunately, the results of intelligence assessment may categorize consumers and be misread to support stereotypes, or they can be constructively used to identify people's needs and direct rehabilitation planning to beneficial goals. This specific assessment can also provide valuable information to consumers, families, and service providers concerning returning to work, especially after a traumatic brain injury (Lichtenberger, Kaufman, & Kaufman, 2008).

"The clinical tests most commonly used to assess intellectual functioning in adolescents and adults have not changed much over the past 60 years" (Kaufman & Kaufman, 2001, p. 84). Intelligent behavior, moreover, is as much a function of drive and incentive as the more traditionally conceived components of intellectual ability, such as abstract and logical thinking, reasoning, judgment, and retention of knowledge (Shertzer & Linden, 1979). Intelligence is not a single, unitary ability but rather a composite of several functions. It is individuals' global capacity to act purposefully, think rationally, and deal effectively with the environment

(Wechsler, 1981). Intelligence is a function of the total personality, and personality characteristics generally affect the direction and extent of the individuals' intellectual development. Affective life and cognitive life, although distinct, are inseparable (Shertzer & Linden, 1979).

No one has seen a thing called "intelligence." Rather, intelligence is inferred from a sample of behaviors. These behaviors include generalization, motor behavior, general information, vocabulary, induction, comprehension, detail recognition, analogies, abstract reasoning, and memory (Salvia & Ysseldyke, 1995). Intelligence can also denote practical problem-solving ability, verbal ability, and social competence, as well as the ability to adapt to life's changing demands (Tyler, 1984). Because of the norm concept discussed in Chapter 5, intelligence test results in rehabilitation assessment must be interpreted cautiously. Most intelligence tests do not include people with disabilities in their standardization sample. Unfortunately, IQ and intelligence have become so value laden in society that persons are labeled on the basis of a small amount of evidence.

Many rehabilitation practitioners have argued that cognitive ability is the most important predictor of job performance (Krug, 2001). But a question lingers: "Why is it that many people who appear to have relatively high intelligence and should have the skills to do a job, do not perform productively at this job?" Personality factors may inhibit job performance, or they may play a significant role in enhancing job predictability. Chapter 9 of this text discusses the subject of personality factors.

Is intelligence related to employment success? People tend, insofar as circumstances permit, to gravitate toward jobs in which they have the ability to compete successfully with others. In turn, having capabilities considerably in excess of those required by a job often causes dissatisfaction because of the lack of challenge and consequent loss of interest in the work. A correlation between intelligence test scores and job success may actually be an artifact, the product of their joint association with class status (McClelland, 1973). Although many employers select some employees who have gone to the "right" schools because they do better, intelligence does not necessarily make people proficient at their jobs. Tyler (1984) explained that

> professional people average higher than skilled workers, skilled workers average higher than unskilled workers. But this might simply be a

result of the fact that it takes more schooling to get into the higher level occupations, and IQ is correlated with school success. (p. 49)

However, within any occupational group, the degree of success attained may depend largely on characteristics other than IQ. Among college students, there is no consistent relationship between scholastic aptitude scores and actual accomplishments, whether in social leadership, the arts, science, music, writing, or speech and drama (McClelland, 1973). Likewise, in routine occupations that require speed and accuracy (whether clerical or semiskilled factory jobs), intelligence measured by an alertness factor rather than a standard time-powered test is more related to success in the learning period.

Precisely what intelligence tests measure has been the subject of dispute since their origin. Wechsler believed that they measure "the capacity of an individual to understand the world about him and his resourcefulness to cope with its challenges" (Shertzer & Linden, 1979, p. 123). However, no intelligence test available today measures innate ability (Shertzer & Linden, 1979; Tyler, 1984). Rather, such tests measure the extent to which an individual's innate potential has been modified or developed within his or her environment. Many factors other than intelligence (e.g., creativity, exploratory interests, economic supports, environmental opportunities) may influence success in intelligence testing. Measured intelligence has been found to both reflect past schooling and predict future school success. The IQ score resulting from such tests could be viewed as "measured intelligence, not necessarily the adaptive intelligence used in everyday living" (Sundberg, 1977, p. 245). The concept of intelligence common to all intelligence tests, however, is the ability to learn.

Along with the ability to learn, another aspect of intelligence is aptitude. Although learning ability may be narrow or wide and specific or general in importance, intelligence is considered to have a wider scope. A reason for this is that intelligence includes a variety of closely related mental abilities that are most useful for predicting general achievement. Verbal and numerical abilities, which are essential in some degree to nearly all forms of achievement, have become the main ingredients of many intelligence tests. Verbal intelligence tests are most like achievement tests and, in that respect, are better suited for predictions of success at the next higher level of learning than for assessing the full range of trainability. Also, the majority of intelligence tests include appraisal of the reasoning factor. These tests are especially useful for discerning the difference between past learning and present capacity. Intelligence testing, therefore, does not provide a comprehensive measure of all aspects of intelligence. Because the concept of intelligence is so complex, any test or assessment procedure attempting to measure all of its theoretical aspects would be too lengthy to be practical. What is measured is the consumer's performance on a series of tasks, and from this performance the amount of "intelligence" that a consumer possesses is inferred. Consequently, intelligence should be regarded as a descriptive, rather than explanatory, concept. It is an expression of an individual's ability at a given point in time in relation to age norms. To be noted is that several new theories of intelligence have emerged in the past 27 years, such as Sternberg's triarchic approach and Gardner's theory of multiple intelligences, but none of these have been successfully adapted into a workable, commercially published IQ test (Kaufman & Kaufman, 2001).

Related to the complex nature of understanding the concept of intelligence is the emerging interest in emotional intelligence. The concept of emotional intelligence is quite different from cognitive intelligence. Beginning with the latter part of the 20th century, this aspect of intelligence became a focal point of research (Zuniga & Fischer, 2010). In fact, a recent research study (June 2011), conducted online, surveyed more than 2,000 nongovernmental hiring managers and human resource professionals in the United States and found the following:

- 71% said they value emotional intelligence more than the employee's IQ.
- 75% of employers are more likely to promote workers with high emotional intelligence over candidates with high IQs.
- The characteristics of employees with high emotional intelligence are more likely to stay calm under pressure, know how to resolve conflict effectively, lead by example, be empathetic, and make more thoughtful occupational decisions.

Emotional intelligence comprises several factors, such as an individual's ability to perceive emotions, understand the meaning of those emotions, and manage and solve emotional problems. In turn, these abilities help a person handle stressful situations, deal with feelings of loneliness, and, importantly, gain an appreciation of others' emotional states. For those with disabilities, moreover, understanding their emotional intelligence may provide insights into their attitudes toward the disability situation. Emotions, behaviors, and attitudes can all be linked together.

For the rehabilitation practitioner, it is important to remember that the reliability of most well-known intelligence tests is high (usually in the 0.80s or 0.90s), but even these figures allow for variation (Sundberg, 1977). Some people change markedly from time to time, especially if they have gone through periods of maladjustment. The IQ score obtained from an intelligence test does not represent a fixed characteristic of the individual. It should be interpreted as a particular score obtained on a particular test at a particular time. This is especially important for younger consumers, for whom test–retest reliabilities are lower (Hood & Johnson, 2007). The attainment of physical growth does not mean that mental, emotional, and psychological growth has ended. For example, an adult at age 40 can learn new things almost as well as a 13-year-old. In fact, an adult who is motivated strongly enough to make up for some slight loss in alertness and adaptability may learn better than a young person. The greatest difference in mental ability between younger and older persons may be in speed rather than accuracy or power (Shertzer & Linden, 1979).

Because of the multitude of abilities and the complexity of mental activities, it is important not to base decisions for rehabilitation planning on any single measure of ability. Several different kinds of evaluation tasks, such as the interview or the job tryout, should be used. Sundberg (1977) believed that any one IQ should be treated as a range rather than as a single score, keeping in mind the reliability or accuracy of the instrument. Also, it is necessary to ask how and where the consumer wants to use a certain capability. Many training environments, for example, do not demand a high level of abilities.

It is also important to remember both that intelligence tests are usually administered for the purpose of making a prediction about future academic performance, and that behaviors or attributes are being assessed by intelligence test items (Salvia & Ysseldyke, 1995). The rehabilitation professional must ask, "What is the relationship between the kinds of behavior sampled by the test and the kinds of behavior I am trying to predict?" The closer the relationship, the better the prediction. In developing the validity of their mental ability tests, test authors usually correlate them with criteria such as *Stanford-Binet Intelligence Scale–Fifth Edition* (Roid, 2003) performances, grades, academic averages, or ratings of teachers and supervisors. Predictive validity coefficients usually fall in the 0.40 to 0.60 range, with grades as the criteria.

Vocational evaluators should give attention during assessment, moreover, to the consumer's practical ability—namely, what does it take for a person with a disability to cope well with new environmental and personal situations? This could be referred to as *practical intelligence*, *contextual intelligence*, or *experiential intelligence*, or, specifically, the ability to interpret information in a changing context or the ability to adapt to a changing environment (Tyler, 1984). Although an intelligence test does not give a comprehensive measure of all aspects of intelligence, it can still evaluate a person's general ability more quickly and economically than many other procedures. Also, the appraisal of ability is usually more accurate than subjective methods and can provide the professional with a beginning understanding of the consumer's ability to learn in a training situation.

Information Required When Using Intelligence Assessment

When considering intelligence assessment for people with disabilities, several factors should be kept in mind.

Conceptualizing the Meaning of Intelligence

Although there are many forms of intelligence, such as linguistic, emotional, and experiential intelligence, in traditional intelligence assessment the examiner may be testing more for competence in verbal and school-acquired cognitive-related areas than for *intelligence* that will help the consumer act purposefully, think rationally, and deal effectively with his or her environment. But if the counselor endorses a more nontraditional understanding of intelligence, then contextual and emotional intelligence are the two areas that the professional should be mainly identifying in vocational assessment.

Contextual intelligence, namely, the ability to adapt to a changing environment, could be appraised by asking such questions as, "How have you managed the changes in your life resulting from your disability? Can you give me some examples of any changes and what you have done to adapt to them?" and "How were you introduced to vocational rehabilitation, and what changes in your life have you made to be here today?"

As stated earlier in this chapter, the consumer's emotional intelligence is a dimension of functioning that is important to identify in order to understand how the consumer is coping with many life demands while managing life adjustment tasks. Five domains of emotional intelligence were emphasized in the research report mentioned earlier:

- Knowing one's emotions (self-awareness and recognizing a feeling as it happens)
- Managing emotions (dealing with feelings so their expression is appropriate)
- Motivating oneself
- Recognizing emotions in others
- Handling relationships

These domains can be explored by listening carefully to the consumer's story communicated during the initial interview, by the counselor's responses to this story, and perhaps by asking such specific questions as

- What are the challenges you are encountering in handling stressful situations associated with your disability, and how do you handle these challenges?
- Has it been difficult to handle the circumstances of your disability, and why or why not?
- When you find yourself in a frustrating situation, what do you usually do to relieve this frustration, especially when it involves someone else?
- Are you aware when you begin to become angry over some event? Also, do you find it easy to recognize anger, or sadness, or happiness in others? When you recognize such emotions, then what do you do?

Interpreting Intelligence Information

Such records are particularly available for consumers who recently have completed formal school programs and whose disability saw its onset either from birth or during the developing years of elementary school, high school, or college. For those who incurred a disability during post–high school or college years, information on intelligence functioning is probably not available. When it is deemed important for the purpose of making a prediction about future performance in an academic, training, or employment setting, then a measure exploring relevant intelligence factors might have to be administered. Interpreting intelligence information from the consumer's record or from a very recently administered instrument also means reviewing the results from a vocational functioning perspective. Do the results suggest mental abilities for learning new, work-related tasks demanding specific mental competencies, such as those involving comprehension, memory, abstract reasoning, and detail recognition?

Selecting an Appropriate Instrument

Traditional tests that are most commonly used to assess intellectual functioning in adults have not changed much over the past 60 years (Kaufman & Kaufman, 2001). When deciding whether to use a measure of assessing intelligence functioning, and which specific measure, the rehabilitation counselor might consider the following two guidelines:

1. Is any information available on the consumer's functioning in this cognitive area? If so, is the information sufficient for vocational assessment goals, or does it need to be updated because of apparent consumer changes due to the disability situation, such as brain injury or a form of neurological illness? Also, for those born with a disability and who have received IQ testing, these persons may have been unfairly labeled. Accompanying this labeling may also have been a focus on what the individual cannot do, instead of identifying those cognitive strengths that can be utilized in vocational rehabilitation. The administration of an appropriate measure might facilitate obtaining this information.

2. What competencies does the counselor have for administering an intelligence measure? The Wechsler and Stanford-Binet IQ tests

require specialized training. After reading the test manual, however, the counselor can administer such tests as are discussed in Chapter 8, that is, the Slosson, the *Peabody Picture Vocabulary Test*, the *Beta III, Raven's Progressive Matrices*, the *Quick-Test*, and the *Kaufman Brief Intelligence Test*. But the question still remains: "Do these measures provide the needed information for vocational planning?" Especially for those with disabilities and who also may represent an ethnic minority group, several charges have been leveled against intelligence assessment measures:

* Anxiety in the testing situation
* Unfairness and lack of relevance of content
* Improper interpretation of scores

Evaluating the consumer's contextual and emotional intelligence may be more useful for predictive purposes when vocational goals focus on employment. But when training goals are also to be considered, then both the consumer and the counselor want the added assurance that the consumer has the cognitive abilities to respond to educational opportunities and tasks, such as verbal, reasoning, comprehension, memory, and detail recognition tasks. Other measures, that is, those described in this chapter, may be necessary. For these individuals with a disability, however, an added understanding of contextual and emotional intelligence factors may be foundational for other domains necessary for training and then work-related productivity.

Who should administer and interpret intelligence tests? Unless the rehabilitation professional has had specialized training, a psychologist or psychological examiner should give the measure and interpret the results. This is particularly true of three of the tests suggested in this chapter: the *Wechsler Adult Intelligence Scale–Fourth Edition* (WAIS-IV; Wechsler, 2008), the *Luria-Nebraska Neuropsychological Battery* (Golden, Purisch, & Hammeke, 1985), and the *Halstead-Reitan Neuropsychological Test Battery* (Reitan, 1993).

The rehabilitation professional should be familiar with these measures, specifically regarding their strengths and deficiencies, as well as the meaning of the test results. Also, the helping professional should understand their relevance to a particular consumer and the consumer's vocational aspirations. This is especially true concerning the validity of scores with regard to the consumer's disability, socioeconomic status, and other variables. Many intelligence measures, for example, rely heavily on the consumer's verbal ability, which is not a well-developed trait in many persons with disabilities.

The other measures suggested in this chapter can be administered and interpreted by rehabilitation professionals with a graduate degree or training in standardized instruments. The manuals of these tests contain clear instructions on administration and interpretation, and the tests themselves take a relatively short time to complete. Their results can be valuable in determining what occupations for training possibilities would not be appropriate for an individual, as well as determining intellectual strengths or competencies for eventual vocational programming.

Issues Involved in Selecting Instruments for a Consumer With a Disability

Timing of Administration

An IQ test should be chosen according to the consumer's educational and life experiences as well as his or her disability-related limitations. Also, when administering an intelligence measure, the rehabilitation professional should consider how long it has been since the consumer took such a test. Records may state that many years have elapsed since the original identification of measured intelligence functioning. Although longitudinal research studies generally have suggested that above the age of 7 years, IQs tend to remain relatively stable over time (Cohen et al., 1996), mental growth can be a continuing and uneven process for many. The creative process, for example, can continue through adulthood and into old age. Another example occurs when deterioration of an individual's basic functioning is suspected because of the presence of head trauma or chronic disease. On the other hand, in some people, intellectual ability can continue to increase as one gets older. For all of these reasons, an update of the consumer's intelligence functioning should be considered.

Problems Found in Intelligence Testing Are Magnified With Persons With Severe Disabilities

If a physical disability limits a consumer's capacity to perform in the areas of social competence or psychomotor functioning, do the results of the test then reflect intelligence, or simply the degree of physical impairment (Schlenoff, 1974)? Each disability has specific and characteristically limiting effects, and consumers with disabilities reflect adaptive and learning behavior aspects of intelligence differently. Consequently, it is necessary that the rehabilitation professional be aware of the problems and limitations that are characteristic of the consumer's severe disability. The initial interview can identify these concerns. Exploring the consumer's physical, social, educational, and occupational history during the initial interview can provide further information on the best possible ways to evaluate intelligence functioning.

For individuals with significant disabilities, the assessment of intelligence is not really a process that is different in "kind" from traditional evaluation but, rather, is different in "extent." At the same time, this testing process can be overwhelming to many consumers, particularly to those who are unaccustomed to testing. To alleviate consumer anxieties, time should be spent on explaining the goals of assessment and the purpose of each IQ test to be used. It is often beneficial to administer at least two intelligence measures. This can provide more comprehensive information for rehabilitation planning. After the preparation, and when two or more IQ measures are to be used, the following sequence is recommended. These recommendations embrace generally all those with significant disabilities; the consumer's physical and mental limitations must be considered, as well as what are appropriate testing accommodations. The following suggestions are focused more on an individual's educational history, past records, and past reading levels as a foundation for the selection and sequence of intelligence measures.

Identifying Intelligence Measures for Consumers

1. For consumers whose records contain no recent information on intelligence functioning, and whose educational background and reading ability are apparently poor:
   a. *Peabody Picture Vocabulary Test–Fourth Edition* (PPVT-IV; Dunn & Dunn, 2007); *Beta III* (Kellogg & Morton, 1999); *Raven's Progressive Matrices* (Raven, Raven, & Court, 2004); *Slosson Intelligence Test–Revised* (SIT-R3; Slosson, Nicholson, & Hibpshman, 1990); or the *Kaufman Brief Intelligence Test– Second Edition* (Kaufman & Kaufman, 2004); and then

    b. the *Wechsler Adult Intelligence Scale–Fourth Edition* (WAIS-IV; Wechsler, 2008)

2. For consumers who (a) have records containing no recent information on intelligence functioning and (b) have records indicating some high school education, any one of the measures identified previously in (1) can be used, but at least the *Beta III* or the *Kaufman Brief Intelligence Test–Second Edition* or the WAIS-IV.

3. For rehabilitation professionals who want an update on intelligence functioning for a consumer who has graduated from high school when interview information suggests a well-developed reading ability or recent educational training:

    a. *Kaufman Brief Intelligence Test–Second Edition*, and then

    b. WAIS-IV

Acknowledging Influences on IQ Development and Stability

Measured intellectual ability represents an interaction between innate ability and such environmental influences as family expectations and culture. Items on an intelligence test tend to reflect the culture of the society in which these tests are used. Culturally fair tests have been developed and tend to be nonverbal for the consumer, with directions that are simple, clear, and often administered orally by the evaluator. Culturally specific tests also have been developed for members of particular groups or subcultures (Cohen et al., 1996).

Considering Individual Differences Within Disability Groups

Earlier in this chapter the importance of selecting a test that is relevant to a specific disability was explained. However, attention must be given to differences among individuals who have the same identified disability. Visual and hearing impairments, for example, can be classified into different types, from someone who is totally blind or deaf to a person who can read efficiently if print is in larger type. Individuals with hearing impairments differ with respect to such variables as magnitude of hearing loss, age of loss onset, and consequential effects of the loss on language skills and social adjustment (Cohen et al., 1996). The Verbal

Comprehensive Index (VCI) can be used in evaluating the intellectual functioning of people with blindness or visual impairments. The rehabilitation professional should be aware, however, of the issues of language development and socialization skills when selecting an appropriate intelligence measure.

IQ Classification Chart

The following table, with information provided by Wechsler (2008), can be used when interpreting scores on traditional intelligence tests:

IQ Classification

130 and above: *Very superior*   80–89: *Low average*

120–129: *Superior*   70–79: *Borderline*

110–119: *High average*   69 and below: *Having mental retardation*

90–109: *Average*

Selected Useful Measures of Intelligence Functioning

This section identifies information on the different measures of intelligence functioning that are useful when evaluating consumers with disabilities. These tests emphasize developed general ability (i.e., achievement) more than the raw aptitude for such development.

Briefly, the WAIS-IV does have selected applications for those with disabilities. The *Peabody Picture Vocabulary Test–Fourth Edition* (PPVT-IV; Dunn & Dunn, 2007) is applicable for persons with mental retardation. The *Quick-Test* (Ammons & Ammons, 1962) is a valuable instrument for identifying a general range of intelligence functioning, although it is not applicable for persons with a visual impairment. The *Slosson Intelligence Test–Revised* (SIT-R3; Slosson, Nicholson, & Hibpshman, 2002) and *Raven's Progressive Matrices* (Raven, Raven, & Court, 2004) are appropriate for all handicaps, although they have limited use with persons with visual and hearing impairments (Siefker, 1996). The *Kaufman Brief*

Intelligence Test–Second Edition (KBIT-2; Kaufman & Kaufman, 2004) is applicable and very useful for several groups of persons with disabilities (Hood & Johnson, 2007).

Wechsler Adult Intelligence Scale– Fourth Edition

The WAIS-IV was revised in 2008 with several new features and benefits and with updated normative data for ages 16 to 90 years, reflecting also the abilities of today's population. This measure assesses general and specific intellectual characteristics, emphasizing a more comprehensive understanding of cognitive functioning. Wechsler (2008) believed that "intelligence is a function of the personality as a whole and is responsive to other factors besides those included under the concept of cognitive abilities. Intelligence tests inevitably measure these factors as well" (p. 8).

The WAIS-IV is a current version of the original WAIS-R and responds to changing societal demographics, emerging clinical needs, and new research in the field. The different updates of the WAIS tests over the past decades represent perhaps the best general adult intelligence test available, as they closely approximate the highest level of professional standards. This 2008 version, moreover, is reported to have five revision goals (http://www.pearsonassessments.com, 2012).

- *Expanded clinical utility* (new special group studies and co-normed with the *Wechsler Memory Scale IV*)
- *Increased developmental appropriateness* (more efficient administration time, reduced vocabulary level, or verbatim instructions, as well as reduced emphasis on motor demands and timed performance)
- *Enhanced user friendliness* (revised instructions, redesigned record form, expanded sample responses, simplified technical manual organization)
- *Improved psychometric properties* (updated norms, expanded full scale IQ range, improved subtest and composite reliability, reduced item bias)
- *Updated structural foundations* (a new measure of fluid intelligence, revised arithmetic and digit-span subtests, improved measures of processing speed, such as reducing fine motor demands)

With a completion time of 60 to 90 minutes for the 10 core subtests, the new WAIS-IV replaces the performance subscales from previous versions with index scores. Two broad scores are generated, which can also be used to summarize general intellectual abilities:

1. Full Scale IQ (FSIQ), which is based on the combined performance of the following indices, representing major components of intelligence.
    a. *Verbal Comprehension Index* (VCI) (Similarities, Vocabulary, Information, and Comprehension subtests)
    b. *Perceptual Reasoning Index* (PRI) (Block Design, Matrix Reasoning, Visual Puzzles [new], Picture Completion, and Figure Weights [new] subtests)
    c. *Working Memory Index* (WMI) (Digit Span, Arithmetic, and Letter-Number Sequencing subtests)
    d. *Processing Speed Index* (PSI) (Symbol Search, Coding, and Cancellation [new] subtests)
2. *General Ability Index* (GAI), which is based only on the nine subtests that the VCI and PRI comprise.

VCI Subtests

Similarities. Explores abstract verbal reasoning by presenting word pairs of increasing difficulty, for example, "In which way are an apple and a pear alike?"

Vocabulary. Words of increasing dificulty are presented both orally and visually. The subject is asked to define each word. This measures the degree to which one has learned and been able to comprehend and verbally express vocabulary.

Information. Questions are presented orally that cover a wide variety of information (events, objects, places, and people) that adults in the American culture should presumably acquire. An effort was made to avoid specialized or academic knowledge. This measures the degree of information acquired from culture.

Comprehension. Many items require the subject to understand and articulate social rules and concepts of solutions to everyday problems. This measures the ability to deal with abstract social conventions, rules, and expressions.

PRI Subtests

Matrix Reasoning. Traditional type of nonverbal task in which the examinee looks at a picture of geometric shapes and either names or points to the correct answer from five response options. This measures nonverbal, abstract problem solving and inductive reasoning.

Picture Completion. Subtest includes color pictures of common objects and settings, each of which is missing an important part. Examinee must identify the missing part by pointing or naming. This measures the ability to quickly perceive visual details.

Block Design. This test consists of increasingly complex designs made from two to nine cubes. Examinee must replicate two-dimensional geometric patterns using two colored cubes. This measures spatial perception, visual abstract processing, and problem solving.

Visual Puzzles (new). This subtest requires no motor skills and is reported to be more reliable than the Object Assembly subtest (http://www.pearsonassessments.com, 2012). The examinee is presented, for example, with three pieces and asked which ones go together to make this puzzle. This measures nonverbal reasoning.

Figure Weights (new). This subtest requires no motor skills and measures quantitative analogical reasoning.

Working Memory Index Subtests

Arithmetic. Many problems are similar to those encountered in elementary school arithmetic. Each problem is to be solved without the use of paper and pencil and is orally presented. This measures concentration while one manipulates mental mathematical problems.

Digit Span. The first task (Digits Forward) includes orally presented lists of two to nine digits that are to be repeated, verbatim, orally. In the second part (Digits Backward), the subject must repeat, backwards, lists of two to eight digits. This measures attention, concentration, and mental control.

Letter-Number Sequencing. This is a series of orally presented letters and numbers that are presented in a mixed-up order. The examinee must reorder and repeat the list by saying the numbers first in ascending order, and then the letters in alphabetical order. This measures attention and working memory.

PSI Subtests

Symbol Search. This subtest includes a series of paired groups of symbols, each pair consisting of a target group and a search group. The examinee indicates, by marking the appropriate box, whether a target symbol appears in the search group. This measures visual perception and speed.

Coding. This measures visual-motor coordination, motor speed, and mental speed.

Cancellation. This subtest measures visual perceptual speed. The examinee is presented with different pictures and is asked by the examiner, at a set start time, to draw a line, for example, through each red square and yellow triangle depicted in one of the pictures.

Although not normed with the population of those with a disability, many of the subtests within the Index groups can provide valuable information on the consumer's career-related strengths. The reduced emphasis in the WAIS-IV on motor demands and timed performance may facilitate the use of this valuable measure with a wider group of those with a disability. Particularly for those who have incurred brain damage, several of the WAIS-IV subtests may suggest the extent of the brain damage, especially in the area of attentional difficulties (http://en.wikipedia.org/wiki/Wechsler Adult Intelligence Scale).

To be noted is the use of shorter versions of the WAIS to form a valid estimate of verbal performance and Full Scale IQ in a shorter amount of time. Although most rehabilitation counselors do not directly administer or interpret the WAIS-R, it is helpful for counselors to become familiar with various short forms of the WAIS. For example, one short version of the Wechsler intelligence test is the *Wechsler Abbreviated Scale of Intelligence* (WASI), an individually administered intelligence test that was introduced in 1999 (Stano, 2004). Consisting of four subtests (Vocabulary, Block Design, Similarities, and Matrix Reasoning), it can be used as a screening device. The manual provides complete directions for administration and scoring. A psychometric technician can administer this test, although graduate-level training is required to interpret the results. To be noted is that all four subtests can be used to develop a Full Scale IQ. These subtests measure both fluid and crystallized intelligence, as well as verbal knowledge and nonverbal reasoning (Stano, 2004). The WASI is easy to use in rehabilitation settings, especially when cognitive screening is indicated. It is soundly constructed, with outstanding psychometric properties, and is available from the Psychological Corporation, San Antonio, TX (Stano, 2004).

The WAIS-IV, with additional software that can save time scoring and reporting results using the practical WAIS-IV Scoring Assistant and Report Writer software, is available from Pearson, 19500 Bulverde Rd., San Antonio, TX 78259-3701; 800/627-7271.

Stanford-Binet Intelligence Scales–Fifth Edition

The *Stanford-Binet Intelligence Scales–Fifth Edition* (SB5) took 7 years to complete. The SB5 is an individually administered, comprehensive intelligence test designed for consumers ages 2 to 85 years and over (Roid, 2003). It consists of five verbal and five nonverbal subtests, a more manageable number for assessing individuals in a rehabilitation setting (Lichtenburger, Kaufman, & Kaufman, 2008). Verbal subtests can require individuals to read, speak, and understand age-appropriate English. Nonverbal subtests expect minimal receptive language and additionally require fine motor coordination. The SB5 uses very few time limits. The full-scale battery normally takes between 45 and 75 minutes to administer; the abbreviated battery takes between 15 and 20 minutes to administer. Typical uses of the SB5 include diagnosing exceptionalities and developmental disabilities in adults, adolescents, and children. The manual states that the nonverbal subtests can be used for evaluating those with hearing impairments, communication disorders, limited English, and other areas in which verbal ability is limited.

Although the administrator of the test should have specialized training and supervision for using this instrument, the SB5 is highly correlated with major cognitive tests, such as the Wechsler Scales. During the test's latest development, studies were conducted with special populations; test fairness with regard to gender, race/ethnicity, and culture were carefully monitored; and the instrument was renormed. Also, the test has broadened the measurement of nonverbal abilities and added items to measure very low-functioning and very high-functioning individuals (Lichtenberger et al., 2008). Consequently, the SB5 appears to have validity for consumers from a great variety of backgrounds. Importantly, the SB5 now includes an appraisal area of Working Memory, useful for those with learning problems, and there is an expanded emphasis on nonverbal intelligence. Scoring software is available. Also, test materials can be viewed easily.

The SB5 is available from PRO-ED, Inc., 8700 Shoal Creek Blvd., Austin, TX 78757.

Slosson Intelligence Test–Revised

The *Slosson Intelligence Test–Revised* (SIT-R3; Slosson et al., 2002) is an individually administered oral test that can be used for initial screening purposes. The test is brief, and scoring is fairly objective. Because the test is oral, it can be used with individuals who are blind, have reading handicaps, have physical disabilities, cannot respond to paper-and-pencil tests, or cannot work effectively under the pressures of a timed test (e.g., those who are on heavy medication, individuals who are "test anxious").

Siders and Wharton (1982) explained that when providing educational services to children with mild disabilities, the SIT-R3 and the PPVT-IV may be used as quick screening devices. Also, if these tests do not rule out a disabling condition, such as mental retardation, they may be followed by a more in-depth exam.

As the manual states, the SIT-R3 has been re-standardized and improved across many areas. It is still designed to be a quick and reliable index of verbal intelligence, with the following areas of improvement:

1. The distribution of items within the item classification system of the SIT-R3 is more even, and the SIT-R3 test items are referenced in contemporary language.
2. The standardization sample is significantly larger and reflects stratification consistent with census data. Validity and reliability studies are more comprehensive.
3. The SIT-R3 permits answers in English or metric measures, where applicable.
4. The deviational Intelligence Quotient (IQ) is extended to a Total Standard Score (TSS).

Although no research is available on its use with adults with disabilities, the SIT-R3 can be used as a screening instrument with a population of those with a disability. Siefker (1996) explained that although the SIT-R3 is a screening instrument that should not be used in final placement decisions, it can estimate the cognitive ability of a person who has a mental illness or mental disability. The examiner should pay particular attention to the consumer's ability to respond to the test items. The SIT-R3 can be administered in 10 to 30 minutes. Because of the brevity of the test, it should be used in vocational assessment only with other supporting information, particularly in situations in which important diagnostic decisions are required.

The SIT-R3 is available from Slosson Educational Publications, PO Box 280, East Aurora, NY 14052, 800/828-4800.

Peabody Picture Vocabulary Test–Fourth Edition

The *Peabody Picture Vocabulary Test–Fourth Edition* (PPVT-IV; Dunn & Dunn, 2007) is an untimed individual intelligence test, orally administered in 11 to 12 minutes or less. Extensively revised, this test measures an individual's receptive (hearing) vocabulary for Standard American English. In addition, it provides a quick estimate of verbal ability or scholastic aptitude. Specifically, the PPVT-IV can be used for assessing the English vocabulary of non–English-speaking individuals and assessing adult verbal ability. No reading is required by the consumer, and scoring is rapid and objective. Item responses are made by pointing. The total score can be converted to a percentile rank, mental age, or standard deviation IQ score. No special training is required to administer, score, or interpret the PPVT-IV.

The national norms of the PPVT-IV have been extended to include ages 2-6 to 90 years of age. This edition was developed from adult norms obtained on 828 persons, ages 19 to 40 years, selected to be nationally representative of geographical regions and major occupational groups (Anastasi, 1988; Siefker, 1996). No people with disabilities were included in the norm population. A technical supplement gives detailed standardization data.

The PPVT-IV provides an estimate of the consumer's verbal intelligence and has been administered to groups that had reading or speech problems, had mental retardation, or were emotionally withdrawn. Because the manner of the consumer's response to stimulus vocabulary is to point in any fashion to one of four pictures that best fits the stimulus word, these tests also apply to rehabilitation consumers who have multiple physical disabilities, but whose hearing and vision are intact. The test also has high interest value, and this can establish good rapport with the consumer. For its administration, the examiner presents a series of pictures to each consumer. There are four pictures to a page, and each is numbered. The examiner states a word describing one of the pictures and asks the consumer to point to or tell the number of the picture that the word describes.

The test is not useful in its present form for people who are blind or deaf but can be useful for people with mental retardation, for whom no modifications in instructions or format are needed. The only possible problem is that the illustrations for about the first 50 items often depict children. This may not be acceptable to the adult with mental retardation.

The PPVT-IV is available from Pearson, 19500 Bulverde Rd., San Antonio, TX 78259, 800/627-7271.

Beta III

The *Beta III* (Kellogg & Morton, 1999) is designed to serve as a measure of the general intellectual ability of persons who are relatively illiterate or non–English speaking. A nonverbal estimate of intelligence is given as a single IQ score. It is designed for individual or group administration. Including instruction, it can be administered in about 30 minutes. Subtests are timed and last from 1½ to 4 minutes. A Spanish translation of the directions for administration is also included in the back of the manual.

The test contains six separately timed tests that measure different aspects of nonverbal ability:

1. Mazes: marking the shortest distance through a maze without crossing any lines.
2. Coding: matching figures with their corresponding numbers.
3. Paper Form Boards: fitting figures together to form squares.
4. Picture Completion: filling in the parts of pictures that have been omitted.
5. Clerical Checking: marking pairs that are alike.
6. Picture Absurdities: identifying drawings that are wrong or foolish.

No reading is required for this test; it is mainly designed for illiterate consumers. All responses are recorded in a non-reusable booklet. The ability to hold a pencil and print numbers and enough dexterity to trace mazes are required for recording the responses. Each subtest includes several demonstration items and at least three practice items, along with instructions requesting that the examiner carefully check the consumer's performance on each item.

This test is not usable in its present form for consumers with severe visual limitations. It can, however, be used effectively with consumers who have mental retardation. The only problem that may arise is the abstract quality of some of the items in several of the subtests. With modifications, the test can also be used with individuals who are deaf, due to the visual content as well as the fact that the test can be individually administered. The problem is in giving the instructions, which could be signed or placed on cards for the consumer to read. The consumer who cannot understand signing and who cannot read could be administered the *Beta III* if the examiner carefully goes over each practice exercise.

The *Beta III* is available from Pearson, 19500 Bulverde Rd., San Antonio, TX 78259, 800/627-7271.

Raven's Progressive Matrices

Raven's Progressive Matrices (Raven, Raven, & Court, 2004) are designed to measure general ability, especially the ability to perceive and use relationships between nonverbal materials. It taps such qualities of the intellect as spatial aptitude, inductive reasoning, and perceptual accuracy. The tasks, or matrices, consist of designs that are incomplete. The individual being tested chooses from several designs or patterns and selects the pattern that best completes the matrix.

Raven's Progressive Matrices are available at three levels and can be used with persons age 5 years or older. The test can be administered individually or in groups and is hand scored. It is easy to administer and relatively brief. Although not useful for individuals with visual impairment, the test is helpful with consumers with physical disabilities or emotional disturbance. There is no time limit to the test, and this is a favorable feature for many consumers who have disabilities.

A literature review indicates no research on use or standardization of *Raven's Progressive Matrices* with the population of persons with disabilities. There are percentiles for children ages 5½ through 11½ years, percentiles specifically for British schoolchildren, and means and standard deviations for several adult groups. This test should be used in conjunction with a vocabulary test, which will provide an index of the general information a consumer has acquired up to the present as well as his or her command of the English language.

Raven's Progressive Matrices are available from Pearson, 19500 Bulverde Rd., San Antonio, TX 78259, 800/627-7271.

Quick-Test

The *Quick-Test* (QT; Ammons & Ammons, 1962) is a carefully standardized individual intelligence test in three forms, based on perceptual–verbal performance. It takes 3 to 10 minutes to administer. Anyone who can see the drawings, hear or read the word items, and signal "yes" or "no" can take this assessment instrument. The consumer is not required to read, write, or speak. With adequate administration, scoring is quick and objective. Item responses are easily scored during the administration of the test. Summary scores, mental ages, tentative IQs, and percentile ranks can be quickly computed or read from tables on the record form and in the manual. The examiner should be aware that the drawings are dated and that the standardization group, although controlled on an exact, simultaneous quota basis for age, gender, and educational level, is not representative of the diverse population currently in the United States.

This test is most helpful for gaining a general understanding of a consumer's perceptual–verbal functioning. The measure should be followed by a more comprehensive test, such as the WAIS-IV, after an estimate of the consumer's functioning has been achieved, although many rehabilitation practitioners use the results of this test to move into an assessment exploration of aptitudes and abilities.

The QT can be used with individuals with hearing impairments, but it is not suitable for those who are blind. The test can also be used to build rapport in the testing situation, to test persons with short attention spans, and to estimate the intelligence of persons with severe physical disabilities (for whom larger and more complicated tests may not be appropriate). Reported reliabilities of single forms of the QT have been high, with a range of 0.78 to 0.97. The QT is designed for quick, efficient estimations of general levels of intellectual ability when circumstances are less than optimal and time is limited.

The QT is available from Psychological Test Specialists, PO Box 9229, Missoula, MT 59807, 406/728-1710.

Kaufman Brief Intelligence Test–Second Edition

An individually administered assessment of verbal and nonverbal intelligence of individuals ages 4 to 90 years, the *Kaufman Brief Intelligence Test–Second Edition* (KBIT-2; Kaufman & Kaufman, 2004) is designed so that it can be administered by the evaluator in just 15 to 30 minutes. It is useful for (a) identifying individuals who may require further evaluation; (b) obtaining a quick estimate of the intellectual ability of adults in institutional settings, such as group homes, rehabilitation clinics, or mental health centers; (c) reevaluating periodically the intellectual status of an adult who previously had been administered a thorough psychological battery; and (d) obtaining information useful for vocational and rehabilitation settings. The test provides three scores: verbal, nonverbal, and overall IQ composite.

The vocabulary (or verbal) subtest measures school-related skills and is divided into two parts: expressive vocabulary (45 items) and definitions (37 items). The nonverbal subtest measures nonverbal skills and the ability to solve new problems (48 matrixes). All matrixes involve pictures and abstract designs rather than words.

The KBIT-2 was normed on a national standardization sample that matched U.S. Census data and included more than 2,000 individuals, ages 4 to 90 years. Concurrent validity was established by analysis with the WAIS-R and the WISC-R. Concerning reliability, both test–retest and internal consistency studies showed 0.93 for the KBIT-2 composite, with equally strong reliability coefficients for the vocabulary and matrixes subtests.

The KBIT-2 is available from Pearson, 19500 Bulverde Rd., San Antonio, TX 78259, 800/627-7271.

The Mental Status Examination

With head injuries and undiagnosed memory problems increasing in the caseloads of rehabilitation counselors (DeVinney, Tansey, Ferrin, & Pruett, 2005), identifying persons who may require additional evaluation prior to vocational plan development can benefit both the consumer and the professional. While psychiatrists or psychologists might perform a more comprehensive mental status examination, the suggested short, structured assessment offered by DeVinney et al. (2005) is designed to be used as a screening tool of an individual's mental state. This administration does not require extensive training and takes approximately 10 to 15 minutes to administer. The symptoms and behaviors observed with certain mental status problems are particularly significant in vocational assessment, since they present an individual's limitations in participating in vocational evaluation (DeVinney et al., 2005). This suggested brief mental status examination is recommended for the counselor's consideration, especially when the professional is concerned about the consumer's mental functioning. This appraisal can be integrated into the initial interview and consists of nine aspects of individual behavior.

- Appearance
  - dress and grooming
  - facial expression
  - posture and gait
  - eye contact
  - physical characteristics
  - motor activity
  - specific mannerisms
- Orientation to time and place
- Speech
  - rate
  - pitch, volume, clarity
- Thinking
  - flow of ideas
  - fund of knowledge
  - quality of associations
  - content (distortions, obsessions, phobias, suicidal ideation, somatic concerns, illusions, hallucinations)
- Attention, concentration
- Memory (immediate, recent, and past)
  - alertness
- Emotional state (response to disability event)
  - mood
  - affect (variability, appropriateness)
- Attitude toward the counselor
- Insight and judgment

This assessment may be used to verify the counselor's impressions, and the above nine aspects of behavior may be recognized by listening carefully to the consumer's responses to counselor questions, such as "Can you describe a typical day for you?" or "What do you think is your greatest difficulty in managing your disability?," and via observation of the consumer's facial and body movements, his or her word selection, how the consumer talks about sensitive topics, and how the consumer responds to the question "How can I help you?"

Neuropsychological Assessment

As previously stated, individuals who have had a head injury or related neurological diagnosis are increasing in number on counselors' caseloads, and there is an accompanying need for the rehabilitation counselor to understand selected dynamics of neuropsychological assessment.

Head injuries can produce a wide array of impairments. The vocational evaluator is not concerned with differential diagnoses in the usual sense. What the evaluator needs is assessment feedback that identifies the full range of cognitive assets and deficits, as a meaningful rehabilitation program can be formulated only through a complete identification of cognitive assets and deficits (Baxter et al., 1985). Assessment results should indicate what consumers know as well as what they do not know. It is most helpful, when possible, to evaluate general intelligence in persons who have brain injuries because this allows the professional to determine whether the consumer has access to previously acquired knowledge. Also, because of the consumer's cognitive deficits, it is often necessary to have evaluation materials with a variety of response modes and that have content presented in different formats (Baxter et al., 1985).

Rehabilitation counselors will initially see persons after diagnosis and in-hospital care who are neurologically impaired and now are undergoing a treatment regimen on an outpatient basis that may include learning new independent living activities and re-establishing career goals. Psychologists and occupational therapists are usually involved in this treatment plan. But the rehabilitation counselor should understand the targets of the neurological assessment with those who have undergone a changed, cognitive status. Ruff and Schraa (2001) identified such targets and evaluated three major cognitive domains:

- Attention and concentration, which include arousal and alertness, selective attention, and speed of processing. Selective attention is the ability to set priorities in information processing.
- Memory and learning, essential in vocational rehabilitation because of the necessity to remember information from day to day. Remote memory functions (information before disability onset) and recent memory (information since disability onset) are also evaluated.
- Executive functioning, which includes decision making ability, maintenance of day-to-day interpersonal relationships, concept formation, and patterns of emotional responsiveness

Many of these target areas that embrace vocational functioning and neuropsychological assessment will identify the deficits that limit the consumer's ability to function independently, and that limit vocational rehabilitation potential (Ruff & Schraa, 2001). Different appraisal instruments are used to determine the consumer's functioning in these areas. Such information should be included in the consumer's case file, and with the consumer's permission, the counselor should have access to an interpretation of the results so that an assessment can be made on what the consumer needs to perform appropriately during vocational assessment and what neurological factors should be considered in vocational planning. Psychologists and other allied health professionals may provide this interpretation. Importantly, the results of neurological testing help the consumer to understand his or her cognitive limitations and residual strengths, and help the rehabilitation counselor to identify assistive methods and modification needs during vocational assessment and the vocational rehabilitation process itself.

The dynamics of cognitive assessment are complex. For the rehabilitation counselor these focus on selected knowledge of intelligence assessment, and the utilization of specific skills that target cognitive functioning. As emphasized in this module, these skills include interpreting existing cognitive records in a vocational rehabilitation perspective and administering appropriate instruments, when needed, to the consumer.

Such skills reside under the umbrella of necessary competency skills in vocational assessment for the rehabilitation counselor.

Two widely used batteries for exploring cognitive deficits in persons with brain injury are the *Luria-Nebraska Neuropsychological Battery* and the *Halstead-Reitan Neuropsychological Test Battery*. Both instruments require specific skills in administration and interpretation that demand specialized preparation.

Luria-Nebraska Neuropsychological Battery

Baxter et al. (1985) explained that the test items on the *Luria-Nebraska Neuropsychological Battery* (Golden, Purisch, & Hammeke, 1985) are divided in such a way that composite scores can be obtained for each of the 11 scales of functioning: Motor, Rhythm, Tactile, Visual, Receptive Language, Expressive Language, Writing, Reading, Arithmetic, Memory, and Intellectual Processes. Items within each scale are designed to measure, in both simple and complex forms, more than the particular ability suggested by the name of the scale. Items from each of the 11 regular scales are used to generate two additional sets of scales. The first of these scales provides a basis for inferring the lateralization and localization of cortical lesions, and the second provides specific information on such basic skills and abilities as visual acuity and naming, phonemic discrimination, simple tactile sensation, and 27 additional areas of cognitive function. Consumer scores are compared to a Critical Level, which is determined on the basis of age and education. The Luria-Nebraska batteries represent efforts to translate directly Luria's (1973) theories of brain–behavior relationships into a standardized test procedure.

Halstead-Reitan Neuropsychological Test Battery

The *Halstead-Reitan Neuropsychological Test Battery* (Reitan, 1993) was devised by Ward Halstead (1947), and development has been continued by Ralph Reitan (Baxter et al., 1985). In its current form, the battery consists of five tests (Category Test, Tactual Performance Test, Speech Sounds Perception Test, Finger Tapping Test, and Seashore Rhythm Test), which are supplemented by Reitan's inclusion of an aphasia examination, a sensory–perceptual examination, the Trail Making Test (parts A and B), and a measure of bilateral grip strength.

Conclusion

In rehabilitation, assessment of the consumer's competence in handling everyday situations can be most valuable. This information can help consumers to appreciate their remaining capacities after a serious trauma has brought extensive physical limitations. Also, many consumers may have no idea about their general ranges of intellectual functioning because they have received no feedback about this capacity for years. An awareness of this information can be a stimulus to a more realistic, individually oriented rehabilitation plan. All the evaluation data should lead to effective, individualized rehabilitation programming.

While an assessment of intellectual functioning can be useful for the development of the consumer's rehabilitation plan—especially one that includes employment training—there are a number of difficulties regarding the selection of IQ tests. Intelligence is an inferred construct, and the evaluator should determine what behaviors are going to be assessed by the test items. Also, most group intelligence tests are not standardized on representative populations, or they may be standardized on volunteer samples that can introduce bias into the standardization. The choice of a test should depend on the rehabilitation professional's training and the purpose for obtaining information on intelligence functioning.

The rehabilitation professional's training is an essential consideration when administering many intelligence assessment measures. As noted earlier in this chapter, specific training is required for the administration of the WAIS-IV, the *Luria-Nebraska Neuropsychological Battery,* and the *Halstead-Reitan Neuropsychological Test Battery.* Educational institutions offer specialized courses in the theory and practice of these instruments.

Rehabilitation psychologists and neuropsychologists who specifically work with populations that have incurred significant cognitive or neurological deficits use these aforementioned tests. When vocational evaluation is conducted with, for example, individuals who are traumatically brain injured, it is important for the neuropsychologist to explain the vocational implications of the test results. If a consumer's consciousness, perception, memory, learning, thinking, and reasoning have been weakened by the injury, as test results indicate, then what are the accompanying vocational restrictions? Head trauma can affect retentive memory, the understanding of meaning and relationships of words and sentences, attention to detail, ability to relate to people, and lucidity of expression. Each limitation can affect satisfactory job performance.

But assessment cannot end with an understanding of the consumer's intelligence potential. Along with identification of areas of consumer interest (explained in Chapter 7), more information on other areas of consumer functioning, such as achievement and personality, is needed. The following chapters identify and describe these assessment approaches.

Chapter 9

Personality Assessment in Vocational Rehabilitation

One of the important goals in rehabilitation is to assist the consumer with a disability in achieving satisfaction in a job or similar productive opportunity. This goal implies more than skill proficiency. Individual needs and motivation, the ability to get along with others, and a capacity to cope with employment-related demands are all aspects of personal functioning that are of major importance for the consumer's suitable job adjustment and success. Moreover, many consumers beginning the rehabilitation process bring with them continued problems of anxiety, difficulties in continuing with a job or training program, and behavioral patterns such as overdependency and aggressiveness. All of these patterns are antithetical to appropriate placement in a job setting. All of these considerations emphasize the need for evaluation of personality functioning in rehabilitation.

Also, if vocational assessment is to be an "empowering experience" for the consumer, then choices or options must be available. Underlying the selection of options is the awareness on the part of the evaluator and consumer of those characteristics that are more suitable for different directions in vocational planning and employment. Additional information about characteristics such as the consumer's emotional reaction to a disability, personal needs and values, and maturity can prove to be very helpful in selecting an assessment approach and structuring individual vocational plans. In their review of the rehabilitation literature, Kaplan and Questad (1980) reported that motivation, self-concept, and acceptance of and adjustment to disability are specific consumer characteristics that are critical for successful rehabilitation outcomes. Self-concept, particularly, is often a very useful predictor of rehabilitation success. Personality assessment plays a significant role in facilitating appropriate choices for the consumer and even reducing uncertainty related to career and employment decisions (Krug, 2008).

In the early days of the rehabilitation movement, when services emphasized physical restoration, the assessment of personality was considered to be irrelevant for most consumers. However, when vocational rehabilitation evolved and began to undertake work with consumers who had mental retardation, severe disabilities, mental illness, alcoholism, and social disadvantages, many counselors resisted working with these populations, claiming that the consumer problems were too severe. When these persons were accepted for rehabilitation services, some counselors were determined to apply the same evaluation procedures that had succeeded with their previous consumers. These approaches largely ignored the personality functioning of the people with disabilities and presumed that an understanding of cognitive ability alone could explain why the consumer would or would not do well at a specific job. When the proportion of failures grew and, out of necessity, the impact of personality functioning on job adjustment was explored, the practice of evaluating a consumer's personality characteristics gradually became more common in vocational rehabilitation. In fact, counselors learned that some personality traits may predispose the consumer to function well in some occupational areas and badly in others.

For those with disabilities, the relationship between personality and career development plays an important role in vocational evaluation approaches. An individual's personality affects career decision making, on-the-job performance, and occupational success, as well as dictating the relative strengths that influence job competencies and job satisfaction (Kjos, 1995). Effectiveness in assessment outcomes is enhanced by the evaluator's ability to identify personality styles and personality disorders that may inhibit or facilitate an individual's adjustment to a disability and achievement of appropriate employment goals.

The purpose of personality assessment in rehabilitation is to identify personality strengths or deficits that influence job demands, including where and how the consumer can function effectively and what training may be needed to enhance the behaviors required for suitable job adjustment (Maki, Pape, & Prout, 1979). In other words, this assessment attempts to reduce uncertainty in making career decisions. Additional information may prove very helpful in developing plans following the assessment process (Krug, 2008). In rehabilitation, the term *personality* refers to consumer information related to typical behaviors, rather than to intellectual attributes. Consequently, personality is defined as "the system whereby the individual characteristically organizes and processes biophysical and environmental inputs to produce behavior in interactions with the larger surrounding systems" (Sundberg, 1977, p. 12).

For the rehabilitation worker, personality is a constellation of interests, needs, values, and behaviors that allows an individual to meet appropriate work rules in a particular job setting. In vocational evaluation, personality assessment should focus on the behaviors necessary for employment or productive output. Work behavior is a complex set of interactions between the consumer and his or her environment (Hursh & Kerns, 1988). Because of these interactions, personality assessment should identify factors that will facilitate adjustment between the consumer and the work environment.

The definition of personality can be extended, however, to include more current research that identifies five dimensions that account for the ways in which we describe others and ourselves. These dimensions "have enjoyed wide acceptance and have assumed an important, perhaps central, role in guiding current thinking about normal range personality" (Krug, 2001, p. 127). The dimensions of extroversion, agreeableness, conscientiousness (willpower), emotional stability, and intellect (openness to experience or culture) form a framework in which to evaluate similarities and differences among various personality measures (Krug, 2001, 2008). These dimensions can also help the evaluator explore characteristics that suggest appropriate work or career adjustment.

With the recognition of such dimensions, there are specific terms related to personality functioning. *Vocational personality* is a term often used in vocational rehabilitation and is a product of a lengthy developmental process that begins at a young age, is a learned entity shaped by rudimentary work experiences, and encompasses the concept of self as a worker as well as motivation to work (Bolton, 1997). It is a reflection of the consumer's basic trait structure. A *trait* is usually observable, stable, and enduring and significantly contributes to the consumer's behaviors. A *state*, however, is a less stable characteristic and more of a transitory exhibition of some personality trait—a temporary predisposition. For example, a consumer may be in an anxious state but is not an anxious person. In vocational rehabilitation, assessment efforts reach out to both traits and states of the consumer with a disability.

A consumer's *vocational functioning* may include the following facets of traits or states:

needs	values
mood	personality style
motivation	self-concept
acceptance of disability	capacity to face one's problems
limitations	attitudes toward self and others
temperament	troubling behaviors
coping behaviors	dysfunctional behaviors

Although the identification of any behaviors that may negatively influence the achievement of vocational goals, and even predispose the consumer to failure, is not ignored during vocational assessment, the emphasis is on those behaviors that are facilitators to vocational adjustment, decision-making, and the attainment of career goals. These behaviors include the personality characteristics identified above. But it is a positive, strength-based understanding of these behaviors that brings to vocational personality assessment a distinctive perspective. During appraisal the rehabilitation counselor is continually asking the question, "What are the personality strengths of my consumer?" Table 9.1 identifies personality traits that are important to recognize during vocational assessment. This table also includes personality measures and possible problem areas related to specific personality traits and, importantly, targets behavioral areas necessary for vocational planning.

Integral to the personality functioning of the individual with a disability or chronic illness is his or her emotional reaction to the experience. Persons with disabilities vary in their abilities to deal with the occupational and possible social losses caused by job-related injuries. The time required for medical treatment, the stress of rehabilitation, the lack of mobility, and concern with possible changing personal appearance may precipitate a number of crises for the individual. The consumer may not be motivated to reach and maintain projected functional levels of performance. Instead, a life of social isolation and dependency on others may be preferred to one in which all the person's energies are exhausted in the attempt to reach a maximum level of occupational and family productivity.

Table 9.1

Identification of Personality Traits

Personality traits	Personality measure	Vocational functioning problem areas
Mood and temperament (general appearance and behavior)	MMPI 16 PF CPI	• Relationship to supervisors and other workers • Frustration tolerance • Adjustment to strains and pressures of work environment

Attitude
  Toward self
  Toward others
    (orientation toward other people)
	PSI Tennessee Self- Concept CPI MBTI RSE	• Sense of responsibility
		• Successful job performance
		• Cooperativeness
		• On-the-job social skills
		• Self-confidence in the work situation
		• Follows instructions and practices work safety
		• Self-presentation (dress, appearance, grooming, posture, method of talking to others

Motivation
  Energy level
  Goal-directedness
	16 PF CPI	• Seeks rehabilitation goals
		• Energy on job
		• Meets work demands, such as punctuality or continuing at task
		• Work habits
		• Response to pleasant or unpleasant tasks
		• Acceptance of work role

Adjustment to disability
  Coping resources
  Capacity to face one's problems
Strengths of client
	PSI MMPI 16 PF CPI	• Reality orientation—accepts limitations
		• Dependent or independent role in work situation
		• Coping mechanisms for dealing with stress on the job

Needs
  Security
  Variety recognition
  Status responsibility
  Creativity
  Achievement
    independence
	16 PF	• Change orientation
		• Adaptability
		• Ability to take risks with self

Values	MIQ SWV	• Clarify work or life goals • Achievement orientation • Work satisfaction

Note. MMPI = *Minnesota Multiphasic Personality Inventory* (Hathaway, McKinley, & Butcher, 1990); 16 PF = *Sixteen Personality Factor Questionnaire* (Cattell, 1986); CPI = *California Psychological Inventory* (Bough & Bradley, 1996); PSI =*Psychological Screening Inventory* (Lanyon, 2010); MBTI = *Myers-Briggs Type Indicator* (Myers & Briggs, 1988); RSE = *Rosenberg Self-Esteem Scale* (Rosenberg, 1979); MIQ = *Minnesota Importance Questionnaire* (Rounds et al., 1981); SWV = *Survey of Work Values* (Wollack et al., 1976).

The experience of the sudden onset of a disability in adulthood can affect one's belief in the world at large, belief in oneself, and belief in the cause-and-effect nature of crisis (Scott, 1998). The disability occurrence forces the realistic appraisal of these beliefs. Many emotions and attitudes surface, consequently, that can impact one's physical adjustment and motivation to pursue further occupational opportunities. Scott (1998) referred to the work of Horowitz (1983), who presents the following phases of recovery from sudden onset of physical disability, and his research is still relevant many years later.

Outcry→ denial→ intrusiveness→ working through → completion

Consumers may *deny* the circumstances of the injury, its severity, the prognosis concerning the restoration of work-related functions, the need for difficult medical interventions, and the temporary or permanent impact on life functioning. The injured worker may state, "I know they are wrong . . . they don't know me, I'm different . . . I'm glad to be alive. Nothing has really changed." These beliefs may be accompanied by the following:

- *Intrusive recollections,* in which the emotional experience is revisited, with intense feelings of helplessness, fear, and anxiety. The consumer's mind seeks reevaluation and integration of the experience through reliving and recalling. These recollections become important to clarification and adaptation (Janoff-Bulman, 1992).
- *Working through,* a phase characterized by counting the personal losses associated with the injury and grieving over these losses, which may take days, weeks, or months, accompanied often by depression. The management of depression is necessary to the overall assessment of the injured worker's status of returning to work. Further factors included in the working-through process leading to eventual life adjustment are the availability of family and social support, and evaluating the meaning behind the onset of disability in a search for control and a need to make sense of a world that simply makes *no sense* (Scott, 1998). Such questions as "Why did I ..." or "If I only had ..." enable the injured worker to confront the disability or disease event and attempt to make sense of it. Self-blame is adaptive when the individual is able to separate the behavior from the person (Dunn, 1994). The consumer, consequently, acknowledges the disability or injury itself, and its implications.

From this stage of acknowledgment or working through, the person begins to adjust to the disability. This adjustment can range from rehabilitation exploration to disengagement from any rehabilitation opportunities. There are many reasons why persons make such choices: satisfaction with work, the presence or absence of therapeutic intervention, the life (or developmental) stage, reaction to previous crises, the personality of the individual before the disability, the consumer's philosophy of life, and the personal meaning the individual makes of the disability injury or chronic illness. When the rehabilitation professional observes that an especially negative reaction to the injury or chronic disease is occurring, these factors should be carefully explored. Also, it should be determined whether the consumer is using symptoms for secondary gain. If the person is actually getting more reinforcement or benefits from being disabled than nondisabled, it will be very difficult to motivate him or her for rehabilitation purposes.

Assessing all of these emotional factors in personality functioning and identifying the degree to which the consumer is coping with the disability can generate invaluable information for the determination of readiness for assessment and eventual rehabilitation planning. Just as emotional reactions differ, coping styles vary as well. The consumer has several choices: minimize the disability through selective inattention, ignoring, denial, or rationalizing of the significance of the injury; make attempts to "master" or "control" the implications of the disability by identifying other compensating abilities and using energy for productive purposes; or simply give up and lead a life of inactivity and passivity. An awareness of the injured person's coping style can influence the direction of rehabilitation intervention.

What is needed in vocational rehabilitation for an appropriate personality evaluation, consequently, is an exploration that includes the consumer's emotional reaction to the disability/chronic illness event and a description of the consumer's behavior in positive, observable, quantifiable, understandable, and functional terms (Field, 1979). Because a rehabilitation counselor is primarily responsible for planning and developing the consumer's rehabilitation process—which also implies collecting relevant and essential information needed for consumer planning—the counselor should be concerned about obtaining information on the consumer's personality or behavior functioning that is vocationally oriented. Consumer planning assumes that the counselor understands the particular behaviors needed to perform certain jobs adequately, so the assessment should focus on the behaviors that the consumer typically shows that are relevant to job situations. The utilization of selected personality measures, work samples, and situational assessment may provide information on those consumer behaviors relevant to career/employment opportunities.

In personality assessment, definite personality patterns or clusters of behavioral problems are not associated with particular disabilities. Problems associated with motivation or interpersonal relationships may be found with consumers having orthopedic problems, visual impairments, or emotional difficulties. However, certain behavioral deficits, such as high distractibility or continued lack of sustained concentration, are very often identified among persons with neurological illnesses or severe emotional problems. Also, medications that are used with certain conditions, particularly mental disorders, may cause passivity or related effects. All of these factors should be considered by the rehabilitation professional, for they may influence the consumer's response to rehabilitation demands.

Collecting Information on Personality Functioning

In vocational rehabilitation, the traditional way to obtain an evaluation of personality functioning resulting from the disability/chronic illness event is to authorize a referral for a *psychological workup* from a psychologist or a psychiatrist. Occasionally an adequately trained and certified vocational evaluator/counselor may also seek to identify a consumer's emotional problem areas, to recognize domains of personality strengths, or to confirm his or her own hunches about the consumer's personality difficulties by using appropriate tests. But usually an approved psychologist administers a battery of tests and then develops a report to be given to the referring agency. The report by the psychiatrist or psychologist usually consists of a brief description of the consumer, a socio-psychological history, and a clinical summary of the present condition. The result is a diagnosis. The report emphasizes the results of the test battery and a summary of consumer behaviors. Unfortunately, these reports often contain information that is not vocationally relevant, or they do not provide an assessment of the consumer's residual emotional strengths that can be used in vocational training or employment. When reading these reports, the rehabilitation professional frequently has to translate the meaning of the described behaviors into vocationally relevant terms.

To assist in the development of the report's credibility, however, the rehabilitation professional might consider asking the referral source the following questions:

1. Has the consumer shown emotional reactions toward the disability that may be obstacles to adequate vocational adjustment?
2. How is the consumer likely to respond in a high-production or high-stress job?
3. Will the consumer respond appropriately to supervision on the job?
4. On a job that brings close association or collaboration with other workers, can the consumer adjust to this demand? Can the consumer, for example, take criticism, get along with others, and, when appropriate, be assertive?
5. How does the consumer understand the daily adjustmental implications of his or her disability?
6. Is the consumer able to work independently, control any tendency toward impulsiveness or continued anxiety, and take responsibility for job-related decisions?

The consumer may be involved in taking personality measures during the vocational assessment by a vocational evaluator. Responses to a personality inventory make up consumers' attempts to describe—for themselves and specific others, such as the rehabilitation professional—the way they see themselves in terms of the behaviors described in each inventory item. Such inventories provide a picture of the extent to which consumers are able to face themselves or are willing to have others see them as they think they are. Personality inventories probe into feelings and attitudes that many people normally conceal and regard as private. It is the rehabilitation professional's responsibility, consequently, to create conditions that assist the consumer in generating information that is useful for self-understanding and self-acceptance.

When the consumer is participating in personality assessment during vocational evaluation, there are different methods for identifying and measuring the personality domains that are applicable for his or her vocational functioning. Many of these methods require specialized training and appropriate certification.

Verbal techniques—Verbal techniques may include many visual stimuli that are presented to the consumer, who gives a verbal response. The *Rorschach* (Rorschach, 1942) and the *Thematic Apperception Test* (TAZ-Z; Murray & Morgan, 1935) are examples of this method. Other projective stimuli may be simple questions, such as, "If you had three wishes, what would you wish for?" and "What did you like most about school or the most recent training?"

Drawing techniques—When professionals are exploring personality traits, such instruments as the *Bender Visual Motor Gestalt Test* (Bender, 1992) and the *Kinetic Drawing System for Family and School* (Knoff & Prout, 1985) may be used. Many consumers find that drawing is a more appropriate expression for their perceptions related to adjustment to disabilities, as well as their reaction to the world around them. The way an individual approaches drawing stimuli often reflects how that person approaches life situations.

Manipulative methods—Toys or similar materials may be used, particularly with younger people, to explore temperaments, moods, or feelings about relationships.

As stated, all of these techniques, however, require a great deal of education and training to administer and interpret correctly. Such training is usually not in the professional preparation of the rehabilitation worker; rather, psychologists are more specifically trained to administer these evaluation tools.

When personality assessment is performed with a consumer, moreover, certain tests described in this chapter may be more useful than others. The main purpose of these measures is to screen the consumer or gain more supportive information for the professional's perceptions acquired during the interview. With these goals in mind, the following approaches are recommended:

Screening or supportive information:

Step 1—*Psychological Screening Inventory* (PSI; Lanyon, 2010)

Step 2—*Rosenberg Self-Esteem Scale* (Rosenberg, 1978)

Step 3—*California Psychological Inventory–1996 Revision* (Gough & Bradley, 1996)

Step 4—*Tennessee Self-Concept Scale* or Myers-Briggs (Fitts & Warren, 1996)

An understanding of the consumer's self-concept is helpful when evaluating attitudes toward self and motivation for rehabilitation. The results of the PSI suggest the ways in which the consumer is reacting behaviorally to the disability. For example, is the consumer showing much discomfort and feeling greatly alienated from others?

Consumer's understanding of needs and personality factors:

Step 1—*Minnesota Importance Questionnaire*

Step 2—16 PF, Form E, or *California Psychological Inventory* or Myers-Briggs

To be useful for rehabilitation planning, the results of these inventories must be interpreted from the perspective of rehabilitation needs and goals. If further information obtained from the 16 PF indicates high scores on assertiveness, conscientiousness, practicality, and controlled personality factors, then this personality style of the consumer in a work or independent living situation might be explored. In other words, the results of the two measures can be interpreted together, and such interpretation enables the consumer to gain added self-insight into rehabilitation strengths and weaknesses.

Differential diagnosis:

Step 1—*Minnesota Multiphasic Personality Inventory*, when appropriate

Step 2—*Tennessee Self-Concept Scale*

Issues to Consider When Collecting Personality Information

The most popular and widely used technique to assess personality is the personality questionnaire. It can be administered to individuals or to groups and usually is easily administered and scored. Questionnaires exist to measure all the different dimensions of personality: attitudes, adjustment, temperament, values, motivation, and anxiety. It is important to note that personality questionnaires and many verbal techniques use the self-report method. Krug (2001) believed that this method is the most highly researched and critically examined mode of measurement, but it is not clear whether the self-report method represents a significant loss in reliability or validity.

Rehabilitation counselors engaged in any personality assessment usually either read reports from personality inventories or administer informal or formal measures. The following are questions that need to be asked when choosing a personality appraisal instrument:

- What is the purpose of the personality measure? What is it designed to do?
- Is the measure designed to appraise traits, states, or some combination thereof?
- Can the instrument be used to gauge the relative strength of various traits? Is it to be used to identify individuals on the basis of the suitability of their personalities for vocational training or vocational adjustment?
- What kinds of ideas does the inventory/questionnaire contain? Are they culture free? Do the items minimize bias toward those with disabilities or who represent a minority ethnic culture or a specific gender? Does the response format enable the consumer to answer readily and confidently?
- Does the test have reported validity and reliability?
- Are the items or tasks to be responded to written clearly and unambiguously?

These questions are asked because there are concerns with using or reviewing personality instruments and results. The standardization samples and test content could be inappropriate for the consumer using the measure. There are differences in the ways consumers with a disability will respond to the instrument itself. Personality inventories can be very threatening to many consumers. Fear of exposing one's perceived deficits and what will happen to the test results are real issues for the consumer.

When engaging in reviewing personality test results or administering a personality instrument, the professional should be aware that there are many ways consumers can avoid the self-revelation emerging from personality methods. The consumer may tend to distort responses in a particular direction, regardless of the instrument's content, to avoid threatening feedback. When responding, they may offer a positive response regardless of which questions are asked. Consumers may wish to produce a certain image and may choose the response that they believe to be socially desirable rather than the response that more accurately reflects their behavior or feelings. The forced-choice technique used in constructing items in a personality questionnaire may facilitate this slanted response. Consumers are asked to pick one or two items most descriptive of them; however, not all possible combinations of stimuli are presented, and a given item may consist of two alternatives of equal social desirability. A situation is created in which the person may have no basis for making a choice.

The counselor should also be aware, when working with consumers from different minority groups, that these individuals may not be accustomed to taking personality inventories as they are presented in current assessment practices. Issues of motivation, test practice, and lack of understanding regarding the purposes of testing may influence the accuracy of test results. When using personality measures with consumers representing diverse ethnic backgrounds, cultural equivalence becomes important. In other words, does the personality construct being measured have equivalent or similar psychological meaning within and across different cultural groups? Inaccurate conclusions may be based on differences in construct meaning or even language bias (Suzuki & Kugler, 1995).

Slanting of responses reflects a dimension of the "fakeability" aspect when taking a personality inventory. To minimize this problem, the professional might explain that in a personality measure, test-takers are describing themselves, and untrue statements can inhibit appropriate rehabilitation planning.

Another suggestion for alleviating these problems associated with self-disclosure is to carefully structure the assessment situation, which emphasizes thoroughly preparing the consumer for the different paper-and-pencil tests to be administrated. This preparation includes explaining the purpose of the particular test, responding to the consumer's possible anxiety, and emphasizing both the importance of obtaining an accurate picture of the consumer for effective rehabilitation planning and the necessity of confidence in the assessment results.

Because these problems can affect the reliability of the personality assessment method, Krug (2008) believed that although using the self-report process in responding to questionnaires and similar formats tends to be less expensive than collecting information by other, traditional methods (i.e., visual, manipulative, and drawing techniques), it is not clear from the research literature, as was stated previously in this chapter, that this self-report method of personality assessment results in significant loss in reliability or validity. In fact, structured personality inventories may represent the best approach currently available to accurately measure relevant personality characteristics. Personality development, however, is not like cognitive development in such areas as verbal and numerical skills. A consumer can respond in very different ways in different contexts. Thus, as Anastasi (1982) stated, "[the] same response to a given question on a personality inventory may have a different significance from one person to another" (p. 527).

In rehabilitation, the professional wants to know how an individual will respond within an independent living, training, or employment situation. Because of this need and the uncertain predictive validity of the personality measure for an individual, the personality test provides an estimate of the consumer's current emotional functioning. From interview information exploring the consumer's past behavior and current emotional functioning in areas other than vocational (e.g., family, social), the rehabilitation professional will be able to have some idea of personality-related problems in a training or work situation. For example, a 35-year-old man who was injured on the job now wants to return to work because he has completed physical rehabilitation treatment. A personality measure may indicate withdrawn or alienated behaviors, but his work experience may have been highly productive. Other factors must be considered, to develop appropriate rehabilitation goals. The consumer's current reaction to the disability, perception of work expectations, environmental influences, and opportunities for work adjustment should all be identified before predictions are made regarding his or her behavior in an employment setting.

Particular attention should be given by the evaluator to the consumer's emotional reaction to the disability/chronic illness. This reaction is often ignored, since during assessment the focus may be dominantly on the consumer's physical functioning and the skills needed to be competitive in the 21st-century labor market. Earlier in this chapter the consumer's emotional reaction was discussed. The pattern of reaction suggested in that section is just one of many that have been developed during the past decades. Concepts of denial, anger, and various styles of coping with the changed reality caused by the disability not only express emotional, cognitive, and behavioral states, but also suggest the consumer's many needs. Recognition of and a timely and appropriate response to these needs can facilitate the consumer's vocational adjustment. Such recognition is another aspect of personality functioning.

Personality Inventories

Many personality inventories currently in use require some training in their administration and interpretation, but do not require training as intensive as the projective measures require. In the following pages, many personality measures are recommended for use in rehabilitation, some of which can be interpreted by the rehabilitation worker. When using these tests, evaluators must remember that test administration, scoring, interpretation, and reporting should be supervised by a person who meets the qualifications defined by state law and the American Psychological Association standards (Sax, 1981). Although the tests listed in this chapter were not developed primarily to predict behavior in work situations, the information they give, combined with an interpretation perspective that is job focused, can be quite useful in rehabilitation.

Along with the description of many widely used personality inventories, it is important to remember that most of these measures are supported by computer programs that score and interpret their results. These results are usually provided immediately. Also, developments in telecommunications technology have led to Internet-based products (Krug, 2001).

Minnesota Multiphasic Personality Inventory–Second Edition

The *Minnesota Multiphasic Personality Inventory–Second Edition* (MMPI-2; Hathaway, McKinley, & Butcher, 1990) is the most widely used personality inventory. Consisting of 567 affirmative statements, the test is designed for adults age 16 years and up and has been developed to assess major psychological characteristics that reflect an individual's social and personal maladjustment, including disabling psychological dysfunction. The inventory items range widely in content, and the measure provides scores on the 10 clinical scales that follow:

1. *Hypochondriasis (Hs)*—33 items derived from patients showing abnormal concern with bodily function.
2. *Depression (D)*—60 items derived from patients showing extreme pessimism, feelings of hopelessness, and slowing of thought and action.
3. *Conversion Hysteria (Hy)*—60 items from neurotic patients using

physical or mental symptoms as a way of unconsciously avoiding difficult conflicts and responsibilities.

4. *Psychopathic Deviate (Pd)*—50 items from patients who show a repeated and flagrant disregard for social customs, an emotional shallowness, and an inability to learn from punishing experiences.

5. *Masculinity–Femininity (MF)*—60 items from patients showing homoeroticism and items differentiating between men and women.

6. *Paranoia (Pa)*—40 items from patients showing abnormal suspiciousness and delusions of grandeur or persecution.

7. *Psychasthenia (Pt)*—48 items based on neurotic patients showing obsessions, compulsion, abnormal fears and guilt, and indecisiveness.

8. *Schizophrenia (Sc)*—78 items from patients who show bizarre or unusual thoughts or behavior, are often withdrawn, and experience delusions and hallucinations.

9. *Hypomania (Ma)*—46 items from patients characterized by emotional excitement, overactivity, and unrealistic flight of ideas.

10. *Social Introversion (O or Si)*—70 items developed from persons in the norm sample showing shyness, little interest in people, and insecurity.

The MMPI-2 has many supplementary scales, such as Anxiety, Repression, Ego Strength, MacAndrew Alcoholism–Revised, True Response Inconsistency, Overcontrolled Hostility, Dominance, Social Responsibility, College Maladjustment, Gender Role–Masculine, Gender Role–Feminine, Post-Traumatic Stress Disorder–Keane, Post-Traumatic Stress Disorder–Schlenger, Shyness/Self-Consciousness, Social Avoidance, Alienation–Self, and others.

In addition, content scales newly developed for the MMPI-2 include Anxiety, Fears, Obsessiveness, Depression, Health Concerns, Bizarre Mentation, Anger, Cynicism, Antisocial Practices, Type A, Low Self-Esteem, Social Discomfort, Family Problems, Work Interference, and Negative Treatment Indicators.

According to the catalogue of the National Computer Systems (1989), the MMPI-2 contains many traditional features of the original test format that remain unchanged: the basic scale set, separate profile forms for male and female subjects, hand-scoring keys, and norms with and without *K* corrects.

Important refinements and modifications have been made in four areas: revised test booklet, restandardized national norms, uniform T scores, and new scales. The MMPI-2 test booklet contains 567 items. Some of these items are from the original MMPI. Many are new and were designed to augment test coverage. Items with sexist wording and outmoded content were modified. The 16 duplicate items were eliminated, and items with "objectionable" content were excluded, thus slightly shortening five of the basic scales. The item order was changed, making it possible to score all of the basic scales from the first 370 items. Items 371 through 567 provide items for supplementary, content, and research measures.

The MMPI-2 norms are much more representative of the present population of the United States than were the original norms. The national reference group is also considerably larger than the original normative group. Experienced users of the MMPI will discover that T scores based on the new norms will not be as deviant as those based on the original norms.

The MMPI-2 incorporates representative samples of only two racial/ethnic minority groups (Black and Native American). An examination of scores and MMPI-2 profiles indicates no substantial mean differences between these ethnic group samples and the general normative sample on the MMPI-2 validity and standard scales (Suzuki & Kugler, 1995).

Scores from the restandardization subjects on eight of the Basic Clinical Scales (omitting scales 5 and 0) are uniform T scores. These scores were introduced because the traditional linear T scores are not strictly comparable from scale to scale due to differences in the distributions. The uniform T scores remove these differences and (unlike normalized T scores) preserve the general shape of the original T-score distributions.

Many volumes have been written about the original inventory, and hundreds of additional scales have been developed beyond the basic scales described above. These scales also stimulated much research with varied types of consumers. Moreover, the manual reports retest reliabilities on normal and abnormal adult samples from the 0.50s to the low 0.90s. Anastasi (1982) explained that certain scales (e.g., Depression) assess behavior that is variable over time, so as to render retest reliability inappropriate.

Anastasi (1982) stated that, in general, the greater the number and magnitude of deviant scores on the MMPI, the more likely it is that the individual has a severe disturbance. Anastasi further believed that the principal applications of the MMPI are to be found in differential diagnosis. This inventory is essentially a clinical instrument, and its proper interpretation calls for considerable psychological sophistication. Although several computerized systems for completely automated profile interpretations have been developed, training is still necessary to interpret the results for consumers. Many of these automated interpretations are largely descriptive summaries, whereas others provide highly interpretive statements.

The MMPI-2 is available in several administration formats: hardcover test booklet, softcover test booklet, and online MICROTEST assessment software. All formats consist of 567 true–false items written at the eighth-grade reading level. Both computer-scorable and hand-scorable answer sheets are available. Item order is the same for all formats. Basic Validity and Clinical Scales can be obtained by scoring the first 370 items.

Vocational Implications

There are many benefits to using the MMPI-2. It is a self-report measure, little time is required for scoring, and the data collected are scored on a variety of scales (Lowman & Richardson, 2008). Caution must be used in the choice of this instrument for certain consumers, as there are certain limitations. As a screening device, other measures described in this chapter might be considered. For many emotionally disturbed individuals, for example, this inventory might simply be too long. Administration in two or three sessions might have to be considered. Also, for many consumers who have no history of emotional disturbance and currently show good adjustment to their disabilities, differential diagnosis might not be necessary.

However, when a consumer is suspected of having strong emotional undercurrents caused by adaptive problems, the MMPI-2 can provide some useful information. For example, with the consumer who reports continued back pain, the MMPI-2 can suggest emotional factors that should be considered when developing rehabilitation plans. Many of the consumers described in Chapter 3 may be using their pain as a source of secondary gain or a reason for their ambivalence. Furthermore, this measure can suggest a level of a person's depression, thus identifying the professional adjustment problems for different types of occupational situations. However, unless a rehabilitation professional has special training, another qualified person should interpret the results of the MMPI-2. When using computer-generated reports on the MMPI-2, the professional should be aware that such data may not be able to integrate all the relevant cultural information.

To be noted is that an MMPI-2 AIS Version 2 software for Windows is available. It is designed to provide the counselor with a comprehensive analysis and interpretation of a scored MMPI-2 protocol. The MMPI-2 AIS is not a scoring program; it allows the helping professional to enter the consumer's T scores for the MMPI-2, and the software determines the best-fit prototypic profile and then generates a summary of the goodness of fit between the consumer's MMPI-2 profile and the prototypic profile.

Availability

The MMPI-2 is available from Pearson, 19500 Bulverde Rd., San Antonio, TX 78259, 800/627-7271.

The Myers-Briggs Type Indicator

The *Myers-Briggs Type Indicator* (MBTI; Myers & Briggs, 1988) was developed by Isabel Briggs Myers and her mother, Katharine Briggs, who, in the 1920s, developed a system of psychological types by conceptualizing their observations and readings (Hood & Johnson, 2007). The measure is based on Jung's concepts of perception and judgment. Each of the several forms of the MBTI are scored on eight scales (four pairs) yielding four bipolar dimensions:

1. Extroversion (E) Versus Introversion (I)—This dimension reflects the individual's perceptual orientation. Extroverts prefer to direct their energy to the outer world of people and things; introverts look inward to their internal and subjective reactions to their environment.

2. Sensing (S) Versus Intuition (N)—People with a sensing preference rely on that which can be perceived and are considered to be oriented toward that which is real (Pittenger, 1993); intuitive people rely primarily on indirect perception, incorporating ideas or associations that are related to perceptions coming from the outside (Hood & Johnson, 2007).

3. Thinking (T) Versus Feeling (F)—A thinking orientation shows a preference for drawing conclusions using an objective, impersonal, logical approach. A feeling individual prefers to make decisions that are based on subjective processes that include emotional reactions to events.

4. Judgment (J) Versus Perception (P)—The judgment-oriented person uses a combination of thinking and feelings when making decisions; the perceptive person often delays judgments as long as possible, preferring to collect information through either a sensing or intuitive process.

A person's MBTI personality type is summarized in four letters; this combination indicates the direction of the person's preference on each of the four dimensions. All possible combinations of the four paired scales result in 16 different personality types. An ESTJ, for example, prefers to organize projects, operations, and people, and then act to get things done. This person takes an objective approach to problem solving, uses thinking capabilities to organize life and work, and usually has little patience with confusion and inefficiency.

Although an individual's type is supposed to remain relatively constant over a lifetime, Cummings (1995) believed that norms on several MBTI dimensions change substantially between childhood and adolescence, as well as during the adult years. Pittenger (1993) explained that a factor analysis of the MBTI has not produced convincing results and that the factors found in the statistical analysis were inconsistent with the MBTI theory. He also believed that there is no evidence to show a positive relation between MBTI type and success in an occupation.

The MBTI is appealing to many evaluators because it has no good or bad scores or good or bad combinations of types. All type combinations can be viewed as having strengths. Each preference includes some positive characteristics, though each also has its problems and blind spots (Hood & Johnson, 2007). It does bring an added dimension to vocational assessment, and it should be used along with interest inventories and other psychological test results.

Vocational Implications

Because one of the most important motivations for a suitable occupational adjustment is a desire for work that is intrinsically interesting and satisfying, and that will permit use of preferred functions and attitudes, one's MBTI type can suggest a match between the individual and a particular job. There is no perfect match between type preferences and work tasks, but good occupational choices can prevent major mismatches. According to type theory, a mismatch causes fatigue and discouragement. Tasks that call on preferred and developed processes require less effort for better performance and can give more satisfaction. The MBTI manual provides extensive information on examples of frequent occupational choices made by each type.

Availability

The MBTI is available from CPP, 1150 Hamilton Court, Menlo Park, CA 94025, 800/624-1765.

Sixteen Personality Factor Questionnaire, Form E

Krug (2008) believed that the *Sixteen Personality Factor Questionnaire* "is one of the most widely used theory-based instruments for assessing normal-range personality characteristics in adults" (p. 159).

Form E is the new "low literate" form of the *Sixteen Personality Factor Questionnaire* (16 PF; Cattell, 1986) and, as in other forms of the 16 PF, the manual states that it is designed to "make available … information about an individual's standing on the majority of primary personality factors" (p. 4). Final scores are given on 16 bipolar primary factors:

A:	Warmth	L:	Vigilance
B:	Reasoning	M:	Abstractedness
C:	Emotional Stability	N:	Privateness
E:	Dominance	O:	Apprehension
F:	Liveliness	Q1:	Openness to Change
G:	Rule-Consciousness	Q2:	Self-Reliance
H:	Social Boldness	Q3:	Perfectionism
I:	Sensitivity	Q4:	Tension

Scores are reported in standard 10 scores (stanines). Form E uses forced-choice items such as, "Would you rather play baseball or go fishing?" The person selects the activity, feeling, preference, and so on that he or she would rather do or be. A few questions, however, require a reasoned, factual answer, for example, "After 2, 3, 4, 5, does 6 come next or does 7 come next?" The 16 PF manual contains no information on the average time needed to complete Form E. The 128-item test is not timed.

When considering this test for persons with disabilities, the publisher estimates that Form E requires between a third- and sixth-grade reading level. Answers are always recorded on a separate answer sheet, which can be either hand or machine scored. Although no information is specifically given, Form E is designed for personality evaluation for persons with a wide range of physical impairments (Elliott, 1995). In its present form, it is not applicable to consumers who are blind. Because of its low reading level, Form E should be usable with people with hearing impairments who read fairly well. Also, a rehabilitation professional who understands basic personality concepts can, after reading the manual carefully, interpret the 16 PF profile to the consumer. Sufficient information on the profile is provided to do this appropriately.

Vocational Implications

Many of the 16 personality factors can be applied to the consumer's rehabilitation planning. Factor C (affected by feelings or emotionally stable), Factor E (assertive or conforming), Factor F (liveliness), and Factor Q2 (self-sufficient or group dependent) are particularly relevant to adjustment issues in a training or occupational situation. Furthermore, the factors can indicate a pattern of adjustment to disability itself, which is a critical variable in successful rehabilitation. Factor H (venturesome or shy) suggests a consumer's change orientation or work flexibility. Also, persons with disabilities who score low on Factor C (affected by feelings or emotionally stable) tend to be low in frustration tolerance pertaining to unsatisfactory work conditions, easily annoyed, and perhaps evasive of necessary job demands.

Moreover, many of the factors in this measure can alert the rehabilitation professional to such consumer characteristics as low energy for work demands (Factor G), strong pessimism about possibilities for job adjustment (Factor F), or continued difficulty in getting along with others, working with people, and accepting supervision (Factor L).

Availability

The 16 PF, Form E, is available from Pearson, 19500 Bulverde Rd., San Antonio, TX 78259, 800/627-7271.

California Psychological Inventory– 1996 Revision

The *California Psychological Inventory* (CPI; Gough & Bradley, 1996) is a multipurpose questionnaire designed to assess normal personality characteristics important in everyday life. It can be used to assist consumers in making vocational plans and when supplementing other clinical tests. It can also be used to understand consumer maladjustments and to evaluate such specific problems as social immaturity and vulnerability to physical illness. The CPI can be given under normal conditions to individuals ages 14 years through adult and includes such basic scales as (a) interpersonal style and manner of dealing with others (dominance, capacity for status, sociability, social presence, self-acceptance, independence, and empathy), (b) cognitive and intellectual functioning (achievement via conformance, achievement via independence, and intellectual efficiency), (c) thinking and behavior (psychological mindedness, flexibility, and femininity/masculinity), (d) internalization and endorsement of normative convention (responsibility, socialization, self-control, good impression, communality, tolerance, and well-being), and (e) special scales and indexes (managerial potential, work orientation, leadership potential index, social maturity index, and creative potential index). The CPI includes the following features: (a) Its 462 items are printed in a reusable text booklet, (b) it can be taken under normal conditions in 45 minutes to 1 hour, and (c) its manual contains extensive reliability and validity information.

Vocational Implications

Many of the CPI factors can be used more specifically for vocational assessment purposes, such as flexibility, responsibility, socialization, tolerance, well-being, work orientation, and social maturity index. These work readiness factors can be identified during rehabilitation planning. This measure, however, is not applicable to individuals with mental retardation.

Availability

The CPI is available from CPP, Inc., 1150 Hamilton Court, Menlo Park, CA 94025.

The Psychological Screening Inventory

Although developed many years ago, the *Psychological Screening Inventory* (PSI; Lanyon, 2010) was updated in 2010 and is designed to meet the need for a brief mental health screening device for situations in which time and professional manpower may be at a premium. It is valuable as a screening device to be used in identifying persons who might profit by receiving more intensive attention. There are five scales in the PSI: Alienation (AL), Social Nonconformity (SN), Discomfort (DI), Expression (EX), and Defensiveness (DE). The combination of these scales is designed to assess the degree of defensiveness characterizing the test-taker's responses.

The PSI consists of 130 personal statements or items to be answered true or false. It is printed on the front and back of a single 8½ × 11 in. sheet. Items are at a fifth- to sixth-grade reading level, and the test can normally be completed in 15 minutes. It can be administered in either group or individual settings, both with a minimum of instructions. In its present form, the test is not usable for persons with visual impairments; however, if a person who is deaf has at least a fifth-grade reading comprehension level, it can be applicable.

Vocational Implications

The PSI can be particularly useful in rehabilitation, because it can provide a beginning awareness of how a consumer is coping with a disability. The scales of alienation, discomfort, and expression are especially valuable for this purpose. For example, the Discomfort scale was designed to assess the personality dimension of anxiety or perceived maladjustment. Persons who score highly on this dimension tend to complain of varied somatic symptoms and admit to many psychological discomforts and difficulties. When a rehabilitation professional wants to understand how the consumer's handling of pain is associated with a disability, this scale provides some suggestions that can be further explored in counseling. An accompanying high score on the Alienation scale may indicate that because of his or her disability, the consumer is withdrawing from family and social involvements. Consequently, high Discomfort and Alienation scores for a consumer with a disability can suggest difficulties in adjustment to the strains and pressures of a work environment or many of the demands of competitive work (e.g., getting along with co-workers, maintaining an adequate production rate).

Availability

The PSI is available from Sigma Assessment Systems, PO Box 610757, Port Huron, MI 48061, 800/265-1285.

Tennessee Self-Concept Scale

The *Tennessee Self-Concept Scale* (TSCS; Fitts & Warren, 1996) was designed to be used with both healthy and maladjusted people. Atkins, Lynch, and Pullo (1982) explained that self-concept involves the dynamic interaction of the consumer's beliefs, needs, body image, sexual identity, values, and expectations. Many of these factors can be explored when interviewing persons with disabilities because understanding self-concept is a critical element in understanding psychological makeup. The TSCS explores many dimensions of self-concept, such as family self, physical self, moral self, and identity.

The scale consists of 90 items, equally divided for positive and negative responses. It is self-administering and requires no instructions beyond those on the inside cover of the test booklet. The answer sheet is arranged so that the subjects respond to every other item and then repeat the procedure to complete the sheet. The Counseling Form answer sheet is easy to interpret because the score sheet can be presented directly to the consumer for interpretation and discussion. However, the manual should be read before any interpretation is given to the consumer. A trained rehabilitation professional should be able to understand the concepts explained in the manual.

This scale has particular use for rehabilitation professionals because it can provide information and suggestions on the consumer's pattern of adjustment to disability. Although no reading level is indicated in the test manual, a review of the items indicates that at least a sixth-grade reading level is necessary. In its present form, the test is not usable for persons with severe visual impairments but is applicable to persons who are deaf if their reading comprehension is at the sixth-grade level or higher. It is important to understand, however, that the normative group for the development of the varied scales did not include the population of those with disabilities. This should be explained to the consumer.

Vocational Implications

Self-concept is an important factor in rehabilitation planning, for it influences the consumer's motivation and is linked to self-confidence in work situations. The Physical Self, Personal Self, and Social Self scales can indicate consumers' attitudes toward their disabilities. A high score on the Family Self scale may suggest a coping resource for the consumer. When the scales (with the exception of the Physical Self scale) reveal high scores, it may indicate to the rehabilitation professional that the consumer has many perceived strengths for adjusting to work situations. These can be explored during counseling with the consumer.

Availability

The *Tennessee Self-Concept Scale* is available from Western Psychological Services, 625 Alaska Ave., Torrance, CA 90503, 800/648-8857.

Rosenberg Self-Esteem Scale

The *Rosenberg Self-Esteem Scale* (RSE; Rosenberg, 1979) is a 10-item scale with one dimension that was originally designed to measure the self-esteem of high school students. However, since its development, the scale has been used with a number of other groups, including adults working in a variety of occupations. One of the RSE's greatest strengths is the amount of research that has been conducted with a wide range of groups on this scale over the years. This research has demonstrated the concurrent, predictive, and construct validity of the RSE. It can also be useful as a screening device for consumers with physical or mental disabilities.

Vocational Implications

The RSE is easy to score and can be particularly beneficial to both the counselor and consumer immediately after the initial interviews. Self-administered, this measure can provide feedback on one's level of self-esteem and whether this state is going to be a significant problem during the vocational assessment process.

Availability

The RSE is available from the Department of Sociology, University of Maryland, 3404 Benjamin, College Park, MD 20742, 301/405-2801.

The Employability Maturity Interview

The *Employability Maturity Interview* (EMI; Roessler & Bolton, 1987) is a structured interview instrument consisting of 10 questions designed to assess readiness for the vocational rehabilitation planning process. It is useful as a brief screening instrument to identify consumers needing additional vocational exploration and employability services. The 10 questions represent four areas: occupational choice, self-appraisal of abilities, orientation to work, and self-appraisal of personality characteristics. The EMI takes between 10 and 15 minutes to administer and another 5 minutes to score. Three factor scores are calculated: General Maturity, Specificity of Goals, and Variety of Interests (Bolton, 1997).

Vocational Implications

This brief measure can be administered before the initial consumer assessment interview to give the counselor an overview of the consumer's awareness of his or her work-related abilities and selected personality dimensions, and even some insight into the consumer's motivation to work. The results of the EMI can be discussed with the consumer during the initial interview and can prompt further exploration of employability issues.

Availability

The EMI is available from the Arkansas and Research Training Center in Vocational Rehabilitation, Fayetteville, AR.

Identifying a Consumer's Values

With the different inventories that explore the varied dimensions of personality functioning, one area that is also important for personality assessment is the evaluation of values. An understanding of a consumer's values will not only highlight the individual's uniqueness but also strongly suggest an added factor that can contribute to job satisfaction. A synonym for the word *value* is *worth,* and when we speak of a consumer's values, the evaluator is talking about whatever the individual prizes or believes is important (Cohen, Swerdlik, & Phillips, 1996).

One of the purposes of vocational assessment is to help the consumer make informed decisions about career opportunities. These decisions are usually based on the consumer's values. Values with high priorities can be the most important determinants of a career choice. There is also considerable variation in the values of ethnic subgroups. Frequently, however, the consumer's values are undefined or unexplored, and persons who have an adult onset of a mental or physical disability may shift their values from pre-onset of the disability. There are specific considerations that should be identified as a framework for exploring the value system of individuals with a disability.

For the person with a disability, the process of changing or shifting values can be an adaptive response to psychological distress emanating from disability-management tasks. Shifting the importance or value of a goal can reduce emotional tension (Mpofu & Bishop, 2006).

The rehabilitation counselor should have a value vocabulary. Though the total number of values that a person possesses is relatively small, they are usually organized into terminal and instrumental groups (Rokeach, 1973). Terminal values are defined as the idealized end state (e.g., self-worth, success, security, a happy and dignified life), and instrumental values are viewed as the desirable attitudes or behaviors for accomplishing terminal values (e.g., honesty, independence, responsibleness). For those with disabilities, the focus in assessment should be more on one's instrumental values, for their identification will assist these persons to understand or to develop reasons for vocational choices. Additional examples of instrumental values are:

comfort	flexibility
working with people	variety
creativity	money
working indoors or outdoors	recognition
autonomy and self-sufficiency	control
altruism	fairness
competent medical and social services	a peaceful life

Instrumental and terminal values should be identified that are salient to the individual person's adjustment, and Mpofu and Bishop

(2006) suggested two measures on disability-related value change that have been developed in the last three decades. One, the *Minnesota Importance Questionnaire,* is briefly discussed later in this chapter. The other, *The Acceptance of Disability Scale* (Linkowski, 1971), can be used, with other personality measures, to evaluate one's personal value status and the choice of interventions to plan vocational functioning after assessment.

But the counselor can use open-ended questions to pinpoint the consumer's values. Some questions that can be asked are the following:

- "What is important to you now that your disability is part of your life?"
- "How did you initially react when you realized you had a disability, and how has this reaction changed over time?"
- "Is your disability a major part of how you view yourself now?" (Mpofu & Bishop, 2006)

Prompted by the rehabilitation counselor, who identifies a range of possible values that the consumer might hold, the consumer prioritizes these values and describes what they mean to him or her. Additional ways for the person with a disability to identify values follow:

- Dream analysis describing someone the consumer admires
- How the consumer prioritized daily and future activities
- Reflecting on choices made in the past

Although understanding a consumer's values may be a lifelong process, there are ways to help a person identify work-related values. Such values include advancement, achievement, altruism, competition, fairness, friendships at work, health, income, independence, interesting work, variety, location of work, people contact, physical appearance, security, work environment, and perhaps predictable work. The evaluator might perceive that many of these values are actually consumer needs. Lock (1988) affirmed that values are related to needs, but they are not the same as needs. "Technically," he states, "a need is a lack of something desirable … values are internal in nature" (p. 237).

There are several ways to identify consumer values, including both informal and formal approaches.

Informal Approach

Similar to the material discussed in the chapter on interest assessment (Chapter 7), the evaluator may ask the consumer such questions as the following, suggested by Mpofu and Bishop (2006):

- Would you work if you didn't have to? Why or why not?
- In what kinds of work situations would you work harder than you ordinarily do?
- In what kinds of work situations would be you be willing to work for less than normal pay?
- Name some people whose work you really admire. Why do you admire the kinds of work they do?
- What is important to you now that your disability is part of your life?
- How did you initially react when you realized you had a disability, and how has this reaction changed over time?
- Is your disability a major part of how you view yourself now?

Simon, Howe, and Kirschenbaum (1972) suggested a sentence completion activity, using sentences such as,

- What I want most in life is …
- I do best when …
- I think my parents would like me to …
- People who know me well think I am …
- I am concerned most about …

The evaluator can generate a list of the values that are important to the consumer. Pierce, Cohen, Anthony, and Cohen (1978) explained that a simple step is to begin by reviewing with the consumer his or her educational and work experience, along with any information gained from interest exploration. Particular emphasis should be placed on the consumer's likes and dislikes. The evaluator may have to compare the consumer's values against a list of values that past experience has shown are important in selecting a job. During this exploration the professional may also ask the consumer about someone he or she admires, or reflect on choices made in the past, or identify important daily activities. In this identification and prioritization, individuals can also describe what a particular value means to them. Moreover, a person's attitudes, interests, feelings, beliefs, activities, and convictions can be further indicators of values. Some of these values hold more meaning than others, and there is a tendency to pursue more vigorously the values that have more meaning to us.

Traditional job value categories are physical, emotional–interpersonal, and intellectual, and each category includes many of the work values identified earlier. Physical values include personal appearance, physical working conditions, physical activities, and salary and benefits. Emotional–interpersonal value categories include job security, emotional–interpersonal working conditions (structure, pressure, amount of supervision, amount of isolation), and emotional–interpersonal activities (amount of interaction with people, what one does with people [such as help or persuade]). Intellectual value categories include the chance for advancement, supply and demand, and such intellectual activities as planning, decision making, computation, and writing (Pierce et al., 1978).

Formal Approach

Measures to identify work values are available, two of which are briefly explained next.

Survey of Work Values

The *Survey of Work Values* (SWV; Wollack, Goodale, Wijting, & Smith, 1976) was designed for those in the range of late adolescence to adulthood. The test measures intrinsic work-related values and extrinsic reward-related values. It includes 54 items and the six scales (9 items per scale) that follow: social status of job, activity preference, upward striving, attitude toward earnings, pride in work, and job involvement.

Minnesota Importance Questionnaire

The *Minnesota Importance Questionnaire* (MIQ; Rounds, Henly, Dawis, Lofquist, & Weiss, as cited in Fouad, Smothers, Kantamnani, & Guillen, 2008) is a measure to assess the vocational needs and values of consumers and reinforce patterns of various occupations. It asks individuals to evaluate 20 different work needs or values in terms of their importance in an ideal job. The 20 needs derive from studies of job satisfaction based on the theory of work adjustment developed by Dawis and Lofquist (1984). The 20 needs have been reduced to six broad factors called values (Achievement, Comfort, Status, Altruism, Safety, Autonomy) by means of factor analysis. Although two forms of the MIQ exist, most people prefer the simplified version, which usually takes about 20 minutes to complete. Reading difficulty level is approximately 6th-grade, and some previous work experience will help consumers identify which needs are most important to them in the ideal job (Fouad et al., 2008). Computer scoring is available through the publisher (University of Minnesota, Minneapolis, MN; Hood & Johnson, 2007).

In summary, Mpofu and Bishop (2006) believed that the individual experience of disability offers a challenge to orient this person's value system to accommodate disability-related tasks and demands. Previously established behavior patterns are disrupted. Preferences, new expectations, and other self-perceptions may reflect the individual's values, which, in turn, suggest rehabilitation interventions.

Conclusion

Personality assessment is one of the most important areas of consumer self-knowledge. I have used all the measures described in this chapter. Other inventories could be suggested, but these measures have proven particularly helpful and are, therefore, recommended. Although tests cannot always accurately describe a consumer's basic underlying motivations, they do provide a sample of behavior. Such indications can facilitate personal insight (Biggs & Keller, 1982). For many consumers, the evaluation process in rehabilitation is not really an end in itself, but can be the first step toward achieving self-awareness. Rehabilitation plans that evolve from vocational assessment build on this self-understanding. Consumers who are aware of their own strengths and weaknesses, and who realize that some deficits may have to be modified before training or job placement occurs, often become more involved in the formulation of rehabilitation plans.

In rehabilitation, effective personality assessment begins with the rehabilitation professional's own awareness of the close relationship between behavioral traits and job-related or other productivity-related adjustment. This awareness enables the rehabilitation professional to make referrals to psychological consultants for personality information on the consumer that will be more specific and relevant to rehabilitation needs. Also, in understanding both the relationship between work and personality and the fundamental ingredients of personality assessment, the rehabilitation professional can generate referral questions or use appropriate evaluation measures that will provide more useful information for rehabilitation planning.

Chapter 10

Understanding Aptitude, Achievement, Work Samples, and Functional Assessments

One of the objectives of vocational assessment is to help consumers understand their strengths and weaknesses in relation to the world of work, while at the same time recognizing the usual demands flowing from most employment opportunities in the 21st-century labor market. These demands involve educational skills, problem-identification and problem-solving skills, perceptual abilities, and the capability to understand and follow directions (Power, 2011). Whether a consumer possesses such skills or has the capability to acquire them is determined through four specific evaluation approaches: aptitude, achievement, work samples, and functional assessments. All of these approaches evaluate whether information gained from educational and work experiences can be a foundation for the development of skills needed in the 21st century and whether the consumer has the potential to develop needed skills.

The rehabilitation counselor does not often conduct aptitude, achievement, or work sample assessments. When this information is not available or needs to be updated, the rehabilitation professional may either request an updated evaluation or administer an appropriate available measure. Prior to utilizing any of these assessment approaches, specific information is needed:

- Does the consumer have educational training records that contain updated information on many abilities or basic skills that can be used for future training or employment? Interest assessment should indicate specific career directions, and within these directions more specific career job opportunities could also be identified. The counselor then recognizes the skills in that particular cluster of opportunities and determines whether the consumer has the requisite potential or learned knowledge for any skill training. For example, the consumer's interest patterns may be more directed to opportunities in the computer field. The skills that are necessary to perform in those jobs need to be identified, and then aptitude, achievement, and work samples can be appraised to determine the consumer's specific learning potential for acquiring the needed skills.

• If assessment measures are not available for the determination of aptitude or potential in certain occupational areas, then are there available resources to do this specific assessment? In today's world of vocational assessment, there is a scarcity of appraisal measures that evaluate particular skills needed for newly developed job titles. Other resources should be used, and in order to achieve validity in a particular assessment domain, the consumer could be referred to another resource. Also, many training schools have been very cooperative about evaluating individuals in their particular areas of interest.

• The consumer, of course, needs to be prepared for this referral. Similar to the rehabilitation counselor's knowledge of resources available to conduct complex dimensions of personality assessment, so the counselor should have information on resources that provide aptitude, achievement, and work samples evaluation in those very specific areas. With this information of available resources, the counselor can then discuss with the consumer the nature of the referred source, how to contact them, and whom to speak to, all of which may ease the consumer's anxiety that can emerge from the unknowns in vocational assessment.

This information suggests that the counselor has decisions to make when exploring aptitude, achievement, and work samples evaluation with the consumer. "What kind of instruments should we use?" and "How will they enhance the consumer's self-understanding about career-related strengths and capabilities?" are questions that interface with the counselor's information on what is needed to know in this particular area of the consumer's vocational functioning. The *need to know* area extends to the counselor's competence in interpreting those reports of aptitude, achievement, and work sample results. Before an explanation of these four approaches is offered, learning styles and their implications for vocational rehabilitation are discussed. Each consumer has developed a unique learning style. This learning style affects the consumer's capacity to acquire, during training, employment-related information and skills. Individuals learn in various ways, and traditional or standardized approaches may not be consistent with a consumer's ability to learn. Learning styles that conflict with the way subject matter is presented during training can severely inhibit vocational and educational progress. Evaluating a consumer's learning style preference can help him or her adapt to training and employment demands.

The majority of learning style assessment tools described in the literature are standardized approaches. A consumer learns best through a combination of the written and spoken word; through charts, pictures, or demonstration; or by the experience of doing a task. Assessment approaches should identify an individual's preferred style. Preferred learning style is a variable that usually depends on the nature of the material to be learned and the personality of the learner. The interview can initially be used to explore the consumer's learning preference. The rehabilitation professional can ask such questions as the following:

- What has been your most enjoyable learning experience? In what kinds of environments do you think you learn new things best?
- Can you remember the best way that you have learned school subjects or job tasks?
- When learning to do some of your favorite spare time activities, what kind of learning style (e.g., the spoken word, seeing things through pictures, actually performing the activity) has been most useful for you?
- How do you prefer to be given instructions to a new assignment: in writing, verbally, by a demonstration, or any combination of these?
- Would any accommodations help you to perform better at school or work?

Kolb (2005) developed the *Learning Style Inventory: Version 3.1* to measure differences in learning styles along the two basic dimensions of abstract–concrete and active–reflective. Test results yield an identification of four statistically prevalent learning styles: (a) convergers (use abstract conceptualization and active experimentation; strength lies in the practical application of ideas), (b) divergers (use concrete experience and reflective observation; strength lies in imaginative ability), (c) assimilators (use abstract conceptualization and reflective observation; strength lies in inductive reasoning), and (d) accommodators (use concrete experience and active experimentation; strength lies in doing things and becoming involved in new experiences).

Behavioral observation is another informal source of information for learning styles assessment. For example, a consumer can be taught how to perform a particular task and allowed to practice without regard to speed and quality. Then, during the actual performance, attention is focused on those factors important to consider for the successful completion of the task. Poor performance may be caused by a learning style problem, although motivation, poor skill-related abilities, and certain environmental factors may also contribute to this performance.

In the context of understanding learning style issues, this chapter will discuss four methods of assessment important to occupational and/ or career exploration. Aptitude, achievement, work sample, and functional assessments generally target the abilities area of consumer functioning. Results from these methods often determine the feasibility of pursuing a consumer's reported interest direction.

Aptitude Assessment

"Aptitude tests are psychometric instruments designed to assess individuals' skills and abilities" (Parker, 2008, p. 123). Although aptitude cannot be directly measured, it can be inferred from the consumer's performance on an evaluation instrument. Multiple aptitudes are required for successful performance in a particular vocational area, and the matching of an individual's aptitudes with the abilities needed for the vocational area is an indicator of potential success in this area. With the information gained from aptitude assessment, the professional has a better opportunity to assist consumers who are trying to choose among training or occupation possibilities. The information gained from this approach can also facilitate the planning of training goals by persons with disabilities (Parker, 2008).

The reliabilities for aptitude and achievement tests tend to cluster in the high 0.80s and low 0.90s. The validity of these tests is also relatively high. For clerical, service, trade, craft, and industrial occupations, the consumer's potential for successful training at different levels can be predicted rather well by tests. Examples of tests that can measure this potential are tests of intellectual abilities, spatial and mechanical abilities, and perceptual accuracy. However, prediction of job proficiency for these occupational groups is much more tenuous. For example, a consumer may take a mechanical aptitude test and score at the 75th percentile. If the group that was used to standardize the scores of this test, called the *norm group*, was made of successful auto mechanics, it might be predicted that this consumer would also be successful as an auto mechanic. This kind of prediction does still involve a subjective judgment, however, because there is no conclusive research evidence that a score at the 75th percentile ensures a high probability of success in auto mechanics. Although aptitude and achievement tests can indicate whether a consumer has the potential or capacity to meet training or occupational demands, these tests do not necessarily predict success. Norms are descriptive, not predictive, in nature, and the evaluator should make a conceptual separation between description and prediction (Parker, 2001).

Unfortunately, norms for these tests often are inappropriate for comparison purposes when used with individuals with disabilities, and this caveat should be considered when interpreting results. Norms can be useful, however, if certain minimum acceptable performance levels are established for various training opportunities or placements into local workshop situations. Many achievement tests, consequently, are based on standards or criteria that have been developed by an organization or a relevant group for a level of performance. Such measures assess what a person can do; they do not provide interpretations regarding one consumer's success as compared to another's. It should be noted that criterion measures include speed of work, quality of work, number of absences, and safety record (Parker, 2001).

Aptitude tests attempt to identify an ability or characteristic—mental or physical, native or acquired—that is believed or known to indicate a consumer's capacity or potential for learning a particular skill or knowledge. They focus on performance capabilities that have been developed without conscious effort. While they can be expensive and time consuming, these tests yield results that suggest the cumulative influence of a multiplicity of daily experiences (Anasatasi, 1982). The following identifies a few of these measures.

O*NET Ability Profiler

Parker (2008) has explained that the *General Aptitude Test Battery* (GATB) has been replaced by the ability profiler (AP) in order to improve the former measure's operational and technical characteristics. Form matching was deleted from the GATB, but the AP incorporates the other 11 of the GATB's 12 subtests. Parker also has stated that the AP has a reduced number of items and subtests, new instructions, reduced speed for certain subtests, improved legibility and comprehension level of all written materials, and a self-interpretable *O*NET Ability Profiler Score Report*. Downloads of test materials, manuals, and scoring software are available at no cost on the website (http://www.onetcenter.org/AP.html).

Differential Aptitude Tests–Fifth Edition, Form C

The *Differential Aptitude Tests–Fifth Edition, Form C* (DAT; Bennett, Seashore, & Wesman, 1990) features two levels that collectively measure the aptitudes of students in Grades 7 through 12, as well as adults. Level 1 is designed primarily for students in Grades 7 through 9; Level 2, for students in Grades 10 through 12. Both levels can be used with adults. Separate norms are given for males and females, and the rationale for separate norms to reduce gender bias is carefully explained to consumers. The test items and the directions, as well as the student report, have been carefully edited with the needs of non–college-bound students in mind, such as those in adult basic education and vocational technical school programs (Siefker, 1996). Reading is called for only when it is a part of the ability being measured.

The tests can be administered in groups and can be hand or machine scored. If the complete battery is given, test administration requires slightly more than 3 hours. The term *differential* implies not only that the test measures different aptitudes but also that differences in score levels within one person's profile are likely to be significant and interpretable. The DAT consists of the following tests: Verbal Reasoning,

Numerical Reasoning, Abstract Reasoning, Perceptual Speed and Accuracy, Mechanical Reasoning, Space Relations, Spelling, and Language Usage. A computerized adaptive edition is also available, which is an integrated battery of eight aptitude tests that provide assistance in educational and vocational guidance. The computer software tailors the test to the consumer's ability level, and this test is administered and scored by the computer. The DAT adaptive software will work on all Apple IIc and IIe computers. It will also work on Apple III, Franklin Ace 1000, and Laser 128 computers with at least 64K memory. The IBM version runs on the IBM PC, XT, AT PS/2, and compatibles.

Siefker (1996) believed that the DAT offers a psychometrically sound and logistically convenient source of information for young people, particularly for the educational and vocational decision-making process. The DAT has been validated extensively against various criteria, such as school grades, related tests, and previous editions of the DAT, but validity studies have not been made using job or training success as criteria (Siefker, 1996).

Omizo (1980) believed from the research findings that several of the variables tested by the DAT series are valid predictors of performance in engineering, mathematics, and science courses. Moreover, reliability coefficients are high and permit interpretation of interest differences with considerable confidence (Anastasi, 1982). The manual provides both percentile and stanine norms.

Although Parker (2008) believed that the DAT is the "best established aptitude test commercially available" (p. 131), it does have limitations and should be used cautiously. There is no information in the manual, for example, on the use of the DAT with the population of persons with disabilities. For educationally deprived individuals, the use of this test for an initial exploration of aptitude is really not appropriate; more basic measures should be used. The DAT is not applicable for persons with visual impairments. The tests, however, do provide valuable information for those consumers with disabilities who have at least a 10th-grade education and who are interested in occupations demanding technical skills—for example, in science and math areas. Also, for those who have completed high school and who are not going to college but are planning occupational careers in technical fields, the DAT can be most useful for assessment purposes.

Vocational Implications

Because of their levels of difficulty, these tests can assist consumers in (a) developing more realistic occupational and training goals, (b) exploring their pool of learned skills that can be drawn upon and used for possible skill transfer following disability onset, (c) finding suggestions for marketable job skills, and (d) exploring their current level of reasoning, mathematics, and language development. Many DAT tests, such as Abstract Reasoning, Numerical Ability, Mechanical Reasoning, and Space Relations, can also be used to explore consumer capabilities in electronics-related occupations (e.g., computer technology, television repair).

Availability

The DAT is available from Pearson, 19500 Bulverde Rd., San Antonio, TX 78259, 800/627-7271.

Armed Services Vocational Aptitude Battery

Targeted to potential military recruits between the ages of 16 and 23, the *Armed Services Vocational Aptitude Battery* (ASVAB), with its many relatively updated forms, is a widely administered instrument that provides test takers with information in the following areas: general science, work knowledge, paragraph comprehension, electronics, auto and shop information, code speed, arithmetic reasoning, mathematics knowledge, mechanical comprehension, and numerical operations. Information on the acceptable reliability and validity of the test is extensive, but the available norms are dated. However, there is restricted access to the measure, and the speediness of 2 of the 10 subtests limits its use for many disability populations (Parker, 2001).

Vocational Implications

There are obvious restrictions in the ASVAB's use with those with severe disabilities and perhaps those who are not considering the military as a career. Yet, selected minority groups were oversampled to provide more of an accurate estimate of their performance (Parker, 2001a). In the subgroup tested area, however, the ASVAB can provide useful information for selected populations.

Availability

Phone 800/323-0513 for information.

Bennett Mechanical Comprehension Test

The *Bennett Mechanical Comprehension Test* (BMCT; Bennett, 1992) was designed to explore aptitude for understanding the mechanical principles involved in a range of practical situations (Aiken, 1997). There is one final score in percentile form for mechanical comprehension. The test is group administered, with each examinee receiving a test booklet and separate answer sheet. Most of the 68 items contain two illustrations and a written question about each illustration dealing with mechanical principles or general physical concepts. Examinees have three choices for each answer.

The Bennett is widely used and is suitable for such groups as high school students, industrial and mechanical job applicants, and candidates for engineering programs. The manual provides percentile norms—including educational levels, specialized training, and prospective job categories—for several groups. Odd–even reliability coefficients of each form have been reported from 0.81 to 0.93. A fourth-grade reading level is necessary, and visual acuity to read standard print and see the details in the illustrations is required. For consumers with limited reading skills, Forms S and T may be administered with tape-recorded instructions and questions. Spanish versions are also available for both regular and oral administration. Form T is the Mechanical Reasoning Test of the DAT.

The test can be completely administered in 40 minutes, including directions and questions. The test itself has a 30-minute time limit. When considering the test for persons with disabilities, the manual states that the test falls within the "fairly easy level of popular magazines." In the manual, no information on persons with disabilities is given. Although not usable in its present form for persons with blindness, this test should be appropriate for consumers who are hearing impaired. Also, the instructions are easy for persons with mental retardation to comprehend, but the concepts evaluated by the test may be too difficult for many of them to grasp. If the rehabilitation worker is planning to give the test to these consumers, then individual administration and sufficient practice during the first two trials should be carefully followed.

Vocational Implications

The BMCT explores training capabilities in mechanical fields and is also recommended as an initial measure for consumers who wish to pursue occupations in one of many technical areas (e.g., computer technology, electronics repair fields).

Availability

The BMCT is available from Pearson, 19500 Bulverde Rd., San Antonio, TX 78259, 800/627-7271.

Minnesota Paper Form Board–Revised

The *Minnesota Paper Form Board–Revised* (MPFB-R) helps the consumer explore aspects of mechanical ability that require the capacity to visualize and manipulate objects in space. The administration time is 20 minutes, and although it is a speed test, it is suitable for group or individual test administration concerning vocational implications. The test is suitable for nonreaders and non–English-speaking populations. It was normed on those in Grades 10 through 12, as well as on industrial applicants and employed workers (Siefker, 1996). This measure is a useful complement to the BMCT.

Availability

This test is available from Pearson, 19500 Bulverde Rd., San Antonio, TX 78259, 800/627-7271.

Career Ability Placement Survey

The *Career Ability Placement Survey* (CAPS; Knapp & Knapp, 1994) contains eight subtests: mechanical reasoning, spatial relations, verbal reasoning, numerical ability, language usage, word knowledge, perceptual speed and accuracy, and manual speed and dexterity. All of these subtests were designed to measure abilities focusing on entry requirements for the majority of jobs in each of 14 occupational clusters. Each subtest is printed on a separate form, and the individually or group-administered battery can be completed in approximately 50 minutes or less. Each subtest has a time limit of 5 minutes. Consumers can score their own tests and convert their raw scores to stanines on a profile sheet in 30 minutes. Mail-in machine scoring is available, and software for onsite scoring can be purchased from the test publisher. This battery of tests is appropriate for persons who at least have a junior high school education and have the ability to read standard print and to use the paper-and-pencil method of marking answers.

The CAPS is available from the EdITS/Educational and Industrial Testing Service, PO Box 7234, San Diego, CA 92167, 800/416-1666.

Minnesota Clerical Test

The *Minnesota Clerical Test* (Andrew, Patterson, & Longstaff, 1992) was designed both to aid in the selection of clerical employees and to advise individuals interested in clerical training. The specific trait measured by the test is the consumer's ability to notice, within a specified time period, the differences between two items. The test consists of two parts: Number Checking and Name Scoring. Each part contains 200 items, with 100 identical and 100 dissimilar pairs. The consumer is to identify and check the identical pairs. No special training is needed to administer and score this test, and the test is hand scored. Although not suitable for consumers who have visual impairments, this test can be adapted for individuals who have hearing impairments.

Percentile norms have been reported in the manual for several large samples of clerical applicants and employed clerical workers, as well as for boys and girls in 8th through 12th grades. Moderately high correlations have been found between scores on this test and ratings by office supervisors and commercial teachers, and with performance records in clerical courses (Anastasi, 1982). Note that the test measures only one aspect of clerical work.

Vocational Implications

This test suggests specific capacities in the clerical area (a good beginning test for many consumers whose stated occupational interest is clerical work).

Availability

The *Minnesota Clerical Test* is available from Pearson, 19500 Bulverde Rd., San Antonio, TX 78259, 800/627-7271.

Hand-Tool Dexterity Test

Because the *Hand-Tool Dexterity Test* (Bennett, 1981) measures gross-motor dexterity, manipulative skill, and the ability to use common hand tools, it is a good complement to the *Crawford Small Parts Dexterity Test.* The test uses an upright wooden frame clamped to a table or workbench in front of the consumer. The person must remove the nuts, bolts, and washers from the left side and mount them on the right side using wrenches and a screwdriver. As there are three different sizes of nuts and bolts, separate tools are required for each. The *Hand-Tool Dexterity Test* is timed, and most individuals can complete it within 5 to 20 minutes. Percentile norms are based on the completion time and are given for such groups as maintenance mechanics, technical trainees, physically injured workers, special education students, vocational training students, and trainees with mental or emotional disabilities (Siefker, 1996). To be noted is that this measure does not work well for people who have visual deficits. It can be used appropriately for consumers who are exploring industrially related employment.

Availability

This test is available from Pearson, 19500 Bulverde Rd., San Antonio, TX 78259, 800/627-7271.

Occupational Aptitude Survey and Interest Schedule– Third Edition (OASIS-3)

This measure contains a separate interest inventory and aptitude battery. The aptitude battery provides five aptitude factors to explore, with the relevant subtest: verbal—vocabulary; numerical—computation; spatial—spatial relations; perceptual—word comparison; and manual dexterity—making marks. Directed to assist adults and students in Grades 8 through 12, it requires 45 minutes to administer. Parker (2008) explained that this battery could be viewed as a reliable short form of the GATB test. Both validity and reliability scores are in the acceptable range. While many test reviewers believe that the OASIS-3 is a valuable tool for vocational exploration, similar to most paper-and-pencil measures for those with a disability, the examiner should carefully read the manual to determine norm appropriateness and administration demands relevant to individual consumers. This measure is used, however, in many student transitioning programs, as it provides information on possible career directions.

Availability

The test is available from PRO-ED, Inc., 8700 Shoal Creek Blvd., Austin, TX 78757.

Achievement Assessment

Achievement evaluation, including standardized tests, is designed to provide an evaluation of the specific information that individuals have learned from their education and life experiences. Such assessments should respond to the skills needed by the consumer in the context of the 21st-century career and occupational worlds. Many careers have new skill requirements and currently are situated in an economic environment that also requires perseverance, adaptability, and humility (Peck, 2010). Multiple skills are usually necessary today for a productive performance in a specific work task, such as tasks requiring verbal comprehension, computational abilities, and manual dexterity. Achievement assessment, moreover, can help determine the consumer's employability, that is, his or her work potential, characterized by the demonstration of necessary work behaviors and the potential to develop work-related skills. Yet in this specific type of assessment there are two particular target areas that provide information which, in turn, forms the basis for the development of needed work skills. They are the consumer's verbal and numerical skills. Verbal achievement is demonstrated in reading and spelling. In numerical achievement, such factors as counting, reading number symbols, and performing written computations are necessary for efficiency in related jobs.

Wide Range Achievement Test–Fourth Edition

The *Wide Range Achievement Test–Fourth Edition* (WRAT-4; Wilkinson & Robertson, 2006) is one of the most frequently used achievement tests. It is designed to be administered individually or in small groups. The fourth edition of the *Wide Range Achievement Test* includes a new subtest, Reading Comprehension, in addition to the original Word Reading, Spelling, and Arithmetic subtests.

Word Reading—Recognizing and naming letters, pronouncing printed words

Reading Comprehension—Reading and understanding the meaning of sentences

Spelling—Writing letters and words from dictation

Arithmetic—Counting, reading number symbols, oral and written computation

The WRAT-4 provides standard scores and percentile ranks by both age and grade, a national stratified sample, scaling and item analysis, and two equivalent test forms. These alternate forms, Gray and Red, can be used for pretesting and posttesting or combined for more comprehensive test results.

The age range for the WRAT-4 is 5 to 95 years. For either the Gray or Red test form, administration is approximately 30 to 45 minutes. This measure can provide a rough indication of a consumer's academic achievement and can serve as an adjunct to intelligence and behavior-adjustment tests administered by rehabilitation professionals.

For many years, the WRAT has found widespread use in rehabilitation facilities; however, the test is not appropriate for consumers with visual impairments. Also, the emphasis on hearing the examiner and the necessity of having to pronounce words correctly on certain parts of the test may place consumers with a hearing impairment at a disadvantage. The WRAT-4, however, is particularly helpful in assessing academic achievement when the consumer has not had recent educational experience and the rehabilitation professional wants to determine basic reading and arithmetic capabilities for possible training. The items in each part of the test are arranged in order of difficulty. For consumers with mental retardation or others for whom many items may be too difficult, an oral section with easier questions is provided with each test.

Vocational Implications

The WRAT-4 explores an adequate level of basic educational skills and development and provides suggestions for the level of possible training. However, the functional application of the scores is not always evident. Yet the WRAT-4 identifies the level of reading comprehension on an absolute scale in relation to age/grade peers. It is particularly helpful in diagnosing learning disabilities in reading, spelling, and arithmetic when used in conjunction with a comprehensive test of general ability. It can identify these deficits during assessment as one explores which academic skills are necessary for competing for employment in this 21st-century labor market.

Availability

The WRAT-4 is available from PAR, Inc., 16204 N. Florida Ave., Lutz, FL 33549.

Adult Basic Learning Examination–Second Edition

The major purposes of the *Adult Basic Learning Examination–Second Edition* (ABLE-2; Karlsen & Gardner, 1986) are to determine the general educational level of adults who have not completed a formal eighth-grade education, diagnose individual strengths, and assist in the development of educational plans. According to the publisher, the second edition of the ABLE is the only adult achievement test designed specifically for adults. The test was written for adults and standardized with adults, reflecting current philosophies regarding adult education. The ABLE provides scores in five areas: vocabulary, reading, spelling, computation, and problem solving (math). This paper-and-pencil test contains three levels: Level I—Grades 1 through 4; Level II—Grades 5 through 8; and Level III—Grades 9 through 12. Each level has two alternate forms. There are five subtests at each level: Vocabulary, Reading, Spelling, Arithmetic, and Computation and Problem Solving. Each test consists of multiple-choice items, as well as items requiring the writing out of the word that is the answer to an arithmetic problem.

The ABLE was designed to be adult oriented in content and was specifically designed for use in connection with adult education classes or job-training programs (Anastasi, 1982). Vocabulary, reading, spelling, and arithmetic are related to adults' everyday lives. The test is administered in group form and can be hand or machine scored. Machine scoring is somewhat impractical because all math problems must first be hand tallied. The total testing time for Levels I and II is about 2½ hours; Level III takes about 3 hours.

Anastasi (1982) indicated that split-half and Kuder–Richardson reliabilities of each test in the ABLE range from 0.80 to 0.96. Correlations between corresponding tests of the ABLE and the *Stanford Achievement*

Test (Psychological Corp., 1988) in the elementary and high school samples range from the 0.60s to the 0.80s.

When a rapid estimate of an adult's level of learning is needed, or when testing time is limited, the ABLE screening battery is a useful alternative to the full ABLE battery. It can be administered in about an hour, yet it provides a reliable measure of an adult's functional reading and mathematics ability. A new edition of the ABLE, for use with individuals whose primary language is Spanish, includes measures of reading and mathematics.

Regarding the use of the test for persons with disabilities, the reading level for each of the three tests gets progressively more difficult. There is no information on individuals with disabilities in the test manual. For persons with severe visual or hearing impairments, the test is not usable in its present form. However, it can be used without modifications for consumers with mental retardation. The parts of the ABLE that are administered orally can be used with persons who are blind if responses are recorded using a Braille answer sheet or typewriter or, in the case of individual administration, given aloud for the test administrator to record. The major problem with the test is the arithmetic parts; although some of the arithmetic problems could be presented orally, many problems require computation using paper and pencil. For individuals who are deaf, major modifications are needed in the orally administered parts. The items read by the examiner could be printed together with the multiple-choice answers found in the test booklets. Consumers who are unusually proficient in signing or lipreading can have the test administered to them by these methods. Although no modifications are necessary, individual administration may be considered for consumers with mental retardation. Extra practice items may also be necessary.

Vocational Implications

The ABLE explores an adequate level of basic educational skills and current levels of reasoning, mathematics, and reading development and assists in the determination of basic job-seeking behaviors, such as completing the interview form.

Availability

The ABLE is available from Pearson, Customer Service, PO Box 599704, San Antonio, TX 78259, 800/328-5999.

Peabody Individual Achievement Test–Revised

The *Peabody Individual Achievement Test–Revised* (PIAT-R; Markwardt, 1998) provides a wide-range screening measure of achievement in the areas of mathematics, reading, spelling, and general information. The test yields six final scores: mathematics, reading recognition, reading comprehension, spelling, general information, and a total score. The PIAT-R is individually administered, and none of the six subtests is timed. All items are presented orally, and the examinee responds by selecting the appropriate number or illustration from four alternatives. The items are contained in two booklets. Results are given in grade scores, percentile ranks, age scores, and standard scores. The length of the test varies with the individual. The manual states, however, that this untimed test usually requires between 30 and 40 minutes to administer and score. A written language composite may be obtained by combining scores on the spelling and written expression subtests.

The PIAT-R is a thorough update of the original 1970 PIAT. In addition to new items, new artwork, redesigned test materials, and new norms, a written expression subtest is offered for screening written language skills. Additional features include an audiocassette tape that may be used by examiners as a guide to the accepted pronunciation for words used in the Reading, Recognition, and Spelling subtests. The test's norms have been updated and represent a national standardization that employed the most recent Bureau of Census projections of the U.S. school population at the time of publication.

No information is given in the test manual on persons with disabilities. The test is not useful in its present form for individuals who have severe visual or hearing impairment; however, for persons with mental retardation, it is very useful in its present form. The usefulness of this test for persons who are blind depends on the extent of the visual disability. The high-contrast black-and-white drawings may be perceived accurately enough to permit the use of the test with consumers who are partially blind. Such consumers should try a few practice items in each section to determine if they can accurately perceive them. Those who cannot should not be given the PIAT-R.

The emphasis on listening to the examiner and the necessity of having to pronounce words correctly on certain parts of the test place persons with deafness at a severe disadvantage on the PIAT-R. However, the visual content of the test has much to offer this group. The questions can be signed, or printed on separate cards and presented one at a time. The person who is hearing impaired and who does not speak very well can easily point to the correct answer or respond by signing.

No modification of this test is necessary for persons with mental retardation. However, it is helpful for the rehabilitation worker to know that the Mathematics subtest requires the consumer to know numbers and some symbols, and that Reading Recognition requires examinees to know letters, identify words, and read and pronounce words aloud. In the Reading Comprehension subtest, the consumer reads a sentence silently and then matches it with the appropriate illustration.

Vocational Implications

The PIAT-R explores an adequate level of basic educational skills, provides the consumer with a pool of learned skills that can be drawn on and used, and suggests educational skill readiness for training.

Availability

The PIAT-R is available from Pearson, 19500 Bulverde Rd., San Antonio, TX 78259, 800/627-7271.

Summary of Achievement and Aptitude Assessment

When working with different consumers in rehabilitation, the following batteries of achievement and aptitude tests are suggested.

Consumers Who Have No Recent Educational Experience and Little Formal Education

Step 1—*Wide Range Achievement Test–Fourth Edition* or *Adult Basic Learning Examination*

Step 2—*Bennett Mechanical Comprehension Test, Minnesota Clerical Test,* or *Minnesota Paper Form Board–Revised* and *Career Ability Placement Survey*

Step 3—*Differential Aptitude Test* series, if appropriate for rehabilitation planning purposes

Consumers Who Have No Recent Educational Experience but Are High School Graduates

    Step 1—*Adult Basic Learning Examination* or *Peabody Individual Achievement Test–Revised*

    Step 2—*Differential Aptitude Test*

    Step 3—*Hand-Tool Dexterity Test*

Work Sample Assessment

Since 1970, the availability of work sample systems has been a significant part of the vocational assessment process. Although many practical tasks and activities are employed by vocational evaluators to explore a consumer's capabilities, the most highly structured technique that provides an exploratory vehicle is the work sample, which can provide a most productive approach to evaluation. With a work sample, one "performs actual portions (or simulations) of jobs or training curricula, using the same materials, tools, and equipment that one utilized in the real work or training setting" (Corthell & Griswald, 1987, p. 58).

Traditionally, work samples have been used with populations for which valid measurement with paper-and-pencil tests is unobtainable. These groups may be low in verbal skills, unable to read, or unable to relate to standard testing situations for any number of reasons.

There are several types of work samples. Some applied work samples are replicated directly—in their entirety—from specific jobs in industry and include the equipment, tasks, raw materials, supplies, and procedures found in the industry setting. Other samples replicate a segment of the essential work factors and tasks, materials, equipment, and supplies that simulate jobs to be performed in the community (Costello, 1991; Hursh & Kerns, 1988; Patterson, 2008). Other types of samples include single-trait or cluster-trait samples. The former evaluates a single worker trait or characteristic that may have relevance to a specific job or many jobs; the latter sample is designed to assess a group of worker traits and contains a number of traits inherent in a job or variety of jobs. The differences among these several types of samples are matters of emphasis: All disclose specific abilities, either by observation or by measurement, and in every case the results of a series of individual work samples are combined to form a profile of consumer potential.

Work samples are usually found in controlled settings, such as the rehabilitation center or laboratory. Nevertheless, there has been quite a bit of discussion regarding the validity, soundness, and appropriateness of the standards provided with work samples because these statistical elements are much more difficult to provide in the case of the work sample than in the case of most psychological tests. The Vocational Evaluation and Work Adjustment Association (VEWAA) explains that because work samples shall be representative of realistic, competitive worker skills (Vocational Evaluation and Work Adjustment Association, 1975), a content validity approach is recommended. The approach incorporates the techniques of (a) approval by a panel of experts, (b) job analysis, and (c) task analysis. Work samples should also be standardized in terms of materials, layout, instructions, and scoring. The best approach for achieving this goal of standardization is to prepare an examiner's manual.

Questions to Ask When Selecting a Work Sample System

Although in-house work samples may be a response to the local labor market, many commercial systems are available that have been standardized and that can be of great assistance to the rehabilitation worker who is exploring vocational potential. An evaluator can be easily confused, however, about which system or systems will best satisfy assessment needs. The following questions have been developed from suggestions provided by Hursh and Kerns (1988) and are representative of the types of questions that can be asked by the evaluator:

> What type of classification system is used by the commercial work samples: trait factor or job cluster?
> Does the manual provide normative information (such as data on the normative population sample) and reliability and validity information?
> If one were to use the particular system, what are the initial costs, equipment maintenance and replacement costs, necessary computer time allotments and printouts, and space requirements? What is the evaluator:evaluee ratio?

Are the behavioral, performance, and physical capacity measures clearly identified?

Are appropriate forms available for recording the reporting observations and recommendations?

Does the system provide a practice orientation period?

Does the system penalize the consumer for low verbal skills or low academic achievement?

Is it necessary to buy the whole package, or can one or more individual components be purchased?

What is the length of time required for the average consumer to complete the work samples in the system?

The Work Sample Evaluation Process

A manual on the particular work sample system should be used, because it can offer uniform procedures for administration, use, and interpretation. The evaluator can also explain the relationship of the particular work samples to available jobs and training opportunities.

Instructions should be given to the consumer prior to beginning a work sample. If the consumer cannot perform the task from these standardized instructions, then a determination will have to be made on what types of instruction will facilitate the consumer's understanding of the task to be performed. The consumer should thoroughly understand what he or she is going to do and how to do it. But an explanation of the instructions can provide valuable information about the consumer's learning preference.

Once the consumer has demonstrated his or her ability to perform the work sample, then performance is measured. If possible, an evaluation should be conducted on the whole person, because an understanding of the consumer's skills and interests may not be enough for successful work adjustment and job progress. Behaviors that are crucial to acquiring and holding jobs in industry include the ability to follow directions, use tools, understand work methods, maintain attention span, have physical stamina, and accept criticism. However, because the environment of the rehabilitation facility differs from an actual work setting, the behaviors of the consumer during the evaluation process may not accurately reflect eventual job-related behaviors.

While the consumer does the work sample, the evaluator observes and records observations on the following:

- explicit behavior factors
- performance factors related to the demands of the task, such as aptitudes and skills
- possible learning style and preferences, as the consumer should adequately learn all aspects of what is to be done before he or she is required to perform the task
- possible indications of interest through observing the consumer's behavior during task performance
- possible job-related needs and potential job modifications for the consumer

Upon completion of the sample, a score is determined regarding how well the consumer has performed relative to others who have taken the sample. A summary of the results of all the actual work samples performed that day should be conducted. This summary is accomplished in terms of the consumer's behaviors, interests, and performance.

After the completion of all the work samples, the daily observations are summarized and a meeting with the consumer is arranged. The following topics are discussed:

- the consumer's reactions to the work sample process, and the work samples the consumer especially liked or disliked
- the consumer's estimate of his or her behavior and performance, and then the consumer's actual behavior and performance
- the consumer's reaction to this information

The evaluator will then write a report and include information on indications of interest, learning preferences, possible vocational aptitudes and skills, and qualities and behaviors that appear to be characteristic of the individual at work.

Advantages and Disadvantages of Work Samples

Using work samples to obtain a comprehensive assessment means that the cultural, educational, and language barriers of vocational potential can be reduced. As consumers realize that they are working on practical tasks, they may accept the assessment activity as being significant to their vocational planning. Work samples may be as close to the reality of work as can be obtained in the rehabilitation facility. Performance of concrete tasks provides direct and immediate information to the evaluator and, in turn, immediate feedback to the individual about his or her performance (Hursh & Kerns, 1988). Botterbusch (1983) explained that a major advantage is that the consumer's motivation is usually enhanced due to the face validity of the work sample (i.e., the work sample looks like an actual job), and performance standards are almost identical to those of actual jobs.

There are disadvantages, however, to using work samples. Although work samples may be an improvement over traditional psychological tests, they are still viewed by many examinees as yet another test; this perception can be quite anxiety provoking for individuals with disabilities. Also, a person's abilities—at a given moment in time within a contrived, time-pressured situation—do not necessarily indicate a success level within a more normal situation. The lack of standardization of many work samples, moreover, may result in very dissimilar results with different evaluators. The work samples should relate to varied available career or employment opportunities in the consumer's geographical area and explore tasks and demands in the current workforce. Also, inconsistent administration and scoring reduces reliability. Work samples may also fail to distinguish between aptitude and achievement. For the evaluator, there is the great responsibility to interpret results in light of how much related experience the consumer has had.

An additional caution when using work samples is explained by Walk (1985). In a work sample system, the tasks are constructed to identify the consumer's skills in a given area. Failure to complete a task successfully usually indicates limited or no ability in the area tested. However, this may not be the case with individuals with disabilities. Failure to successfully complete a task could mean, instead, that certain characteristics of the task itself, coupled with the disability, interact, leading to failure. As Walk (1985) stated, "A reviewer must be careful to distinguish the two" (p. 29).

Selected Work Sample Systems

The following information identifies selected work sample systems that are used in many vocational evaluation facilities. Some facilities, moreover, will use several of the currently available systems, while others may only use one or two because of consumer and budget considerations.

McCarron-Dial Evaluation System

The *McCarron-Dial Evaluation System* (MDS; McCarron & Dial, 1973) consists of eight separate instruments that assess six neuropsychological factors: verbal, cognitive, sensory, motor, emotional, and integration coping (adaptive behavior). It provides predictive information regarding work potential and suggests rehabilitation strategies related to central nervous system damage. Three days of training are required at Dallas and selected sites, and training is available at McCarron-Dial Systems, PO Box 45628, Dallas, TX 75245, 214/634-2863.

Micro-Tower

This system has 13 work samples, is group administered, and evaluates 8 of the 11 aptitudes within 5 aptitude cluster areas (motor skills, clerical perception, spatial, numerical, and verbal). Each of these areas is assessed by specific tests. The system takes 3 to 5 days to complete and may be taken while seated or standing, requiring, however, the use of at least one hand. Each work sample is divided into a learning practice period and the actual performance. It may be used for individuals with all types of disabilities (Hursh & Kerns, 1988), except for consumers with moderate to severe mental retardation. *Micro-Tower* is available from the ICD Rehabilitation and Research Center, 340 East 24th St., New York, NY 10010.

Table 10.1 identifies available selected work sample systems that can be used in agency settings for consumers with varied disabilities. Some of the samples require specialized training.

Functional Assessment

Terms such as *functional assessment, behavioral assessment, physical capacities assessment*, and *functional capacities assessment* have been used to describe the assessment of work behaviors (Patterson, 2008). While used interchangeably, each of these terms can have a different meaning depending on how the professional is using the term, or the setting in

Table 10.1
Selected Work Sample Systems

Sample system	Developer	Description	Training
McCarron-Dial Evaluation System (MDS)	McCarron-Dial Systems PO Box 45628 Dallas, TX 75245 214/247-5945	Consists of eight separate instruments that assess six neuropsychologic factors: verbal, cognitive, sensory, motor, emotional, and integration coping (adaptive behavior); provides predictive information regarding work potential and suggests rehabilitation strategies for disabilities related to central nervous system damage.	Training of 3 days required at Dallas and selected sites
Micro-Tower	Micro-Tower Institutional Services, ICD Rehabilitation and Research Center 340 East 24th St. New York, NY 10010	Provides 13 work samples for persons who are educable and have retardation through those in the normal range, adolescents, and adults; takes 3 to 5 days to complete; instructions presented on cassette tape with opportunity for questions and supplemental instructions; administered to 5 to 10 people at a time; each work sample divided into a learning practice period; group discussion conducted at end of each day; profile of scores in five aptitude areas provided: verbal, numerical, motor, spatial, and clerical perception; norms provided; testing of jobs from DOT given.	Not required, but available at ICD (Institute for Disabled) or at purchaser's agency at their cost
Valpar	Valpar International Corporation PO Box 5767 Tucson, AZ 85703	Valpar 22 are component work samples that consist of generalized work-like tasks. Each sample is administered, scored, and interpreted independently.	Contact Valpar

which it is used (Patterson, 2008). The targeted areas of functional assessment measures are usually the following:

- Individual preferences
- Individual strengths
- Work history
- Functional use of academics (to what extent the consumer uses reading, time-telling, money, and writing skills)
- Following directions
- Behavior (concerning age-appropriateness, appropriateness to situation and location, interfering with work tasks, ability to engage others in social interactions, moods, and what prompts challenging behaviors)
- Learning style (what methods seem to work best when teaching the consumer a new skill)
- Social skills/interactions
- Communication skills—both expressive and receptive
- Work endurance/stamina
- Medical/physical status and management
- Orientation/mobility skills
- Fine- and gross-motor coordination skills
- Work-related skills/concerns (independent transportation to and from work, personal hygiene, motivation to complete an activity, problem-solving skills)
- Transportation needs (current access to training or employment)
- Current financial information and concerns

While it is a challenging process to apply measurement principles to functioning, the basis for functional assessment emerges from a disablement model created by the World Health Organization (Granger, Gilewski, & Carlin, 2010) that includes such dimensions as physical independence, mobility, occupation, social integration, orientation, and economic self-sufficiency. Functional skills help to achieve these goals.

Selected Functional Assessment Measures

As identified by Patterson (2008) and Saladin (2008), there are several measures that can identify many of these dimensions, three of which are the following:

Minnesota Satisfactoriness Scales

Minnesota Satisfactoriness Scales (Gibson, Weiss, Dawis, & Lofquist, 1970), an observer rating system based on the Minnesota Theory of Work Adjustment, is a theory of vocational adjustment for people with disabilities (Bolton, 1986). This can be completed by an employer or trainer in 5 minutes and has five subscales: Performance, Conformance, Personal Adjustment, Dependability, and General Satisfactoriness. An excellent vocational counseling tool (Patterson, 2008), it is available from Vocational Psychology Research, N657 Elliott Hall, University of Minnesota, Minneapolis, MN 55455; e-mail: vpr@tc.umn.edu

Functional Assessment Inventory

The *Functional Assessment Inventory* is intended to help counselors obtain a comprehensive view of an individual with a disability prior to beginning rehabilitation planning. It consists of 30 behavioral items ranging from physical capacities to work history and work habits. This measure also has items related to potential vocational strengths possessed by the consumer and two summary questions related to an overall assessment of severity of disability and likelihood that the individual can acquire and hold a job (Crewe & Athelstan, 1984). It is available from the Rehabilitation Resource, University of Wisconsin–Stout, PO Box 790, Menomonie, WI 54751; e-mail: http://www.chd.uwstout.edu/svri/pwi/trr/orderform.html

Functional Skills Screening Inventory

The *Functional Skills Screening Inventory* (Becker, Schur, Pacletti-Schelp, & Hammer, 1984) was developed for use with individuals with moderate to severe disabilities. It evaluates basic functional skills and concepts, personal care, communication, domestic skills, work and community living skills, and social awareness. The instrument emphasizes the consumer's assets, rather than only targeting deficits. It also relies on observer ratings and informant data and consequently may have a high degree of subjectivity (Saladin, 2008).

Conclusion

There are several aptitude-related measures (i.e., APTICOM, *Talent Assessment Program,* and *Aviator*) that are computer based and are described in Chapter 11. Significantly, however, achievement tests can also occasionally be developed by rehabilitation workers to quickly evaluate a consumer's daily living and employment-related skills. Although such tests are of the "homemade" variety, they can be more criterion referenced, containing test items that are closely associated with the consumer's daily life demands. These tests, which may include selected work samples, have not been standardized but can still provide much useful information for rehabilitation planning purposes.

Achievement, aptitude, and work sample assessments are useful approaches to help the consumer achieve a better knowledge of work-related strengths and weaknesses. Fortunately, many standardized tests are already available to provide an evaluation of achievement- and aptitude-related skills. If the rehabilitation worker uses these measures according to their specific directions, information can be gained about the consumer that is invaluable for rehabilitation planning.

Chapter 11

Self-Assessment and Other Selected Approaches in Assessment

Legislative policies, entrepreneurial efforts by rehabilitation professionals, and the growth of technology have all contributed to the development of assessment approaches beyond the traditional paper-and-pencil testing methods. The emphases on consumer participation in the vocational evaluation process and feedback during this process have also fueled the implementation of innovative appraisal strategies. These methods have further focused on providing information to help those consumers for whom standardized methods are not that useful. An important, integral component of three of these approaches is self-assessment.

Self-assessment is an important, even vital, part of career exploration. Such an exploration demands an in-depth investigation targeted at reconciling the consumer's perceptions of self and his or her career prospects. It is the act of knowing one's self and the world of careers and how the two can interact to obtain needed and desired outcomes. In fact, career exploration is among the most central and commonly studied mechanisms in the career development literature (Porfeli & Skorikov, 2010).

Since self-assessment can be both cost effective and consumer empowering, vocational evaluators and rehabilitation counselors are using self-assessment strategies with consumers more and more frequently, and the demand for them is growing. Prince, Most, and Silver (2003) believed that "the market for self-help career assessment has exploded over the past 30 years" (p. 40). In self-exploration, information is sought about a variety of personal qualities and attitudes that are relevant to vocational planning, including values, interests, education, abilities, and lifestyle preferences, and the assessment is a detailed, careful analysis of these qualities. The assessment is actually taking a personal inventory in which personal information is identified and then prioritized for usefulness in exploring and appraising career directions. The assessment can identify patterns of what worked well for the consumer and what did not, so that as the consumer focuses on job and career opportunities, choices will be based on current needs and preferences.

Self-assessment tools are usually less expensive, require less time to complete, and facilitate consumer involvement. Active participation is a key ingredient of successful career planning. It is often difficult for the consumer, however, to distinguish from among the rapidly expanding self-assessment options those that have been professionally developed and validated and those that have not. Many of these options present a challenge because "they are being developed with powerful technology that allows for sophisticated assessment administration and interpretation previously available only through professional counseling" (Prince et al., 2003, p. 44). The instruments also vary considerably in quality and level of sophistication, and in many cases, the evidence may be lacking that they have been validated for self-directed use. It should be noted, moreover, that when using these tools, the evaluator should be careful when working with consumers who have limited verbal ability, goal instability, and low self-confidence and motivation. These individuals may need mediated assistance to follow through with decision-making efforts.

Two other chapters in this book identify self-assessment activities. Chapter 7, "Interest Assessment in Vocational Rehabilitation," discusses a specialized approach to consumer interest exploration that demands personal reflection and evaluation. Chapter 9, "Personality Assessment in Vocational Rehabilitation," suggests using sentence-completion exercises when exploring consumer values. During the consumer interview, moreover, the evaluator can ask open-ended questions that may stimulate personal reflection and awareness of many issues that may provide important information for vocational assessment and rehabilitation planning.

The Interview Guide for Consumers With Functional Limitations, the Independent Living Assessment, and the Employment Readiness Scale (see the Appendix and the forms located on the CD-ROM) are three self-assessment tools for consumers with disabilities. Although developed many years ago, they still provide valuable information that can facilitate self-exploration. The Interview Guide for Consumers With Functional Limitations was developed for persons with low verbal skills and disabilities and is a comprehensive interview guide. The Independent Living Assessment instrument is particularly useful for people who may be in transition from an institutionalized environment to community-based living. It explores such important living areas as meeting daily demands when living in an apartment or other group setting and includes a review of some of the domains of financial responsibility. The Employment Readiness Scale is particularly useful for evaluating employment expectations and can be taken immediately after the initial assessment interview. Similar to other self-assessment measures, all of these instruments help consumers to realize that they are valuable partners during the assessment process and that their input can be an important determinant for eventual job or career planning.

This chapter will discuss three other selected vocational assessment approaches, namely, transferable skills evaluation, portfolio evaluation, and computer-based assessment. Each strategy has its own distinctive methods and provides an opportunity to gather insights about the realities of the consumer's career-related strengths and limitations. For consumers who challenge the reliability and validity of standardized, traditional instruments because of cultural considerations or severe disability-related limitations, these approaches, with their self-assessment perspective, specifically transferable skills and the consumer portfolio, may be more relevant for obtaining useful assessment information.

Transferable Skills Assessment

One of the practical ways to explore the consumer's abilities in relation to employability goals is transferable skills assessment. Such an exploration encourages consumer participation and provides an opportunity for an individual to receive immediate feedback on career-related strengths. It is an exercise in consumer empowerment, allowing the consumer to believe that he or she has some control during the assessment process.

Transferable skills are skills that have been used on one job and can be applied to alternative jobs, and they are most applicable to consumers who have a work history. This assessment is based on observable, objective work histories. Work histories, of course, can be misinterpreted, but this skills analysis is less prone to test anxiety or the effects of disability than work samples or most standardized paper-and-pencil tests (Patterson, 2008).

Skills Analysis

Skills analysis has a long and diverse history, and its development has been facilitated by business and industry. The concept of transferable skills analysis was popularized by the book *What Color Is Your Parachute?* (Bolles, 2004), which prompted counselors to look for *similarities* among skills, rather than differences. This form of assessment has received increased attention from evaluators because employers are looking for people with particular competencies and not necessarily with special interests. Consumers also want job situations in which they use the skills that are important to them. If individuals with disabilities are to become more marketable in the competitive job environment, then they should be clear about their skills. People are hired on the basis of their qualifications—a mix of experience, skills, knowledge, attitudes, and abilities—and how well their qualifications match what is needed on the job.

A skill is simply an ability to do something. It may be a natural ability or one acquired through training or education. Skills have been classified into the following categories:

- *Adaptive skills*—Adaptive skills are the self-management skills and personality orientations an individual brings to the job. Examples of such skills include attention to detail, cooperation, concentration, empathy, enthusiasm, punctuality, reliability, spontaneity, and tolerance.
- *Functional skills*—Functional skills are generic behaviors related to people, data, and things that are brought into play in a work environment. Examples of such skills include synthesizing, mentoring, working with precision tools, analyzing, negotiating, manipulating, computing, supervising, operating, compiling, consulting, controlling, copying, persuading, and handling.
- *Specific content skills*—Specific content skills are competencies that enable an individual to perform a specific job according to the employer's expectations. These are skills related to a given discipline,

such as a mechanic knowing the parts of an engine or a physical therapist understanding the different components of the human body.

Another way to think about job-related skills is to organize them by Holland (1977) types, such as the following:

- *Realistic*—Assembling, participating in physical activities or outdoor activities, building, and operating tools or machinery
- *Artistic*—Formulating ideas, inventing, designing, composing or playing music, and expressing feelings and thoughts
- *Enterprising*—Managing money, developing a budget, seeing a problem and acting to solve it, organizing people, making decisions, taking risks, selling, and persuading
- *Investigative*—Calculating, researching, analyzing, diagnosing, experimenting, and observing
- *Social*—Helping, listening, motivating, counseling, consulting, and working on a team
- *Conventional*—Keeping records, comparing, attending to details, classifying, and organizing things

There are still further approaches to group work skills, groupings that may be more specific to assessment needs and useful for the counselor, for example, according to working condition and roles (Sikula, 1994):

- *Management skills*—Analyzing, negotiating, directing, solving, evaluating, expediting, synthesizing, researching, producing, organizing, supervising, delegating, making decisions, taking on responsibility, promoting change
- *Communication skills*—Organizing, reasoning, writing, listening, explaining, cooperating, collaborating
- *Research and investigation skills*—Reviewing, collecting data, diagnosing, synthesizing, designing, interviewing, identifying problems and needs
- *Financial skills*—Calculating, working under stress, handling detail work, concentrating, budgeting, projecting, counting
- *Manual skills*—Assembling, building, repairing, fixing, operating, monitoring, cutting, operating tools or machinery, setting up

- *Human relations skills*—Coordinating, counseling, guiding, leading, understanding others' feelings, expressing appropriately one's feelings, teaching, listening accurately, establishing rapport, interviewing, influencing
- *Clerical skills*—Recommending, computing, examining, evaluating, filing, improving, recording, following directions
- *Technical skills*—Designing, financing, evaluating data, calculating, aligning, verifying, adjusting
- *Public relations skills*—Working under stress, conducting, planning, informing the public, maintaining a favorable image, consulting, writing, representing, researching
- *Selling skills*—Working under stress, promoting, persuading, contacting, reviewing and inspecting products, working with people, informing buyers, determining value
- *Critical-thinking skills*—Identifying critical issues, defining a problem, applying general principles that explain experiences, analyzing data, applying appropriate criteria to strategies, comparing, making decisions

Another grouping goes by classification of work environments (Roe & Lunneborg, 1984):

- *Service*—Serving and attending to the personal needs and welfare of others
- *Business contact*—Persuading other people, face-to-face sale of goods and services
- *Organization*—Efficient functioning of commercial enterprises and government activities
- *Technology*—Production, maintenance, transportation of commodities and utilities
- *Outdoors*—Cultivation, preservation, gathering of natural resources and animal welfare
- *Science*—Scientific theory and its application to real-world problems
- *General culture*—Primarily concerned with the preservation and transmission of the general culture and heritage
- *Arts and entertainment*—Use of special skills in the creative arts and the world of entertainment

Also, skills may be recognized by identifying and examining a consumer's most satisfying accomplishments. Skills lead to these accomplishments, and by exploring these accomplishments, a pattern of skills may be recognized that an individual uses and enjoys using. To be noted is that accomplishments may be completed activities, goals, projects, or jobs held. Embedded in these overall accomplishments are the following:

- *Basic skills*—Reading, writing, arithmetic, listening, speaking
- *Thinking skills*—Creative thinking, decision making, problem solving, seeing things in the mind's eye, knowing how to learn, reasoning
- *Skills inherent in personal qualities*—Responsibility, sociability, self-management

Skills, of course, can be acquired. Most skills are developed from education, but the level of a consumer's educational attainment does not necessarily limit the skills that can be attained. A person with an undergraduate degree in history, for example, may display a vast array of achievable skills, but the degree itself does not denote necessarily the level of skill attainment. Skills can also be derived from work and leisure experiences. What is important for the evaluator is to assist consumers to identify their skills for general self-assessment.

There are different approaches to identify information on a person's transferable skills, such as questionnaires, interviews, and the use of the consumer interview, during which the consumer is asked, for example, to describe something that he or she is proud of having completed, and then the skills are listed that were required to complete it. Another method is to ask the consumer to write a story about one of his or her accomplishments and then list the skills used. Still another approach is to provide consumers with an already designed checklist. A variety of checklists have been developed, many of which are found in career development and counseling texts. Examples of three measures follow.

- Bolles's (2004) *What Color Is Your Parachute?* contains an inventory that is quite useful in assessment situations when exploring transferable skills.
- *A Skills Inventory,* an adaptation of a skills inventory created by Bolles (1989), was developed by Robert Lock (1992) and follows

the Holland typology of Realistic, Investigative, Artistic, Social, Enterprising, and Conventional. A workbook of student activities titled "Taking Charge of Your Career Direction" that contains the inventory also has useful information on adaptive, functional, and specific content skills that the consumer can identify while taking the inventory.

• Patterson (2008) explained that the *Vocational Diagnosis and Assessment of Residual Employability* (VDARE) system was developed to identify residual employability potential (e.g., transferable skills). Although the VDARE was originally developed for use in providing expert testimony in disability adjudication cases, it can be used as a tool for vocational counseling. The VDARE process includes such steps as

❖ listing the relevant jobs held by an individual,

❖ recording the worker trait factors and identifying a Work Field code,

❖ generating the Pre-Vocational Profile by recording the worker trait code that mirrors the highest level of functioning for each trait, respectively, across the entire work history (Havranek, Field, & Grimes, 2005),

❖ identifying the Residual Functional Capacity Profile by determining the changes in functioning that result from the disability,

❖ reviewing similar or related jobs, and

❖ evaluating the availability of the potential jobs within the local labor market.

• The VDARE may identify alternative jobs, including previously performed jobs or jobs in which the individual has expressed an interest. Or, the results may indicate types of rehabilitation services that are needed for the individual to return to work. The Transferability of Work Skills Worksheet used in the VDARE process is available from E & F Publishing, 1135 Cedar Shoals Drive, Athens, GA 30605.

Step-by-Step Procedure of Identifying Skills

Whereas an established checklist can provide insightful information for identifying transferable skills, a more informal method can be quite useful for assisting consumers during a self-assessment for future career options. The following is a suggested, sequential approach:

Step 1. The evaluator asks the consumer to discuss, describe, or explain his or her work and leisure experiences. A review of these experiences will reveal a pattern of skills that may have been used repeatedly. This description can be facilitated by asking the following questions:

- What were the most important skills for your different jobs?
- What was the happiest role for you during work or leisure activities?
- What skills and abilities did you need for this kind of work?

If each work and leisure activity is discussed in detail, a pattern of skills will emerge. The more details that are gathered from memory and from the memory of other people's positive responses, the more skills will be identified with confidence. A question that emerges from this identification is the following: Could any of these skills be used in another setting?

Step 2. Once the in-depth work history is completed, the evaluator can develop a transferable skills and abilities profile (Saxon & Spitznagel, 1995) that is structured in the following manner:

Job (from work history)
Skills and Abilities
   1.
   2.
   3.
   4.
   5.

Job (from work history)
Skills and Abilities
   1.
   2.
   3.
   4.
   5.

Step 3. The evaluator determines the consumer's current interest pattern, identifying the consumer's stated and measured interests (see Chapter 7).

Step 4. The counselor finds the *Guide for Occupational Exploration* (GOE; JIST, 1998a) work group that is appropriate for the consumer's job history, skills, and abilities from the profile developed in Step 2. The work group presents the skills and abilities that may be needed for jobs that relate to the consumer's interest pattern and the pattern of skills and abilities that make up the consumer's profile. With the GOE, all jobs are divided into 66 work groups.

Step 5. In completing Step 4, the evaluator must consider the consumer's disabling condition in relation to his or her residual vocational functioning capacity. Skills and abilities that have been lost or limited by the disabling condition must be reflected in the consumer's transferable skills and abilities profile (Saxon & Spitznagel, 1995).

Step 6. The counselor needs to check the local labor market. The jobs that are identified as job matches from previous activities are only "suggestions" and should be evaluated using common sense and good judgment. These job suggestions should be compared to jobs that actually exist in the local or regional labor market.

This six-step process includes an analysis of a consumer's previous work history and leisure activities, the demand characteristics of jobs within that work history, and the consumer's current level of functioning (which may have been affected by illness or injury). With the reduction in job functioning because of disability-related factors, this process requires that additional or alternate job titles be identified. These jobs need to be consistent with the worker's level of functioning, while taking into account previous work skills and leisure activities.

An assumption for the completion of either a structured transferable skills inventory or the six-step approach is that consumers possess the self-confidence to identify skills accumulated throughout their employment history. Consumers may doubt their abilities or may be skeptical about possessing any skills. However, many consumers realize that they have many more skills than they had previously acknowledged. The issue of self-confidence, consequently, may need attention before the exploration of transferable skills can proceed.

Portfolio Assessment

In harmony with the emphasis on active involvement by the consumer in the vocational evaluation process, more attention is being given to the role of portfolio assessment in rehabilitation and career planning. As the Thirtieth Institute on Rehabilitation Issues (IRI; 2003) noted, changes in workplace realities are requiring consumers to take responsibility, when feasible, for their own career development. Portfolios are an appropriate way to create a more interactive and engaging experience for the consumer and are gaining wider acceptance among assessment professionals.

A vocational evaluation portfolio "is a collection of items or samples that demonstrate one's work-related competencies, achievement, values, experiences, and aspirations" (Merz & Koch, 1999, p. 241). With their emphasis on reflection and self-assessment, portfolios organize collections of information, such as assessment results, accommodation needs, career or employment plans, personal reflections, and work samples that highlight the consumer's skills, abilities, and unique talents (IRI, 2003). They are an aspect of performance-based assessment, and the contents of each portfolio are highly individualized.

In vocational evaluation, a portfolio serves as both process and product. It can store relevant career information and can function as a comprehensive informational and planning document. There are two types of portfolios: working and presentation. Their purpose is to assist in employment or career planning and facilitate achievement of employment or career goals. The presentation portfolio functions as a product, sums up the particular process itself, and communicates the consumer's competence, knowledge, or skills in the employment or career area. As a process, with the working portfolio the consumer decides what to include in the portfolio and continuously updates and revises the material to depict the current situation (Merz & Koch, 1999).

Because of its emphasis on reflection, self-awareness, and consumer choice, a portfolio can (a) help consumers better understand themselves and their personal strengths, (b) identify previously unrecognized skills, and (c) help monitor progress over time. The portfolio extends the dimensions of self-assessment to embrace self-evaluation and self-growth. It helps the consumer to take some control during the assessment process. Although portfolios may not sample the whole domain of the assessment experience, the accuracy of the information is generally quite valid and improves with use (Koch & Merz, 2001; Merz & Koch, 1999). All in all, portfolios "discover, develop, and document employability" (Merz & Koch, 1999, p. 242).

Developing a Portfolio

Portfolios can be introduced to consumers with the message that they are tools for integrating assessment data, learning self-appraisal strategies, identifying job and career requirements, and identifying gaps in knowledge or skills that can be remedied through rehabilitation planning and interventions. The evaluator needs to emphasize that consumer participation is necessary, and that the portfolio will be individualized, flexible, and based on information found in assessment instruments, job or career requirements, and the consumer's vocational experiences.

Following this orientation, seven steps are suggested for portfolio development and use so that the portfolio is easy and logical to follow from beginning to end.

Step 1. The consumer should decide what form the evaluation and career development portfolio will take. The most popular format is the hard copy, or paper, portfolio, although the electronic portfolio, or e-portfolio, is gaining more widespread use. The latter uses electronic or digital technology and allows the consumer to collect and organize portfolio artifacts using media tools such as video, audio, and graphics (Barrett, 2001; IRI, 2003). It permits more flexibility in presentation, enables an individual to view its content in an easy-to-use interface, and creates a three-dimensional picture of the individual that is not always possible with paper.

Step 2. The consumer identifies and documents the perceived purpose or goals of the vocational evaluation process, which then becomes the purpose of the portfolio.

Step 3. The evaluator helps the consumer engage in a prelearning activity that includes exploring such questions as, "What do I know about myself?" and "What would I like to learn about myself?" This information is recorded on a form supplied by the agency and then is added to the portfolio (IRI, 2003).

Step 4. The consumer is encouraged to decide what additional documents to include in the portfolio. It should contain all aspects of the individual's career development, such as self-assessment reflections; any update of specific employment or career goals; vocational interest results; previous training and education; employment-related experiences; test results that have identified vocational, career, or employment skills (information often acquired from evaluation experiences, e.g., situational assessments, paper-and-pencil measures, work samples, transferable skills worksheets); and letters of recommendation.

It is suggested that the consumer organize the accumulated portfolio content material under the headings "Understanding Self," which can include reports of assessment results, perceived strengths and skills, certifications, acquired training and education documents, and self-awareness reflections on vocational history and information learned during the evaluation; "Career Exploration," which includes collected information on training and job requirements, employment availability, and career opportunities; and "Decision-Making Plans," which includes an identification of short- and long-term employment or career goals and an overall career plan. More information on specific outlines for this vocational planning is found in Chapter 14.

Step 5. Once the content of the portfolio is chosen, the collection of information proceeds. These data are updated regularly as the consumer proceeds through the assessment process, especially when new skills and additional evaluation results are gained.

Step 6. During the collection and organization of information, the evaluator encourages the consumer to engage in an analysis of the information. Which vocational-related themes emerge and what the data reveal about strengths and career or employment potential are areas that could be explored. This analysis is ongoing during portfolio development, and side-by-side comparisons are made with training, employment, and career requirements. Connections should be made, and when discrepancies are identified, plans should be developed to resolve the differences.

Step 7. When the collection of information nears completion, plans should be made for maximizing the consumer's vocational potential. Usually this is a joint effort by the evaluator and the consumer, with the latter providing feedback from self-analysis exercises. This planning should reflect informed career decisions—decisions that echo the individual's unique interests, skills, talents, and abilities.

All of these suggested steps imply continued interaction between the evaluator and consumer. Portfolio development is also an ongoing project, but when it is presented as a product that has organized assessment results and other personal materials, and contains information on the links between these data and the requirements and opportunities of selected careers, then the portfolio is a document that can bridge consumer potential with career, job, or training realities.

Computer-Based Vocational Assessment

For more than 40 years, computer applications to administer, score, and interpret tests have been used (Sampson, Purgar, & Shy, 2003). Computer-based tests include self-help instruments that extensively involve the consumer in administration, scoring, and interpretation and can be delivered via a personal computer. Also, Internet-based tests can be used anywhere that the consumer has access to the Internet (Sampson et al., 2003).

The greatest stimulus to the growth of computer-assisted assessment has been the development of the desktop microcomputer, which has upheld the promise of in-office computerized test administration combined with quick and accurate test data interpretation (Cohen, Swerdlik, & Phillips, 1996). Rehabilitation professionals were first introduced to computers as a means to score psychological test instruments used in the counseling process (Golter & Golter, 1986). Computers also have been used to help individuals with disabilities take psychometric tests—for example, through voice-operated response units (Growick, 1983).

Although the emergence of computerized assessment has not been without controversy, advocates of computer use see computerized testing, scoring, and interpretation as being more reliable, cost effective, and sophisticated. It also allows for more complex handling of variables and the production of highly sophisticated reports from a statistical standpoint (Brown, 1991). Computerized assessment facilitates the economy of professional time, with usually a negligible time lag between the administration of a test and its scoring and interpretation. A computer program also has the capacity to combine data that are more accurate than the capacities of humans. In addition, computers provide the potential for systematically gathering and accessing extensive normative databases that transcend the capacities of human test interpreters (Cohen et al., 1996).

Golter and Golter (1986) explained that computer applications are of two types: consumer assessment and job matching. Consumer assessment is mainly oriented to computerized psychological testing for determining vocational interests, attitudes, and personalities. Such information can be scored quickly via computer, and a profile of test results can be generated for use in the counseling process. Computer systems, including voice-operated response units that record oral responses for persons with impaired hand function or limited writing skills, can also be used to administer tests (p. 160). These systems have additional capabilities, many of which were identified by Niles and Harris-Bowlsbey (2005).

- Inventory administration and interpretation
- Monitoring progress of the user throughout the vocational and career management process
- Database searches
- Linking resources

Sampson et al. (2003) identified three categorizations of computer-based test interpretation: descriptive, clinician modeled, and clinical actuarial. Descriptive interpretations develop statements based on test scores; clinician models generate statements by "simulating the judgment of a renowned clinician, and clinical-actuarial interpretations generate narrative statements and clinical hypotheses based on empirical research for particular score patterns" (p. 25).

Components of a Computer Assessment System

Maze (1984) identified three areas of computer systems that have application to vocational assessment: self-assessment components, occupation selection, and informational components.

Self-Assessment Components

As stated previously, computers provide an effective medium for administering and scoring evaluative instruments. Assessment instruments can be scored instantaneously, and the results can be explained to the consumer without delay. Subjective exercises can also be administered by the computer, with prompts and extra assistance for those who have difficulty understanding the instruction. As Maze (1984) stated, "Consumers' responses can then be compiled and printed out by the computer in a format that facilitates self-understanding. Any self-assessment topic can be computerized, including aptitude, abilities, skills, interests, work preferences, values, and personality types" (p. 159).

Occupation Selection

To bring more reality into the consumer's vocational evaluation, computers are able to sort occupational titles and select appropriate vocational categories. Maze (1984) believed that, in general, computers are more accurate than counselors, as they can retain hundreds of titles and accurate details about each occupation simultaneously in their memories. They also sort objectively by applying only the screening criteria programmed into them for the sorting process, without regard to gender, race, or socioeconomic status. In other words, computers open up career options and are able to present a wide selection of relevant titles. In fact, many assessment components offer occupational titles as part of their results; the two components can be separate, as when an instrument produces personality types or goal statements that are later translated into occupations, or they can be combined, as they are in many computerized interest inventories (Maze, 1984).

Informational Components

Computers are excellent information-retrieval devices. A computer can score the information, retrieve parts of the information simultaneously, and provide a printed copy for the consumer. Computerized information can include facts about educational programs, industries, occupations, financial aid, job openings, and bibliographic materials.

Computerized career information systems provide a wide array of information regarding employment and specific jobs. These systems are online databases in which comprehensive information regarding various occupations is provided. This information can include detailed descriptions of the occupation, educational requirements for entry into the occupation, and extensive information regarding the day-to-day activities of persons engaged in the occupation (Brown, 1991).

Emerging from computer-assisted self-assessment activities are different types of scoring reports. These reports represent computer output options and can include (a) simple scoring reports that provide test scores, either listed or drawn on a profile; (b) extended scoring reports that provide key statistical information about the results, as well as the relationships between the various subtests or scales (this scoring is very useful for intelligence, ability, and vocational interest tests); and (c) interpretive reports that provide a written interpretation of test findings. The report can give both descriptive and screening information.

Decisions to Make About Computer Use

After determining the components of a computerized assessment system, the quality of each system should be evaluated. Maze (1984) offered a checklist for developing guidelines for computer use in career guidance, adopted for use in vocational evaluation. The following questions are to be asked by the rehabilitation professional when attempting to choose among different systems and components for use in vocational evaluation.

Questions Related to Computer Systems

- What do you perceive as the essential elements in the vocational assessment process? What role is the system intended to play in this process?
- Which assessment instruments does the system offer? Can these instruments be taken either online (at the computer) or offline (on paper with entry of scores into the computer)?
- What are the outcomes the system intends to achieve, and what population is it intended to serve?
- Is the assessment material presented in an interesting and lively manner? How often will it need updating?
- Is the assessment material relevant to your consumer population, and is the assessment material developed at an appropriate reading level? Is normative information provided on the assessment system?
- Are the assessment and job-matching components effective in selecting relevant occupations or educational programs?
- Are there aids to self-assessment that help the consumer answer questions accurately?
- Do the assessment modules make full use of the interactive capabilities of the computer?
- Is the interpretation accurate, usable, and understandable?
- Is the occupational and educational information localized to your region or state? Is it possible to add data?
- What philosophy is used in interpreting the data?
- How is the system intended to be used? How easy is the program to use? To what extent is the program interactive? Does the system allow individuals to change or rethink answers? Are corrections allowed for simple mistakes? How much time does the average

user need? How many sessions do most users need to complete a useful assessment?

- Is the system adaptable to the complex evaluation needs of your consumers?
- Does the manual explain the objectives and logical structure for each assessment component?
- To what extent have the software packages been tested by a variety of users?
- Are there assessment exercises available for special populations?
- Does the system actually keep the data as up-to-date as it claims, and are the updates produced on a dependable schedule?
- Is information provided in the user manual on such issues as concurrent and predictive validity? Has this information been well researched?
- Does the user manual provide information on whether criterion groups are used to determine the ratings of skills and values of occupational groups?
- Is knowledge provided about computerized estimates of skills, interests, or values and their reliability over time?
- Does the system provide a way to determine whether an individual is faking answers or responses?
- What are the professional credentials of the system developers?
- Does the system run on machines already available on site?
- Is the system supported by a reputable, stable organization?
- What is the cost of the system compared to that of the competition?

Questions Related to a Consumer

- Does the consumer have the verbal ability necessary to use the system?
- Is the consumer motivated to use computer systems and relatively free from negative thinking, significant anxiety, depression, and decisional anxiety? Consumers who have negative thinking about themselves and low expectations from assessment are unlikely to benefit from computer system usage, since they may distort the information they receive.
- Does the consumer have some basic skills in the use of computers—skills that can be taught if the consumer has the necessary learning potential?

To use information generated by a computer system, the professional should have, of course, knowledge of computer-assisted software; an understanding of how the assessment results can be integrated with other data, such as educational and work histories; and the experience required to prepare the consumer to use a computer-based assessment system. The following guidelines are recommended:

1. Inform the consumer as to why a specific computer system is recommended. This includes using the particular system manual to illustrate the assessment goals of the system, and what approaches are offered to achieve these goals.
2. Communicate your expectations to the consumer regarding his or her participation in the system and your role as a source of support for the consumer.
3. Conduct a trial run on the computer system with the consumer and answer any questions of concern.
4. Convey the confidentiality of the results and how these results will assist in achieving self-understanding. An emphasis on confidentiality and on the consumer being as *open* as possible when responding to the computer-based exercises can enhance the reliability of this assessment approach.

The comprehensiveness of these computer-based assessment systems, and the large amount of information that is contained in each system, can stimulate their usage for consumers who have the potential to benefit from them. Their interactiveness further sends the message that the consumer assumes a degree of ownership for the assessment process. Also, these systems offer multiple databases and suggest multiple ways to use assessment information. This increased knowledge suggests that the satisfaction and even the certainty of an eventual occupational choice might be enhanced.

Computer Programs for Vocational Assessment

The questions in the previous section should be applied to the list of selected computer-assisted assessment systems that follows. This list is not exhaustive, but the systems that are described have been used frequently in assessment work with consumers.

Aviator

This is Valpar's newest aptitude and interest computer-based assessment system. Aviator is a criterion-referenced battery of short tests whose scores relate to work-related factors of the U.S. Department of Labor's *Revised Handbook for Analyzing Jobs*. It also contains a basic math and language curriculum typical of schools in the United States, Grades 4 through 12. Skills are measured in the academic areas of reading, math, vocabulary, and spelling, as well as other cognitive skills, such as editing, eye–hand coordination, problem solving, color and size discrimination, and short-term visual memory. Test takers progress through the academic tests from the relatively easier, early grade levels through increasingly advanced content levels by correctly answering a minimum number of items within each grade level. Aviator's O*Net database is based on the U.S. Department of Labor's O*Net. Aviator's Standard Occupational Database was derived from the U.S. Department of Labor's collection of 12,700 jobs using the 66 interest areas of the *Guide for Occupational Exploration* as a filter. Both the Pro 3000 and Aviator systems are available at the Valpar International Corporation, PO Box 5767, Tucson, AZ 85703, 800/528-7070.

System of Interactive Guidance and Information Program

Available as of July 2004 from the Valpar Corporation, the *System of Interactive Guidance and Information Program* (SIGI) is an educational and career-planning software system that integrates self-assessment with in-depth and up-to-date career information. It is easy to use and provides students and adults with a realistic view of educational and career options.

The six interrelated subsystems are the heart of the SIGI system; they provide a system of value clarification and disseminate occupational and educational information. Each of these subsystems offers a critical question and helps the student answer it through a series of statements and questions. The questions and answers form the distinctive steps in decision making that a consumer would also follow in future decisions. The subsystems are as follows:

1. *Values.* Examines 10 occupational values and weighs the importance of each one. The values are income, independence, interest field, variety, security, leisure, leadership, helping others, prestige, and early entry.

2. *Locate.* Assigns specifications to five values at a time and gets lists of occupations that meet specifications. The consumer is provided with exercises devised to explore the consequences of the value choices.

3. *Compare.* Asks pointed questions and obtains specific information about occupations of interest. Such questions include occupational description, education and training requirements, income based on national averages, personal satisfaction, conditions of work, opportunities, and outlook.

4. *Prediction.* Estimates probabilities of getting various marks in key courses of preparatory programs for occupations. The predictions are based on local data that may include test scores, self-estimates, and other local predictors.

5. *Planning.* Presents displays of programs that describe each selected occupation and how to access it.

6. *Strategy.* Evaluates occupations in terms of the rewards they offer and the risks of trying to enter them.

The database from which the information is taken in the various steps is continually updated and reviewed. Regional differences are considered in the review process. The SIGI was developed to supplement and complement the work of the rehabilitation professional. The flexibility of the SIGI in adapting to local resources is an attractive part of the system.

APTICOM Aptitude Test Battery

The APTICOM Aptitude Test Battery (Vocational Research Institute, 1989)—a portable computerized desktop testing console—was designed to measure vocational aptitudes studied by the U.S. Department of Labor. This government agency is exploring how performance on measures of these aptitudes is related to job performance. The APTICOM Aptitude Test Battery includes 11 separate tests that are all administered on a wedge-shaped computerized testing console, which automatically determines the test being administered, times the test, shuts down at the end of the standardized testing period, and scores results. This system is intended for adolescents and adults reading at the fourth-grade level or above. Each test is preceded by a practice phase during which the consumer must demonstrate a functional understanding of test demands. In the overall battery, only 2 of 11 tests require the ability to read test items, and all 11 tests are administered with standardized oral instruction. Total administration time ranges between 70 and 90 minutes (Harris, 1982). The vehicle for relating APTICOM aptitude scores to jobs involves linkage with the Occupational Aptitude Pattern (OAP) structure based on the *General Aptitude Test Battery* (GATB). When the APTICOM testing console is connected to a computer printer, a printout is generated that lists the consumer's 11 raw and corresponding standardized test scores, 10 aptitude scores (computed by APTICOM) via the combination of appropriately weighted test scores, and all of the OAPs and work groups for which critical normative cutoffs have been attained (Harris, 1982). This system is unique in that it is totally contained in a personal computer without a keyboard or monitor (Parker, 2008).

A new APTICOM A5 has been developed that allows for customized reports and selection of norm populations ranging from ninth grade to the adult employed. This new system also allows for downloading consumer data to a personal computer disk. All existing APTICOMs are upgradable to A5 specifications.

The APTICOM also provides an inventory of occupational interests in 12 areas: artistic, scientific, plants and animals, protective, mechanical, industrial, business detail, selling, accommodating, humanitarian, lead and influence, and physical performing. This interest inventory is yoked to APTICOM's aptitude component to supply consumers and rehabilitation workers with an efficient means of starting the process of occupational exploration with accurate information refined down to the *Guide for Occupational Exploration* (GOE; Harrington & O'Shea, 1984) work group level. Information about this system is available from the Vocational Research Institute, 1845 Walnut St., Suite 660, Philadelphia, PA 19103, 800/874-5387.

Talent Assessment Program

The Talent Assessment Program (TAP; Talent Assessment, Inc., 1985) measures functional aptitudes and relates them to specific types of work. It has a series of 10 hands-on assessment tests using real work materials in which aptitudes for visualization and retention, discrimination, and dexterity are determined. The test results are correlated both to the DOT and to the worker groups of the GOE. Norms are nondiscriminatory and apply to all population groups. To eliminate discrimination risks with nonreaders who are blind, as well as with individuals with learning disabilities, reading is not required and verbal instructions are normally used. Written instructions are provided for hearing impaired persons. The tests can be used as an initial screening device in conjunction with other work evaluation assessment programs. The TAP software allows for easy modifications of test scores and retesting, serves consumer information for future revival, and allows for input from other assessment instruments. It can be used with Windows R, 95, 96, ME, 2000, and XP.

The Instant Report Instant Summary System (IRIS), a five-disk scoring, placement search, and report-writing program, is available as part of the TAP system. The scoring disk scores and profiles the TAP results, provides a summary of strength areas, and relates those strengths to jobs. The job search disks look for jobs in the general market, in those areas specified as appropriate for individuals with disabilities, or in specific local job markets. This system is available from Talent Assessment, PO Box 5087, Jacksonville, FL 32247, 800/634-1472.

The DISCOVER Program

This program was developed by the American College Testing Program (1989) to assist counselors in providing career guidance to students in Grades 7 through 12. The system contains 20 modules, each of which is completed during one class period, although the student has the option to spend more time on any one module. A college and adult version has also been developed.

The system consists of the following modules: (a) entry, (b) clarifying values, (c) values and occupations, (d) effective decision making, (e) decision making in careers, (f) organization of occupational world, (g) browsing occupations, (h) reviewing interests and strengths, (i) making a list of occupations to explore, (j) getting information about occupations, (k) narrowing a list of occupations, and (l) exploring specific career plans. These modules can be grouped into four components: (a) self-assessment (Self-Information), (b) identification of occupational alternatives (Strategies for Identifying Occupations), (c) review of occupational information (Occupational Information), and (d) identification of educational alternatives (Searches for Educational Institutions). Information about the DISCOVER Program is available at 800/498-6068.

CareerScope 6.0

This system measures both aptitude and interest in a completely user-friendly environment and is designed as a self-administered system that measures both aptitude and interest through valid and reliable assessment tasks. It is a briefer computerized version of APTICOM. The results are instrumental in helping an individual begin the career or educational planning process. There is a new multimedia Introduction (CS Intro) that provides evaluees with a brief introduction to the Career-Scope interest and aptitude assessment. Additionally, the audio feature, which guides consumers through the assessment process, can now be set as a default administration template.

The Interest Inventory measures and identifies a user's attraction to careers that correspond to the U.S. Department of Labor's Interest Areas. These areas are artistic, plants and animals, mechanical, business detail, accommodating, lead and influence, scientific, protective, industrial, selling, humanitarian, and physical performing. The results from the Interest Inventory are compiled into a comprehensive Individual Profile Analysis (IPA). The IPA objectively identifies each consumer's most significant interest area preferences.

Critical aptitudes measured by CareerScope are general learning ability, verbal aptitude, numerical aptitude, spatial aptitude, form perception, and clerical perception.

This system allows for the assessment of one or many people at the same time, and evaluees can proceed at their own comfortable pace. The self-administered tasks take 60 minutes or less to complete. CareerScope is self-administered, with each consumer working at a different work station. All that is required is minimal proficiency with a mouse and a fourth-grade reading level. The system features easy-to-follow instructions, step-by-step practice items, and lively animated graphics to help guide the evaluee through the assessment process. Each activity begins with exercises to familiarize users with the assessment tasks, to increase their confidence before starting.

The system is available from Vocational Research Institute, 1845 Walnut St., Suite 660, Philadelphia, PA 19103, 800/874-5387.

Disadvantages of Computer-Assisted Programs

There are several problems and concerns associated with using computers. Krug (2008), in discussing personality assessment, said that the concerns relate most often to (a) the technical quality of the systems that so far have been produced, (b) the lack of available validity information, (c) the dangers to consumers if the systems are administered or supervised by unqualified persons, and (d) the fear that gradually the assessment report may replace the professional's input about the consumer.

Most systems for job matching and vocational evaluation require a professional who has the qualifications to operate the system for the consumer. Also, some designers of computer applications in rehabilitation may inadvertently limit the range of occupations considered by a consumer on the basis of disability type. A database may only identify selected jobs obtained by persons with disabilities. From the perspective of the consumer, especially someone who is not experienced in using computers, a computer-administered test may be in itself an intimidating experience. Many consumers may also be restricted in their ability to articulate appropriate data for input into the computer.

For tests originally developed for paper-and-pencil administration that are now developed for computerized administration, there is the question of equivalence. Relatively few studies have tested the equivalence factor, but findings range from major to relatively moderate differences as a function of format. If the rehabilitation professional doubts the equivalency of a particular mode of test administration, the questionable method should not be used (Cohen et al., 1996). However, not all computer-administered evaluation tests have a paper-and-pencil predecessor.

The appropriate application of computer-assisted evaluation measures depends, consequently, on the judgment and professional experience of the rehabilitation professional. Computer-derived information does not consider how jobs can be modified (as is required under the ADA of 1990) or how assistive technology can be applied to promote greater accessibility to jobs. The evaluator becomes an important component by taking job information and identifying how modifications may be made. Although no governmental regulation exists for these products—and opinion is divided as to whether such regulation should be introduced— the evaluator should be discriminating as to which products are appropriate for consumers with disabilities. The validity of the program needs to be ascertained carefully. Gati (1994) recommended that professionals contribute to the effective use of computer-assisted programs by (a) constructively criticizing available systems; (b) participating in the selection of the systems to be used by their consumers; (c) designing diagnostic prescreening procedures regarding who should be encouraged to use the available programs, when they should be used, and which systems are appropriate; and (d) discussing with the consumer, integrating, and interpreting the information received from the computer systems. All of these steps make the process more meaningful to the individual.

Selected Ethical Issues Related to Computer-Assisted Programs

Ethical principles of vocational evaluation are certainly applicable to the use of computer-assisted programs, and two particular ethical issues are especially relevant, namely, the nature of the measure comprising a computer-assisted program and the evaluator's or practitioner's competencies in using these programs. The testing standards, for example, developed by the American Educational Research Association (AERA), the American Psychological Association (APA), and the National Career Development Association (NCDA) describe important guidelines for the ethical use of computer-assisted programs in assessment. If the measure is a test, then those standards apply (Sampson et al., 2003). But many measures appear to be checklists or questionnaires and may not be subject to the standards identified by the AERA, APA, and NCDA (Sampson et al., 2003).

Qualifications for competent use of computer-assisted evaluation programs have been identified by Sampson et al. (2003) and are summarized in the following list. Completion of a degree or a specific credential may not be sufficient for the ethical use of these programs, especially for interpretive reports. The following competencies are required, as is supervised experience in using the selected measure.

- An understanding of the construct or behavior being measured.
- An understanding of the test, including the theoretical basis (if any), item selection and scale construction, standardization, reliability, validity, and utility.
- An understanding of test interpretation, including scale interpretation and recommended interventions based on scale scores (Sampson et al., 2003).
- The ability to identify evidence of validity factors and understand the concept of equivalence of test forms.

All in all, there are many possibilities for the use of computer-assisted programs in vocational evaluation. They encourage active involvement by the consumer, but the professional must exercise caution. Particular competencies are necessary, and consumers must be carefully prepared for the experience.

Conclusion

The self-assessment approaches, including transferable skills and consumer portfolio methods, discussed in this chapter especially provide the opportunity for cultural factors to be considered during the vocational evaluation process. Each consumer presents a unique background when beginning the assessment process, and a self-assessment strategy facilitates feedback on this uniqueness. The consumer, through participation, does not become an object of the assessment process but functions as a partner, taking control of his or her own career development.

Chapter 12

Assessment With an Environmental Focus: Situational, the Family, and Assistive Technology

Human behavior is a product not only of the individual with a disability but also of the environment (Savickas et al., 2009). In the 21st century, this career/work environment is rapidly changing. More and more, today's employment involves short-term goals, worker flexibility and adaptability, and the management of complex restraints within the worker's personal, social, and family domains. The globalization process and rapidly improving technologies are requiring persons to develop skills and competencies that differ substantially from the knowledge and abilities required by 20th-century occupations (Savickas et al., 2009). For effective work adjustment, these phenomena demand that individuals with a disability pay close attention to what 21st-century career environments require, and how these same environments can be used to learn more about one's lifelong learning abilities. What consumers need to know in coping with rapidly changing work requirements, and how and what they can do to enhance their marketability, may be partially found in environment-based strategies used during assessment.

Accompanying these work-related 21st-century changes is a paradigm shift occurring in vocational rehabilitation. This paradigm includes the themes of empowerment and individuality, which are incorporated into newer approaches to assessment. Evaluation approaches are also being integrated into community settings, which may include industrial and other service-related sites that offer situational assessment, a family environment that can influence the assessment process, and assistive technology strategies that can facilitate the person's performance during evaluation. Using these environmental resources has caused rehabilitation professionals to rethink and reconceptualize how vocational evaluation is conducted, especially for populations with disabilities, who historically have been viewed as difficult to serve.

Traditional forms of assessment, such as paper-and-pencil tests and work samples, have dominated, and they continue to do so in the general vocational evaluation of persons with disabilities. I have frequently stated in this book that when these measures are used with selected populations, such as those with severe disabilities or who represent ethnic minorities, there are problems related to reliability and validity. In the past, vocational assessment has also been viewed as a linear process, which identified abilities, aptitudes, and interests at usually one point in time. Historically, the vocational assessment process is based on a predictive model, which is not only developed from norm-referenced measures that yield information about an individual's standing relative to other persons, but is also a model that, for those who are very difficult to place in appropriate employment settings, is discriminatory and, all too often, exclusionary.

As identified in Chapter 5, vocational assessment concerns should also focus on domain-referenced measures and on criterion-referenced methods integral to a service delivery approach that can identify and measure environmental variables that affect employability and the development of employment outcomes, and make a difference in maintaining employment. Such variables include personal factors (e.g., finances), workplace factors (e.g., employer attitude, co-worker attitude, accessible worksite, technology, benefits, labor market trends), and community factors (e.g., housing, transportation, support network, accessible community, training opportunities; Farley & Bolton, 1994). Consequently, more of an ecological assessment approach, conducted in an environment in which there is a close, interactive relationship between evaluation and training, may provide consumers with severe disabilities or for whom traditional methods are not applicable a greater opportunity to succeed in the vocational rehabilitation system.

This chapter will discuss two assessment approaches (i.e., situational assessment and family assessment) offered in the context of the individual's available environment, and explain how these approaches can facilitate the achievement of rehabilitation goals. The chapter will also include a discussion of assistive technology. These three target areas of vocational evaluation are developed from the premise that vocational performance is a function of both situation and person variables. These variables contribute to assisting individuals with a disability live a career life shaped by a global economy and supported by information technology (Savickas et al., 2009).

Situational Assessment and Supported Employment

Situational assessment and supported employment are interrelated. In fact, the terms *situational assessment, community-based situational assessment, job tryouts, on-the-job evaluation,* and *supported employment evaluation* are "often used interchangeably" (Patterson, 2008, p. 330).

A supported employment model was introduced in the early 1980s that proposed that the consumer be placed on the job and then receive specific training and selected assessment by a professional staff person on site. The Rehabilitation Act Amendments of 1992 (P.L. 93-112) defined supported employment as

> competitive work in integrated settings for individuals with severe handicaps for whom competitive employment has not traditionally occurred, or for whom competitive employment has been interrupted or intermittent as a result of severe disability, and who, because of their handicap, need on-going support services to perform such work. (p. 1811)

The basic nature of supported employment is characterized by intensive, initial training of persons with severe vocational disabilities in natural work environments, with the provision of continuing support, social integration at the work site with nondisabled individuals who are not paid caregivers, and integration into the industry. Supported employment can take a variety of forms. Such models strive to offer immediate opportunities for work and preparation rather than emphasizing readiness and preparation (Rogan & Hagner, 1990). These models include (a) the individual placement approach, in which individuals are placed in regular community jobs and support is provided at the work site as needed; (b) the enclave approach, which consists of a small group (commonly eight individuals), trained and supervised together in the midst of an ordinary, mainstream work environment; (c) the mobile crew approach, in which a single-purpose business is established by a service provider, such as janitorial or grounds-keeping services, and crews of about five work under an individual supervisor; and (d) the bench-work approach, which offers more individualized, supervisory attention than the other approaches and frequently addresses behavioral problems that exceed a mobile crew's ability to respond. In most of these approaches, support for the consumer is continuous and long term.

Although the overall concern of an evaluator in supported employment is advocacy for integration, both the demand and the opportunity are present to conduct or supervise a vocational assessment while the consumer is engaged in training. Using supported employment sites for vocational evaluation therefore requires an environment-based approach in which both consumers and prospective work environments are assessed. As Parker, Szymanski, and Hanley-Maxwell (1989) explained, "The term *ecological* or *environment,* when used to describe a framework for assessment and intervention, reflects an underlying assumption that individuals interact with their environments and that both change as a result of the interaction" (p. 29). A consumer's ability to learn from an optimal training experience is ascertained in a format that includes opportunities for consumers to learn and practice what they are expected to perform (Irvin & Halpern, 1979). Individual assessment information gathered from a wide range of services is coupled with a job analysis of various possible jobs and a behavioral analysis of specific consumer setting characteristics. In other words, an individual's abilities are identified, and a match is then attempted between those abilities and the specific skills required on particular jobs. As Schalock and Karan (1979) noted, "The subsequent remediation provided is designed to alleviate or ameliorate any existing basic ability deficits" (p. 39). The focus of vocational assessment in supported employment then shifts from a prediction orientation—a psychometric approach—to an ability-training orientation that fosters the remediation of skill deficiencies and the development of skills needed to sustain employment (Schalock & Karan, 1979). This evaluation emphasizes the importance of direct assessment of actual skills and behaviors over a period of time and in the actual work environment (Halpern & Fuhrer, 1984). Such a shift in perspective underscores the fact that vocational assessment is not merely an event yielding data but a highly dynamic process charged with meaning for both evaluator and consumer.

Situational assessment, an integral part of supported employment, is essentially the observation of people in work settings. It involves a practice of observing, evaluating, and reporting over a period of time. During this assessment, a consumer's behavior and work performance while working in a job situation with other employees are observed. The emphasis is on the evaluation of work behaviors, especially total work function and not just a potential skill performance. It is a systematic observation that takes place in a realistic and controlled working environment.

For situational assessment to be effective, an appropriate site should be used, adequate supervision provided, and a means used to gather information that, in turn, can be translated into rehabilitation planning. Because the observational approach is the basis of situational assessment, these observations must be carefully planned and scheduled, and well-designed rating and observation forms should be used. This demands that the rehabilitation professional understand the work evaluation opportunities in respective agencies, the experience and educational background of the staff, and what kinds of ratings are used to record the situational assessment information.

Situational assessments can also be used in-house, developed to provide a means of helping consumers understand their work abilities and behaviors that are not identified by existing paper-and-pencil measures, or used within the consumer's available employment community. Whatever the setting for situational assessment, pertinent information about the consumer as he or she relates to the work environment should be collected. Much of this information responds to the question "Can my consumer do the job and possess, or be able to learn, the work skills necessary to be productive in this specific work environment?"

Goals for Situational Assessment

Assessment is usually an ongoing process within the context of supported employment. Just as the demands and requirements of a job can change, so can consumers change as they learn new adjustment behaviors or acquire new physical and restorative functions. The goals for situational assessment are as follows:

1. The identification of the consumer's employment goals and vocational interests or preferences. Some consumers, by virtue of their need for supported employment, may have difficulty articulating appropriate goals.
2. The identification of the consumer's entry behaviors in relation to those required by the existing job.
3. The identification of the resources, such as people, places, things, and activities, that consumers need in order to be successful in the work environment, given their present skill level or projected skill level (Cohen & Anthony, 1984). This may also include an estimate of the quantity and quality of remedial resources that are needed to facilitate the acquisition of necessary work behavior by the consumer, as well as an appraisal of modifications and assistive devices that will enable the consumer to maximize productivity. An understanding of resources also includes an assessment of the ongoing need for support that may increase independent productivity and how this information integrates into a work or rehabilitation plan.
4. The appraisal of the consumer's work performance, especially those problem behaviors or skill deficits that impede job adjustment and productivity. This appraisal should also focus on (a) specific work adjustment behaviors, (b) interpersonal skills, (c) productivity, and (d) job skills (Hursh & Kerns, 1988).
5. From the assessment information learned during the consumer's job training, the formulation of a rehabilitation remedial program that proceeds on a step-by-step basis toward specific behavioral objectives related to actual job demands.
6. An exploration of the consumer's satisfaction with a particular job in supported employment.
7. The identification of such social factors as co-workers' attitudes; the extent of supervisory support or encouragement; the degree of work stress or pressure involved; an understanding of the physical setting that specifically includes lighting, temperature, and task variety; and an awareness of the financial rewards and the ability and training requirements of the particular job. Transportation resources to and from the work site should also be considered.

For the rehabilitation worker who endorses these goals, the evaluation derives meaning both from the belief that jobs and supports should be structured around individuals rather than the belief that individuals should be placed into existing programs or slots (Rogan & Hagner, 1990) and from the specific behavioral objectives to be achieved. Jobs are viewed, moreover, within the context of situational assessment as complex sets of behaviors that should be broken down into sequential component parts (Schalock & Karan, 1979). To achieve the assessment goals, therefore, the evaluation process should be kept simple so that the consumer, the supervisor, and the evaluator can easily understand and quickly communicate to each other what is of diagnostic significance. Also, the evaluation can frequently be tailored to fit the specific characteristics of the setting and the target behaviors.

Situational assessment, moreover, can be a dynamic approach to use during vocational evaluation if the consumer has the potential to learn, adapt to, and function effectively in a setting that also requires skills needed in the 21st-century world of occupational careers. The hands-on experience includes interaction with co-workers, when possible, and may provide information on such work skills needed in this century as:

- Coping with changes and tolerating ambiguity
- Interacting competently and positively with diverse co-workers
- Learning to use select technology
- Using a combination of skills needed to perform one job in the work situation or to respond to "a series of employers who need projects completed" (Savickas, 2012, p. 13).

Though situational assessment does have disadvantages, such as being resource intensive, time-consuming, and logistically difficult to arrange (MacDonald-Wilson, Rogers, & Anthony, 2001), Patterson (2008) identified several benefits, namely:

- This resource can increase self-awareness of strengths and limitations.
- The work is real, and the consumer may have the opportunity to be hired.
- There is less concern with validity and reliability because when the consumer performs the job according to employer expectations, this usually indicates that the individual can do the job.

The Situational Assessment Process

A key to effective assessment outcomes in supported employment is the identification of an appropriate job site. Many evaluators prefer to identify the employment, training, or assessment resource after the consumer's initial interview, in harmony with the "fit the job opportunity to the consumer's needs" principle. Such a potential placement presumes that the evaluator already has many resources available during the initial consumer interview. This availability also facilitates the individual's own work motivation, but it does not mean that consumers will only be placed stereotypically in certain job opportunities. Stereotyping is always a danger when helping those with severe disabilities find productive employment. Even so, when balancing the realities of available supported employment sites with job resources to be developed, leaning toward the direction of having resources available when initially discussing supported employment with the consumer is more feasible.

There are many strategies for developing situational assessment sites. They include identifying businesses with targeted job positions, such as large businesses (e.g., hospitals, factories, department stores, nursing homes), which often have several departments within one facility that can be used for situational sites. Other strategies can include contacting the personnel director by phone, describing the supported employment and situational assessment programs, scheduling an appointment to visit, and visiting the personnel director to observe in the identified departments the different tasks required, the work environment "climate," and job-duty schedules. When visiting the identified department, the professional can determine the jobs best suited for situational assessment and observe co-workers performing those jobs. Once the job site is finalized, situational assessments can be scheduled as the consumer is training and working on the job.

Several subsequent steps take place during the consumer interview. This interview facilitates a further understanding of the job-related potentials of the consumer when the decision is mutually made that the consumer is a candidate for supported employment. This particular decision emerges from responses to questions such as the following:

- What vocational assessment approach is most in harmony with the consumer's cultural, educational, and work experiences?
- What goals does the consumer articulate in the assessment process?

- What approaches are available to the evaluator and consumer?
- Does the consumer have distinctive needs that would best be met with one specific assessment approach rather than another?
- Will situational assessment evaluate those behaviors and potential for future training or work performances that cannot be validly and reliably assessed by other instruments or measures?
- Will this approach enhance the consumer's participation in the vocational assessment process, and provide that person with a sense of ownership in the assessment results?
- Can confidentiality be maintained about assessment results?
- Have job sites been developed in the community that can be used for this method of vocational assessment? How can they be accessed, and have cooperative relationships been established with employers who are willing to participate in this evaluation, and with supervisors within the job site who would conduct a behavioral observation of needed performance behaviors?

During this exploration-and-response session, the evaluator has the opportunity to encourage the consumer's choice making. This process comprises developing assessment goals, gathering information, and considering a range of options for evaluation approaches (Kosciulek, 2004). Informed choice, mandated by the Rehabilitation Act Amendments of 1998, stipulates that consumers must be active and full partners in the vocational rehabilitation process, with such participation leading to meaningful choices. The communication of information is crucial, however, to exercising informed choice. The evaluator should carefully discuss with the consumer the different approaches in vocational assessment, and if the professional believes that situational assessment would be an effective appraisal strategy and the consumer agrees, then different sites can be identified. The consumer's feedback is solicited for an evaluation of this information. With this feedback and participation, the consumer assumes a shared responsibility for the outcome of the choice with the assessment provider (Kosciulek, 2004).

It should be noted that while a structured interview can be a valuable source of information, these office interviews may offer a restricted sample of consumer behavior. Not all consumers can respond to the verbal interview formats, as they require developed communication and introspection skills. Other ways to solicit consumer feedback are to visit with the consumer at home, to listen to the expectations of family members, or to review information from secondary sources, such as past Individualized Education Programs (IEPs) or personnel files (Rogan & Hagner, 1990).

During the consumer interview, obtain the following information. First, once the evaluator understands the consumer's main occupational interests, the evaluator can begin to identify the job environments in which to pursue training and work adjustment. Physical or mental conditions may limit the repertoires of work, educational, and leisure experiences for many consumers who are candidates for supported employment, and these consumers may be unaware, consequently, of their range of interests. The job or situational assessment site itself may have to be the resource for interest assessment if no interests or very few are elicited from consumers. Because this interest exploration is often conducted concurrently with the identification of different assessment approaches and determination of situational assessment sites, the informed choice process may become quite restricted, at least in the beginning of the vocational evaluation process.

Furthermore, tasks during the interview focus on collecting information related to work readiness, as discussed in Chapter 2, as well as exploring what kinds of jobs would be satisfactory to an individual. Many of the questions suggested in the psychological, physical, occupational, and socio-environmental areas can be either used or adapted for the initial interview. During this interview, the rehabilitation worker can also determine whether the consumer recognizes that there are quality standards for work performance and can accept them as reasonable.

In this interview exchange, the interviewer should focus on the way the consumer learns. The rehabilitation professional may have access to the consumer's records, which explain the consumer's learning style. In other words, it is important to determine whether the consumer acquires information primarily via reading, demonstration, or hearing. Each individual has a learning-style preference, and the identification of this preference can strongly facilitate adequate work adjustment.

Next, the interviewer should explore whether a job analysis of the proposed work environments has been conducted. This analysis is similar to the one explained in Chapter 13. The interviewer should give particular attention to an analysis of possible social interactions and the social climate of the job or situation assessment site. A great deal of informal interaction occurs in any work setting, and a considerable amount of support is available within work environments that can be used for workers with severe disabilities (Rogan & Hagner, 1990).

The rehabilitation worker then needs to identify the resources and activities that are available to consumers and that can assist individuals in achieving an appropriate adjustment in the work setting. Such resources are, for example, the consumer's family, neighbors, or relatives, or community programs that provide ongoing support to consumers. An approach to understanding family dynamics is suggested in the second section of this chapter. Also, community programs such as group counseling can be educational in nature and help consumers address certain skill deficits, as well as learn how to remediate deficits and build on existing strengths. This information may have to be collected apart from the structured interview, and the consumer's significant others may be excellent resources.

Following the identification of resources, the rehabilitation worker and the consumer can develop an assessment plan that may consist of general job modifications, such as job restructuring, assistive technology aids, or the addition of job-coach support (Parker et al., 1989). But the necessary focus of this plan is the specific strategy to be used in the job-site assessment. Usually this strategy is to conduct systematic observations at the job site. When discussing with the consumer the observation plan, consider the following important behaviors to observe. These behaviors can involve

- appearance
  - ◈ hygiene, grooming, and dress
  - ◈ personal complaints
  - ◈ odd or inappropriate behaviors
- attendance and punctuality
- supervisory relationships
  - ◈ amount of supervision required during and after initial instruction period
  - ◈ recognition and acceptance of supervisors' authority
  - ◈ reactions to criticism and pressure by supervisors
  - ◈ amount of tension aroused by close supervision
  - ◈ requests for assistance from supervisor
- perseverance
  - ◈ ability to cope with work problems (frustration and tolerance)

- ❖ steadiness of work
- ❖ distractibility
- ❖ vitality of work-energy output
- ❖ stamina or 8-hour work capacity
- ❖ limitations—physical, mental, or both
- co-worker relationships
  - ❖ irritating habits
  - ❖ communications skills as related to work needs
  - ❖ social skills in relation to co-workers
- generalization of work habits
  - ❖ conformity to shop rules and safety practices
  - ❖ reactions to change in work assignment
  - ❖ acceptance of and resistance to work tasks
  - ❖ work methods and organization of tools and materials
  - ❖ production output

The schedule for observing behaviors will usually depend on the job situation and who is available to observe and record the appropriate information. The ideal person, when possible, is the consumer's supervisor, because the use of this "natural support" might serve to validate any concurrent assessment by the rehabilitation professional. An observer is needed who has realistic expectations of the consumer's work potential and who can relate effectively to the consumer. The timing of the observations further depends on feedback from the person doing the observations. Observations should be accomplished in short time periods, unobtrusively during the consumer's workday, and the information should be recorded, if possible, at each day's conclusion.

As for recording procedures, rating scales and checklists are very useful in this assessment, and they are most helpful if they are similar to measures used in business and industry. These scales are also useful in planning future training or employment with consumers because they can facilitate communication between the professional and the consumer. A variety of vocational behavior checklists and rating scales have emerged that contain, for example, social–interpersonal skill items expressed in terms of observable behaviors. Several of the checklists also include specification of conditions under which relevant behavior is to occur (Foss, Bullis, & Vilhaver, 1984).

Many times, because of the individuality of consumer behavior and the uniqueness of supported employment sites, composing one's own evaluation form is the most feasible way for an evaluator to collect necessary information. The Situational Assessment Supervisor Evaluation (see the Appendix and the forms located on the CD-ROM) is a suggested form I developed. Frequently, checklists are also developed with employer input, because in-house points of view can often be more realistic regarding behavioral performance goals for consumers.

When using a checklist, the evaluator should link behaviors to work performance conditions: identifying when and where the behavior occurred, how often the behavior occurred, the duration of the behavior, the frequency of the behavior, and who was involved. Also, the observed behavior should relate to the performance criterion established. For example, is the behavior performed 50% of the time, and is it appropriate to industry standards (Hursh & Kerns, 1988)? It should be noted, however, that the rating scale method of assessment has some serious flaws. Reliability is often a problem, item scoring is subjective, and the measures that result from ratings are typically limited to descriptions of the conditions under which a person functions.

In attempting to remediate job-related limitations, the evaluator should solicit consumer feedback about his or her awareness of observed limitations, or any discrepancies between the job or task demands in the situational assessment site and the consumer's individual abilities or characteristics. These discrepancies may relate to specific work skills and abilities, or required task-related social behaviors. With this information, suggest a behavior-oriented approach as a plan for possible improvement. This specific strategy might follow such guidelines as determining the problem, taking a baseline count of how many times the individual exhibits the selected behavior within a given time period, identifying a reinforcer, and setting a goal for appropriate behavior occurrence.

Periodically during the situational assessment, the rehabilitation professional should appraise the consumer's job satisfaction. It is frequently less clear how those with severe disabilities, who have never experienced the "world of work" and who may have led lives cut off from the mainstream of society, view their working experiences. One approach to exploring job satisfaction is to ask the following questions:

- How do you feel at the end of a working day?
- Does your job underuse or overstrain your abilities?
- Do you daydream about having a different job?
- Do you feel unappreciated at work?

- What do you like and dislike about your job?
- Would you be happy to do the same job if it paid less?
- If you were not working at your job, which would you miss most—the money, the work itself, or the company of your co-workers?

Evaluation, training, and job performance are factors that go together when assessment information is needed for individuals with severe disabilities or for those for whom traditional assessment approaches are not appropriate. The content areas for evaluation suggested in this chapter provide a structure to the assessment process. Although there are disadvantages to conducting vocational evaluation within supported employment (e.g., the work offered at the job site may be too simple, too difficult, or not congruent with the consumer's interests), and inaccurate conclusions about the consumer's work behavior may be drawn (Pruitt, 1986; Sax & Pell, 1985), this opportunity may be the most appropriate way to learn about consumers' productivity. It is important to remember that assessment conducted within supported employment is not an end in itself; it is a springboard for future training or continued employment.

Assessment of Family Dynamics

Family involvement in the rehabilitation process has become a topic of importance in recent years (Power & Dell Orto, 2004; Sutton, 1985). Disability is actually a family affair, and the consumer's performance in vocational rehabilitation is a function of both the person and the family environment. Progress toward rehabilitation goals cannot be achieved without considering and evaluating the family influences that can facilitate this progress.

An appraisal of what it is in family life that influences the family member with a disability can become the basis for the development of appropriate intervention strategies. Without an understanding of the family situation, intervention approaches often go awry (Power, Dell Orto, & Gibbons, 1988). When contact with the family is possible, an identification is needed of the family factors that may disrupt the consumer's rehabilitation. Unfortunately, rehabilitation professionals have been reluctant to have any involvement with families, and their role and functions with the family in the rehabilitation process are issues that are seldom addressed in the literature (Power & Dell Orto, 1986).

One of the main reasons for the uncertainty harbored by rehabilitation professionals over interaction with the family is the professionals' understanding that attention to the consumer's family is not encouraged by most state and private vocational rehabilitation agencies. However, such contact really requires only a small, additional expenditure of time and money for a potentially great return. For many rehabilitation professionals, assessment of the family can frequently be accomplished during office visits with the consumer. A family meeting may be initiated during the beginning interview, when both eligibility for vocational rehabilitation and the extent of services are being determined. Such a meeting can be particularly beneficial when the rehabilitation helper has doubts about the consumer's sincerity about pursuing the rehabilitation process, or perceives that there may be factors within the consumer's home environment that are detrimental to the achievement of rehabilitation goals.

For these and other reasons, such as when the consumer states that the family is seeking information on the vocational rehabilitation process or on resources that will assist them in their adjustment efforts, the helper realizes that contact with the family would serve a most beneficial purpose, and a meeting is discussed. When consumers are living with their families or the families are easily accessible, the consumer's permission can be obtained to bring family members to the next agency visit. All the family members or significant others with whom the consumer lives should be invited, when possible, to this agency meeting. Each person can have an influence on the consumer's vocational rehabilitation. The focus of assistance is still primarily on the consumer, and the purpose of the initial family visit is both to help the consumer and to identify obstacles and those persons who can facilitate or hinder the rehabilitation process.

Family assessment is usually conducted within a brief time frame. The rapid flow of consumers through vocational assessment systems usually necessitates short-term intervention. Because families can often be seen only briefly, or because assessment information may need to be obtained at only one meeting, this meeting must be carefully designed to make effective use of this limited assessment opportunity.

To facilitate the family's verbal expression of important information, the helper needs to exercise such basic communication skills as (a) attentiveness, (b) a nonjudgmental attitude, (c) understandable words, (d) verbal reinforcers such as "I see" or "Yes," (e) reflections back to clarify the family's statements, and (f) phrasing of tentative interpretations to elicit genuine feedback from family members (Okun, 1987). The helper should not assume anything and should ask only what he or she believes the family members can answer, so that they feel competent and productive. Also, the helper should ask questions that family members can handle emotionally at the time (Satir, 1967). In other words, the helper must create a setting during the family meeting in which people can seek information about their concerns and, perhaps for the first time, risk sharing their emotions.

Areas of Family Dynamics

Eight areas of family dynamics need to be explored if an appropriate evaluation is to be made on the family's role during the vocational rehabilitation process.

What has the family done so far to respond to the disability or illness? The helper can ascertain whether family members have encouraged the consumer to participate in the process of vocational rehabilitation. Furthermore, he or she can determine whether the family has made plans for dealing with problems associated with the disability (e.g., identifying other financial resources when family income has been reduced, shifting home responsibilities so that a family member may obtain at least a part-time job to alleviate economic hardship). Exploring these concerns with families can be difficult for evaluators, and the following questions are suggested:

- Can you describe your family life since the occurrence of the disability or illness?
- What are the differences in your family life since the beginning of the disability or illness?
- What are your feelings about having your husband or wife at home?

What information does the family have about the disability or illness? The counselor can also explore whether family members are aware of what the consumer can still do in the home, what community resources may be used for respite care, whether various work options are available to the consumer, and what the different phases of the rehabilitation process are. Information about the disability may already have been given by health professionals, but family members, because of their anxieties, may not have processed information very well during their conferences with physicians (Polinko, 1985).

What is the unique composition of the family, and what are the strengths and pitfalls inherent in that structure that would influence the consumer's rehabilitation? To identify the presence of family dynamics that may promote the consumer's vocational rehabilitation, the counselor should be aware of several indicators during the visit: warm and trusting attitudes shown in familial interactions; open and mutual respect demonstrated toward each family member; honest dialogue between family members about any adjustmental concerns; and assumption of personal responsibility, when appropriate, for the consumer's treatment and rehabilitation needs. Included in this exploration should be an identification of who the family spokesperson is and who the principal caregivers for the consumer are (Doherty & Baird, 1983).

On the other hand, the meeting might reveal confusion and disagreement about events affecting family life, conflicts over the performance of family responsibilities, or family communication that reveals distorted or unrealistic views of family members toward one another. Family members may also be angry because the presence of the disability has interfered with their lifestyles, privacy, vacations, future plans, or amount of time spent together. Much of the anger may have existed prior to the onset of disability, and the disability itself may only have exacerbated long-standing family feelings. The anger may take the form of neglecting the consumer's treatment and vocational needs or excluding the person with a disability from family activities.

What is the perceived threat to family functioning because of the disability? This is an important area to explore in any family assessment, because all families are especially vulnerable to unwelcome stress and prolonged anxiety after the occurrence of a disability or illness. For example, if a disability causes unemployment of the principal family wage earner, how does the family make up for this deficit? This is just one of many issues that emerge with a disability in a family. In other words, how does family life change because of the disability? An awareness of what happens to a family in a disability situation can make a difference in whether family members can be used for the eventual rehabilitation of the person with a disability.

What are the resources available to the family? These resources include both those available from within the family and those external to the family members. They include financial resources; the availability and willingness of extended family members to help; and the presence of community support systems, such as respite care, child day care, or programs for the elderly. The availability of these resources can make a difference in the family's adjustment to a trauma. Family members frequently state that the main reason they have adapted to a disability and become a source of help to the ill family member is that support external to the family itself is available.

What secondary gain issues interrupt the rehabilitation process? Examples of such issues are financial disincentives to the continuation of employment, or family influences that actually oppose work activities. Exploring these issues with families may be difficult, but during evaluation they should be explored. The following questions might be helpful:

- Has life in your family been better for you since the occurrence of your injury?
- What kind of financial benefits are you receiving now?
- What do you believe your family's reaction is to the fact that you are not working?
- Does your family expect you to return to work?

Are family beliefs about the maintenance of role responsibilities in the home and in the world of work acting as deciding factors for employment reentry? Families that communicate attitudes of essential worth to the consumer help to stabilize his or her self-concept, foster a positive attitude toward the future, and facilitate maintenance of rehabilitation gains. During assessment, these issues can be explored with consumers by asking questions such as the following:

- Do you still perform your customary duties around the home? Do you still participate with your family in social activities?
- Could you please describe what happened in your family life yesterday?
- What kinds of things does your family expect you to do, especially around the house?

What are family needs as the consumer begins the rehabilitation process? An awareness of these needs provides relevant suggestions on how rehabilitation professionals can assist the family during the time of consumer transition. These include the need (a) to receive concrete services (e.g., available community resources, financial information); (b) to be listened to and understood as a concerned person who is attempting to cope with a disability; (c) to process information already communicated by health professionals; (d) to care for himself or herself; (e) to recognize potential problems that may develop from the consumer's involvement in the rehabilitation process (e.g., transportation, negative attitudes from peers or employers); and (f) to learn information about the rehabilitation process as it applies to the family member with a disability.

During the initial phase of the rehabilitation process, many families are reluctant to voice their needs in the above areas, and these needs may have to be anticipated. The recognition of family concerns by professionals can help considerably in a family's adjustment efforts and in their assistance in promoting rehabilitation goals for the consumer. The consumer's involvement in vocational rehabilitation is a critical time for most families, and the rehabilitation professional can facilitate the family's cooperative efforts by asking them certain questions. For example, a professional can ask the following questions:

- How do you feel about your family member beginning vocational rehabilitation? Do you foresee any problems?
- What is family life going to be like, now that your family member is starting vocational rehabilitation?
- What services do you believe your family needs now to help the family member during his or her involvement in the rehabilitation process?

In summary, families are a potential resource for the vocational assessment and rehabilitation of persons with disabilities. Family involvement could be a continued, dynamic process. Certain family members may consent to playing a significant role after employment has been achieved. But families of those with a disability need options, not prescriptions. They need to become aware of different career choices following the assessment process. Such knowledge facilitates their being a valuable partner in vocational rehabilitation.

Assistive Technology

Encompassing many diverse activities, assistive technology (AT) is a resource that assists individuals with functional limitations to reach their maximum potential through the use of AT products, services, or related technology services (Langton, 1993; Thirtieth Institute on Rehabilitation Issues [IRI], 2003). The available resources can include technology information resources, adaptive aids and devices, technical assistance, and specialized staff (Langton, 1993; Langton, Smith, Lown, & Chatham, 1998).

The definition of assistive technology most frequently used is "any item, piece of equipment, or product system, whether acquired commercially off the shelf, modified, or customized, that is used to increase, maintain, or improve functional capability of individuals with disabilities" (U.S. Technology-Related Assistance of Individuals with Disabilities Act of 1988).

Assistive technology, consequently, has both a legal and functional definition. It is a resource that can help individuals with functional limitations reach their maximum potential through the use of products, services, or related technology. Enders (2002) explained that disability is actually a complex interaction between an individual and the environment, mediated by tools, skills, and interaction with other people. Technology is often the interface between the person and the environment. The ability to access and use technology can play a pivotal role in functionally redefining disability, and in bridging the wide gulf between the meaning of a significant disability to the disability community and what it means in the labor market.

The benefits of using assistive technology are many:

- It shifts the focus from primarily assessing performance to interactive problem solving that seeks ways to determine how to maximize someone's capabilities.
- When assistive aids are available, it becomes possible to explore even more ways to accomplish a task, thus widening employment/career opportunities.
- Use of assistive resources within the assessment process offers the potential to enhance successful outcomes and increase the value of the assessment phase of the rehabilitation process.
- Technology helps to empower consumers by increasing their life and work choices.

Rehabilitation counselors "constitute one group of professionals who play key roles in facilitating the match between individuals with disabilities and assistive technology" (Scherer & Sax, 2010, p. 231). The assessment process is often the best place for vocational exploration, assessment, and assistive technology to come together (IRI, 2003). This presumes that any potential technology-related needs are identified and the potential benefits of assistive technology are recognized. Also, those with more severe disabilities present not only vocational needs but also basic life skills needs that are inextricably linked to achieving successful employment/career outcomes (IRI, 2003). The increased availability of assistive technology options, however, has facilitated the process of matching a person with the most appropriate device. Those with disabilities have varying needs, preferences, past experiences, and exposure to technologies, and different expectations for quality of life, sense of well-being, and future career functioning (Scherer & Sax, 2010). All of these influences interact when the use of assistive technology is explored.

The International Classification of Functioning, Disability and Health (ICF; WHO, 2001) identifies selected domains of consumer activities and participation, and then gives examples of assistive technology and other supports. A familiarity with this identification can enhance the awareness of feasible ways to enhance consumer performance during assessment.

ICF Activities and Participation and Suggested Assistive Devices/Resources

- *Learning and applying knowledge*—learning, applying the knowledge that is learned, thinking, solving problems, and making decisions (note taking, real-time captioning services, personal digital assistant [PDA] and laptop computers, audio recording devices, computer software, electronic calculators)
- *General tasks and demands*—carrying out single or multiple tasks, organizing routines, and handling stress (personal assistance, service animals, timers, memory aids)
- *Communication*—communicating by language, signs, and symbols, including receiving and producing messages, carrying on conversations, and using communication devices and techniques (sign language interpreters, electronic and manual communication devices, computer input and output devices, modified telephones)
- *Mobility*—changing body position or location or transferring from one place to another by carrying, moving, or manipulating objects;

by walking, running, or climbing; and by using various forms of transportation (manual and power wheelchairs, canes and walkers, transfer boards, vehicle modifications, lifts, relief maps, global positioning system [GPS])

- *Interpersonal interactions and relationships*—basic and complex interactions with people (strangers, friends, relatives, family members, and lovers) in a contextually and socially appropriate manner (manual and electronic communication devices, life skills coach, sexual aids)
- *Major life areas*—tasks and actions required to engage in education and employment and to conduct economic transactions (remote control devices, customized work stations, structural modifications, alternative computer access)
- *Community, social, and civic life*—actions and tasks required to engage in organized social life outside the family, in community, social, and civic areas of life (signaling and alerting devices, noise-reduction devices, adapted recreational and leisure devices, transportation accommodations; Scherer & Glueckauf, 2005)

Assistive technology resources and services should be provided prior to vocational assessment or incorporated as an integral part of vocational assessment. These resources should also be an option at any time during vocational assessment. The *role* of the rehabilitation counselor is usually not to provide the assistive technology devices but to be *aware* of the consumer's needs for these resources and to *know the community resources* to which the consumer may be referred. The following are suggestions for the counselor for using assistive technology, developed by the 30th Institute on Rehabilitation Issues (2003).

Making Preevaluation Preparations

- Review referral information to determine if technology needs are indicated.
- Identify functional limitations or problems that may require accommodations during assessment. Feedback from the consumer can facilitate this communication.
- Ensure that all test and instructional materials that are likely to be used are available in appropriate formats.
- Ensure that the process of assessment is completely accessible for individuals with disabilities.

Conducting the Initial Interview

- Determine whether the individual uses or has used any assistive devices.
- Determine the need for involving a technology specialist. This may be necessary for those with severe disabilities.
- Determine the consumer's attitude toward using AT or workplace accommodations. If any reluctance is noted, this should be explored before considering the use of assistive technology.

Developing the Evaluation Plan

- Arrange for any consultation or other involvement of technology specialists if AT needs have been identified. The counselor should, of course, be familiar with the AT resource.
- If the need for assistive technology aids/devices is noted, make a referral to an appropriate resource.
- If formats of tests and assessment activities are not appropriate for the individual, consider that other assessment instruments or alternate formats may be needed. Computer-assisted assessment should be explored.

Administering Assessment Tasks and Activities

- AT resources are implemented and the consumer is ready for evaluation.
- Observe any difficulties the individual experiences in performing assessment tasks/activities. Be prepared to modify the task or activity to obtain the optimal possible performance, when such intervention is possible.
- Permit the consumer to use any device necessary to complete the assessment.
- Focus more on the consumer's ability to perform essential functions and less on norms.

The initial consumer interview provides an opportunity, consequently, to explore the individual's assistive technology needs. With their identification and other succeeding activities, the counselor is preparing the consumer to take advantage of a referral to an AT resource. This resource should be able to select an intervention and device for a given consumer. The counselor, due to limited time and support, may not be able to match specific aids to consumer needs.

A balance is needed, however, among consumer needs and preferences, quality service delivery, and time effectiveness and cost-efficiency (Scherer & Sax, 2010). But the availability of a knowledgeable rehabilitation counselor, who understands the importance of assistive technology and how it can considerably enhance assessment opportunities for those with moderate to severe disabilities, as well as recognizing the value of a consumer-driven process, is key to a quality assessment experience for the person with a disability. A consumer-driven process implies that the needs of the consumer are carefully explored—a process that demands listening to the consumer's expectations and being aware of how these needs/expectations can be met by technology.

Both computer-assisted assessment and the appropriate use of assistive technology resources speak to counselor responsiveness. These opportunities also enlarge assessment possibilities for consumers for whom traditional approaches may be too limited. They offer appraisal approaches that can be highly individualized and personal. Both services can enable individuals with varied functional limitations to accomplish tasks and perform functions that they otherwise might be unable to do.

In summary, several factors should be emphasized. Langton (1993) believed that when initially exploring the use of assistive technology with consumers, evaluators should consider such basic functional capacities as communication, mobility, motor skills, strength and endurance, sensory issues, cognition and memory, academic achievement, and self-care skills. When employing AT in vocational assessment, moreover, the evaluator is engaging in an interactive, problem-solving activity that seeks to maximize the individual's capabilities (IRI, 2003). Assistive technology, consequently, should open up work adjustment and career possibilities rather than narrowing choices. These possibilities can be explored during the initial interview, when potential technology needs are identified. Then, during evaluation planning, those needs are incorporated into the plan, including arranging for any specialized services. The consumer's attitude toward using AT or workplace accommodations should also be identified.

As the assessment process continues after developing the evaluation plan, if immediate need for AT is identified, technology specialists may have to be contacted or arrangements made for necessary equipment. When administering evaluation tasks and activities, the focus should be on the consumer's ability to perform essential functions, and observations should be conducted to ascertain if the consumer is experiencing difficulties when performing assessment tasks. If so, the tasks or activity may have to be modified to achieve optimal performance (IRI, 2003).

It is feasible to explore both assistive technology in selected work areas and those career alternative areas in which technology resources are available. Recommendations following the assessment process should be developed with the consumer's feedback and problem-solving interactions to identify possible use of assistive technology in order to acquire resources or services needed to achieve work-related or career goals (Langton, 1993). These recommendations should be built on the consumer's vocational strengths, including interests, and job analysis strategies might have to be used to explore ways to make accommodations or use AT devices to compensate for loss of function and to maximize vocational potential.

In assistive technology, the choice of services can range from low-tech to high-tech and inexpensive, off-the-shelf products to expensive, custom-made equipment. For example, voice recognition software packages are available now for less than $200, as well as ScanSoft's Dragon Naturally-Speaking Preferred, which sells for about $200. Also available are such low-tech options as Plexiglas keyboard covers that slip over the keys and prevent computer users from pressing more than one key at a time. There are also armrests that attach to a desk or chair and stabilize the arm and wrist while typing. Both resources are available through specialty vendors for $50 and up.

Realistically, in assistive technology the vocational evaluator usually has two roles, namely, to identify needed consumer areas for assistive technology and to coordinate its use. Evaluators may not be technology specialists, but they should have a link to referral sources, vocational evaluation programs, and specialized technology service providers. They can coordinate other service delivery staff, such as rehabilitation engineers, speech–language pathologists, and occupational therapists. This integration will often depend on both the interest and the capability of the evaluator. But particular areas of assistive technology, such as writing, seating and positioning, and work site accommodations, may require specialized expertise. Making arrangements for this assistance can be difficult, especially with the short time frames found in many vocational assessments. It is important, therefore, to begin to identify assistive technology needs during the initial interview with the consumer. Additional options can then be revealed to the consumer during the assessment process, which in turn facilitates further options for eventual work site accommodation. Two selected resources for assistive technology follow:

The Computer/Electronic Accommodations Program (CAP), 703/693-5160; TTY 703/693-6189

The Helen A. Keller Institute for Human Disabilities, 703/993-3670; http://k:hd.gse.grav.edu

Conclusion

The three resources identified in this chapter, namely, situational assessment, the available family, and assistive technology, facilitate the process of helping the consumer confront some realistic demands in the 21st-century career world. Both the available family and assistive technology, moreover, provide valuable consumer support. For those with especially severe disabilities, marketing themselves will be extremely difficult without this support. The evaluator will discover that utilizing these environmental-based resources will help consumers to compete for both training and employment opportunities in this century.

Chapter 13

Transition Assessment
With Adolescents

Transition is a broad concept, and each transition varies in how it affects the adjustment or realignment of life goals. The transitional changes caused by a serious mental or physical disability, moreover, influence the consumer's family, occupational, and leisure worlds. But vocational and career assessments provide an opportunity to understand the impact of disability-related transitions. Whether the transition is developmental or results from events emerging from a life-threatening diagnosis or accident, an evaluation of selected career-related characteristics associated with the transition is crucial to the affected person's life adjustment. Importantly, assessment also provides the opportunity for someone to become more marketable in the 21st-century labor world.

The vocational assessment concepts and approaches explained in this book embrace all those with a physical or mental disability. The book's chapters focus on all consumers seeking vocational rehabilitation services, without giving special attention to the young person born with a disability or incurring a chronic illness or disability in early childhood or adolescence. This chapter will provide that particular attention, targeting the population of young and/or school-age persons who are beginning to develop a picture of themselves and, for some, gaining an early understanding of their role in the world of work. Especially for those transition-aged consumers who become eligible for vocational rehabilitation services, this chapter will discuss the characteristics that will facilitate transition planning and lead to eventual career adjustment.

The literature reveals, however, alarming statistics about the career development of people with childhood onset of disability. This early onset is associated with a diminished likelihood of completing high school and entering employment (Moore, Konrod, Yang, Ng, & Doherty, 2011). Especially for students with emotional and behavioral disorders (EBD), when the focus is on employability, many of these young persons lack actual job experience while in high school and consequently experience a notable rate of unemployment or low-paying and unsatisfying jobs several years after leaving high school (Curtin & Garcia, 2011). Furthermore, though postsecondary education is a vital opportunity for high school graduates, only about 37% of persons with disabilities enroll in postsecondary institutions (i.e., community colleges and vocational technical schools; Dutta, Kundu, & Schiro-Geist, 2009).

But since the early 1980s, considerable legislation has been passed that helps young people with disabilities make a successful transition from school to work and to community functioning (Levinson, 1994). In 1990 the requirement for the provision of Transition Services was added to the Individuals with Disabilities Education Act (IDEA). Community and school-based programs have been created to reach out to these young people and provide them with opportunities to learn the skills needed for occupational or higher education entry. There are mixed feelings, however, about their effectiveness (Herbert, Lorenz, & Trusty, 2010). Several programs have been both useful and helpful. Others have been perceived as perhaps less effective because of many obstacles: lack of funding to support state rehabilitation services, lack of cooperation/collaboration among team members who implement a transition plan, poor understanding of the professional competencies needed for transition assessment and planning, inadequate family expectations, and a lack of career exploratory experiences for young persons with a disability (Herbert et al., 2010).

This chapter will consider many of these barriers as it responds to several questions that frame a feasible vocational assessment intervention for this young population. This intervention becomes an important tool in helping students achieve realistic occupational goals and the skills to operationalize those aspirations (Herbert et al., 2010). The six questions are as follows:

1. What are current definitions of transitional assessment for this specific population?
2. What are the purposes of transitional assessment?
3. What are important issues that establish a foundation for understanding the young consumer with a disability?

4. What are the domains of transition assessment?
5. What are the guidelines for selecting transition assessment methods?
6. What are selected current practices in transition assessment and a proposed program for this assessment?

Current Definitions of Transition Assessment

Clark, as cited in Rojewski (2002), defined transition as "a planned, continuous process of obtaining, organizing, and using information to assist individuals with disabilities of all ages and their families in making critical transitions in students' lives both successful and satisfying" (p. 79).

The State Board of Education and the New Hampshire Department of Education (2010) define transition services as "a coordinated set of activities for a student with a disability, designed within an outcome-oriented process, and based upon the individual student's needs, which promotes movement from school to post-school activities" (p. 1). Adapted by practitioners in many states, the above definition implies a coordinated set of activities designed within a result-oriented process that is focused on improving the academic and functional performance of the child with a disability to facilitate the child's movement from school to postschool activities. These activities include postsecondary education, vocational education, integrated employment (including supported employment), continuing and adult education, adult services, and independent living or community participation based on a student's needs and taking into account his or her preferences and interests. Also, these activities may involve instruction, related services, community experiences, the development of employment and other postschool adult living objectives, and, when appropriate, the acquisition of daily living skills and functional vocational evaluation (New Hampshire Dept. of Education, 2010).

These two definitions are the engines that drive the transition assessment process. They identify the scope of this process, and the definitions have the themes of comprehensiveness, holism, school-based delivery of services, and person-centered planning that utilizes natural supports and an interdisciplinary team. This team may consist of school administrators, school counselors, transition counselors or coordinators, and selected family members. The themes of comprehensiveness and holism, moreover, particularly shape the vocational transition assessment process. This process should also be unique to a specific individual, be formulated to reduce anxiety and encourage growth, and provide many opportunities for self-discovery and learning about the world of work (Rojewski, 2002). It is important to note in these definitions, however, that what is implied in transition assessment is not only an evaluation for future training or employment, but an appraisal for *living* in the community. This concept of community includes varied settings.

Purposes of Transitional Assessment

The purpose of transitional assessment should be viewed within the context of a relationship perspective and the realities of the 21st-century labor market. Transitional assessment is relational. Its process attempts to achieve consumer self-understanding, encouraging knowledge of the self, and to involve significant personnel in the consumer's life space. During the evaluation, feedback may be solicited from family members and school personnel on their perception of the consumer's occupational or career-related strengths. Transition-aged consumers are urged to facilitate this feedback so that realistic transition assessment approaches may be designed. Moreover, collaboration and cooperation among personnel who have some responsibility in implementing the transition plan are absolutely necessary. The Individuals with Disabilities Education Improvement Act of 2004 mandates involvement from relevant parties that can establish a natural linkage between, for example, schools and state rehabilitation programs (Herbert et al., 2010).

Yet, the demands of the current labor market must be considered when developing both a transitional assessment approach and the resulting transitional assessment plan. Although many young people today are having a difficult time securing stable employment, young people with disabilities are finding it even more difficult to launch a stable career. Today there is generally an absence of long-term security in most employment settings. The worker should have adaptable, marketable skills and be willing to update those skills. The consumer's motivation and ability to learn and work in diverse employment environments should be included in the evaluation areas.

Furthermore, the 21st-century worker should cultivate such skills as social intelligence, adaptive thinking, cross-cultural competencies, computational thinking, and literacy to understand technology. If the assessment process for the transitioning young adult is going to make a difference in that consumer's beginning occupational/career life, then this evaluation process should include an awareness of what is realistically possible for training and employment. The focus of the transitional evaluation, consequently, is on the potential of the young person to develop skills and to use work-related behaviors in order to become marketable in the future career world.

With this information, the following purposes of transitional assessment were identified by Sitlington, Neubert, Bejon, Lombard, and Leconte (1996):

- To help students and families think about their life after high school and identify long-range goals
- To design the assessment process within the school experience to ensure that students identify and perhaps gain the skills and connections they need to achieve designated goals
- To determine the individual's level of career development when planning transition assessment activities
- To help young people with disabilities identify their interests, strengths, and abilities in relation to postsecondary goals, such as employment opportunities, postsecondary education and training opportunities, independent living situations, community involvement, and personal and social goals
- To determine appropriate placements within educational, vocational, and community settings that facilitate the achievement of these postsecondary goals
- To identify the accommodations, supports, and services individuals will need to attain and maintain their postsecondary goals

The perspective, consequently, for transition assessment includes not only appropriate planning but also skill identification and development. A product of this assessment could also be establishment of a foundation for building career self-efficacy and self-determination (Herbert et al., 2010). To attain these goals, the vocational evaluator may need to play many roles, such as helping special educators, transitional and supported employment specialists, and rehabilitation counselors to include a broader assessment domain in transition planning. The roles also include working with other transition team members who can provide career or vocational assessment information. Collaboration with educational professionals who are involved in the career development and planning of the young person with a disability is a key responsibility for the vocational evaluator.

Important Issues in Transition Assessment

Important issues in transition assessment include (a) understanding the career service needs of young people with disabilities, (b) the dynamics of family involvement during the transition assessment process, (c) factors in the 21st-century labor market identified as influencing the transition process and planning, (d) collaboration among professionals involved in the transition assessment process and planning, and (e) the necessity for long-term strategies. The following discussion elaborates on each of these issues.

Understanding the Career Service Needs of Young People With Disabilities

Manage Stigma

Young people with disabilities experience stigmatization. Everyday experiences reinforce the message that young people with disabilities are less desirable and less valued than their more typical counterparts. Overly sympathetic responses, maintaining prevailing stereotypes, avoidance reactions, diminished interactions with peers, disability harassment, and negative social experiences are all experiences of stigmatization (Moore et al., 2011). This stigmatization can result in feelings of shame, inferiority, and low self-esteem, and these feelings can diminish life opportunities as young people reduce their career and life aspirations. But a transition assessment process that emphasizes the consumer's strengths is a stepping stone for the young person in building a positive identity. This strength orientation can also help the person to develop a valuable resource for coping with a disability. Furthermore, highly supportive families with realistic but hopeful expectations, and access to institutions, professionals, and significant others who do not label the family member in a stigmatizing way, are of additional help in reducing negative feelings (Moore et al., 2010).

Understand the Dynamics of the Workplace

Earlier placement into educational and vocational contexts may be less than ideal for the well-being of transition-aged persons and may result in inferior vocational development experiences (Moore et al., 2010). Involvement in career resources that are integral to the assessment process and offer normalizing experiences, that is, situational assessment sites, can begin to respond to this need for job-related knowledge.

Receive Support

With the young consumer, support can take many forms, such as acceptance and encouragement for involvement in assessment, respect for the consumer's choices as detailed in the transition plan, and the appropriate exchange of information about training and career opportunities. What is also important is the consumer's perception of support available to him or her.

Gain a Sense of Accomplishment in Pursuing Occupational or Career-Related Tasks

Adolescents with a disability usually have little confidence in their abilities to make productive career plans. This is true of many nondisabled young people, but because of their lack of exposure to or isolation from training and workplace requirements, and perhaps little valuable information about self, those with disabilities have not yet developed any measure of career efficacy. Career efficacy is self-confidence gained by performing specific career-related tasks. But transitional assessment should be an opportunity to successfully complete certain tasks and thus begin to develop self-confidence.

Maintain Structure

Usually adolescents with a significant mental or physical disability operate best in a structured, organized environment. Imparting information clearly within an orderly evaluation or training environment will facilitate a relevant response to assessment tasks.

These five needs are generally idiosyncratic to those young people with disabilities and do not exclude the other needs of young people, such as security, contact with peers, acceptance, and enjoyment.

Dynamics of Family Involvement During the Transition Process

A young consumer's available family can be integral to this person's adjustment during the assessment process and then eventual planning. Certain dynamics within the family, such as conflict and enmeshment, may impede an individual's career development. Research suggests that parental attitudes regarding specific careers, career exploration, and occupational plans may affect the young person's choices during the process of transition assessment (Keller & Whiston, 2008). Family members, moreover, may assume a variety of roles that can enhance the adolescent's ability to reach a satisfying training or occupational outcome. They can provide emotional support, help in the cultivation of relationships that lead to natural supports in the community, and help the young person to understand the strengths and limitations associated with the disability and the resulting accommodations that may be needed for both productive assessment and appropriate transitional planning. Family involvement, when it is possible, can be important, therefore, throughout the entire transition process. In actuality, family members can become case monitors, providing praise and encouragement and partnering with their family member to confront such hurdles as discrimination, episodic bouts of lowered motivation, and maintaining one's initiative during self-exploration while facing the realization of limited choices (Stuart, 2008).

Factors in the 21st-Century Labor Market

The changes, whether expected or planned, sudden or unwelcome, are a continued hallmark of the 21st-century career and employment worlds. The reorganization of work, technological and scientific advances, and the extensive use of part-time workers tied to production cycles are phenomena that should be considered when targeting the evaluation of possible skills and work-related behaviors during the assessment process (Power, 2010). The following are added factors that should be explored during transition assessment:

- The potential for career resilience, that is, the flexibility implied when considering participating in a 21st-century workforce that may demand diverse responses to changing economic situations
- The potential for adaptability, namely, the assumption that a worker understands how to apply acquired job skills to different work tasks or is willing to learn new skills. These skills may include working interpersonally as a member of a team.

However, because of the nature of the young person's disability, the potential to learn many new skills may only be the ideal. But as stated earlier, the focus during assessment should be on the *possible*. Helping the individual to recognize how to maximize his or her strengths should be one of the hallmarks of an effective transitional assessment.

Collaboration Among Professionals

It is again emphasized that transitional assessment and planning are best understood from a relational perspective. A continuum of services is needed for effective implementation of the transitional plan, and this requires linkages between the consumer's family, school administrators, evaluators, and state-based transition specialists. Such linkages necessitate an understanding of each other's roles and collaboration among these professionals. This connection can begin with the assessment process, as a comprehensive evaluation also includes utilizing such community-based resources for job shadowing, on-the-job tryouts, and other situational assessments. Collaboration means, consequently, dialogue, motivation, and understanding.

Necessity for Long-Term Assessment Strategies

In the 21st-century labor market, many individuals are finding that long-term job security is a thing of the past. When the consumer begins to understand that a self-assessment is periodically necessary during one's career journey, and periodic self-exploration may identify what is needed to compete successfully for employment opportunities, then these specific self-directed skills can be used many times in order to adjust to changing training and job demands. Self-assessment approaches should begin during the initial transition assessment. The evaluation methods should not only promote self-understanding but also begin to establish those skills for exploring one's own capabilities and how they harmonize with specific training and changing occupational tasks. Self-assessment approaches are included in the transitional assessment format explained later in this chapter.

The five issues in transition assessment discussed previously both frame and influence the development of the transitional assessment picture that will be drawn in this chapter. Assessment, for example, is not going to be relevant without an understanding of the young consumer's needs, available support, and family influences. Assessment will not connect with this consumer unless it is structured and organized, conveys an opportunity for accomplishment and career efficacy, and communicates the realities of the 21st-century career world. All of these issues also set the stage for explaining the domains, selection guidelines, and practices of transition assessment.

The Domains of Transition Assessment

This assessment should be comprehensive and embrace the domains of the transition-age consumer's psychological, social, educational/academic, physical/medical, and vocational functioning (Levinson, 1994). More specifically, this assessment can target the following:

- Intelligence and cognitive abilities
- Needs, values, and temperament
- Computational skills
- Socialization skills
- Emotional development and mental health
- Independent and interdependent living skills
- Physical functions of vision, hearing, strength, endurance, and dexterity
- Needed family or other supports, as well as needed linkages with support services
- Adaptive skills
- Vocational interests, aptitude, career maturity, and any developed work habits
- Interpersonal relationships
- Self-determination
- Communication skills of speaking, listening, reading, and writing

- Daily living areas, such as the ability to perform household tasks, manage own money, use local transportation systems, and maintain personal grooming and hygiene

All of these domains suggest a holistic transition assessment approach. An exploration of each domain can provide feedback to the young consumer about his or her career-related strengths, possible occupational-related behavioral limitations, and further information about career possibilities. All of this knowledge establishes a foundation for self-understanding.

Guidelines for Selecting Transitional Assessment Approaches

The choice of an approach will depend on the assessment resources available, the competence of those conducting the evaluation, who does the assessment, the developmental stage of the young person with a disability, the severity of the disability, and properties of a particular instrument, such as readability, cognitive demands, cultural or environmental bias, and appropriate norms. Assessments may begin at age 14; regardless, assessment and other programming needs should be identified and conducted early in the student's life. Vocational assessments are then performed at designated developmental stages. As students learn more about their abilities, values, interests, and basic skills, they can move closer to having the ability to make a realistic vocational choice (Thirtieth Institute on Rehabilitation Issues [IRI], 2003). Sitlington, Neubert, and Leconte (1997) identified the following guidelines.

- Assessment methods must be tailored to the types of information needed and the decisions to be made regarding transition planning and various postsecondary outcomes.
- The specific methods selected must be appropriate for the individual's learning characteristics, including cultural and linguistic differences.
- Assessment methods must incorporate assistive technology or accommodations that will allow an individual to demonstrate his or her abilities and potential.

- Assessment methods must occur in environments that resemble actual vocational training, employment, independent living, or community environments.
- Assessment methods must produce outcomes that contribute to ongoing development, planning, and implementation of "next steps" in the individuals' transition process.
- Assessment methods must be varied and include a sequence of activities that sample an individual's behavior and skills over time.
- Assessment data must be verified by more than one method and by more than one person.
- Assessment data must be synthesized and interpreted in a way that is tailored to individuals with disabilities, their families, and transition team members.
- Assessment data and the result of the assessment process must be documented in a format that can be used to facilitate transition planning.

Highlights of these guidelines include that (a) vocational assessment for transitioning students should be done in multidisciplinary groups that include a specialist in assistive technology; (b) real work assessments should be conducted, when possible, that can provide information on environmental variables that are impossible to duplicate in the classroom or with a paper-and-pencil test; and (c) because readiness for the transition from school to work may occur via multiple pathways, the student must be assessed across settings, situations, and relationships (Phillips, Bleustein, Jobin-Davis, & White, 2002). These guidelines further imply that the transition assessment information must be communicated in an understandable format and be regularly updated. Many school-based and vocational rehabilitation resources use "Transition Profiles," which facilitate nonduplicative transfer of important assessment information, are completed by the Individualized Education Program team, and are coordinated by students' special education teachers (IRI, 2003).

As described in Rojewski (2002), Sitlington et al. suggested that an individualized assessment plan be developed for all students, following guidelines developed from a series of questions:

> What do I already know about this student that would be
> helpful in developing postsecondary outcomes?

What information do I need to know about this individual to
   identify postsecondary goals?
What methods will provide this information?
How will the assessment data be collected and used in the
   planning process?

Selected Current Practices in Transition Assessment

Appropriate assessment strategies are essential for helping young people
with disabilities improve their self-confidence and experience a sense
of accomplishment when performing career-related tasks. Both being
involved in the evaluation process and understanding the meaningful
results of this evaluation can help to build this career efficacy. Productive evaluation approaches should also yield information that can be incorporated into the transition plan for the student. Assessment, consequently, is a key intervention for the adolescent student transitioning to
other opportunities after high school.

Concerned about which specific career assessment areas were being addressed in high school, Herbert et al. (2010) surveyed nearly 400
high school personnel and state vocational rehabilitation counselors using an online questionnaire. Results indicated that seven content areas
were identified:

Career interests
Work values
Career decision-making skills
Aptitude
Personality
Achievement
World of work

To obtain consumer information in these areas, multiple methods
were used, such as individual paper-and-pencil career tests, online career assessment, job shadowing, training in job-seeking skills, and on-
the-job tryouts. Vocational interest measurement was the dominant assessment area, followed by aptitude and achievement evaluation.

All of the collected evaluation information, moreover, provided
the material for designing transitional programs. This design included

empowerment-focused, age-appropriate, and community-based processes. There were also multiple goals for these assessment programs, such as helping the transition-aged consumer to plan for independent living situations, vocational and academic opportunities, or immediate employment settings. Feedback to the author, however, indicated that many agencies, when designing a transitional assessment intervention, use three levels of assessment domains as an individual framework for the evaluation:

- *Level One:* Could include a review of existing information (intelligence and achievement data from the most current reports, student interviews, interest assessments, temperament assessments, and aptitude testing).
- *Level Two:* Targets young persons with a disability who are having difficulty making a career choice, clarifying their interests, preparing for adult living, or contemplating leaving school as a dropout. This could expand to include assessments targeting information on one's work-related behaviors, general career maturity, and daily or independent living skills.
- *Level Three:* Includes students who need additional assistance with identifying long-term employment, education, and/or independent living goals, when earlier assessments were inconclusive, or for those with significant disabilities.

The level determination is made by the appropriate professional who is responsible for the young person's transition process. Following this identification, a progression of assessment activities is planned, with each activity to be implemented, when possible, by a multidisciplinary team. These activities include the consumer interview and selected additional sources of formal and informal evaluation approaches.

A Proposed Specific Program

Using information from selected assessment programs (which are usually conducted in a school setting) for transition-aged young persons with a disability, the following evaluation intervention is suggested that comprises several guidelines previously identified in this chapter. Those guidelines include (a) collaboration of professionals both in planning and during the actual administration of the evaluation, (b) a holistic approach that embraces the living and learning areas of consumer functioning, (c) multiple assessment methods used to identify characteristics needed for appropriate transition planning, (d) that the evaluation itself takes place in a context that closely resembles actual vocational measurement and training, (e) that the assessment data are synthesized and then interpreted in a manner specific to each transition-aged individual (this interpretation should emphasize the consumer's career-related strengths and identify the factors necessary to operationalize transition planning), and (f) that assistive technology be available during the assessment process.

Transition Planning Inventory

The *Transition Planning Inventory* (TPI; Clark & Patton, 2006) should be completed by a family member, an appropriate school person (i.e., teacher or counselor), and the transition-aged individual. It covers such consumer living areas as the following:

Employment
Community participation
Further education/training
Health
Daily living
Self-determination
Leisure activities
Communication
Interpersonal relations

The information from these nine areas is then tabulated into a profile form of the transition-aged student. This profile provides an overview of the consumer's abilities in daily living and pursuing further training or education, employment, community participation, and communication. It also gives information on the family member's and school-related professional's perception of the consumer's health, self-determination, and quality of interpersonal relationships. Thus, the TPI establishes a foundation for understanding which living and working domains should be emphasized in transition planning. One of the attractive, engaging properties of this inventory is that it requires input from the young consumer, a beginning step for this person to take some responsibility during the transition assessment. But the information suggested by the inventory also develops a framework around which is constructed those assessment approaches that will be utilized for this specific consumer. This information also helps the interviewer to further understand the issues that must be considered in transition planning. The *Transition Planning Inventory* is available from PRO-ED, Inc., 8700 Shoal Creek Blvd., Austin, TX 78757-6897, 800/897-3202.

The Consumer Assessment Interview

Chapter 6 discussed the dynamics of an assessment interview. In it I suggested many questions that can be asked that will solicit information useful for transition planning. Specifically, as the young consumer responds and explains his or her life story, the following areas might be explored:

Age, sex, and developmental stage of life
Culture, race, ethnicity, and language
Gender role
Previous education and work experiences
Awareness of career opportunities
Perceived career obstacles arising from the disability
Emotional responses to disability
Independence and socialization skills
Social supports and perceptions of available support
Linkages to these supports
Personal meaning of disability

To solicit information in these areas, specific questions should be asked sometime during the interview, and many of these questions are identified in Chapter 6. Some other questions—ones tailored to the needs and goals of the transition-aged consumer—are the following:

Can you tell me about the people in your life who have helped you to be here today?
What are the most important events in your life until now?
What have been the most important things that have happened to you?
What is your life like today? What are your greatest accomplishments so far?
What are your dreams for the future?

What could prevent you from reaching your dreams?

What has to happen in order for you to move forward toward your dreams?

What are the first things we must do to help you achieve your goals? Who can help?

What is most important to you right now?

Responses to these nine questions could further facilitate the sharing of personal perceptions, lifestyle preferences, expectations, career-related values, and coping resources that become the building materials for a sustainable career structure. For the transition-aged consumer, the interview is, consequently, a non-normative measure that is also uniquely valuable for collecting information to design the next steps following assessment for one's career journey. Further, it is an important opportunity to identify those living and working areas of the young person that should be addressed as the assessment experience continues.

Informal and Formal Assessment Approaches

Informal and formal approaches can provide information that supports data gained from the interview or offer new insights into current consumer functioning and what is needed to develop a realistic transition plan.

Informal Assessment. Informal assessment includes not only the interview but also direct observation, questionnaires, and environmental or situational analyses. These methods should encourage the consumer's self-understanding and ownership of evaluation results. It is important to note that the informal approaches should also include activities that the consumer can readily understand, are appropriate for any cultural and linguistic differences, and consider the learning characteristics of the young person with a disability. Furthermore, these approaches both target the young consumer's interest and values areas of life functioning and include situational and job analyses.

Interest Identification. Because information about aptitudes and career-related abilities and achievement can be gained from the young person's school and/or training records, the focus of recommendations for informal assessment is on the exploration of the consumer's interests and values. As stated earlier, recent research (Herbert et al., 2010) has indicated that for this transition population, interest measurement is the dominant area among seven assessment domains utilized in evaluation programs. Among the informal approaches of situational analysis and direct observation that may yield interest identification, further interest information may be obtained by a specialized approach to interest assessment, as described in Chapter 7 of this text. This approach involves six steps that include asking specific questions, categorizing the information, and identifying the educational and occupational requirements of the dominant interest areas.

Also, using card sorts is a nonstandardized approach to sorting almost any array of topics. Occupational card sorts consist of occupational titles listed on small cards. "Consumers are simply asked to sort the cards into three piles: those they like, those they are indifferent to, and those they dislike. A next step could be for the consumer to take one of the piles and sort it into smaller piles based on any common themes that might have influenced him/her placing the cards into the broader category" (Gysbers, Heppner, & Johnston, 2009, p. 205).

Value Identification

The consumer interview, questionnaires, and card sorts can also provide information on the transition-aged person's values. Chapter 9 explains and the Interview Guide for Consumers With Functional Limitations (see the Appendix and the form located on the CD-ROM) shows an informal approach to value identification. Frequently, a consumer's values surface while the young person is discussing educational, leisure, and previous work experiences. Such values as salary, interaction with co-workers, seeking a sense of accomplishment, security, fairness, and location of work may be suggested as the individual discusses these experiences. But the disclosure of values may be the catalyst for and the motivation for the consumer's pursuit of dominant interest choices.

Values and interests, though related, are two distinct concepts. Moreover, gender plays a major role in career-related values. Men are more likely to espouse extrinsic values, and women are more likely to embrace social values (Duffy & Sedlacek, 2007). But the dialogue between the counselor and the transition-aged person with a disability, particularly during the individual's brief narration of his or her life story in the interview, may suggest significant career-related personal values and a willingness to engage in assessment activities (Crooker, Niija, & Mischkowski, 2008).

Situational Analysis

Situational assessment is another method for obtaining career-related interest information and is explained in Chapter 12. But the assessment approach will not be useful for planning unless a job analysis is conducted about available employment or career opportunities in the consumer's community, prior to the selection of a situational assessment site. This analysis is guided by the consumer's career interest preferences and a matching of these preferences to those career opportunities. This analysis can provide a perspective for the evaluation and could be an excellent resource for a situational assessment site.

Job Analysis

Job analysis is the identification of worker activities and skills required to complete a set of associated actions or operations that make up a job. It is different from job restructuring, which is the act of assembling identified worker activities from one set of jobs in order to build a different set of jobs, for the purpose of accomplishing the same product or output. Preceding the process of job analysis are two recommended steps that provide a foundation for the analysis:

Step 1. Identify the particular available jobs in the community or possible employment or career options for the consumer. The state employment office, the Chamber of Commerce, and local civic organizations are a few resources for job openings; career guidebooks are further resources for those not immediately entering employment. If available, placement personnel and career counselors are also a valuable source of information.

Step 2. Identify the two categories of job analysis elements that are required for the analysis of any job. Those categories are as follows:

- Work performed, including (a) worker functions; (b) work fields (specific methods characteristic of machines, tools, equipment, or work aids, such as drafting, riveting, sawing, installing, and repairing); (c) machines, tools, equipment, and work aids; and (d) materials, products, subject matter, and services.
- Worker traits, including training time, aptitudes, temperaments, interests, and physical demands and environmental conditions.

This two-step analysis yields information about the major tasks, settings, and worker qualifications of a specific job.

Another approach to this analysis follows these guidelines:

- *Job name or title*—In describing a job, particular attention should be given to what differentiates this job from others. Although several titles may be used for a particular job, distinctive tasks must be emphasized. For example, a clerical job might involve taking dictation, typing, photocopying, and filing. These functions could be given titles. It is important to consider precisely which functions any given job demands.
- *Tasks the worker performs*—Counselors and consumers must be aware of the skills required for doing the job and may consider the following questions:
  - What three or four work activities are really necessary to accomplish the purpose of the job?
  - What is the relationship between tasks, and is there a special sequence that the tasks must follow?
  - Do the tasks necessitate sitting, standing, crawling, walking, climbing, running, stopping, kneeling, lifting, carrying, pushing, pulling, fingering, talking, seeing, listening, feeling, or cooperation? To what degree does the job require muscular discrimination, depth of vision, color perception, the understanding of oral and written instructions, arithmetical computation, oral expression, intelligence, and the ability to work with people? All of these characteristics may be rated according to how important they are to the job. Note that the characteristics required to perform the job, not the characteristics of the present worker on the job, are rated.
  - What are the personality characteristics that are required or hoped for in order to perform the job successfully?
  - To do this job, is previous training or experience required? If so, how much, and is vocational, technical, or on-the-job training required?
  - What levels of required training and mental capabilities are necessary for performing the job adequately? For example, how complex is the job, and how much is required in terms of re-

sponsibility for the work of others, equipment, materials, and safety? Also, to what degree are initiative, adaptability, mental alertness, and judgment required?

❖ What specific knowledge is required for this job? This may include knowledge of machines, processes, materials, techniques, or policy and government regulations.

- *Methods required for the worker to perform job tasks*—What tools, materials, and equipment are used? What are the methods and processes used?
- *Physical setting of the job*—This includes the pay scale, the hours and shifts, and the standards for productive output. How would one describe the physical conditions of the job setting: hot, cold, damp, inside, outside, underground, wet, humid, dry, air conditioned, dirty, greasy, or noisy? Does the job environment have vibrations, hazards, odors, high places, sudden temperature changes, toxic conditions, solitary conditions, or crowded conditions?

All of this information must be considered in the context of the possibilities of job restructuring and the use of assistive technology. Without these accommodations, many young people with disabilities are eliminated from possible jobs.

Formal Assessment. Because frequently many informal measures are limited by the evaluator's knowledge of employment or career opportunities, stereotypes, or the questionnaire's own limitations in relevant content, selected formal approaches may be more helpful for self-understanding and career exploration goals. They are standardized, have a history of practical application, and if appropriate for the specific consumer, considerably widen the awareness of possible career choices.

The measurement focus of formal assessment in this chapter, highlighting useful information for transition planning, will be on adaptive behavior, interest, values, aptitude, and skills. In these areas, particular measurement tools are recommended.

Adaptive Behavior. The *Vineland Adaptive Behavior Scales–Second Edition* suggests the type and amount of support an individual may need. Consisting of a semistructured interview and a questionnaire, it also identifies the personal and social skills used in daily situations.

Interest Assessment. Results from this assessment should be coordinated with results from abilities tests, knowledge gained from the initial interview, medical reports, and, if possible, results from situational assessment. Chapter 7 of this text describes many useful measures, particularly,

> www. careercrusing.com
> www.bridges.com
> *Self-Directed Search*
> *Reading-Free Vocational Interest Inventory–Second Edition*
> *Picture Interest Career Survey*
> *Career Exploration Inventory*
> *Geist Picture Interest Inventory–Revised*

Added to this information is the *Wide Range Interest and Occupation Test–Second Edition* (WRIOT-2; Glutting & Wilkinson, 2003). The software of this test is compatible with Windows XP, VISTA, and Windows 7. This test contains 238 full-color pictures to help persons with disabilities determine whether they like, dislike, or are undecided about the different work situations depicted. It covers a full range of occupations, and the results indicate the strengths of interests, preferred functional duties, level of training, and working conditions. There are also extended descriptions of the consumer's interest areas.

CareerScope, Version 10 (Vocational Research Institute, Philadelphia, PA, 2010) is widely used in assessment programs and identifies both aptitudes and interests and is correlated with the O*NET and DOT Occupations/Groups. It can be completed online.

To be noted is that interest inventories can usually be used with assistive technology devices and do not compromise the inventory's reliability.

Values Assessment. Chapter 9 of this text identifies two measures, the *Survey of Work Values* (Wollack, Goodale, Wijting, & Smith, 1976) and the *Minnesota Importance Questionnaire* (Rounds, Henly, Dawis, Lofquist, & Weiss, 1981). If available to the professional, they can be used to supplement what is gained by using informal approaches that yield information about the consumer's values.

Aptitude Assessment. If records are lacking on the young consumer's aptitude-related strengths, then the following could be helpful.

- *Armed Services Vocational Aptitude Battery* (ASVAB)
- *Occupational Aptitude Survey and Interest Schedule–Aptitude*

Survey: Third Edition (OASIS-AS:3). It also contains a separate interest inventory and an aptitude battery. It is explained in Chapter 10 of this text.

- *Kaufman Functional Academic Skills Test* (Kaufman & Kaufman, 1994). Designed especially for transition-aged youth and adults, this test allows for verbal and motor responses and provides age-based standard scores of arithmetic and reading, as well as a composite score. This measure is best used as a supplement to other cognitive or adaptive assessments, and focuses on content appropriate for adult independent living.

Skills Assessment. Many young transition-aged consumers may not yet have had the opportunity to develop specific work content or special knowledge skills but have developed functional and adaptive skills. Functional skills are competencies that enable an individual to relate to people, data, and things in some combination according to personal preferences and appropriate to his or her potential (Power, 2011). They emerge with growth and development in educational, training, and vocational activities (Sikula, 1994). Some examples are:

achieving
constructing
managing
applying
installing
reasoning
choosing
investigating
communicating
maintaining

Adaptive skills are competencies that enable individuals to manage themselves in response to change and to accept and adjust to the physical, interpersonal, and organizational demands that arise in training or employment (Sikula, 1994). These skills are acquired in the early developmental years, originating in one's family and then reinforced in school and adult situations. Some examples are:

adaptable
enterprising

competent

healthy

dependable

honest

efficient

trustworthy

To collect information about functional and adaptive skills, the previously mentioned *Vineland Adaptive Behavior Scales* is appropriate. Resources such as *What Color Is Your Parachute?* (Bolles, 2009) and *Taking Charge of Your Career Direction* (Lock, 2005) contain helpful checklists and inventories. But if young people with disabilities are to be competitive in the 21st-century labor market, they must have the capacity to learn new skills or possess those skills needed in the current economy. Skill identification can be a beginning step to enhance a consumer's marketability.

In summary, both informal and formal assessment, necessary components of a transitional assessment program, provide an opportunity for young transition-aged consumers to learn about their career needs, strengths, and self-attributes, such as interests, abilities, and values. But for the consumer to participate actively in these assessments, he or she should be adequately prepared for the assessment experience. Encouraging the young person to be honest with him- or herself, indicating how the assessment results will be used, communicating that assessment may be "better seen as questions for the client than as answers" (Mastie, 1994, p. 40), and explaining carefully the purpose of each measure and the professional's role in this assessment may all be significant steps toward promoting participation and empowerment in the consumer.

Integrating and Interpreting Assessment Results

The last suggested steps in this proposed specific transitional program are integrating evaluation results and communicating these findings to the young consumer. Chapter 14 of this text provides detailed information on this interpretive communication, and the following, developed by Power (2011), is a format for integrating these results that can be used during the assessment interpretation session.

1. Organize background information (age, gender, culture, education, work, disability history, etc.).

2. Gather and prioritize appraisal results in the following areas: values, interests, skills, abilities, aptitudes, personality strengths.

3. Identify the dominant interest area and then relate the prioritized values, interest areas, skills, abilities, aptitudes, and personality strengths to the dominant interest area.

4. Develop a composite consumer picture from identification of the dominant interest area (item 3 above) and relevant factors, such as any supportive or nonsupportive family influence, the environmental context in which an eventual career decision will be made, cultural influences on a potential career choice, and disability-related factors.

5. Develop a hypothesis that would become the driving force of the search for career information (e.g., Would career exploration and an eventual career choice in this dominant interest area be realistic?).

Conclusion

The transition assessment process is ongoing, consumer centered, and tailored to each person's particular circumstances and needs. Although assessment models have been developed that are formulated around general guidelines for preparing young people with disabilities to engage in the transition from school to career, assessment plans should be created that respond to individual career and educational plans. Importantly, the National Occupational Information Coordinating Committee (NOICC) has established national guidelines "that provide competencies needed by individuals who are at various life stages (elementary, middle, high school, and adult) in three major areas of development: self-development, educational and occupational exploration, and career planning" (Rojewski, 2002, p. 89). This generic framework begins 4 to 5 years prior to high school completion, then includes a phase 2 to 3 years prior to high school completion, and concludes 1 year prior to high school completion. Each phase comprises an assessment or completed assessment plan, initial and ongoing assessments, development and completion of a career portfolio, and the identification of the skills or training necessary to achieve the results of the assessments.

Apart from this generic framework, however, assessment for the transition-aged young person should provide information both for transition planning and to enhance the individual's self-understanding and employment marketability. The 21st century presents a challenge for all those with disabilities, and it will be difficult for this population to compete successfully for available jobs or to develop a productive career path. Workforce skills have been redefined. The suggested evaluation program in this chapter targets the young person's potential to learn the necessary skills, the development of which can become integral to the transition plan. This proposed program emphasizes that once the person's potential is recognized, the possible may become probable.

Chapter 14

Interpreting Assessment Information and Identifying Occupational Resources

One of the most important aspects of vocational assessment is the way the rehabilitation professional communicates to the consumer the information gained from the evaluation. This communication involves interpreting test data in an understandable way, helping consumers to make decisions about their future plans, and perhaps alleviating some difficulties that might be obstacles to effective rehabilitation planning (such as unrealistic vocational aspirations or poor motivations for training). For consumers with disabilities, reporting assessment data may be crucial to making a decision regarding which course will lead to possible employment. For the professional, this interpretation session demands skills in integrating assessment data about the abilities, education, and motivation of individuals with what is known about the nature of various occupations (Shertzer & Linden, 1979).

These skills include the ability to provide accurate interpretation and to focus on the impact of cultural differences on the assessment results. The results themselves are not information. Information is that which evolves from the data interpretation (Donnell, Robertson, & Tansey, 2010). There are factors external to the actual evaluation measures, and interpretation may be significantly influenced by cultural and linguistic differences. Furthermore, the consumer's acculturation, language, ethnicity, and beliefs about careers may shape both the assessment administration and an understanding of the results (Donnell et al., 2010).

Rehabilitation assessment should be part of the continued counseling process in order for the consumer to reach productive goals, and the rehabilitation professional often has to interpret test information gained from nonvocational sources (such as a psychiatrist or psychologist) into vocational terms. This vocational translation includes knowledge of customary instruments used by nonvocational sources, such as medically based agencies, in order to make test results meaningful to the consumer. Some of the principles underlying this interpretation are explained in this chapter.

This chapter explains the types of interpretation involved in rehabilitation assessment, identifies the general principles involved in interpreting and communicating assessment information to the consumer, discusses the actual situation of communicating evaluative information to consumers, indicates the special problems that often occur in the interpretative session, and offers some responses to questions. The role of the rehabilitation professional in developing resources for occupational information that can be used when communicating interpretation information and when developing the assessment report is also discussed. Selected occupational literature is identified, along with ways to generate knowledge about the local world of work.

Types of Interpretation

Goldman (1971) identified four types of interpretation—descriptive, genetic, predictive, and evaluative—all of which fit within the structure of rehabilitation assessment.

Descriptive

This interpretation asks such questions as, What kind of person is this consumer? What are his or her hobbies, vocational interests, particular capabilities, and personal strengths? What does the evaluation reveal about this consumer, especially when the person is compared to other people on specific test scores, such as aptitude functioning? Does the consumer do better in one area than another?

Genetic

In this aspect of interpretation, various reasons are explored as to why or how the consumer is functioning in a certain manner. For example, if the consumer has a work history in outdoor activities, but interest testing reveals that he or she actually has little interest in this area, then the reasons for this discrepancy could be explored. Low aptitude scores can also be discussed. Particular obstacles, either from the consumer's environment (e.g., family) or from within the consumer (e.g., attitude, emotional disposition), can be identified. Such obstacles might represent reasons why the consumer is against a particular vocational direction, especially when evaluation strongly suggests an exploration of the area.

Predictive

Many factors can confound or facilitate vocational or training success. Prediction should be done cautiously during the reporting of evaluation data because of such realities as motivation, the consumer's own adjustment to disability, and environmental forces influencing the consumer as he or she moves from medical treatment or inactivity to more active involvement in the rehabilitation process. If interpreted properly, most evaluation information suggests reasons why a certain vocational direction is feasible for the consumer. Soliciting consumers' feedback during interpretation can also facilitate their awareness of what is needed for effective adjustment to training or to employment.

Evaluative

In this area of interpretation, the emphasis is more on such objective considerations as specific behavioral and ability-related job demands, what the O*NET identifies as job qualifications (Hanson, Matheson, & Borman, 2001; Thirtieth Institute on Rehabilitation Issues [IRI], 2003), and which occupations are particularly in demand in the consumer's geographical area. The results from the assessment are then compared or matched to this objective information. From this comparison, the professional can begin to determine what occupation or level of training would be more feasible to enter and how long a course of vocational training should be pursued. This area of interpretation, however, necessitates value judgments by the rehabilitation professional, which in turn generate recommendations for the consumer.

In reporting evaluation information, all of these varied kinds of interpretation are used. When considering the interpretation of assessment results, the validities of evaluation measures must be carefully identified. If an instrument has a low predictive ability and has been used in evaluation, then this should be discussed when communicating the results to the consumer. As explained in Chapter 5, the validity issue is a continuing problem when using traditional assessment tools with individuals who have disabilities, as this population probably was not included in the norm group; although these measures may be strong in content validity (which has reasonably good descriptive use during the interpretation session), they should not be used for prediction.

General Principles of Interpretation

Many guidelines make the interpretation session an effective experience for both the rehabilitation worker and the consumer. It is important for the evaluator to remember that test scores identify how well individuals perform at the time of testing, not why they perform as they do. The causes of a person's test performance may emerge from an exploration of the consumer's learning history, an understanding of the environment in which the individual developed, the events or influences that the individual encountered, and the person's response to these influences (Anastasi, 1992).

Communicating Evaluation Information and Results

The rehabilitation worker should communicate evaluation information at the level of the consumer's understanding. Ideally, at this time in the evaluation process, the professional has some knowledge of the consumer's mental abilities as well as the deficits that may limit the consumer's capability of understanding important assessment facts. People who have chronic anxiety or who have been showing continued resistance to exploring new alternatives for life planning often have a difficult time endorsing assessment feedback. In these instances, the consumer's point of view, attitudes, or goals can be used as a point of reference or departure. When preparing for the interpretive session, the professional can then identify information that may be favorable or unfavorable to the consumer's point of reference. Once this "for-and-against" evidence has been summarized, an explanation can be offered as to why the consumer should shift goals or consider a certain direction for rehabilitation planning. In other words, the inventory or test results that are the most positive, and perhaps most consistent with the consumer's self-image and the easiest to understand, should be explained first. The interpretation process should begin with a focus on what is personally meaningful to the consumer, in the context of an awareness of the linguistic differences and the specific learning style of the consumer. Test interpretation should be a meaningful learning experience for the person with a disability. Simply sharing assessment information verbally may not always be in harmony with how the consumer retains this information. Visual aids that illustrate test results may be more effective for many individuals.

Using Alternative Recommendations

The recommendations that are offered in this reporting of the information session should be made in terms of alternatives so that the consumer can then make a choice. It is the consumer who basically interprets the test information (Biggs & Keller, 1982), but it is the professional who must understand the different options that are available to the consumer. Knowing how to use the DOT and O*NET is an invaluable asset in assessment. These resources, especially the O*NET, identify the many occupational choices available in the labor market and give the requirements for each job. The discussion of alternatives or the exploration of different job options feasible for the consumer reflects the professional's experience in handling job-related information and knowing the different opportunities that may exist within the consumer's community.

Encouraging Consumer Participation

Promoting consumer involvement ensures that the consumer will appropriately evaluate the test results (Biggs & Keller, 1982). This entails feedback and exploration of consumer questions. Although it might be easier for the rehabilitation professional simply to present the test results or other related information to the consumer without soliciting any feedback and then make recommendations without allowing much time to deal with the consumer's response, this approach will usually not facilitate realistic rehabilitation planning. If consumers participate in gaining an understanding of assessment results, they will be likely to introduce new information about themselves from other sources and to produce new insights regarding the significance of all the information (Goldman, 1971). The more consumers contribute to the results provided by the assessment measures and the more the rehabilitation professional is "consumer centered" (emphasizing the consumer's feelings about assessment data), the more accepting consumers will be of the conclusions and their implications regarding future activities. The consumer who is involved in reporting evaluation information stands a better chance of remembering accurately what is communicated. The evaluator's avoidance of jargon and technical terms can facilitate this involvement.

Emphasizing the Importance of Professional and Consumer Perception of Test Results

It is not the test information itself but the rehabilitation professional's and consumer's perceptions of these results that are important. One of the emphases in reporting evaluation results should be on the attitudes and readiness of consumers to use the information being given in the session. For this reason, the professional should also be aware of consumers' views toward themselves and toward the rehabilitation process, their expectations about the assessment process, and the feasibility of future job-related productivity. Some consumers, for example, may see no need to learn more about themselves or to explore options that are even marginally different from their present lifestyle. The consumer also may still be attempting to adjust emotionally to the disability. Consequently, the consumer who perceives that there is little hope for a satisfying life may have quite a low self-concept. The consumer's perception of test scores is often associated with his or her self-view. Consumers have great difficulty accepting information that conflicts with their self-concept. It is the professional's responsibility to facilitate the kind of interaction that leads the consumer to a more accurate perception of assessment data.

Another issue related to the communication and perception of test results is bias. Bias is reflected in minimizing the differences among different racial/ethnic groups (Dana, 2008), or stereotyping the career possibilities for someone with a specific disability because of preconceived beliefs about "what is occupationally best for the person with a particular impairment." These stereotypes especially surface during the *recommendations phase* of the interpretation session. The professional's awareness of these unwarranted beliefs and a careful review of the evaluation results to identify all career possibilities may both help to minimize prejudice.

Avoiding Persuasive Methods

During this information-imparting session, the professional should avoid persuasive methods that might convey brusqueness or aggressiveness. The evaluation data should speak for themselves and be the motivational tool for rehabilitation planning—not the professional's personality alone. Of course, the professional provides suggestions, options, attractive choices, and reasonable alternatives. However, it is the consumer who makes the final decision about whether to act on recommendations. One of the goals of this session is not to force the professional's interpretation of assessment data upon consumers but, rather, to allow consumers to relate this new information to their view of previous experiences and rehabilitation expectations. It is helpful if the evaluation information is presented to the consumer as objectively as possible. A statement such as "Eight out of 10 consumers with scores like yours have a good chance of succeeding in this electronics program" is preferable to one that begins "You should …" or "I believe …" or "If these were my scores, I would…."

Maintaining Professional Knowledge of Tests and Assessment Approaches

The professional should be as familiar as possible with the different tests, measures, or approaches used during the consumer's evaluation. Such questions as "How well and what does this instrument measure?" and "What do the scores mean?" should be answered before the interpretation session with the consumer. This information can be obtained from the test manual or, when testing was done by another source, such as a psychologist, this information should be received from that person. Moreover, rehabilitation professionals can learn a great deal about a particular paper-and-pencil test by taking the same tests that are used with their consumers in vocational assessment. Associated with this principle is the belief that consumers should understand which test is being interpreted and what it measures.

All of these issues, however, connect with the professional's competencies for understanding the needs of persons with disabilities, the wide variety of assessment approaches and measures that can respond to evaluative needs, and the cultural differences among consumers. These differences speak to the necessity for selecting culturally appropriate measures, and an awareness of how certain ethnic factors, such as traditional family beliefs about careers, the influences of social class on decision-making, and acculturation, affect one's test-taking responses.

Avoiding Confrontation With Unanticipated Negative Information

The consumer should not be confronted with unanticipated negative information. Instead, the professional should balance negatives with positives by, for example, saying, "On the one hand, your scores in the mechanical aptitude suggest that you would have a difficult time succeeding in training in that area. But on the other hand, your clerical aptitude is very high and merits serious attention for future planning."

Communication of Test Results in a Holistic Perspective

Information on test results should be presented not only in the context of what is already known about the consumer but also with a holistic viewpoint. Interview data and information gathered from school records, previous employment experience, and earlier test results can provide a background for understanding existing evaluation results. A comparison of past and recently acquired information may identify areas of consumer growth or regression. Because disability trauma represents a major transition of life functioning for most consumers, an understanding of pre-onset emotional, physical, and cognitive strengths can establish a direction for the interpretation session. The interpretation session may also be an opportunity to explain the interaction between the consumer's physical, emotional, and cognitive functions. Assessment planning usually incorporates planning in all these areas. The results of each area should be explained in the context of not only cultural/ethnic influences but also how one functioning area, such as cognition-related results, is influenced by another functioning area.

All in all, these principles emphasize that the interpretation session is both a teaching and counseling opportunity for the rehabilitation professional; for the consumer, it is primarily a learning situation. During the session, consumers have the chance to explore alternatives, to discuss their own views about the meaning of the evaluation results, and to gain added self-understanding that might be needed for subsequent life-planning decisions; however, the professional also has the opportunity to learn more about the consumer. The extent of this learning depends on how the evaluation information has been communicated, how the goals of the evaluation process have been formulated earlier with the consumer, and how consumers themselves respond to the learning of this newly discovered information.

The Interpretation Session

The interpretation session with the consumer should be structured so that the rehabilitation professional has a clear idea of what is to be accomplished. For example, if the goal is to formulate rehabilitation plans for the consumer, this aim becomes a perspective for the organization of evaluation results. When structuring this session, attention should be given to (a) emphasizing capabilities that can be used in vocational planning, (b) the order in which assessment data will be discussed, (c) how the professional will deal with negative information generated by the evaluation, and (d) what particular data will be used for vocational planning. Also, information should not be forced on the consumer but should be related to his or her previous experiences. Assessment results should be presented in such a way that consumers are encouraged to follow an appropriate rehabilitation direction. All of this demands preparation; when this planning is done, evaluation reporting becomes much more effective.

The interpretation session can be structured into four phases.

Introduction: Facilitating the Consumer's Comfort Level

At the beginning of the session, the professional should help the consumer feel at ease and receptive toward assessment information. Reviewing the goals of evaluation and soliciting responses from the consumer on how he or she felt about the evaluation can help reduce feelings of anxiety. Consumers are usually anxious because of the evaluative and judgmental aspects of assessment. For example, they may fear that tests will reveal bad news. Consumers may also perceive that the results may change their expectations about a certain area of training. Providing them with the opportunity to talk about these concerns may give the professional some ideas about how to present the evaluation results. When the professional provides the chance for consumers to express their thoughts and uses an active listening style to show that he or she is genuinely interested in what is being said, then the consumers' cooperation in acting upon assessment information is frequently promoted. Consumers may have many concerns about evaluation information. Asking them about how they felt during the time that the tests were administered achieves an understanding of attitudinal factors that may have influenced them during the assessment procedures (Miller, 1982).

Discussing Original Purposes of Vocational Assessment and Tests

When the professional believes that the consumer is receptive to listening to the evaluation results, the original purposes of the vocational assessment and what tests or measures were used should then be discussed. Interest tests should be identified first, because their information usually is less threatening to the consumer and can establish a direction for the feedback of the other evaluation data in the personality, aptitude, and intelligence areas. It is also important to review the particular assessment tools used in all the evaluation areas, discussing why they were selected and what they measure. Furthermore, concepts such as norms, percentiles, percentile ranks, and stanines may need to be thoroughly explained (Miller, 1982).

Explaining the Results of Each Assessment Area

After reviewing all the measures used for evaluation, the professional can explain the results of each assessment area, beginning with interest inventories. The consumer is usually shown the interest profile, for example, and told about the information it presents, and then particular results are identified. In this phase of test reporting, statistical data or test-score numbers must be translated for the consumer. Percentiles probably are the safest and most informative numbers to use, provided the consumer understands (a) that they refer not to the percentage of questions answered correctly but to the percentage of people whose performances the consumer has equaled or surpassed and (b) specifically, who the people are to whom the consumer is being compared.

A definite description of the comparison or norm group is particularly important in making the meaning of test results clear. The reporting of numbers should be minimized when communicating test results and, if used, should only be done incidentally. One suggestion for a response is "Your results are similar to those people who...."

After providing the interest assessment information, the consumer should be asked about his or her relevant feelings or reflections. Two questions that solicit consumer responses are "Do you feel these results present an accurate picture of you?" and "Is this information a surprise to you?" The consumer should be able to understand the assessment results and talk about what they mean to him or her.

After the interest results are given, achievement and ability or work results can be reported. Frequently, the interest results are encouraging to the consumer and set the stage for a very productive reporting session. Any negative data should be communicated carefully. In reporting these results, the professional should emphasize the information that identifies the consumer's vocational strengths and the patterns of strengths and weaknesses interpreted in terms of educational and work history. It is important to present this information objectively, using norm comparisons when they are available. Attention should also be given to the consistency of the results with the consumer's past and present levels of functioning. Two questions need to be answered in light of the achievement and ability results: (a) Do the results suggest that the consumer could handle the work or training required at other, higher levels? and (b) What does this information mean in terms of an occupational choice?

Because assessment reporting has already identified general areas of interest, it is most helpful now if the professional suggests particular interest areas, respective occupations, and the physical, emotional, and intellectual qualifications for each area. In this regard, O*NET is a valuable resource. Before the interpretation session, the professional can examine the consumer's assessment results and use O*NET to consider different occupations and the qualifications that are appropriate to these results. (This resource is further described in the last section of this chapter.)

After these results have been explained and the information has been related to the consumer's past experience, statements about vocational goals, prior interest exploration, and overall feedback should again be solicited from the consumer. It is necessary for the consumer to understand the results as they relate to future rehabilitation planning. Encouraging the exploration of feelings and perceptions regarding this data should further facilitate this comprehension.

Following this interaction, the intelligence test results can be communicated if these measures have been used in assessment. The rehabilitation professional should be cautious about giving the consumer a definite IQ score. When consumers receive all the evaluation results, they tend to remember just their IQ score, which distorts its meaning for rehabilitation planning. Also, the score can vary to a small degree, depending on both testing conditions and the consumer's current level of functioning. Rather than report the IQ number, a range (such as *Average*, *Bright Normal*, or *Superior*) can be given.

Personality assessment then follows, and frequently this part of the interpretation session is very threatening to consumers. To alleviate some of the consumer's anxiety, the purpose of each test and what it measures can be explained. Furthermore, the professional should avoid terminology that has unfavorable emotional connotations, such as "neurosis" or "emotional instability." The particular test results can also be related to occupational goals or job requirements. Often, these personality measures reveal negative information about the consumer that may have the consumer's apparent troubled past as its source. The professional should decide whether these data have any relevant bearing on current rehabilitation planning. For example, test results or evaluations might reveal that the consumer has certain phobias or experiences severe anxiety, both of which may affect work adjustment. Therefore, the professional may recommend counseling before any training is pursued. Such a recommendation may be a sensitive issue and presumes that the evaluator has a positive relationship with the consumer and the reasons for the recommendation are prudently given, emphasizing that counseling may facilitate work/career adjustment. In this area of interpretation, it is also particularly important for the professional to identify personality strengths that relate strongly to work functioning. Limitations that might affect employment must also be presented, but these are more readily acknowledged when viewed through the perception of some strong personality assets.

Concluding the Interpretation Session

When terminating the reporting of assessment information, the rehabilitation professional should keep in mind the results that are important for rehabilitation planning. This information should again be identified in summary fashion, and then rehabilitation directions for training or employment can be suggested. Consumers should be asked to provide some feedback on what they have learned from the evaluation and what results they consider to be the most important. They should leave the interpretation session with an understanding of themselves that raises hope and strong expectations for their futures. This often demands that rehabilitation professionals frequently repeat in the interpretation session those results that show capabilities for employment; however, it is time well spent. The results often become motivational factors for later rehabilitation involvement. The professional should remember that the interpretation of test results usually leads to the development of rehabilitation plans. Any planning should involve the consumer, and options need to be explored with the consumer. Table 14.1 shows a summary of an actual interpretation session.

Special Concerns in Interpretation

Problems often arise during the interpretation session, and problems that are not handled promptly can lessen or negate the effectiveness of this important part of assessment. Three concerns frequently occur when the professional provides feedback on evaluation results.

Contradictory Test Scores

Occasionally, evaluation measures may give different scores on the same factor or individual trait. How can those differences be reconciled? For example, can the discrepancy between the results of two interest

Table 14.1
Summary of Interpretation Session

Phase	Tasks
First phase (Introduction)	1. Know about measures that need to be interpreted to the client. 2. Establish a relationship. 3. Review goals of evaluation for the client.
Second phase	1. Give the client an opportunity to talk about the assessment experience. 2. Summarize in a general manner the overall results of evaluation, emphasizing positive test results. 3. Solicit feedback from the client.
Third phase	1. Interpret carefully each evaluation measure—Interest, Aptitude/Ability, Intelligence, and Personality. Use such guidelines as norms, percentiles, and so on. 2. Solicit feedback about the client's feelings concerning the results. 3. Deal with such problems as contradictory test scores, reluctance, and unrealistic vocational aspirations. 4. Suggest particular interest areas, respective occupations, and qualifications for each in the physical, emotional, and intellectual areas.
Fourth phase (Conclusion)	1. Summarize results for the client and discuss how this information can relate to rehabilitation planning. 2. Ask the client for further feedback, especially about what has been learned from the evaluation experience. 3. Develop rehabilitation plans.

inventories be resolved when one of them shows a high score in business-related activities and the other a low score? In responding to these differences, three basic viewpoints can be considered, as identified by Goldman (1971).

Differences Among the Tests

There may be differences in the types of items found on paper-and-pencil tests, for example, free choice versus forced choice. The latter might be more irritating because of the necessity of making choices, even when the consumer feels no preference among the alternative choices. Often, the norm groups used in developing normative data for the tests are quite different from one another in both age and intelligence levels. The characteristics that each test measures might also be quite different. The *Quick-Test* (Ammons & Ammons, 1962), for example, measures school ability and then provides an IQ score; the *Shipley Institute of Living Scale* (Shipley, Gruber, Martin, & Klein, 2009) includes both Verbal and Abstract Reasoning and then gives an IQ score. The same consumer taking both tests may score lower on the Shipley test because of less developed abstract reasoning ability.

Differences Within the Individual

On different occasions during rehabilitation assessment, a consumer may function physically and psychologically in different ways. Fatigue, the presence of mental distractions, situational anxiety, acute stress, and motivation can all be sources for the difference in scores on measures evaluating the same area. When the professional notes this difference, he or she should explore with the consumer reasons for the discrepancy.

Differences in Test Administration and Scoring

Occasionally, the conditions in the testing room or environment (e.g., temperature that is too hot or cold) represent inhibiting factors to test performance. Sometimes, the test administrators may increase anxiety because of the way they present themselves, whereas others try to relax consumers before a testing experience. These realities may contribute to a difference in the way a consumer handles test items. Consequently, scores on the same measure may differ. Again, the professional should ask the consumer for reasons why the scores are different, especially when there is little difference between the tests themselves.

Reluctance to Believe Test Scores or Follow the Professional's Recommendations

During the interpretation session, the consumer may seem unwilling to believe the assessment results, challenge these results often during the interpretation session, or be reluctant to act on this information. Such behaviors as making excuses or speaking negatively about the assessment process may be two indications of the consumer's anxiety over accepting responsibility for the evaluation results and then taking action. Irrational beliefs about recommended career directions ("I do not want to do this for the rest of my life," "Because of my disability, my career options may be either hopeless or very limited," "The requirements to begin training in that field are impossible") may inhibit the consumer's endorsement of the assessment results (Gysbers, Heppner, & Johnston, 2009).

This reluctance or resistance needs attention because one of the goals of the interpretation session is to use the assessment data to help consumers become motivated enough to pursue appropriate rehabilitation goals. The first step in alleviating this concern is to identify the source of the reluctance. The consumer's responses can be influenced by hostility toward the professional as an authority figure, assessment information that apparently goes against the consumer's self-concept, or the consumer's predetermined resolve to follow a course of action, regardless of the evaluation results. Also, because of past failure experiences, the consumer may lack the flexibility to take risks or attempt new ventures suggested by evaluation results and rehabilitation planning. Change is viewed as very threatening, and there is a marked hesitancy to try new directions. Whatever the reason, the source of the consumer's reluctance should be explored and identified.

During this exploration and possible identification of the source of the resistance, empathy with the consumer can be a beginning step toward alleviating the consumer's negative mind-set. When the consumer is aware that the rehabilitation professional is an active listener who expresses warmth, sincerity, and genuine interest, there may be some willingness to discuss obstacles to accepting evaluation results and recommendations. But Gysbers et al. (2009) believed that it will take more than empathy or reflection of feelings to facilitate responses from a reluctant consumer. The professional must also attempt to *join* with the consumer. This connection may be accomplished by recognizing and appreciating the consumer's total life struggles; identifying the individual's areas of pain, difficulty, or stress; and reframing the life experience with a disability. A new description of the life experience can be offered by emphasizing the consumer strengths that have been revealed by the assessment process and how these strengths link to possible career opportunities.

The training and occupational alternatives suggested by evaluation information often have to be made attractive to the consumer. Any suggested course of action must be perceived by the consumer as personally rewarding. Providing emotional support for consumers who hesitate to take a risk, while at the same time emphasizing the assets revealed by the evaluation, may generate movement toward rehabilitation goals. Frequently, when consumers gain confidence in their professionals, they are motivated to overcome apparent obstacles to vocational planning. For example, a consumer's family can influence reluctance; many consumers are afraid to counter family members' expectations. It takes a considerable amount of courage for the consumer to tell the family that he or she is going to follow a certain direction in rehabilitation, even when the family does not endorse the choice. When the consumer believes that a certain course of action is the most appropriate, trusts the rehabilitation professional, and feels that this training or the next step in the rehabilitation process will eventually bring personal satisfaction, he or she may follow this direction over the family's wishes.

Unrealistic Vocational Aspirations

Unrealistic vocational aspirations often arise during the interpretation session. Because of the consumer's insufficient awareness of his or her abilities, limited exposure to the working world, or fear of certain training areas that lead to employment, the consumer's own perception of the best rehabilitation goals may be very different from what the evaluation information suggests. When this problem inhibits appropriate rehabilitation planning, the professional must explore carefully with the consumers their educational and work histories, levels of skill proficiency suggested by the evaluation results, and feasible training or employment possibilities. After the identification of the consumer's work-related qualifications, various employment alternatives can be presented, based on emotional, physical, and intellectual qualifications. The DOT and O*NET provide information on job requirements and working conditions. The professional should also know about salary and promotional possibilities. If this information is given in relationship to the consumer's training and job capabilities, emphasizing as many employment alternatives as possible, the consumer will at least have a considerable amount of useful information for making a choice.

It is the consumer's responsibility to make the decision about which vocational direction should be pursued. When the rehabilitation professional is patient, identifies the sources of the consumer's unrealistic vocational goals, and attempts to make rehabilitation alternatives as appealing as possible, there is a greater possibility that the consumer will consider carefully the professional's recommendations. Many times, it is also helpful for consumers to talk to someone in a field toward which they may be unrealistically aspiring. This reality exposure helps consumers to confront personal options and obtain some concrete information on their feasibility. Often, these encounters help to break down consumers' resistance and allow them to acknowledge the impracticality of an initial vocational choice. Moreover, workers can also recommend that the consumer meet people in those occupations or training opportunities that are more in harmony with the evaluation results.

The Professional's Role in Developing Occupational Information

Knowledge of occupational resources and local opportunities for employment considerably enhances the credibility of the interpretation of test results for consumers. Goldman (1972) suggested that if counselors, for example, continue to use tests, they must also collect information about available local job and career opportunities. This makes interpretive statements more meaningful and brings a perspective for understanding assessment results. Using varied occupational information resources can provide a more realistic picture of evaluation results, which adds more credibility to rehabilitation planning. During the interpretive session, it is also important to increase the consumer's options for training or employment. Knowledge of occupational resources facilitates the exploration of alternatives.

Obtaining career information usually occurs following consumer vocational assessment. At this time, there are the following concerns, as suggested by Niles and Harris-Bowlsbey (2005).

- Is this consumer ready to learn information and deal with it effectively?
- What limitations does the consumer potentially have with regard to using the career data effectively? Cognitive impairments and family and cultural expectations may keep the consumer with a disability from utilizing this information.
- What kinds of data, and how much, will be the most helpful?

- What approach (personal contact, print material, or computers and web sites) will be most appropriate, considering the disability situation?

Resources for Career Information

One key issue for rehabilitation counselors today in managing career information is identifying the real needs consumers have for career information (Gysbers, Heppner, & Johnston, 2009). Not all consumers with a disability, however, have a need for career information. Disability onset, with appropriate accommodations made in the workplace, may not interrupt the regimen and demands of one's occupational career. But recognition of assistive technology resources may support and extend the consumer's communication of career needs and expectations and knowledge of career opportunities. Identifying the consumer's needs in this area will involve asking questions upon gaining some assessment results:

- Considering your understanding of many of the assessment results, what information do you have about their connection to training and occupational opportunities?
- What needs do you think you have now that could be met by learning further career information?

Another key issue in utilizing career information is the consumer's motivation to use this information productively. Many consumers will initially present themselves for rehabilitation planning, engage in assessment, but hesitate at learning more about their career-related choices or opportunities because they believe that such information is a prelude to making a career decision. They believe they are not ready to make that decision, often for several reasons. The consumer might still be in the process of emotionally adjusting to the personal and environmental circumstances of the mental or physical impairment. Or, secondary gain issues might diminish an active desire to make a career choice in a reasonable time frame. Attractive monetary compensation associated with the disability, or family expectations that pressure the consumer to make a career decision, are two other possible causes of the consumer's hesitancy. These factors associated with the consumer's motivation can imply that the timing of the career information process should be considered. Otherwise, the consumer may not profitably use the information (Power, 2011).

But if the professional believes that the consumer is ready for this type of information, there are many resources to identify. Currently, print materials are still the most important source of occupational information. Though printed materials are relatively easy to develop, the use of the Internet and the availability of computerized systems to disseminate information have increasingly reduced the importance of printed materials in the 21st century (Isaacson & Brown, 2000).

When seeking information about possible career or employment opportunities, specific guidelines have been developed by the National Vocational Guidance Association (Fredrickson, 1982) that help the professional to evaluate the relevancy of published or Internet-available career information. Those resources that pertain to career assessment are as follows:

1. Duties and nature of work
2. Work setting and conditions
3. Personal qualifications
4. Social and psychological factors
5. Preparation required
6. Special requirements
7. Methods of entering the field
8. Earnings and other benefits
9. Usual advancement possibilities

There are four basic ways to obtain information about career resources:

1. *Personal experiences*—This may be accomplished by obtaining a part-time or full-time job, doing volunteer work, spending a day observing a job performance, and participating in work/study experiences and job-shadowing programs.
2. *Talking with people/interviewing to solicit information*—Personal interviews may provide information that cannot be obtained from printed sources and also can broaden the network of useful contacts.

3. *Printed material*—Isaacson and Brown (2000) highlighted the National Career Development Association's three general categories of print publications, as shown in Table 14.2.

Online Resources

The Internet is a connection of computer networks, and its most popular branch, the World Wide Web, provides occupational information that is expanding in its availability (Lock, 2005). Though not yet a science

Table 14.2
National Career Development Association's Categories of Print Publications

Category	Items covered	Examples
Vocational	Occupations Trends and outlook Job training Employment opportunities	• Specific information about jobs
Educational	Status and trends Schools and colleges	
	• Private vocational-technical schools	• *2008/2010 Postsecondary Sourcebooks for Community Colleges, Technical, Trade, and Business Schools* (Wintergreen-Orchard House)
	• Four-year colleges and universities	• *Black American Colleges and Universities: Profile of Two-Year, Four-Year, and Professional Schools* (Hill & Wilson, 1994) • *College Admissions Data Handbook* (French, 2001) • *College Planning and Search Handbook* (ACT, 1999)
	Scholarships, fellowships, grants, and loans	
Career/Personal	Planning Adjustment to work Theory Assessment Computer/Internet systems	• Resumes, how to look for job, etc. • Interest, aptitude, testing, etc.

Note. Adapted from *Career Information, Career Counseling, and Career Development* (7th ed.), by L. Isaacson and D. Brown, 2000, Boston: Allyn & Bacon.

but more of an art, the Internet can complement sources of career information (Gysbers, Heppner, & Johnston, 2009). Most companies dealing with occupational information maintain sites on the Web and through this medium provide extensive career information.

Lock (2005) identified selected sites that provide occupational information.

- *Occupational Outlook Handbook* (http://www.bls.gov/ooh). This publication is available online as well as in print.
- *Occupational Outlook Quarterly* (http://www.bls.gov/ooq). This publication supplements the *Occupational Outlook Handbook* four times a year and covers topics about careers.
- *Career Guide to Industries* (http://www.bls.gov/oco/cg). This is the online version of the U.S. Department of Labor's book of the same title. The site gives information on career by industry and the employment needs of the industries it covers.
- *America's Career InfoNet* (http://www.acinet.org). This website has links to the following sources of occupational information: general outlook, wages and trends, employers, state profiles, and career exploration.
- *State-based career information delivery systems.* Each state provides information about occupations and educational programs within that state. Click on "State Job Banks" on the America's Career InfoNet home page (http://www.acinet.org), and then scroll to the state you want.
- *Discover* (http://www.act.org/discover). This site is a comprehensive system containing four units (Learning About Self and Work, Choose Occupations, Plan My Education, and Plan for Work). The Choose Occupations database has information on more than 500 occupations, updated each year, and these occupations can be selected by indicating educational entry levels and other significant criteria. The Discover System is a very useful system for the career-planning process.
- *Career Information System* (CIS). This system operates on a national basis through 121 state agencies. Nearly 500 occupations are described in the CIS file, and basic information is provided on those occupations.

- *System of Interactive Guidance and Information* (SIGI Plus). This tool is useful for constructing occupational alternatives based on self-assessment information (work-related values, interest, skills, and level of education). Twenty-seven questions about one or two occupations at a time are asked, facilitating the consumer's involvement in this system.

O*NET—The Occupational Information Network

The Occupational Information Network (O*NET) is the resource that the Department of Labor (DOL) is supporting to supersede the *Dictionary of Occupational Titles* (DOT) to reflect the work requirements of the 21st-century economy. It is an occupational resource that has yet to realize its full potential but currently does provide a comprehensive, flexible source of occupational information (Hanson et al., 2001). Because of the progress in job analysis technology and in understanding the occupational requirements and the characteristics of workers needed to fulfill these requirements, there was a need to update occupational information and to reach out to a larger audience of potential users, that is, job seekers, especially those representing an ethnic minority; training specialists; career and rehabilitation counselors; displaced workers; and state and federal labor and manpower specialists (Hanson et al., 2001).

The O*NET is significantly different from the DOT. The former consists of standardized, numerical descriptions of occupational requirements and worker characteristics, and the latter resource contains narrative descriptions. Hanson et al. (2001) believed that "O*NET job description information is also likely to be more accessible to consumers than was the DOT information" (p. 298). Behavioral anchors accompany all of the descriptor level rating scales. With a focus primarily on the person performing the tasks, rather than on the tasks performed, more complex types of information are available, such as levels of job stress, exposure to hazards, and organizational influences.

The database of the O*NET contains "descriptors" or key skills, abilities, knowledge, and other characteristics associated with more than 950 occupations. Its online application, O*NET online (http://online.onetcenter.org), provides easy public access to the database (IRI, 2003). The O*NET user can find occupations to explore, search for occupations that use designated skills, look at related occupations, view occupation summaries and details, create and print customized reports outlining O*NET search results, connect to other online career information resources, and access comprehensive and context-sensitive help information (IRI, 2003).

There are four general group descriptors, namely, worker characteristics, worker requirements, experience requirements or needed occupational preparation, and occupational requirements. Worker characteristics in the O*NET comprise abilities, occupational interests and values, and work styles, while worker requirements include basic skills and cross-functional skills, the latter focusing on general performance domains such as problem solving, resource management, and knowledge. There are 11 categories of knowledge requirements descriptors. Occupational preparation includes variables indicating that a person has performed previously similar work or "obtained education or training associated with the knowledges or skills required" (Hanson et al., 2001, p. 291). Finally, the O*NET occupational requirements focus on the work itself, the activities in which workers are engaged, and the context in which these activities are carried out. Examples of occupational requirements are getting and evaluating information, performing physical work tasks, selling or influencing, and coordinating others' work in the context of the demands of interpersonal relationships, types of work settings, and structural job characteristics, such as routine versus challenging work and degree of automation. All of this information is provided through summary, details, and custom reports.

For those with disabilities, O*NET information can help persons to focus on what they can do, and not on what they cannot do. This information also provides assistance in overcoming barriers by providing easy access to knowledge of accommodations. The O*NET system also contains a set of career exploration and assessment tools that help individuals to identify occupations that match their work-related interests and abilities and what they consider important on the job.

The consumer's use of the O*NET system enhances the values of empowerment and lifelong learning. Its easy access provides the consumer with an opportunity to match abilities to appropriate jobs. The 9 physical ability descriptors, 10 perceptual ability descriptors, and 10 psychomotor ability descriptors focus on specificity when matching jobs with individuals, and each descriptor includes ratings of its importance and the ability level required for each occupation (Hanson et al., 2001).

A useful resource is the *O*NET Dictionary of Occupational Titles, Fourth Edition* (2007), available from JIST Publishing, 875 Montreal Way, St. Paul, MN 55102. It contains updated job descriptions and data, and all of the newest jobs listed in the latest O*NET database. Descriptions and data are included for nearly 95% of the jobs, covering almost 100% of the workforce. Featured information highlights a job's requisite education, training, and experience level; annual earnings; projected growth; and number of annual openings, and the skills, abilities, and knowledge needed to performed listed jobs. This source organizes the government's vast O*NET version of 11 databases on jobs into one easy-to use book. This book also includes a special section called "Six Easy Ways to Find O*NET Jobs of Interest" to help readers determine careers that interest them most.

Complete Guide for Occupational Exploration

This excellent resource for evaluators who are preparing an interpretation session provides an easy-to-use method of identifying general clusters of occupations and specific job titles. There are 12 major interest areas (e.g., Artistic, Scientific, Plants and Animals, Mechanical). Each of these is broken down into more specific subgroups of related jobs. The 12 major interest areas and 66 work groups provide general information on the occupations within each group, including skills required, type of work, education required, and other details. This volume includes the entire new and revised job titles listed in the 1991 edition of the DOT.

The *Complete Guide for Occupational Exploration* (JIST, 1993) greatly facilitates the exploration of career and employment alternatives based on general interests, previous experience, training, and other factors. This book uses standard cross-referencing systems that allow the evaluator to obtain more information on career areas or specific job titles. It can be an important tool for the evaluator who is interpreting assessment results and needs readily understandable information about work and careers with which to match evaluation results.

The *Complete Guide for Occupational Exploration* can be obtained from JIST Publishing, 875 Montreal Way, St. Paul, MN 55102, 800/328-1452.

The Enhanced Guide for Occupational Exploration–Second Edition

In this edition (Maze & Mayall, 1995), more job descriptions have been added, comprising 95% of the workforce, and 793 new job descriptions and revised data for all coded information have been included. Obsolete jobs and those employing few people were eliminated in this enhanced edition to make room for new jobs, high-tech jobs, and jobs employing large numbers of people.

Three other resources can be quite useful for the interpretation session: the *Occupational Outlook Handbook* (Bureau of Labor Statistics, 2010–2011); the *Occupational Outlook Quarterly* (2011), also published by the Bureau of Labor Statistics (2011), providing updated information related to the Handbook and other relevant outlook data; and the *Career Guide to Industries* (2010–2011 Edition).

Occupational Outlook Handbook

Occupational Outlook Handbook (2010–2011) is a publication of the U.S. Bureau of Labor Statistics. This Handbook has been a nationally recognized source of career information since the late 1940s and is available from the U.S. Government Printing Office and the Department of Labor. It provides detailed information about hundreds of occupations, covering seven out of eight jobs in the economy. For each occupation, the Handbook begins with a section that highlights key occupational characteristics, followed by sections with information about the nature of the work, typical working conditions, employment of salaried and self-employed workers, requirements for entry and opportunities for advancement, earnings, related occupations, and sources of additional information. There also is a section on job outlook that provides each occupation's projected employment change over the next decade as compared to projected growth for all occupations.

Career Guide to Industries

The *Career Guide to Industries* (2010–2011) was developed as a companion publication to the Handbook in the early 1990s. It analyzes employment change from an industry perspective, providing information about many industries. For each industry, the *Career Guide* describes the nature of the industry, typical working conditions, earnings, expected job prospects, training and advancement, and key occupations employed in the industry. In addition, the *Career Guide* provides the reader with links to information about the job market in each state.

The Handbook and the *Career Guide* can be accessed on the Internet at http://www.bls.gov/ooh and http://www.bls.gov/oco/cg, respectively.

Occupational Outlook Quarterly

The *Occupational Outlook Quarterly* is published by the U.S. Department of Labor. This document updates readers on current occupational developments between editions of the *Occupational Outlook Handbook*. It also organizes and synthesizes information printed elsewhere, and reviews new career planning techniques (Power, 2011).

There are also additional occupational resources developed by commercial publishers. These publishers print hundreds of books on careers, and previously stated vocational and educational sources are in this grouping:

- *Career books,* intended for the general public and published as self-help guides. An example of these books is *What Color Is Your Parachute?* (Bolles, 2009).
- *Directories,* providing employer and particular geographic area information, as well as other useful data. An example of one of these sources is the *Encyclopedia of Associations* (2008). A guide to national and international nonprofit organizations, these volumes include information on location, size, and objectives of more than 14,500 trade associations, professional societies, labor unions, and fraternal and patriotic organizations. This resource is available from Electronic Search Assistance, 27500 Drake Rd., Farmington Hills, MI 48331.
- *Newspapers.* These can regularly provide information on labor markets, employment projections, and up-to-date information about local and regional trends (Luzzo, 2002).
- *Informational videos.* Available at Career Centers or public libraries, individuals who are currently employed in different careers are interviewed and provide important information about occupations and work environments (Luzzo, 2002).

Approaches for Generating Information on Local Working Opportunities

The rehabilitation professional should be familiar with the varied resources that provide information on local job opportunities perhaps available to the consumer. Some resources include:

- Private and independent schools
- Apprenticeships (the best source of information is the regional representative for apprenticeships in the consumer's area)
- Professional and trade associations and labor unions
- State and private employment agencies
- Local newspapers
- The Chamber of Commerce

Conclusion

A central aim of rehabilitation assessment is to identify the consumer's vocational strengths. Communication of the evaluation results is a necessary step in the consumer's overall assessment approach. This includes both identification of the individual's assets and relevant career information and formulation of appropriate plans. This communication also demands certain skills, and the manner in which the rehabilitation professional uses these skills during the interpretive session often determines whether the consumer will achieve his or her rehabilitation goals. The formulation of appropriate plans will be discussed in the next chapter.

Chapter 15

Vocational Assessment of Industrially Injured Workers and Selected Relevant Issues

A staggering amount of time and money is spent each year attending to the needs of industrially injured workers. Insurance companies have spent billions of dollars on employee benefits for disability insurance, including medical and surgical expenses for costs incurred as a result of on-the-job injuries, reimbursement for miles traveled to obtain services, payment of two thirds of injured workers' average gross weekly pay, stipulated dollar amounts awarded to workers who have lost the function of a body part, and compensation for the pursuit of a vocational rehabilitation program for workers who are unable to return to their usual employment. These awards and compensation coverages, however, vary widely from state to state.

In response to the growing incidence of workers who sustain catastrophic injuries, private rehabilitation firms were established to assist consumers with rehabilitation goals. Working closely with insurance companies that provide compensation coverage, these private resources employ personnel to evaluate the rehabilitation potential of their consumers, provide counseling for disability-related adjustmental concerns, and when possible generate job placement opportunities.

Vocational rehabilitation in the private, profit-making sector usually involves many types of consumers: (a) the consumer who returns to his or her former employer in the same or in a modified job, (b) the person with a disability who would like the same job but with a different employer or a different job in the same field or industry, (c) the consumer who wishes to be retrained for new employment, and (d) the consumer who needs independent living. The range of disabilities in the private sector includes orthopedic problems; back injury is the most prevalent problem, and frequently there are other difficulties associated with the disability. The industrially injured worker may have other significant concerns, such as lowered motivation to return to work because of secondary, monetary gains; conflicts among service providers; and such hidden disabilities as learning problems and substance abuse. These concerns can affect performance in vocational training and may influence the choice of an occupational career. The combination of a preexisting condition and the current injury often produces magnified effects. Further, many industrially injured workers receive tax-free compensation, and these payments diminish the incentives to participate in a vocational rehabilitation program.

Consumers are most often referred from insurance companies, litigation having been frequently involved, and they are usually unemployed as a direct result of the disability. Further, injured consumers more often have substantial work history and acceptable work habits but usually experience pain that may develop into a chronic pain syndrome (Stewart & Vander Kolk, 1989). From their experience, Stewart and Vander Kolk reported that individuals with an injury need relatively timely, fast-paced, intensive, and comprehensive rehabilitation services.

Time is a critical factor, particularly in workers' compensation rehabilitation. Speed of service is a paramount consideration when developing assessment approaches for this industrially injured population. A speedy return to work, for example, has always been a major factor in judging the success of insurance rehabilitation. Evaluation approaches should be chosen that are quick and easy to administer and score. Vocational assessment may have to be conducted in 1 or 2 days. The sooner services begin, the sooner the individual may return to employment.

It is also important to choose assessment approaches that will stand up to legal scrutiny. Attorneys are becoming more sophisticated in their knowledge of standardized tests and "are starting to challenge test results with more incisive cross-examination questions" (Olson, 1992, p. 102). It is important to note that the referral for assessment services is usually not made until the consumer's permanent restrictions or limitations have been defined by an attending medical provider, a physical capacity evaluation, or possibly a defense medical exam (Welch &

Condon, 2011). Olson further explained that most workers' compensation systems require that claimants meet certain criteria to be eligible for vocational rehabilitation services, including that (a) as a result of the injury, consumers cannot return to the job they had at the time of the injury and (b) consumers must be able to benefit from vocational rehabilitation. Eligibility determination is often based both on an analysis of the job the consumer had at the time of the injury and on a transferable skills analysis.

The vocational rehabilitation process pursued in this sector of human service is developed from models used by the federal–state rehabilitation system. Restoration of loss (physical, financial, emotional) is the main purpose of both the insurance system and insurance rehabilitation. However, the rehabilitation professional in private practice generates services "from specific referral instructions that may not be necessarily related to the total rehabilitation needs of the injured person" (Workman, 1983, p. 306). But many services require extensive evaluation and training in job-seeking skills. Another alternative is for assessment to be conducted only as part of a professional's preparation for trial testimony, during which no other services are provided. Job placement is a central goal for most efforts in the private, profit-making sector. Sanchez (1981), in defining vocational rehabilitation for the California workers' compensation system, stated that it is "the process of restoring the injured worker to the competitive labor market at a wage level as close as practical to his/her pre-injury level as soon as possible" (p. 131).

Vocational assessment, consequently, is necessary to help the injured worker attain gainful employment. The professional performs this assessment using a number of steps and diverse approaches. The steps for determining eligibility for vocational services and suggested approaches are as follows:

1. Review the medical report.
2. Conduct the initial interview.
3. Complete transferable skills assessment and other selected measures for evaluation.
4. Complete a labor market analysis.
5. Complete a job analysis.
6. Develop the Rehabilitation Plan.

A major goal of this assessment is to determine the individual's employability. An expeditious appraisal of the injured worker's life situation, behavioral characteristics, and residual physical and intellectual capabilities is key to the evaluation process. Frequently, this process occurs while the consumer is receiving benefits or involved in litigation, and during this time, family influences may act as obstacles to rehabilitation goals. There are many factors that can affect an injured worker's successful return to employment.

Earlier chapters in this book provide more detailed information on the various assessment approaches, each of which can be used for different occupational objectives. Testing, for example, can help identify whether a worker is still able to perform the job he or she had at the time of the injury, as well as options for job modification. Specialized tests that are designed for people with disabilities (developmental disabilities, blindness, deafness), however, are infrequently used in working with this population (Olson, 1992).

The previously mentioned six steps of an assessment process for the industrially injured worker stimulate the following responsibilities for the evaluator:

1. Become medically familiar with the types of disabilities that are common in insurance rehabilitation.
2. Obtain complete information regarding the rules and regulations governing the system or jurisdiction in which one is working, and become familiar with insurance and insurance terminology.
3. Recognize time and financial guidelines that are available. An evaluation program with individuals who already have a work history may have to be completed in a day or two.
4. Think in terms of returning the worker to the job or employer he or she had at the time of the injury.
5. Be familiar with the emotional aspects of loss, because many injured workers go through the grieving process for an extended period of time.
6. Phrase recommendations in terms of what they will cost in both time and money. Dollar savings to the insurance company and cost effectiveness are essential ingredients for vocational planning with injured workers.

Using the six assessment steps as a structure to explain the evaluation process for this population, the following sections elaborate on each of these steps.

Suggested Vocational Assessment Steps

Review the Medical Report

The appropriate use of medical information is invaluable to vocational evaluation and planning. Medical professionals are responsible for evaluating the physical limitations an injury may present. Often, direct contact with the professionals who have provided or are providing medical treatment to the consumer is critical in determining specific injury-related limitations. When the rehabilitation professional carefully reviews the consumer's medical report, any residual capacities should be identified so that possible transferable skills can be evaluated.

The following outline shows the specific areas that should be covered in the medical report:

1. Functional limitations
   a. What work activities are possible?
   b. What is the consumer's tolerance for work activity?
   c. What are the consumer's concerns about the limitations he or she may experience at work?
   d. What assistive technology resources can be provided that will respond to physical limitations and facilitate work adjustment?
   e. What is the consumer's current level of performance in strength, climbing, stooping, reaching, talking, and seeing?
   f. What consumer abilities can be developed, perhaps with the use of devices, to compensate for the disability? Has there been substantial deterioration in all possible physical areas that could have been used for work?
   g. Does the consumer have secondary or multiple disabilities with which to cope?
   h. What is the consumer's current level of response to work location, cold, heat, humidity, noise, hazards, and atmospheric conditions?

2. Diagnosis. Readiness for work activities.
3. Prognosis
   a. Will the condition worsen or improve?
   b. Is the condition chronic or temporary?
4. Medication
   a. Is medication taken regularly, and can the consumer function independently of it?
   b. What are the effects of medication on working (e.g., does it cause drowsiness or lethargy)?

Understanding the consumer's medical report can be the first step in formulating realistic rehabilitation plans. Through this awareness, the rehabilitation professional can further comprehend whether (a) the current disability status precludes employment, even with the use of assistive technology, (b) the consumer is unable to work full time because of a mental or physical condition, or (c) the person can work full time but must have a sedentary job with low stress and close supervision or have necessary job accommodations. This report may also indicate whether the consumer is limited to occupations requiring light physical activity but is still able to work full time or whether the consumer is minimally restricted in terms of the type of work that he or she can do.

In many instances, however, rehabilitation professionals will have specific questions, which may have to be given directly to the physician. Such questions can also address how assistive technology can compensate for physical restrictions. Medical report forms are not designed to completely cover every specific situation. It often helps if the examining physician's attention is directed to the things for which specific kinds of information are needed.

Conduct the Initial Interview

The format suggested for the initial interview is semistructured, in which topics and questions are specified but there is flexibility as to in what sequence the topics are to be explored and the extent to which particular interview techniques—such as how and when questions are asked—are used (Berven, 2008). The interview is the beginning medium through which this evaluation is conducted. It can help determine the vocational objectives that are feasible for the consumer and is the most critical point in the rehabilitation professional's involvement with the injured worker. The rehabilitation professional must explore whether the industrially injured worker is prepared to reenter the work situation or is even motivated enough to consider such possibilities and, if so, what training or similar preparation is needed to facilitate this return. A down-to-earth assessment should be made of the factors that affect employability. Chapter 1 identifies significant areas for understanding employability issues, questions that may be asked to assess a person's potential for employment, and the positive and negative indictors suggesting the pros and cons of employability for a specific consumer.

The Interview Session

The interview must be as comprehensive as possible in order to ultimately save time in the rehabilitation process. Chapter 6 discusses the use of the interview for assessment purposes and identifies the many areas that need to be explored. For industrially injured consumers, Chapter 6 presents further considerations and modifications of the interview structure. The following a recommended format for this interview that can generate information for rehabilitation purposes.

Preinterview Period

Before meeting with the consumer, the evaluator should review all relevant case materials, such as medical reports and work history. If there are any missing data, identify topics requiring additional exploration or validation, and stress such topics during the interview. For example, if the consumer's records contain very little information about prior work history, explore this area carefully. Make a list of questions to ask the consumer to clarify any confusing, incomplete, or contradictory information (Olson, 1992).

Beginning the Interview

The consumer's self-perception as a worker is particularly relevant to employability concerns. To assist consumers in evaluating feelings about themselves, encourage them to talk about the accident and its emotional impact and the needs that accompany some of their beliefs that they cannot return to their previous jobs. Early in the interview situation, consumers should also discuss their life situations since the accidents, as well as their own employment expectations. It is helpful if the injured worker can identify any compensatory work-related skills and realizations that he or she gained from the previous work experience. This discussion may include topics such as the following:

- What was the most satisfying experience in the consumer's previous job?
- What is he or she looking for in a job?
- What are the present limitations to continuing work?

Conducting the Interview

With the development of information on the consumer's current living situation and an awareness of the consumer's feelings and attitudes about working again, explore additional factors for rehabilitation planning. The following list highlights important areas and suggests questions to solicit the respective information.

- The consumer's wage at the time of injury and the actual, previous work pattern, including specific duties, abilities, qualifications, physical demands, and equipment and machinery used (*Can you tell me something about what you did at your previous job? What skills do you believe you acquired at your previous job?*)
- Complete work history, explaining any gaps in employment and licenses or training that the consumer may have had in addition to his or her formal education (*Let's discuss your work history, and can you tell me about any training you have had associated with your previous jobs?*)
- Preexisting physical and mental conditions and the effect of those conditions on the consumer's employability (*Are you aware of any physical or mental conditions that were present before the injury that would now affect your ability to be employed again?*)
- Physical and mental conditions caused by the injury or occupational disease and their effect on the consumer's employability (*What is the nature of your injury and disability? How does it physically or mentally affect your ability to be employed? What work-related activities or situations would tend to aggravate your disability or impair your general health?*)

- Identification of applicable work skills acquired through nonwork or related hobbies (*Are there any hobbies or leisure activities that you engage in from which you have acquired skills that you could use at a future job?*)
- Vocational goal (*What kind of a job would you like to have? What are your preferences for certain types of work activities, such as clerical, outdoor, or service occupations? Is there any relationship between your education or training and career possibilities?*)
- Significant consumer factors (*What are your current legal involvements, and should vocational training or employment be delayed until these are resolved? What are your transportation needs? Are there any problems in using community resources? If necessary, can you relocate? What is the attitude of your family toward reemployment, and what influences on rehabilitation do they bring? What specific activities or environments aggravate your disabling condition? Are there unique or particular financial needs that resulted from the accident and the disability? Are current benefits adequate to meet financial obligations? What is your perspective on the physical restrictions received as a result of the injury?*)
- Significant occupational and job factors (*What credentials [education, training, memberships, licenses, certificates] do you have for further employment? Do you believe you are capable now of meeting attendance, promptness, and speed of production demands in any future job?*)
- Getting a job (*Are you able to prepare a personal information package for prospective employers? Do you feel you have the motivation to contact employers as well as make telephone inquiries and applications? How do you feel about participating in a job interview?*)

Communication during the interview should provide some initial suggestions for the most feasible vocational objectives. With an objective in mind, the rehabilitation professional in the private, for-profit sector can then plan, when necessary, a more detailed or formalized exploration of the injured worker's interests, aptitudes, and current labor market opportunities. The following guidelines for different possible vocational goals can be used to assist in identifying these objectives.

1. **Modified job.** The onset of a disability represents a discontinuity in what was previously a fairly constant self-concept and environmental

interaction. The consumer's emotional reaction to the disability event should be explored because often temperaments must be recognized to evaluate ongoing applicability to the modified occupational environment. This adjustment includes the abilities to handle job pressure, interact appropriately with fellow workers, and meet new job demands willingly. A job analysis should also be conducted and appropriate modifications made according to the willingness of the employer, the nature of the work environment, and the availability of technology to make the modifications.

2. **Other work with the same employer.** An essential evaluation for this objective is an analysis of transferable skills. Although the consumer may have a defined physical impairment that prevents return to the same job, many skills and aptitudes remain entirely unaffected. These residual capabilities can be quantified and recombined to meet the requirements of a different job (Weinstein, 1983). Field and Sink (1980), in their development of an evaluation approach titled "Vocational Diagnosis and Assessment of Residual Employability," highlighted five methods of skill identification and skill transference that enable the professional to quantify the consumer's residual occupation-related assets:

* Measurement by valid tests
* Measurement by job history
* Measurement by worker's expressed preference
* Measurement by medical report
* A combination of these methods

Assessment by valid tests, job history, and expressed preference (determination of vocational interest) are discussed in other chapters of this book. In addition, specific worker traits associated with past occupations should be identified. Sink and Field (1980) developed a manual method of compiling this data, in which the professional collects and summarizes the job demand characteristics of the individual's work experience, using the trait–factor profiles of the O*NET and *Dictionary of Occupational Titles* (DOT; U.S. Department of Labor, 1991). Once a composite profile is produced, it is altered to reflect the consumer's current, postinjury functional capacities (Weinstein, 1983). The profile is stated in the language of jobs and is consistent with traits that were characteristic of the individual prior to the injury. After the skill identification, a job analysis of opportunities still available with the previous employer should be made, and an evaluation of the consumer's emotional adjustment to the disability should be conducted.

3. **Direct job placement.** To facilitate direct job placement, it is necessary to complete an assessment of residual and transferable skills, an evaluation of the consumer's emotional adjustment to disability, an analysis of jobs currently available in the labor market, and an analysis of the consumer's job-getting and job-keeping behaviors, especially the manner in which the person with a disability may present him- or herself in a job interview situation. The same assessment should be conducted for on-the-job training or formal training.

4. **Self-employment.** The same assessment as used in direct job placement can be given, with particular emphasis on both the consumer's capabilities to meet the distinctive demands of self-employment (independence, knowledge of business management) and the feasibility of the environment in which the consumer intends to establish a business.

With many consumers, previous employers may be able to give valuable information about the consumer's work capabilities. Much of this exploration can be done while the consumer is still involved in litigation or compensation settlements. The injured worker may delay any decision about rehabilitation planning until the litigation or settlement decision is reached. However, vocational exploration should still be pursued, if for no other reason than to help the consumer realize that he or she possesses work-related capabilities. This awareness can be a motivating factor for return to employment and a foundation for assessment and rehabilitation planning.

Complete the Transferable Skills Assessment and Other Selected Measures for Evaluation

Chapter 11 explains the dynamics of skills assessment and includes a step-by-step procedure to identify skills. Specific measures are also recommended, and added to these recommendations is the Occupational

Access System (OASYS; available from VERTEK, Inc.; Brown, McDaniel, & Couch, 1994), a computerized approach to the transferable skills assessment described in the Vocational Diagnosis and Assessment of Residual Employability (VDARE) system (Patterson, 2008). This system includes all the required databases, such as the DOT database and a database of national and state wage estimates and employment projections. Any additions, deletions, or changes in job analysis are updated at least annually (Patterson, 2008).

For the industrially injured worker, other selected measures should focus on abilities and interest assessment. This consumer might have to search for employment in a field considerably different than the one he or she was in at injury occurrence. For example, many consumers who have incurred a significant on-the-job back injury may have to look in another occupational field for future job opportunities. Chapter 7 has information on current interest assessment measures. The *Strong, Kuder DD,* and the *Wide Range Interest Occupation Test–Second Edition* (WRIOT-2), which are particularly recommended, are explained in either Chapter 7 or Chapter 10.

For ability measures, Chapter 10 identifies a selection of tests that could be appropriate when relevant to the education level of the consumer. But as Patterson (2008) stated, all of these tests "may not reflect the influences of the social-organizational structure of the work environment" (p. 311). With some types of disabilities, this information may be important to understand if the worker is going to make a successful job adjustment.

Complete Labor Market and Job Analyses

Following the review of assessment results, private, for-profit or related counselors should consult labor market surveys to ascertain available employment opportunities in the consumer's geographical area. The local employment service office, Chamber of Commerce, rehabilitation service office, or civic or service organizations may have published information on current, local labor market information. Acquisition of this knowledge will then help the professional to conduct an analysis of jobs that are available and generally in harmony with the consumer's physical, mental, and emotional abilities. Of course, the use of assistive technology and job restructuring must always be considered an important possibility during the analysis itself. Chapter 13 explains a proposed job analysis approach.

Develop the Assessment Report or Rehabilitation Plan

Agencies will usually have developed their own report, but all the reports appear to include the following:

- demographic information;
- rationale for the assessment and highlighted assessment results;
- medical/physical information;
- past employment information and employment at the time of the injury;
- educational history, including the identification of vocational skills;
- supporting labor market information; and
- occupational possibilities.

The format for an assessment report does not include such information as extensive medical/physical information, past employment at the time of injury, or extensive educational history. An assessment report must usually respond to the needs of the referring agency and insurance companies. State agencies may also require information in the above areas. See the section titled "The Assessment Report," later in this chapter, for an explanation of the suggested format.

The tools and process of evaluation with injured workers demand a knowledge of the workers' compensation system, an ability to select appropriately from different approaches to determine both eligibility for vocational rehabilitation services and capability to return to work, an awareness of psychosocial factors influencing the consumer's rehabilitation, and an understanding of the medical limitations caused by the injury. Readiness for employability is a focal point in assessment with the injured worker. Determination of readiness includes knowledge of such issues as incentives, disincentives, legal involvement, financial factors, medical support, family involvement, and the Americans with Disabilities Act of 1990 (ADA) legislation with regard to evaluation of need for accommodations, definition of disability, and eligibility requirements under each area of legislation.

Preparation for Court Testimony

Since the 1970s, increased demands have been made on rehabilitation professionals to present quantifiable evidence for insurance companies, attorneys, claims agents, physicians, and Social Security hearings. Professionals in the private, for-profit sector of rehabilitation who serve those with industrial injuries are more inclined to solicit legal advice than are other rehabilitation professionals; therefore, they may find themselves making court appearances quite frequently.

When providing these services for consumers, the rehabilitation professional confronts a new variety of responsibilities. These responsibilities require the professional to be well prepared to give court testimony about the consumer, as well as to have a well-developed knowledge of vocational evaluation. In the eyes of the court, the professional is an expert and will have to answer a wide range of questions concerning the occupational possibilities of the consumer in an objective and unbiased manner.

Expert witness work involves the use of a vocational rehabilitation professional to assess an individual "who has experienced an injury to determine the effects of the injury on the person's ability to work and earn money" (Choppa & Shafer, 1992, p. 135). Forensic rehabilitation involves the use of assessment for Social Security Disability Insurance (SSDI) determination, workers' compensation employability determination, long-term disability determination, and personal injuries and capability to return to work. Personal injuries may include auto and other types of accidents, professional malpractice, product liability, and injuries resulting from a crime.

To perform successful expert witness work, the evaluator should have an in-depth knowledge of the labor market and training facilities, an ability to perform accurate job analyses, good knowledge of community resources, an understanding of how medical aspects of disabilities affect employment, and comprehensive knowledge of how the legal system works (Owings, 1992). This work focuses on determining whether wage-earning capacity has been lost, the extent of the loss, and how much it will cost to eliminate or minimize that loss. The eventual outcome of expert witness work is usually an oral or written presentation of information gathered (Choppa & Shafer, 1992).

In conducting forensic rehabilitation, the evaluator may be tempted to take sides because he or she has been retained by either the defense or the plaintiff. However, the evaluator should be careful to avoid favoring the viewpoint of either the defense or the plaintiff. The value of an expert's testimony is severely compromised if it can be demonstrated that the expert witness favors the side that has hired him or her. Objectivity should be maintained, and the evaluator needs to provide realistic information that is not edited to fit the viewpoint of either the defense or the plaintiff. Ethical guidelines, consequently, must be followed closely. Accepted codes of ethics and professional standards are established by many rehabilitation-related organizations, including the National Rehabilitation Association, the Vocational Evaluation and Work Adjustment Association, and state licensing boards (Choppa & Shafer, 1992).

Sink and King (1978) identified the many questions that may be asked of rehabilitation professionals when testifying on behalf of their consumers. The questions suggest the type of preparation required to make an adequate court presentation. Godley (1978) suggested that such questions could be prepared and reviewed by the professional and attorney before the court appearance. The following outline, which can be followed by the professional when preparing court testimony, contains information originally stated by Sink and King:

Questions for the Rehabilitation Professional (Vocational Expert)

- Do you have knowledge of physical and mental disabilities and their relationship to employment potential, as well as of jobs and their requirements common to the labor market? How did you obtain this information?
- Have you had experience in job analysis, and can you give examples of local industries in which you have observed and analyzed jobs?
- Have you talked to your consumer's employer? Would this employer hire the consumer?

- If a job is possible with the employer, what would be the salary level, career ladder sequence, and length of time between steps? What would be the anticipated income in 1 year? In 5 years?

Questions Relating to the Consumer

- Can you describe the details of your consumer's previous employment, including work performed; tools used; supervision given and received; communication skills required; temperament, interests, physical demands, and intelligence needed for the job; typical salaries for such jobs; working hours and days; mode of transportation to and from work; and use of arms, hands, fingers, legs, back, and so on?
- Can you define for the court the occupational significance of both physical and mental conditions as defined by the physician? Please also define the consumer's daily (social, avocational, recreational) activities, including work around the house and care for or play with children or grandchildren, and whether or not the consumer drives, attends religious services, or goes shopping.
- Can you describe for the court the occupationally significant characteristics of the jobs the consumer has held and the relationship of the consumer's physical (or mental) conditions to these jobs?
- Are there any jobs in the labor market that may be done by the consumer without additional training, or are there jobs in which the consumer could be employed with additional training or education? If so, what are they and where are they located?
- If training or education is needed, is the consumer qualified for acceptance into training or educational programs? What kind of training or education is required, how long is it, what is the cost, and what are the qualifications for training?
- What are the consumer's perceptions of going back to work, not working, the physical limitations as stated by the physician, and being trained or educated for another job?
- If the consumer has had a vocational evaluation, describe the types of psychological tests or work samples administered during the assessment process. What are they supposed to evaluate, what are they supposed to measure, and what is their validity? To what kinds of skills or jobs do the work samples relate? If you did not

administer the tests or work samples, what are the qualifications of those individuals who did so?

Sink and King (1978) explained that the questions should be answered in terms of magnitude, frequency, and duration. To obtain the information requested by many of the questions, the consumer may be observed or questioned. The O*NET or DOT should be used for classification of job title, worker trait group arrangements, physical demands, working conditions, general educational development, specific vocational preparation, aptitudes, interests, and temperaments. The rehabilitation professional should also have a job market survey that applies to the consumer's living area.

The Assessment Report

The final report is an important outcome of the assessment process for the rehabilitation professional who has referred the consumer to a vocational evaluation agency or conducted a vocational evaluation for a consumer who has been industrially injured and sponsored by an insurance company. Some written documentation of the assessment process, particularly the findings and recommendations, is usually required to purchase services. This document is the foundation for the individual rehabilitation plan, which is usually developed later with the consumer. The assessment report is written by the assessment agency following their guidelines and a format that conveys the expectations of the consumer, the referring rehabilitation professional, and the evaluators who managed the assessment process itself. This section will discuss issues related to the assessment report, identify the dynamics of rehabilitation planning, and suggest a model that captures the important factors for appropriate, timely, and effective planning. The key words for both the report and rehabilitation planning are *communication* and *consumer involvement*. Because of new, Internet-enabled communication, it is now much easier for all rehabilitation professionals and consumers to have better, ongoing communication (Thirtieth Institute on Rehabilitation Issues [IRI], 2003).

The written report is integral to the communication of test results. Most professionals learn to write reports through on-the-job training, and such training is often influenced by theoretical orientations, agency expectations, and previous writing education. Consequently, brevity and conciseness are traditionally missing from these reports. Reports frequently provide information that the reader already knows or suggest unrealistic plans for the consumer. In addition, many reports neglect the needs of those who will read and act upon the report's recommendations. Because the assessment report gathers employability-related information, it should be accurate, objective, and maintain a simple, direct style that promotes readability. Good, clear writing in which unnecessary words and jargon are avoided communicates information most effectively.

The *Employment and Community Services Standards Manual for 2002*, from the Commission on the Accreditation of Rehabilitation Facilities (CARF), offers general guidelines for all written vocational assessment reports. These guidelines state that the report should

- answer the referral questions,
- be shared with the person seeking employment,
- be disseminated in a timely manner to agencies and individuals responsible for implementing the report recommendations, and
- be relevant to the desired employment outcome (IRI, 2003).

Although reports will vary in format according to the guidelines of each agency, they should contain the following components:

- Opening paragraph
- Behavior during assessment
- Assessment methods and measures used
- Assessment results
- Recommendations (short and long term)
- Conclusion

The report should be written in a positive tone, focusing on those findings that will facilitate vocational development and eventual appropriate employment (IRI, 2003). When realistic or negative findings are reported, these could be balanced with perceived consumer strengths. All of the information provided in the report should empower the consumer to make informed choices. In addition, the report writer should provide a professional interpretation of the results that includes future implications, options, and value of the data in relation to already-identified vocational goals.

Visual reports that incorporate such elements as pictures and diagrams are now being used to stimulate or enhance communication between the consumer and rehabilitation professional (IRI, 2003). Visual reports do not require special skills, and a good software package can create a very communicative report. Software packages such as Microsoft Word, Microsoft Excel, and Corel WordPerfect Suite are resources that provide word processing and spreadsheets. The visual report offers for many consumers a more meaningful way to understand the assessment information.

When the referring professional receives the assessment report, the following questions should be considered:

- Did the report answer specific questions?
- Was the evaluation directed to areas that were needed for rehabilitation planning?
- Are there unresolved discrepancies among the reported evaluation test results?
- Does the report integrate all the information into a picture of the consumer that shows the consumer's well-developed skills, behaviors, needs, and limitations that are usable for appropriate vocational planning?
- Does the report provide information that attempts to identify the most important aspect of the consumer's personality that allows the consumer to function as well as he or she is functioning at the present time? What prevents the consumer from functioning more effectively?
- What are the recommendations for the consumer? Are they too broad or too specific? Are options given? Are the recommendations consistent with the test results? Are they realistic?

The Suggested Format for the Vocational Assessment Report (see the Appendix and the forms located on the CD-ROM) provides a structure for the assessment report that has the potential to be more relevant than traditional formats.

Vocational/Career Planning

This section develops and explains a rehabilitation planning model that can be used in professional practice. During the entire assessment process, much information is generated about consumer vocational-related functioning. The assessment report, described in an earlier section of this chapter, utilizes this information to generate a report that is usually sent to the referral agency that originally requested the vocational evaluation. It highlights the short-term goals and recommendations. The vocational/career plan, however, is developed by the referral agency, which might be a state rehabilitation office, a school, or an insurance company. Information from the vocational assessment report is usually incorporated into this overall plan for the consumer. Many agencies may use the vocational assessment report, authored by the evaluation agency, as a substitute for the more comprehensive career plan, but the career plan should not be confused with the vocational assessment report. The latter is foundational to the career journey of the consumer. The former can change over time, and frequently occupational knowledge of available resources is used by the referring agency to expand previously stated short- and long-term goals and recommendations.

Gysbers, Heppner, and Johnston (2009) believe that the vocational/career plan should be viewed as an ever-evolving process and should contain plans of action, "concrete objective steps for doing something differently from the way one did it before" (p. 280). Carkhuff (1971) built vocational planning around the terms *exploration, understanding,* and *action.* The consumer explores the relationship of vocational objectives to his or her personal capabilities, interests, and situation, and attempts to understand the way these different factors influence vocational potential. This personalized understanding also helps the consumer and the professional to eventually develop the steps of the rehabilitation plan.

What Is Necessary for Effective Planning?

During the interpretation of test or assessment results, the ideas and information that are generated (ideally by both the professional and the consumer) represent different directions or ways to reach an achievable career goal. Adequate and meaningful planning necessitates that the professional be both knowledgeable and skillful regarding consumer involvement; the job market, training, and requirements; and the acquisition of specific competencies, including plan development that identifies an overall goal and objectives that are formulated to be specific, observable, time specific, and achievable (Gysbers et al., 2009).

1. Involvement of the consumer

One of the underlying principles in this book is that input or consumer participation should be solicited at the very beginning of the assessment process. Evaluators can set the stage for developing goals and making plans as early as the first sessions. It should be communicated early on that goals and plans of action are expected outcomes of assessment (Gysbers et al., 2009). Earlier chapters identify various ways to accomplish this early communication, including the careful explanation of possible rehabilitation goals, the identification of consumer assets, and the opportunity to explore different options or alternatives for satisfaction in rehabilitation. All of these methods can stimulate early consumer participation in the assessment process. Such participation is an instrumental activity that promotes consumer decision making, responsibility, problem solving, and self-direction.

Consumer involvement is essential during the interpretation session of evaluation results; it can provoke further input into the planning phase of vocational evaluation. If there has been consumer involvement during assessment, such areas as consumer needs and values will usually be identified. A discussion of the assessment results that relate to employment/career needs and values is crucial for appropriate rehabilitation planning, and most of this information from consumers has to be generated from personal feedback rather than from psychometric measures. Further, when consumers participate in the vocational planning process, many potential problems relevant to reaching rehabilitation goals may be anticipated. In all stages of rehabilitation, the professional and consumer must work together (insofar as this is functionally possible for the consumer) in the development of rehabilitation plans. This involvement has been a long-standing objective of evaluation and was reinforced by the Rehabilitation Act Amendments of 1992 (Bongiorno, 1993). If this participation is not enthusiastically promoted, a wide gap may develop between consumer expectations and the professional's perception of realistic opportunities available to the consumer.

2. Knowledge of the job market, training, and requirements

Rehabilitation planning demands an extensive awareness of occupational resources, such as information on the O*NET, the DOT, the *Occupational Outlook Handbook* (U.S. Department of Labor, 1990), and publications that identify job requirements and employment conditions and assist in the development of an overall career goal and specific objectives to be placed into a realistic perspective. This perspective enables the rehabilitation professional to generate alternatives or options relevant to training and eventual employment. Roessler (2006) believed that "knowledge of work routines, requisites, and rewards has a direct effect on the individual's preferences, values, and self-concept regarding different types of work" (p. 172).

3. Acquisition of specific competencies

For effective vocational planning, the rehabilitation professional should possess the following skills:

- An understanding of the problems that impair consumer efforts to obtain work. These problems can pertain to work experience, job availability, or the disability itself.
- Knowledge of the world of work. To select a vocational objective, consumers also need to understand job requirements and local employment conditions. The professional must possess this information and be able to communicate it effectively to the consumer (Roessler, 2006).
- An understanding on how to formulate employment, training, or career goals and objectives into a plan that emphasizes that goal/objective attainment can be reasonable, that progress can be documented, and that this process is according to the needs of each consumer.

A Proposed Planning Model

Encouraging consumer involvement and updating one's knowledge of career opportunities in the current job market are just two of the many professional competencies needed for developing an appropriate rehabilitation plan. This plan is an individualized working document that identifies and explains an overall career goal and describes information for the provision of appropriate services and support, and it can be updated regularly to capture any changes. It should be easy to use, culturally appropriate, and legally sound (Macy & Rusch, 2010). This evaluation plan, in identifying short- and long-term career objectives that are in harmony with 21st-century labor market information, establishes a foundation from which additional services can be suggested in the comprehensive plan. It is important to note that most agencies and educational institutions working with people with disabilities and state offices of special education and/or vocational rehabilitation have their own specific, individualized forms for educational and/or rehabilitation planning. A review of these forms suggests the following common themes:

- The assembling of appropriate information, which can include data from the referral case, vocational assessment results, medical and educational records, special considerations (medications, needed aids, job modifications required), and selected environmental resources, such as family or previous employers.
- The identification of a career goal with stated objectives and resources to achieve this goal. These are meaningful services and outcomes that relate to an appropriate career.
- A beginning and completion time for the stated interventions.

Gathering data collected from the vocational evaluation and other sources is foundational to the development of a comprehensive rehabilitation plan for the consumer. This information is reviewed and a basis is established for the identification of an overall career goal and the activities necessary to achieve this goal. Chapter 6 discusses different approaches to reviewing and organizing this information.

The following is a suggested additional method to organize this data—a method perhaps more suitable for rehabilitation plan development.

1. Identify important background and demographic information.
2. Identify any thematic patterns from the assessment of the consumer's interests, values, work experience, potential skills, aptitudes and abilities, and personality strengths.
3. Identify dominant interest areas and then relate them to any thematic patterns of values, potential ability and aptitude-related

skills, work experience, and personality strengths. The professional wants to appraise whether the thematic patterns are supportive of the dominant interests.

4. Consider such special issues as family and cultural influences, environmental situations (geographic location, finances, medications, need for assistive devices, or possibility for job restructuring) and how each issue is relevant to the dominant interest areas.

5. Develop a composite picture of the consumer, incorporating Steps 3 and 4. This composite picture then helps pinpoint the overall career goal.

6. Develop an overall career goal. Though this may change because of disability or environmentally related circumstances, it should also be in harmony with occupational information that includes current occupational requirements and job availability.

The process of developing an overall career goal and the specific objectives to achieve that goal are preparatory to constructing the vocational rehabilitation plan. During the plan's development, there are important issues to consider, such as consumer feedback during the identification of the career goal and the objectives to reach that goal. The goal itself should respond to the career needs of the individual with a disability. Though the goal may change over time, its initial formulation should also be realistic. To achieve this realism is often a product of the continued interaction between the consumers, concerned family members or significant others, and the professional. Consumer feedback can also generate consumer motivation to implement the plan. Gysbers et al. (2009) believed that this goal-setting stage may be an important time to also help consumers from a minority ethnic background who are taking nontraditional life paths to problem solve probable economic barriers that may prevent them from reaching desired goals.

Objectives must be time specific, observable, and measurable—the individual should be able to realistically achieve them in a certain amount of time (Macy & Rusch, 2010). *Measurability* refers to behaviors that can be easily evaluated whether they were completed or not. These objectives represent various means or activities to attain the end goal and can include specific available services, for example, "to identify an employer in the consumer's area of interest, as well as in one's geographical area, and to discuss information about job opportunities and requirements," or "to attend a job club group at the local community mental health center." However, services should not be identified unless they are financially feasible.

Assistive devices or other necessary accommodations, as well as where and how they can be obtained, should be clearly stated. It is important to establish timelines and to identify personnel who will periodically evaluate any progress toward the completion of the objectives. The rehabilitation plan is an outcome-based document that should provoke such questions as the following:

- Does the overall career goal need to be revised?
- Should more objectives be added so that the career goal becomes more achievable?
- Do the existing objectives need to be revised?
- Does the consumer still agree to the use of certain objectives and services to meet the stated goal?

List a reinforcement that responds to the action identified in the objective, and discuss an appealing and motivating reinforcement with the consumer by asking questions such as "What can make a difference in accomplishing the objective?" or "What can really motivate you to work hard for this objective?" Note that reinforcers relate to individual consumer needs.

Identify personnel to evaluate the plan and determine whether timelines are being met and necessary services are being provided. Frequently, rehabilitation plans gradually lose their effectiveness because there is no follow-up on the implementation and completion of the objectives. Ask the consumer for feedback on who should monitor the planning document. The Proposed Structure for the Vocational/Career Plan form (see the Appendix and the forms located on the CD-ROM) provides a format for the rehabilitation plan and addresses the issues previously stated.

Conclusion

Motivation is often a dominant rehabilitation concern about the injured worker. Rehabilitation will be difficult if the worker has been employed for many years but now is influenced by compensation benefits and family pressures to not return to a job. This motivation variable is a distinctive focus in evaluation efforts with industrially injured consumers. If the consumer possesses all the necessary prerequisites and is ready for immediate placement, the rehabilitation process will run smoothly. If the person with a disability is not ready, then attention must be given to all the barriers that may prevent the consumer from working again. Skill development, resolution of emotional feelings, and cooperation from the family should all be attended to if the worker is to achieve rehabilitation goals. Thus, the evaluation period becomes not only a time to identify job readiness factors but also an opportunity for the rehabilitation professional to counsel the injured worker and help him or her begin to understand new options for productivity.

During rehabilitation planning, the professional uses many types of skills—communicative, diagnostic, and the appropriate retrieval of occupational information. An important goal in the development of many plans, however, is not simply placement in training or employment but also feasible career development (Vandergoot, Swirsky, & Rice, 1982). During the planning session, the consumer should learn the many possible options that are available, taking into consideration the consumer's competencies and values. As assessment helps a consumer identify the strengths and assets that apply to the world of employment or independent living, planning shows the consumer how these capabilities relate to different rehabilitation options. When the professional knows about employment and training resources as well as occupational requirements, the planning session and document that incorporate this information become more valuable for the consumer.

Description of Forms on the CD-ROM

Interview Guide for Consumers With Functional Limitations

This guide explores consumer vocational functioning domains that usually are not evaluated by traditional assessment measures. The form is a self-assessment tool to be taken by the individual with a disability, and it provides information that may encourage further evaluation in specific areas. It can be administered during or immediately after the initial consumer assessment interview, when rapport has been established between the professional and consumer and the latter person understands the purposes of assessment. Both these individuals should have a copy of the Guide during its administration, as the consumer will respond to all the items but may have questions while completing the Guide, or may have difficulty reading or understanding some of the items. This Guide may be particularly appropriate for those with a significant disability and who also represent an ethnic minority group, a population for whom many standardized assessment methods may not be appropriate.

Interview Guide for Consumers With Functional Limitations

Interests

Everyone likes to do certain types of activities more than others. This is true of hobbies, sports, school subjects, and jobs. Knowing your interests will help you choose a career and succeed in it.

In almost everything people do, there are different activities—some that we like and others that we don't like. Usually, we are more successful when we enjoy things than when we don't.

Most workers prefer activities in one or more of 10 interest areas. After you have read over and understand all of the activities, select the one that you think you would like best on a job. Then circle the number next to the activity you have chosen.

1. Activities dealing with things and objects
2. Activities involving business contact with people
3. Activities of a routine, definite, organized nature
4. Activities that involve direct personal contact, to help people or deal with them for other purposes
5. Activities that bring recognition or appreciation by others
6. Activities concerned with people and the communication of ideas
7. Activities of a scientific and technical nature
8. Activities of an unusual, indefinite nature that require creative imagination
9. Activities that are nonsocial and involve the use of machines, processes, or methods
10. Activities that bring personal satisfaction from working on or producing things

General Education Level

The things taught in school help us to do better in nearly every part of our lives. Imagine trying to order food in a restaurant if you couldn't read, trying to make change if you couldn't count, or figuring out how a new toy goes together if you couldn't think through the steps!

Almost every job requires that you have some of the same general skills that schools teach. Some jobs require many of these skills, whereas others require fewer of them. You are asked to rate yourself in the following three areas. Enter your self-rating below:

Reasoning: I can _____

Mathematics: I can _____

Language: I can _____

Comments: _____

© 2013 by PRO-ED, Inc.   #13938C

Independent Living Assessment

Independent Living Assessment

I. Independent Living
Goal: To discriminate ability for safe independent living within an apartment setting

A. Hygiene, personal cleanliness, and clothing
1. How did you dress today?
2. Did the weather outside influence your choice of clothes?
3. Do you like to take a bath or a shower?
4. Can you describe to me your routine for bathing or showering and dressing?
5. How do you shop for clothes? Do you like to go by yourself or with a friend?
6. When is it important to wash your hands?
7. How often do you brush your teeth?
8. How often do you wash your hair?
9. How do you handle hygiene when you have your period?

B. Apartment cleanliness and care
1. Do you do all of your own housekeeping? If you need help with housekeeping, whom do you ask and how?
2. What would you do if your toilet backed up onto the bathroom floor?
3. Where is the garbage kept?
4. What would you do if you saw bugs in your apartment?
5. Who would you call if
   a. the sink was clogged?
   b. something was broken?
   c. the heat was not working?
6. Do you have a special day to do your laundry? Do you do it with assistance or independently?

C. Kitchen skills
1. What are your favorite meals to cook?
2. Tell me about the word nutrition.
3. Do you shop for food on your own or with another person?
4. Can you show me where you keep
   a. TV dinners?
   b. hamburger and other meats?
   c. cheese?
   d. unopened cans of fruit?
   e. open cans of food?
   f. milk?
   g. cereal?
5. What happens to food when the refrigerator does not cool it down properly?
6. How can you tell if food is spoiled?

© 2013 by PRO-ED, Inc.   #13938C   (continue)

This form can be administered either immediately before or immediately after the formal assessment process and consists of questions that can be asked by the professional, particularly of those with a severe disability and who wish to live independently. The obtained information can be eventually used for vocational planning, and the professional can also select the questions that are to be asked. Many of the consumer's responses are facilitated when the consumer can look at a copy of the form as the professional asks the questions.

Employment Readiness Scale

Employment Readiness Scale

Name: _____ Date: _____

Directions
This is a survey used to learn about the many feelings people have toward working. Please fill in the blanks below. Then read the statements on the following pages and circle the number in the column that explains the way you feel about the statement.

Highest grade of education you have completed: _____ Age: _____

	This is true for me all the time	This is usually true for me all the time	This is usually not true for me all the time	This is not true for me at all
1. When working, I move at a steady pace.	4	3	2	1
2. If I watch someone do something that I know is wrong, I will forget it because it does not affect me.	4	3	2	1
3. I believe that safety is important.	4	3	2	1
4. I like to work around machinery.	4	3	2	1
5. People can depend on me.	4	3	2	1
6. I feel people are against me.	4	3	2	1
7. I feel I could succeed at a job.	4	3	2	1
8. I like to look neat at work and away from work.	4	3	2	1
9. I am willing to study when I am not working in order to learn better how to do my job.	4	3	2	1
10. I am willing to get dirty when I work.	4	3	2	1
11. Once I am given something to do, I want to complete it.	4	3	2	1
12. I respect people in authority.	4	3	2	1
13. I think children should work for their spending money.	4	3	2	1
14. I can get along with people.	4	3	2	1
15. I enjoy taking on more responsibility.	4	3	2	1
16. I dislike most other people.	4	3	2	1
17. I would like to be good at what I do.	4	3	2	1
18. I would like to improve myself.	4	3	2	1
19. I am willing to work a 40-hour week.	4	3	2	1
20. My work is important to my employer.	4	3	2	1
21. I feel like I could develop a feeling of belonging to a company.	4	3	2	1
22. I believe in being on time for work.	4	3	2	1
23. I am willing to get up early in the morning to come to work.	4	3	2	1
24. I want to support myself.	4	3	2	1
25. I am willing to work past my regular hours for more money.	4	3	2	1
26. The kind of job I want is one that pays well for very little work.	4	3	2	1
27. I would hate to live on welfare.	4	3	2	1

© 2013 by PRO-ED, Inc.   #13938C   (continue)

This form is to be completed by the consumer and can be done so either at the beginning of the assessment process or during the conclusion of this process. The form is a self-assessment tool, and it explores the consumer's perceptions about many employment demands. The information obtained from the form is usually more reliable if consumers complete the form themselves but the professional is available to answer any questions during its administration. Yet there may be occasions, because of disability limitations, when the professional will have to read the items and direct the consumer to his or her response. In such situations, each person should have a copy of the form.

Suggested Format
for the Vocational Assessment Report

This recommended format can be used by the professional as a structure to communicate assessment results to both the consumer and the referring agency. It should be completed at the conclusion of the vocational assessment process, when all the results are available. During the session when the professional communicates these assessment results to the consumer, the format can be used not only to communicate important information but also to solicit valuable consumer feedback that may provide significant

insights into short-term and long-term recommendations. Such mutual involvement enhances the validity of the report's recommendations.

Proposed Structure
for the Vocational/Career Plan

Following completion of vocational assessment, and usually after the reporting of the evaluation results, a vocational/career plan is developed identifying the goals and objectives of this plan. A copy of the plan should also be given to the consumer, allowing the consumer to provide any feedback related to the plan. This feedback may include the consumer's response to the feasibility of the objectives and the steps needed to achieve them.

Suggested Situational Assessment Supervisor Evaluation Form

To be completed by the consumer's situational assessment supervisor or a related person, this form pinpoints the occupational behaviors that are important to evaluate during this specific approach to evaluation. The form should be completed on a regular schedule, either weekly or monthly, and can also be used by the supervisor as a guide to identify behaviors that are necessary for appropriate work adjustment. The results can also be discussed with the consumer after the form's completion.

Suggested Situational Assessment Supervisor Evaluation Form

Consumer's name: _____

Evaluator: _____

Period Covered: _____

Date of First Evaluation: _____

Rating Key

A – Strong Area
B – No Problems
C – Work Behavior Needs Improvement
D – Change Possible for Work Behavior
E – Change Appears Doubtful for Work Behavior

Category	Rating
1. Relationship With Supervisor	
Comfortable	_____
Anxious	_____
Benefits from instruction	_____
Appropriateness of personal relations with supervisor	_____
Open and clear communication with supervisor on work site	_____
2. Work-Related Factors	
Productivity is consistently high	_____
Cooperates with others on work tasks	_____
Understands and follows through on instructions	_____
Work accomplished is consistently acceptable	_____
3. Personal Work Behaviors	
Attendance	_____
Punctuality	_____
Grooming	_____
Dress	_____
Levels of energy	_____
Motivation to perform tasks	_____
Recognizes work as different from school, home, and recreation	_____
Relations with co-workers/works well with co-workers	_____
Accepts unpleasant tasks	_____
Organizes work	_____
Adapts to changes in the work situation	_____
Shows ability to learn	_____
Communicates with supervisors and co-workers clearly	_____
Acceptable frustration tolerance	_____
Awareness of rules and safety precautions	_____
Inappropriate work behaviors	_____

(continued)

© 2013 by PRO-ED, Inc.   #13938C

# References

ACT. (1999). *The career planning survey*. Iowa City, IA: Author.

Ahadi, S. (1991). The use of API career factors as Holland occupational types. *Educational and Psychological Measurement, 51*, 167–172.

Aiken, L. R. (1997). *Psychological testing and assessment* (9th ed.). Needham Heights, MA: Allyn & Bacon.

Alston, R. J., & McCowan, C. J. (1994). Aptitude assessment and African American consumers: The interplay between culture and psychometrics in rehabilitation. *Journal of Rehabilitation, 60*, 41–46.

American College Testing Program. (1989). *The DISCOVER program*. Hunt Valley, MD: Discover Center.

Americans with Disabilities Act of 1990, 42 U.S.C. § 12101 *et seq.*

Ammons, R. B., & Ammons, C. H. (1962). *The quick-test*. Missoula, MT: Psychological Tests Specialists.

An, S., Roessler, R., & McMahon, B. (2011). Workplace discrimination and Americans with psychiatric disabilities: A comparative study. *Rehabilitation Counseling Bulletin, 55*(1), 7–19.

Anastasi, A. (1982). *Psychological testing*. New York, NY: Macmillan.

Anastasi, A. (1988). *Psychological testing* (6th ed.). New York, NY: Macmillan.

Anastasi, A. (1992). What counselors should know about the use and interpretation of psychological tests. *Journal of Counseling and Development, 70*, 610–615.

Andrew, D. M., Patterson, D. G., & Longstaff, H. P. (1992). *Minnesota clerical test*. San Antonio, TX: Pearson.

Anthony, W. A. (1979). *The principles of psychiatric rehabilitation*. Amherst, MA: Human Resource Development Press.

Anthony, W. A., Howell, J., & Danley, K. S. (1984). Vocational rehabilitation of the psychiatrically disabled. In M. Mirabi (Ed.), *The chronically mentally ill: Research and services* (pp. 215–237). New York, NY: Spectrum.

Araoz, D., & Carrese, M. (1996). *Solution-oriented brief therapy for adjustment disorders*. New York, NY: Brunner/Mazel.

Arkowitz, H., Westra, H., Miller, W., & Rollnick, S. (2007). *Motivational interviewing in the treatment of psychological problems*. New York, NY: Guilford Press.

Athanasou, J. A., & Van Esbroeck, R. (2007). Multilateral perspectives on vocational interests. *International Journal for Educational and Vocational Guidance, 7*, 1–3.

Atkins, B. J. (1988). An asset-oriented approach to cross-cultural issues: Blacks in rehabilitation. *Journal of Applied Rehabilitation Counseling, 19*(4), 45–53.

Atkins, B., Lynch, R., & Pullo, R. (1982). A definition of psychosocial aspects of disability: A synthesis of the literature. *Vocational Evaluation and Work Adjustment Bulletin, 15*, 55–61.

Barrett, H. C. (2001). *Collaborative planning for electronic portfolios: Asking strategic questions*. Anchorage, AL: University of Alaska.

Baxter, R., Cohen, S., & Ylvisaker, M. (1985). Comprehensive cognitive assessment. In M. Ylvisaker (Ed.), *Head injury rehabilitation: Children and adolescents* (pp. 247–274). Austin, TX: PRO-ED.

Becker, L., Schur, S., Pacletti-Schelp, M., & Hammer, E. (1984). *The functional skills screening inventory.* Amarillo, TX: Functional Resources Enterprises.

Becker, R. (2000). *Reading-free vocational interest inventory-2.* Columbus, OH: Elbern.

Beley, W., & Felker, S. (1981). Comprehensive vocational evaluation for clients with psychiatric impairments. *Rehabilitation Literature, 42,* 194–201.

Belkin, L. (2009, October 4). The new gender gap. *The New York Times Magazine,* pp. 11–12.

Bender, L. (1992). *Bender visual motor gestalt test.* New York, NY: American Orthopsychiatric Association.

Bennett, G. K. (1981). *Hand-tool dexterity test.* San Antonio, TX: Pearson.

Bennett, G. K. (1992). *Bennett mechanical comprehension test.* San Antonio, TX: Pearson.

Bennett, G. K., Seashore, H. G., & Wesman, A. G. (1990). *Differential aptitude tests–Fifth edition.* San Antonio, TX: Pearson.

Berven, N. (2008). Assessment interviewing, In B. Bolton & R. Parker (Eds.), *Handbook of measurement and evaluation in rehabilitation* (4th ed., pp. 241–260). Austin, TX: PRO-ED.

Berven, N. L. (1997). Professional practice: Assessment. In D. Maki & T. Riggar (Eds.), *Rehabilitation counseling* (pp. 151–169). New York, NY: Springer.

Betz, N., & Weiss, D. (2008). Validity. In B. Bolton & R. Parker (Eds.), *Handbook of measurement and evaluation in rehabilitation* (4th ed., pp. 57–86). Austin, TX: PRO-ED.

Biggs, D., & Keller, K. (1982). A cognitive approach to using tests in counseling. *The Personnel and Guidance Journal, 60,* 528–532.

Bitter, J. A. (1968). Toward a concept of job readiness. *Rehabilitation Literature, 28,* 201–203.

Blackwell, T. L., Autry, T. L., & Guglielmo, D. E. (2001). Ethical issues in disclosure of test data. *Rehabilitation Counseling Bulletin, 49*(3), 161–169.

Boland, J. M., & Alonso, G. (1982). A comparison: Independent living rehabilitation and vocational rehabilitation. *Journal of Rehabilitation, 48,* 50–59.

Bolles, R. (1989). *How to create a picture of your ideal job or next career.* Berkeley, CA: Ten Speed Press.

Bolles, R. (2004). *What color is your parachute?* Berkeley, CA: Ten Speed Press.

Bolles, R. (2009). *What color is your parachute?* Berkeley, CA: Ten Speed Press.

Bolton, B. (1997, Summer/Fall). Vocationally oriented personality assessment for vocational rehabilitation programs. *Vocational Evaluation and Work Adjustment Bulletin,* 63–67.

Bolton, B. (1986). Minnesota satisfactoriness scales. In D. J. Keyser & R.C. Sweetland (Eds.), *Test critiques* (Vol. 4, pp. 434–439). Austin, TX: PRO-ED.

Bolton, B. (1982). *Vocational adjustment of disabled persons.* Austin, TX: PRO-ED.

Bolton, B. (1979). *Rehabilitation counseling research.* Baltimore, MD: University Park Press.

Bolton, B., Parker, R., & Brookings, J. (2008). Scores and norms. In B. Bolton & R. Parker (Eds.), *Handbook of measurement and evaluation in rehabilitation* (4th ed., pp. 3–30). Austin, TX: PRO-ED.

Bongiorno, P. (1993). Summary of the Rehabilitation Act Amendments of 1992. *Journal of Job Placement, 9,* 26–31.

Bordin, E. D. (1943). A theory of vocational interests as dynamic phenomena. *Educational and Psychological Measurement, 3,* 49–65.

Botterbusch, K. (1983). *A comparison of computerized job matching systems.* Menomonie, WI: University of Wisconsin–Stout, Materials Development Center.

Bowman, S. (1995). Career intervention strategies and assessment issues for African Americans. In F. L. Leong (Ed.), *Career development and vocational behavior of racial and ethnic minorities* (pp. 137–164). Mahwah, NJ: Erlbaum.

Brady, R. (2007). *Picture interest career survey.* Indianapolis, IN: JIST.

Bronzaft, A. L. (1991). Career, marriage, and family aspirations of young black college women. *Journal of Negro Education, 60*(1), 110–118.

Brown, C., McDanel, R., & Couch, R. (1994). *Vocational evaluation systems and software: A consumer's guide.* Menomonie, WI: University of Wisconsin–Stout, Rehabilitation Resources.

Brown, D. T. (1991, Winter). Computerized techniques in career assessment. *Career Planning and Adult Development Journal, 6,* 27–34.

Bruyere, S. (2000). Statistics about people with disabilities and employment. Retrieved from http://www.dol.gov/odep/pube/ek01/stats.htm.

Bruyere, S., & O'Keefe, J. (1994). *Implications of the Americans with Disabilities Act for psychology.* New York, NY: Springer.

Bureau of Labor Statistics. (2010–2011). *Career guide to industries.* Washington, DC: U.S. Government Printing Office.

Bureau of Labor Statistics. (2010). *News.* Washington, DC: United States Department of Labor.

Bureau of Labor Statistics. (2011). *Occupational outlook quarterly.* Washington, DC: U.S. Department of Labor.

Campbell, L. R. (1991). Enhancing diversity: A multicultural employment perspective. In S. Walker, F. Belgrave, R. W. Nicholls, & K. A. Turner (Eds.), *Future frontiers in the employment of minority persons with disabilities* (pp. 38–47). Washington, DC: Howard University Research and Training Center.

Carkhuff, R. R. (1969). *Helping and human relations.* New York, NY: Holt, Rinehart & Winston.

Carkhuff, R. (1971). *The development of human resources.* New York, NY: Holt, Rinehart & Winston.

Carkhuff, R. R., & Anthony, W. A. (1979). *The skills of helping.* Amherst, MA: Human Resource Development Press.

Cartwright, B., & Fleming, C. (2010). Multicultural and diversity considerations in the new Code of Professional Ethics for Rehabilitation Counselors. *Rehabilitation Counseling Bulletin, 53*(4), 213–217.

Cattell, R. B. (1986). *Sixteen personality factor questionnaire.* San Antonio, TX: Pearson.

Chope, K. (2008). Annual review: Practice and research in career counseling and development–2007. *The Career Development Quarterly, 57,* 98–173.

Choppa, A. J., & Shafer, K. (1992). Introduction to personal injury and expert witness work. In J. M. Siefker (Ed.), *Vocational evaluation in private sector rehabilitation* (pp. 135–168). Menomonie, WI: University of Wisconsin–Stout.

Clark, G., & Patton, J. (2006). *Transition planning inventory–Updated version.* Austin, TX: PRO-ED.

Cohen, B. F., & Anthony, W. A. (1984). Functional assessment in psychiatric rehabilitation. In A. Halpern & M. Fuhrer (Eds.), *Functional assessment in rehabilitation* (pp. 79–100). Baltimore, MD: Brookes.

Cohen, R., Swerdlik, M., & Phillips, S. (1996). *Psychological testing and assessment* (3rd ed.). Mountain View, CA: Mayfield.

Commission on Accreditation of Rehabilitation Facilities. (2003). *The Rehabilitation Accreditation Commission 2000 employment and community services standards manual.* Tucson, AZ: CARF.

Corthell, D., & Griswald, P. P. (Eds.). (1987). *The use of vocational evaluation in VR.* 14th Institute on Rehabilitation Issues. Menomonie, WI: University of Wisconsin–Stout, Research and Training Center.

Costello, J. (1991). *Fundamentals of vocational assessment.* Tucson, AZ: RPM Press.

Cottone, R., & Tarvydas, V. (1998). *Ethical and professional issues in counseling.* Columbus, OH: Merrill.

Crewe, N., & Athelstan, G. (1984). *Functional assessment inventory manual.* Menomonie, WI: University of Wisconsin–Stout, Research and Training Center.

Crewe, N. M., & Athelstan, G. T. (1978). Functional assessment inventory. In B. Bolton & D. W. Cook (Eds.), *Rehabilitation client assessment* (pp. 389–399). Baltimore, MD: University Park Press.

Crooker, J., Niija, Y., & Mischkowski, D. (2008). Why does writing about values reduce defensiveness? Self-affirmation and the role of positive other directed feelings. *Psychological Science: Research, Theory, and Application in Psychology and Related Sciences, 19*(7), 740–747.

Cummings, W. H. (1995). Age group differences and estimated frequencies of the Myers–Briggs Type Indicator preferences. *Measurement and Evaluation in Counseling and Development, 2,* 69–77.

Curtin, K., & Garcia, J. (2011). Improving work performances for adolescents with emotional and behavioral disorders: A comparison of two work-based learning interventions. *Journal of Rehabilitation, 77*(1), 31–39.

Cutts, C. (1977). Test review—The Self-Directed Search. *Measurement and Evaluation in Guidance, 10,* 117–120.

Dana, R. H. (2001). Multicultural issues in assessment. In B. Bolton (Ed.), *Handbook of measurement and evaluation in rehabilitation* (pp. 449–470). Gaithersburg, MD: Aspen.

Dana, R. H. (2008). Multicultural issues in assessment. In B. Bolton & R. Parker (Eds.), *Handbook of measurement and evaluation in rehabilitation* (4th ed., pp. 569–587). Austin, TX: PRO-ED.

Dawis, R. V., & Lofquist, L. H. (1984*). A psychological theory of work adjustment: An individual-differences model and its applications.* Minneapolis, MN: University of Minnesota.

De Kleijn-deVrankrijker, M. (2003). The long way from the International Classification of Impairments, Disabilities and Handicaps (ICIDH) to the International Classification of Functioning, Disability and Health (ICF). *Disability and Rehabilitation, 25,* 561–564.

Devinney, D., Kamnetz, B., Chan, F., & Hattori, K. (1998, Spring). Wechsler scale short forms in vocational assessment and evaluation settings. *Vocational Evaluation and Work Adjustment Journal,* 4–10.

Devinney, D., Tansey, T., Ferrin, J., & Pruett, S. (2005). The mini-mental status examination: A screening tool for rehabilitation counselors and vocational evaluators. *Journal of Applied Rehabilitation Counseling, 36,* 16–23.

Doherty, W., & Baird, M. (1983). *Family therapy and family medicine.* New York, NY: Guilford.

Dolliver, R., & Nelson, R. (1975). Assumptions regarding vocational counseling. *Vocational Guidance Quarterly, 24,* 12–19.

Donnell, C., Robertson, S., & Tansey, T. (2010). Measures of culture and diversity in rehabilitation and health assessment. In E. Mpofu & T. Oakland (Eds.), *Rehabilitation and health assessment* (pp. 67–92). New York, NY: Springer.

Dowd, L. R. (1993). *Glossary of terminology for vocational assessment, evaluation, and work adjustment.* Menomonie, WI: University of Wisconsin–Stout.

Draper, W., Reid, C., & McMahon, B. (2011). Work discrimination and the perception of disability. *Rehabilitation Counseling Bulletin, 55*(1), 29–37.

Duffy, R., & Sedlacek, W. (2007). What is most important to students' long-term career choices?: Analyzing 10 year trends and group differences. *Journal of Career Development Quarterly, 55,* 359–364.

Dunn, D. (1994). Positive meaning and illusions following disability: Reality negotiation, normative interpretation, and value change. *Journal of Social Behavior and Personality, 9*(5), 123–138.

Dunn, L. M., & Dunn, L. (2007). *Peabody picture vocabulary test–Fourth edition.* San Antonio, TX: Pearson.

Dutta, A., Kundu, M., & Schiro-Geist, C. (2009). Coordination of postsecondary transition services for students with disabilities. *Journal of Rehabilitation, 75*(1), 10–17.

Duys, D., Ward, J., Maxwell, J., & Eaton-Comerford, L. (2008). Job market: Tiedemann's perspective revisited. *Career Development Quarterly, 56,* 232–241.

Eaton, M. (1979, April/May/June). Obstacles to the vocational rehabilitation of individuals receiving worker's compensation. *Journal of Rehabilitation, 45,* 59–63.

Ebener, D. J., & Smedema, S. M. (2011). Physical disability and substance use disorders: A convergence of adaptation and recovery. *Rehabilitation Counseling Bulletin, 54*(3), 131–141.

Elliott, T. (1995). Personality assessment in SCI rehabilitation: Assessment of nonpathological personality characteristics. *SCI Psychological Process, 8*(4), 139–144.

Elliott, T., Kurylo, M., & Rivera, P. (2002). Positive growth following acquired physical disability. In C. R. Snyder & S. Lopez (Eds.), *Handbook of positive psychology* (pp. 687–699). New York, NY: Oxford University Press.

Enders, A. (2002). *Technology and the employment of persons with disabilities.* Unpublished manuscript.

Enright, M., Conyers, L., & Szymanski, E. (1996). Career and career-related educational concerns of college students with disabilities. *Journal of Counseling and Development, 75,* 103–114.

Farley, R. C., & Bolton, B. (1994). *Developing an employability assessment and planning program.* Fayetteville, AR: Arkansas Research and Training Center in Vocational Rehabilitation.

Farley, R. C., Little, N. D., Bolton, B., & Chunn, J. (1993). *Employability assessment and planning in rehabilitation and educational settings.* Fayetteville, AR: Arkansas Research and Training Center in Vocational Rehabilitation.

Farley, R. C., & Rubin, S. E. (2006). The intake interview. In R. T. Roessler & S. E. Rubin (Eds.), *Case management and rehabilitation counseling* (4th ed., pp. 51–74). Austin, TX: PRO-ED.

Fayne, L. J. (1989). Vocational evaluation of traumatically head injured individuals: Critical factors for consideration. *Vocational Evaluation and Assessment Bulletin, 3,* 1–2.

Feist-Price, S., Harley, D., & Alston, R. (1996). A cross-cultural perspective for vocational evaluation and assessment. *Vocational Evaluation and Work Adjustment Bulletin, 29*(2), 48–54.

Feldman, M. (2006). Learning disabilities. In A. Dell Orto & R. Marinelli (Eds.), *Encyclopedia of disability and rehabilitation* (pp. 434–436). New York, NY: Simon & Schuster MacMillan.

Field, T. (1979). The psychological assessment of vocational functioning. *Journal of Applied Rehabilitation Counseling, 10,* 124–129.

Field, T., & Sink, J. (1980). *The employer's manual.* Athens, GA: Udare Service Bureau.

Fitts, W. H., & Warren, W. (1996). *Tennessee self-concept scale–Second edition.* Nashville, TN: Counselor Recordings and Tests.

Flores, L. Y., Spanierman, L. B., & Obasi, E. M. (2003). Ethical and professional issues in career assessment with diverse racial and ethnic groups. *Journal of Career Assessment, 11*(1), 76–95.

Flowers, C., Griffin-Dixon, C., & Trevino, B. (1997). Cultural pluralism: Contexts of practice. In D. R. Maki & T. G. Riggar (Eds.), *Rehabilitation counseling—Profession and practice* (pp. 124–138). New York, NY: Springer.

Foss, G., Bullis, M. D., & Vilhaver, D. A. (1984). Assessment and training of job-related social competence for mentally retarded adolescents and adults. In A. Halpern & M. Fuhrer (Eds.), *Functional assessment in rehabilitation* (pp. 145–158). Baltimore, MD: Brookes.

Fouad, N. (1993). Cross-cultural vocational assessment. *The Career Development Quarterly, 42,* 4–13.

Fouad, N., Smothers, M., Kantamneni, N., & Guillen, A. (2008). Vocational inventories. In B. Bolton & R. Parker (Eds.), *Handbook of measurement and evaluation in rehabilitation* (4th ed., pp. 209–234). Austin, TX: PRO-ED.

Fredrickson, R. (1982). *Career information.* Englewood Cliffs, NJ: Prentice Hall.

French, K. (2001). *College admissions data handbook.* Itasca, IL: Wintergreen Orchard House.

Friel, T., & Carkhuff, R. (1974). *The art of developing a career.* Amherst, MA: Human Resource Development Press.

Gallagher, J., & Wiener, W. (2008). Assessment of individuals with visual impairments. In B. Bolton & R. Parker (Eds.), *Handbook of measurement and evaluation in rehabilitation* (4th ed., pp. 437–458). Austin, TX: PRO-ED.

Gati, I. (1994). Computer-assisted career counseling: Dilemmas, problems, and possible solutions. *Journal of Counseling and Development, 73,* 51–56.

Geist, H. J. (1988). *Geist picture interest inventory* (Rev. ed.). Los Angeles, CA: Western Psychological Services.

Gibson, D., Weiss, D., Dawis, R., & Lofquist, L. (1970). Manual of the Minnesota Satisfactoriness Scales. In D. Gibson, D. Weiss, R. Dawis, & L. Lofquist (Eds.), *Minnesota studies in vocational rehabilitation* (Vol. 27, Bulletin 53). Minneapolis, MN: University of Minnesota.

Glisson, C., Iannucci-Waller, J., Johnson, L., & Thomas, S. (2004). *The new paradigms in IRI.* Unpublished manuscript. Washington, DC: Rehabilitation Services Administration.

Glutting, J., & Wilkinson, G. (2003). *Wide range interest and occupation test–Second edition.* San Antonio, TX: Pearson.

Godley, S. (1978). Topical review. *Vocational Evaluation and Work Adjustment Bulletin, 11,* 51–57.

Golden, C. J., Purisch, A. D., & Hammeke, T. A. (1985). *Luria-Nebraska neuropsychological battery.* Los Angeles, CA: Western Psychological Services.

Goldman, L. (1971). *Using tests in counseling* (2nd ed.). Santa Monica, CA: Goodyear.

Goldman, L. (1972). Tests and counseling: The marriage that failed. *Measurement and Evaluation in Guidance, 4,* 213–220.

Goleman, D. (2005). *Emotional intelligence.* New York, NY: Bantam Books.

Golter, G. D., & Golter, M. C. (1986). Rehabilitation and computerization. In E. G. Pan, S. S. Newman, T. E. Backer, & C. L. Vash (Eds.), *Annual review of rehabilitation* (Vol. 5, pp. 151–169). New York, NY: Springer.

Gordon, R. P., Stump, K., & Glaser, B. A. (1996). Assessment of individuals with hearing impairments: Equity in testing procedures and accommodations. *Measurement and Evaluation in Counseling and Development, 29,* 111–118.

Gorski, T. T. (1990). The Cenaps model of relapse prevention: Basic principles and procedures. *Journal of Psychoactive Drugs, 22,* 125–133.

Gough, H. G. (1987). *California psychological inventory.* Palo Alto, CA: Consulting Psychologists Press.

Graham, J. R. (1993). *MMPI-2—Assessing personality and psychopathology* (2nd ed.). New York, NY: Oxford University Press.

Granger C., Cotter, A., Hamilton, B., & Fiedler, R. (1993), Functional assessment scales: A study of persons after stroke. *Archives of Physical Medicine and Rehabilitation, 71,* 870–875.

Granger, C., Gilewski, M., & Carlin, M. (2010). Measures of functional performance. In E. Mpofu & T. Oakland (Eds.), *Rehabilitation and health assessment* (pp. 547–568). New York, NY: Springer.

Grevious, L. (1985). A comparison of occupational aspirations of urban black college students. *Journal of Negro Education, 54,* 35–42.

Grier-Reed, T., & Ganuza, Z. (2011, Spring). Constructivism and career decision self-efficacy for Asian Americans and African Americans. *Journal of Counseling and Development, 89*(2), 200–205.

Griffths, R. (1977). The prediction of psychiatric patient's work adjustment in the community. *British Journal of Social and Clinical Psychology, 16,* 165–173.

Griggs, S. A. (1985). Counseling for individual learning styles. *Journal of Counseling and Development, 64,* 202–205.

Groth-Marnat, G. (2003). *Handbook of psychological assessment* (4th ed.). Hoboken, NJ: Wiley.

Grove, B., Leslie, L., & Scott, R. (1999). *Making partnerships work for rehabilitation and employment.* Brighton, UK: Pavilion.

Growick, B. (1983). *Computers in vocational rehabilitation: Current trends and future applications.* Washington, DC: National Rehabilitation Information Center.

Gysbers, N., Heppner, M., & Johnston, J. (2009). *Career counseling: Contexts, processes, and techniques.* Boston, MA: Allyn & Bacon.

Hall, J., & Parker, K. (2010). Stuck in a loop: Individual and system barriers for job seekers with disabilities. *Career Development Quarterly, 58,* 246–256.

Halpern, A. S., & Fuhrer, M. J. (1984). *Functional assessment in rehabilitation.* Baltimore, MD: Brookes.

Halstead, W. (1947). *Brain and intelligence.* Chicago, IL: University of Chicago Press.

Hammill, D. D., Pearson, N. A., & Wiederholt, J. L. (2009). *The comprehensive test of nonverbal intelligence–Second edition.* Austin, TX: PRO-ED.

Hanson, M. A., Matheson, L., & Borman, W. (2001). The O*NET Occupational Information System. In B. F. Bolton (Ed.), *Handbook of measurement and evaluation in rehabilitation* (pp. 281–301). Gaithersburg, MD: Aspen.

Harrington, T. F. (1997). Career development theory. In T. G. Harrington (Ed.), *Handbook of career planning* (2nd ed., pp. 3–40). Austin, TX: PRO-ED.

Harrington, T. F., & O'Shea, A. J. (2008). *Guide to occupational exploration* (2nd ed.). San Antonio, TX: Pearson.

Harrington, T. F., & O'Shea, A. J. (2008). *Career decision-making system–Revised.* San Antonio, TX: Pearson.

Harris, J. A. (1982). Innovations in vocational evaluations and work adjustment: APTICOM—A computerized multiple aptitude testing instrument for cost and time effective vocational evaluation. *Vocational Evaluation and Work Adjustment Bulletin, 4,* 161–162.

Hartung, P. J. (2002). Cultural context in career theory and practice: Role salience and values. *Career Development Quarterly, 51,* 12–25.

Hathaway, S., McKinley, C., & Butcher, J. (1990). *Minnesota multiphasic personality inventory–Second edition.* Minneapolis, MN: National Computer Systems.

Havranek, J., Field, T., & Grimes, J. (2005). *Vocational assessment: Evaluating employment potential* (4th ed.). Athens, GA: Elliott & Fitzpatrick.

Heath, S. B. (1989). Oral and literate traditions among black Americans living in poverty. *American Psychologist, 44,* 367–373.

Helms, J. E. (1992). Why is there no study of cultural equivalence in standardized cognitive ability testing? *American Psychologist, 47,* 1083–1101.

Herbert, J., Lorenz, D., & Trusty, J. (2010). Career assessment practices for high school students with disabilities and perceived value reported by transition personnel. *Journal of Rehabilitation, 76*(9), 18–26.

Hershenson, D. (1990). A theoretical model for rehabilitation counseling. *Rehabilitation Counseling Bulletin, 33,* 268–278.

Hill, L., & Wilson, R. (Eds.). (1994). *Black American colleges and universities: Profiles of two-year, four-year, and professional schools.* Farmington Hills, MI: Gale Group.

Holland, J. (1959). A theory of vocational choice. *Journal of Counseling Psychologists, 6,* 35–45.

Holland, J. (1977). *You and your career.* Odessa, FL: Psychological Assessment Resources.

Holland, J. (1994). *The self-directed search.* San Antonio, TX: Psychological Corp.

Holzbauer, J. J., & Berven, N. L. (1999, Summer). Issues in vocational evaluation and testing related to the Americans with Disabilities Act. *Vocational Evaluation and Work Adjustment Bulletin,* pp. 83–96.

Hood, A. B., & Johnson, R. W. (2007). *Assessment in counseling* (4th ed.). Alexandria, VA: American Counseling Association.

Horowitz, M. (1983). Psychological response to serious life events. In S. Brazacita (Ed.), *The denial of stress* (pp. 129–159). New York, NY: International Universities Press.

Houser, J., Hampton, N., & Carriken, C. (2000). Implementing the empowerment concept in rehabilitation: Contributions of social role theory. *Journal of Applied Rehabilitation Counseling, 31*(2), 18–23.

Hoyt, K. (1986). Ohio vocational interest survey, microcomputer version. San Antonio, TX: Psychological Corp.

Hursh, N. (1989). *Assessing vocational capacity of learning disabled adults.* Unpublished manuscript, Boston University.

Hursh, N. C., & Kerns, A. F. (1988). *Vocational evaluation in special education.* Austin, TX: PRO-ED.

Hurst, R. (2003). The international disability rights movement and the ICF. *Disability and Rehabilitation, 25,* 572–576.

Interdisciplinary Council on Vocational Evaluation/Assessment. (1994). *A position statement by the vocational evaluation and work adjustment association.* Colorado Springs, CO: Author.

Irvin, L. K., & Halpern, H. S. (1979). A process model of diagnostic assessment. In

G.T. Bellamy, G. O'Connor, & O. Karan (Eds.), *Vocational rehabilitation of severely handicapped persons* (pp. 55–70). Baltimore, MD: University Park Press.

Isaacson, L., & Brown, D. (2000). *Career information, career counseling, and career development* (7th ed.). Boston, MA: Allyn & Bacon.

Isaacson, L. E., & Brown, D. (1997). *Career information, career counseling, and career development.* Needham Heights, MA: Allyn & Bacon.

Janoff-Bulman, R. (1992). *Shattered assumptions.* New York, NY: Free Press.

JIST. (1993). *Complete guide for occupational exploration.* Indianapolis, IN: JIST Works.

JIST. (1998a). *Guide for occupational exploration.* Indianapolis, IN: JIST Works.

Johansson, C. B. (2003). *Career assessment inventory–Enhanced version.* San Antonio, TX: Pearson.

Kaplan, S., & Questad, L. (1980). Client characteristics in rehabilitation studies: A literature review. *Journal of Applied Rehabilitation Counseling, 11,* 165–168.

Karlsen, B., & Gardner, E. F. (1986). *Adult basic learning examination.* New York, NY: Psychological Corp.

Kaufman, A., & Kaufman, N. (1994). *Functional academic skills test* (FAST). San Antonio, TX: Pearson.

Kaufman, A. S., & Kaufman, N. L. (1994). *Kaufman functional academic skills test.* Bloomington, MN: Pearson Assessments.

Kaufman, A. S., & Kaufman, N. L. (2004). *Kaufman brief intelligence test–Second edition.* San Antonio, TX: Pearson.

Kaufman, J. C., & Kaufman, A. S. (2001). Intelligence testing. In B. F. Bolton (Ed.), *Handbook of measurement and evaluation in rehabilitation* (pp. 79–102). Belmont, CA: Aspen.

Keller, B., & Whiston, S. (2008). The role of parental influences on young adolescents' career development. *Journal of Career Assessment, 16*(2), 198–217.

Kellogg, C. E., & Morton, N. W. (1999). *Revised beta examination–Beta III.* San Antonio, TX: Pearson.

Kjos, D. (1995). Linking career information to personality disorders. *Journal of Counseling and Development, 73,* 592–596.

Knapp, L. F., & Knapp, R. R. (1994). *Career ability placement survey.* San Diego, CA: EdITS/Educational and Industrial Testing Service.

Knefelkamp, L. L., & Slepitza, R. (1976). A cognitive-developmental model of career development—An adaptation of the Perry scheme. *Counseling Psychology, 6,* 53–58.

Knoff, H. M., & Prout, T. (1985). *Kinetic drawing system for family and school: A handbook.* Los Angeles, CA: Western Psychological Services.

Koch, L. (1998, March). *Increasing client involvement in the vocational rehabilitation process: An expectations approach.* Paper presented at the meeting of the National Counselor Association, Vancouver, WA.

Koch, L. C., & Merz, M. A. (2001, Spring). The career portfolio: An assessment tool for actively involving consumers in vocational rehabilitation. *National Vocational Evaluation and Work Adjustment Journal, 33,* 39–45.

Kolb, A., & Kolb, D. (1999). *The learning style inventory–Version 3.1.* Boston, MA: Hay Group.

Koscuilek, J. F. (2009). Empowering life choices of people with disabilities through career counseling. In N. G. Gysber, M. Heppner, & J. Johnston (Eds.), *Career counseling: Process, issues, and techniques* (3rd ed., pp. 125–136). Boston, MA: Allyn & Bacon.

Kroll, L. G. (1984). LDs—What happens when they are no longer children? *Academic Therapist, 20,* 133–148.

Krug, S. E. (2001). Assessment of personality. In B. Bolton (Ed.), *Handbook of measurement and evaluation in rehabilitation* (3rd ed., pp. 125–142). Belmont, CA: Aspen.

Krug, S. (2008). Assessment of personality. In B. Bolton & R. Parker (Eds.), *Handbook of measurement and evaluation in rehabilitation* (4th ed., pp. 151–173). Austin, TX: PRO-ED.

Kuder, F., Diamond, E., & Zytowski, H. (1985). *Kuder occupational interest survey–Form DD*. Chicago, IL: Science Research Associates.

Langton, A. J. (1993, Spring). Making more effective use of assistive technology in the vocational evaluation process. *Vocational Evaluation and Work Adjustment Bulletin*, 13–18.

Langton, A. J., Smith, F., Lown, N. F., & Chatham, L. J. (1998). *Guide to using assistive technology in assessment and vocational evaluation*. West Columbia, SC: South Carolina Vocational Rehabilitation Department, Center for Rehabilitation Technology Services.

Lanyon, R. I. (2010). *Psychological screening inventory*. Port Huron, MI: Sigma Assessment Systems.

Leconte, P. J., Castleberry, M., King, S., & West, L. (1995). Critical issues in assessment: Let's take the mystery out of assessment for vocational preparation, career development, and transition. *Diagnostique, 20*, 33–51.

Lent, R. W., Brown, S. D., & Hackett, G. (1994). Toward a unifying social cognitive theory of career and academic interest, choice, and performance. *Journal of Vocational Behavior, 45*, 79–122.

Leong, F. T., & Hartung, P. J. (2000). Cross-cultural career assessment: Review and prospects for the new millennium. *Journal of Career Assessment, 5*, 183–202.

Levinson, E. M. (1994). Current vocational assessment models for students with disabilities. *Journal of Counseling and Development, 73*, 94–101.

Lewis, T. F., & Osborn, C. J. (2004). Solution-focused counseling and motivational interviewing: A consideration of confluence. *Journal of Counseling and Development, 82*, 38–48.

Lichtenberger, E., Kaufman, J., & Kaufman, A. (2008). Intelligence testing. In B. Bolton & R. Parker (Eds.), *Handbook of measurement and evaluation in rehabilitation* (4th ed., pp. 91–115) Austin, TX: PRO-ED.

Linkowski, D. (1971). A scale to measure acceptance of disability. *Rehabilitation Counseling Bulletin, 14*, 235–244.

Liptak, J. (2007). *Career exploration inventory*. Indianapolis, IN: JIST.

Lock, R. D. (1988). *Taking charge of your career direction*. Pacific Grove, CA: Brooks/Cole.

Lock, R. D. (1992). *Taking charge of your career direction* (2nd ed.). Pacific Grove, CA: Brooks/Cole.

Lock, R. (2005). *Taking charge of your career direction: Career planning guide, Book 1* (5th ed.). Belmont, CA: Thomson/Brooks/Cole.

Lofquist, L. H., & Dawes, R. (1969). *Adjustment to work: A psychological view of man's problems in a work-oriented society*. New York: Appleton-Century-Crofts.

Lonner, W. J., & Sundberg, N. D. (1985). Assessment in cross-cultural counseling and therapy. In P. Pedersen (Ed.), *Handbook of cross-cultural counseling and therapy* (pp. 199–206). Westport, CT: Greenwood Press.

Lowman, R., & Richardson, L. (2008). Assessment of psychopathology. In B. Bolton & R. Parker (Eds.). *Handbook of measurement and evaluation in rehabilitation* (4th ed., pp. 175–201). Austin, TX: PRO-ED.

Luria, A. R. (1973). *The working brain*. New York: Basic Books.

Luzzo, D. (2002). *Making career decisions that count* (2nd ed.). Upper Saddle River, NJ: Prentice Hall.

Lysaker, P., Bell, M., Bryson, G., & Zito, W. (1993). *Rater's guide for the work behavior inventory: Rehabilitation, research, and development service.* West Haven, CT: Department of Veteran Affairs.

Lynch, R. (1979). Vocational rehabilitation of worker's compensation clients. *Journal of Applied Rehabilitation Counseling, 9,* 164–167.

MacDonald-Wilson, K., & Nimec, P. (2008). Assessment in psychiatric rehabilitation. In B. Bolton & R. Parker (Eds.), *Handbook of measurement and evaluation in rehabilitation* (4th ed., pp. 527–562). Austin, TX: PRO-ED.

MacKay, W. (1975). The decision fallacy: Is it if or when? *Vocational Guidance Quarterly, 23,* 227–231.

Macy, M., & Rusch, F. (2010). Life care planning evaluation. In E. Mpofu & T. Oakland (Eds.), *Rehabilitation and health assessment* (pp. 297–312). New York, NY: Springer.

Maki, D. (1986). Foundations of applied rehabilitation counseling. In T. F. Riggar, D. Maki, & A. Wolf (Eds.), *Applied rehabilitation counseling* (pp. 3–11). New York, NY: Springer.

Maki, D., Pape, D., & Prout, H. (1979). Personality evaluations: A tool of the rehabilitation counselor. *Journal of Applied Rehabilitation Counseling, 10,* 119–123.

Maki, D. R., & Riggar, T. F. (2003). *Handbook of rehabilitation counseling.* New York, NY: Springer.

Manthey, T., Jackson, C., & Evans-Brown, P. (2011). Motivation interviewing and vocational rehabilitation: A review with recommendations for administrators and counselors. *Journal of Applied Rehabilitation Counseling, 42*(1), 3–11.

Markwardt, F. C. (1998). *Peabody individual achievement test–Revised.* Circle Pines, MN: American Guidance Service.

Marrone, J., Horgan, J., Scripture, D., & Grossman, M. (1984). Serving the severely psychiatrically disabled client within the VR system. *Psychosocial Rehabilitation Journal, 8*(2), 5–23.

Marshall, C. A., Leung, P., Johnson, S., & Busby, H. (2003). Ethical practice and cultural factors in rehabilitation. *Rehabilitation Education, 17*(1), 55–65.

Mastie, M. (1994). Using assessment instruments in career counseling: Career assessment as compass, credential, process and empowerment. In J. Kapes, M. Mastie, & E. Whitfield (Eds.), *A counselor's guide to career assessment instruments* (3rd ed., pp. 31–40). Alexandria, VA: National Career Development Association.

Matkin, R. (1980). Legal and ethical issues in vocational assessment. *Vocational Evaluation and Work Adjustment Bulletin, 13,* 57–60.

Maze, M. (1984). How to select a computerized guidance system. *Journal of Counseling and Development, 63,* 158–161.

Maze, M., & Mayall, D. (1995). *The enhanced guide for occupational exploration* (2nd ed.). Indianapolis, IN: JIST.

McCarron, L., & Dial, J. (1973). *The McCarron-Dial evaluation system.* Dallas, TX: MDS.

McCarthy, H. (2010). A modest festschrift and insider perspective on Beatrice Wright's contribution to rehabilitation theory and practice. *Rehabilitation Counseling Bulletin, 54*(2), 67–81.

McClelland, D. (1973). Testing for competence rather than for intelligence. *American Psychologist, 28,* 1–14.

McCue, M. (1989). The role of assessment in the vocational rehabilitation of adults with specific learning disabilities. *Rehabilitation Counseling Bulletin, 31*(1), 18–35.

McDonald-Wilson, K., Rogers, E., & Anthony, W. (2001). Unique issues in assessing work function among individuals with psychiatric disabilities. *Journal of Occupational Rehabilitation, 11,* 217–232.

Menchetti, B. M., & Rusch, F. R. (1988). Vocational evaluation and eligibility for rehabilitation services. In P. Wehman & E. S. Moon (Eds.), *Vocational rehabilitation and supported employment* (pp. 79–90). Baltimore, MD: Brookes.

Merz, M. A., & Koch, L. C. (1999). Portfolios: A tool for including clients in assessment and planning. *National forum on issues in vocational assessment—The issues papers* (pp. 241–243). Menomonie, WI: Materials Development Center.

Miller, G. M. (1982). Deriving meaning from standardized tests: Interpreting test results to clients. *Measurement and Evaluation in Guidance, 15,* 87–93.

Miller, G., & deShazer, S. (1998). Have you heard the latest rumor about…? Solution-focused brief therapy as a rumor. *Family Process, 32,* 363–377.

Miller, W. R., & Rollnick, S. (2002). *Motivational interviewing* (2nd ed.). New York: Guilford Press.

Mooney, R., & Gordon, L. (1950). *Mooney problem checklist.* San Antonio, TX: Pearson.

Moore, D., & Keferl, J. (2008, Summer). Vocational rehabilitation and substance use disorders. *Journal of Applied Rehabilitation Counseling, 39*(2), 3–4.

Moore, M., Konrod, A., Yang, Y., Ng, E., & Doherty, A. (2011). The vocational well-being of workers with childhood onset of disability: Life satisfaction and perceived workplace discrimination. *Journal of Vocational Behavior.* doi:10.1016/ j.jvb. 2011.03.019

Morrison, J. (1993). *The first interview.* New York, NY: Guilford.

Moyers, T., Martin, T., Manuel, J., Miller, W., & Ernst, D. (2007). *Motivational interviewing integrity scale, 3.0.* Albuquerque, NM: Center on Alcoholism, Substance Abuse, and Addictions.

Mpofu, T., & Bishop, M. (2006). Value change and adjustment to disability: Implications for rehabilitation education, practice, and research. *Rehabilitation Education, 20,* 147–161.

Mpofu, E., & Oakland, T. (Eds.). (2010). *Rehabilitation and health assessment.* New York, NY: Springer.

Murray, S. (1990, Winter). Role of vocational evaluation in psychiatric rehabilitation. *Vocational Evaluation and Work Adjustment Bulletin,* pp. 149–153.

Musante, S. E. (1983, Spring). Issues relevant to the vocational evaluation of the traumatically head injured client. *Vocational Evaluation and Work Adjustment Bulletin,* pp. 45–68.

Myers, I. B., & Briggs, K. C. (1988). *Myers-Briggs type indicator.* Palo Alto, CA: CPP.

Naglieri, J. A. (2009). *The Naglieri nonverbal ability test–Second edition.* San Antonio, TX: Pearson.

National Computer Systems. (1989). *Professional assessment services.* Minneapolis, MN: Author.

Neff, W. (1966). Problems of work evaluation. *The Personnel and Guidance Journal, 44,* 682–688.

Nester, M. (1994). Psychometric testing and reasonable accommodation for persons with disabilities. In S. M. Bruyere & J. O'Keefe (Eds.), *Implications of the Americans with Disabilities Act for psychology* (pp. 25–35). New York, NY: Springer.

Neukrug, E. (1999). *The world of the counselor: An experiential workbook.* Pacific Grove, CA: Brooks/Cole.

New Hampshire Dept. of Education. (2010). *Transition planning: Helping students plan for the future.* Concord, NH: VR Administrative Offices, Regional office—http://www.ed.state.nh.us/vr.

News. (2004, August). U.S. Bureau of Labor Statistics publication, U.S. Department of Labor, Washington, DC.

Niles, S., & Harris-Bowlsbey, J. (2005). *Career development interventions in the 21st century.* Upper Saddle River, NJ: Pearson Prentice Hall.

Okun, B. G. (1987). *Effective helping: Interviewing and counseling techniques.* Monterey, CA: Brooks/Cole.

Olson, L. (1992). Use of vocational evaluation in the workers' compensation system. In J. M. Siefker (Ed.), *Vocational evaluation in private sector rehabilitation* (pp. 99–134). Menomonie, WI: University of Wisconsin–Stout.

Omizo, M. (1980). The differential aptitude tests as predictors of success in a high school for engineering program. *Educational Technology Measurement, 40,* 197–203.

Overton, T. (2012). *Assessing learners with special needs: An applied approach* (7th ed.). San Antonio, TX: Pearson.

Owings, S. (1992). Using vocational evaluation in determining employability, wage loss, lost earning capacity, and other aspects of expert witness work. In J. M. Siefker (Ed.), *Vocational evaluation in private sector rehabilitation* (pp. 169–194). Menomonie, WI: University of Wisconsin–Stout.

Owings, S., & Siefker, J. (1991, Fall). Criterion-referenced scoring vs. norming: A critical discussion. *Vocational Evaluation and Work Adjustment Bulletin,* pp. 109–111.

Pack-Brown, S., Thomas, T., & Seymour, J. (2008). Infusing professional ethics into counselor education programs: A multicultural/social justice perspective. *Journal of Counseling and Development, 86,* 296–302.

Paniagua, F. A. (1994). *Assessing and treating culturally diverse consumers.* Thousand Oaks, CA: Sage.

Parker, R. (2001). *Occupational aptitude survey and interest schedule–Third edition.* Austin, TX: PRO-ED.

Parker, R. M. (2008). Aptitude testing. In B. Bolton (Ed.), *Handbook of measurement and evaluation in rehabilitation* (4th ed., pp. 121–150). Austin, TX: PRO-ED.

Parker, R., Hansmann, S., & Schaller, J. (2010). Vocational assessment and disability. In E. M. Szymanski & R. M. Parker (Eds.), *Work and disability* (3rd ed., pp. 203–244). Austin, TX: PRO-ED.

Parker, R. M., & Schaller, J. (1996). Issues in vocational assessment and disability. In E. Szymanski & R. Parker (Eds.), *Work and disability* (pp. 127–164). Austin, TX: PRO-ED.

Parker, R. M., Szymanski, E. M., & Hanley-Maxwell, C. (1989). Ecological assessment in supported employment. *Journal of Applied Rehabilitation Counseling, 2,* 26–33.

Patterson, J. (2008). Assessment of work behavior. In B. Bolton & R. Parker (Eds.), *Handbook of measurement and evaluation in rehabilitation* (4th ed., pp. 309–335). Austin, TX: PRO-ED.

Payton, C. R. (1985). Addressing the special needs of minority women. *New Directions for Student Services, 29,* 75–90.

Peck, D. (2010, March 10). How a new joblessness era will transform America. *The Atlantic,* pp. 40–56.

Pekerti, A. (2008, June). The independent family-centric career: Career perspectives of the overseas Chinese in Indonesia. *Career Development Quarterly, 4,* 362–375.

Peterson, D., Mpofu, E., & Oakland, T. (2010). Concepts and models in disability, functioning, and health. In E. Mpofu & T. Oakland (Eds.), *Rehabilitation and health assessment* (pp. 3–26). New York, NY: Springer.

Phillips, J. (1978). Occupational interest inventories: An often untapped resource. *Journal of Applied Rehabilitation Counseling, 9,* 10–16.

Phillips, S. D., Bleustein, D. L., Jobin-Davis, K., & White, S. F. (2002). Preparation for the school-to-work transition: The views of high school students. *Journal of Vocational Behavior, 61*(2), 202–216.

Pichette, E. F., Accordino, M. P., Hamilton, M. R., Rosenthal, D. A., & Wilson, K. (2002, Spring/Summer). Susceptibility to racial and ethnic bias in intake interviews: Implications for vocational evaluators. *Vocational Evaluation and Work Adjustment Journal,* pp. 17–28.

Pickman, A. (1994). *The complete guide to outplacement counseling.* Hillsdale, NJ: Erlbaum.

Pierce, R. M., Cohen, M. R., Anthony, W. A., & Cohen, B. F. (1978). *The skills of career counseling.* Austin, TX: PRO-ED.

Pittenger, D. J. (1993, Fall). Measuring the MBTI and coming up short. *Journal of Career Planning and Employment,* 49–53.

Polinko, R. (1985). Working with the family: The acute phase. In M. Ylvisaker (Ed.), *Head injury rehabilitation: Children and adolescents* (pp. 91–116). Austin, TX: PRO-ED.

Ponterotto, J., Casas, J., Suzuki, L., & Alexander, C. (Eds.). (1995). *Handbook of multicultural counseling.* Thousand Oaks, CA: Sage.

Porfeli, E., & Skorikov, V. (2010). Specific and diverse career exploration during late adolescence. *Journal of Career Assessment, 18*(1), 46–58.

Power, P. W. (1988). An assessment approach to family intervention. In P. Power, A. Dell Orto, & M. Gibbons (Eds.), *Family interventions throughout chronic illness and disability* (pp. 5–223). New York, NY: Springer.

Power, P. W. (2011). *A guide to career management and programming for adults with disabilities: A 21st century perspective.* Austin, TX: PRO-ED.

Power, P. W., & Dell Orto, A. E. (1986). Families, illness & disability: The roles of the rehabilitation counselor. *Journal of Applied Rehabilitation Counseling, 17,* 41–44.

Power, P. W., & Dell Orto, A. E. (2004). *Families living with chronic illness and disability.* New York, NY: Springer.

Power, P. W., Dell Orto, A. E., & Gibbons, M. B. (1988). *Family interventions throughout chronic illness and disability.* New York, NY: Springer.

Prince, J. P., Most, R. B., & Silver, D. G. (2003). Self-help career assessment: Ethical and professional issues. *Journal of Career Assessment, 11,* 40–58.

Prince, J. P., Uemora, A. K., Chao, G. S., & Gonzales, G. M. (1992). *Using career interest inventories with multicultural consumers* (pp. 2–12, 26–31). Moravia, NY: Chronicle Guidance Publications.

Proctor, B., Prevatt, D., Adams, K., Hurst, A., & Petscher, Y. (2006). Study skills profiles of normal-achieving and academically-struggling college students. *Journal of College Student Development, 47*(1), 37–51.

Pruitt, W. A. (1986). *Vocational evaluation.* Menomonie, WI: Walt Pruitt.

Raven, J. C. (1986). *Raven's progressive matrices.* San Antonio, TX: Pearson.

Rayman, J. R. (1990, April). *Ethics in choosing and using assessment instruments.* Paper presented at the Maryland Career Development Association Conference, Columbia.

Rehabilitation Act of 1973, 29 U.S.C. § 701 *et seq.*

Rehabilitation Act Amendments of 1992, 29 U.S.C. § 701 *et seq.*

Reitan, R. M. (1993). *Halstead-Reitan neuropsychological test battery.* Tucson, AZ: Reitan Neuropsychology Laboratory/Press.

Roe, A., & Lunneborg, P. (1984). Personality development and career choice. In D. Brown & L. Brooks (Eds.), *Career choice and development* (2nd ed., pp. 68–101). San Francisco, CA: Jossey-Bass.

Roessler, R. (2002). Improving job tenure outcomes for people with disabilities: The 3M model. *Rehabilitation Counseling Bulletin, 45*(4), 207–212.

Roessler, R., & Bolton, B. (1987). *The employability maturity interview.* Fayetteville, AR: Arkansas Research and Training Center in Vocational Rehabilitation.

Roessler, R., & Rubin, S. (2006). *Case management and rehabilitation counseling: Procedures and techniques* (4th ed). Austin, TX: PRO-ED.

Rogan, P., & Hagner, D. (1990). Vocational evaluation in supported employment. *Journal of Rehabilitation, 56,* 45–51.

Rogers, E., Hursh, N., Kielhofner, G., & Spaniol, L. (1990). *Situational assessment: Scales to assess work adjustment and interpersonal skills.* Boston, MA: Center for Psychiatric Rehabilitation, Boston University.

Roid, G. (2003). *Stanford-Binet intelligence scale–Fifth edition.* Itasca, IL: Riverside.

Rojewski, J. W. (2002). Career assessment for adolescents with mild disabilities: Critical concerns for transition planning. *Career Development for Exceptional Individuals, 25,* 73–95.

Rokeach, M. (1973). *The nature of values.* New York, NY: Free Press.

Rorschach, H. J. (1942). *Psycho-diagnostics: A diagnostic test based on perception* (P. Lemkau & B. Kronenberg, Trans.). Berne: Huber (1st German ed. published 1921; U.S. distributor, Grune & Stratton).

Rosenberg, M. (1979). *Conceiving the self.* New York, NY: Basic Books.

Rotter, J., Lah, M., & Rafferty, T. (1992) *Rotter incomplete sentence blank–Second edition.* San Antonio, TX: Pearson.

Rounds, J. B., Jr., Henly, G. A., Dawis, R. V., Lofquist, L. H., & Weiss, D. J. (1981). *Manual for the Minnesota Importance Questionnaire: A measure of vocational needs and values.* Minneapolis, MN: Vocational Psychology Research, University of Minnesota.

Rowe, H. A. (1995). *Work readiness profile.* Camberwell, Victoria, Australia: Australian Council for Research Limited.

Rubin, S. E., & Porter, T. (1979). Rehabilitation counselor and vocational evaluator competencies. *Journal of Rehabilitation, 45,* 42–45.

Rubin, S. W., & Emener, W. G. (1979). Recent rehabilitation counselor role changes and role strain: A pilot investigation. *Journal of Applied Rehabilitation Counseling, 10,* 142–147.

Ruff, R., & Schraa, J. (2001). Neurological assessment. In B. Bolton (Ed.), *Handbook of measurement and evaluation in rehabilitation* (3rd ed., pp. 233–254). Gaithersburg, MD: Aspen.

Ruff, R., & Schraa, J. (2008). Neuropsychological assessment. In B. Bolton & R. Parker (Eds.), *Handbook of measurement and rehabilitation* (4th ed., pp. 283–306). Austin, TX: PRO-ED.

RUST Statement Revised. (1990). *Responsibilities of users of standardized tests.* Alexandria, VA: American Association for Counseling and Development.

Saladin, S. (2008). Assessment of individuals who are deaf or hard of hearing. In B. Bolton & R. Parker (Eds.), *Handbook of measurement and evaluation in rehabilitation* (4th ed., pp. 463–489). Austin, TX: PRO-ED.

Saladin, S., Parker, R., & Bolton, B. (2012), Assessment in rehabilitation counseling. In R. M. Parker & J. B. Patterson (Eds.), *Rehabilitation counseling: Basics and beyond* (5th ed., pp. 285–306). Austin, TX: PRO-ED.

Salomone, P. R. (1996). Career counseling and job placement: Theory and practice. In E. M. Szymanski & R. M. Parker (Eds.), *Work and disability* (pp. 365–415). Austin, TX: PRO-ED.

Salvia, J., & Ysseldyke, J. (1995). *Assessment* (6th ed.). Boston, MA: Houghton Mifflin.

Sampson, J., Dozier, V., & Colvin, G. (2011). Translating career theory to practice: The risk of unintentional social justice. *Journal of Counseling and Development, 89,* 326–337.

Sampson, J. P., Purgar, M. P., & Shy, J. D. (2003). Computer-based test interpretation in career assessment: Ethical and professional issues. *Journal of Career Assessment, 11*(1), 22–39.

Sanchez, I. (1981). *The California workers' compensation rehabilitation system.* New York, NY: Macmillan.

Sankovsky, R. (1969). *State of the art in vocational evaluation: Report of a national survey.* Pittsburgh, PA: University of Pittsburgh, School of Education.

Sarason, S. B. (1984). If it can be studied or developed, shouldn't it be? *American Psychologist, 39,* 477–485.

Satir, V. (1967). *Conjoint family therapy.* Palo Alto, CA: Science and Behavior Books.

Sattler, J. M. (1993). *Assessment of children* (3rd ed.). San Diego, CA: Jerome M. Sattler.

Saunders, J., & Leahy, M. (2010). Empirical influences on the 2010 Code of Professional Ethics for Rehabilitation counselors. *Rehabilitation Counseling Bulletin, 53*(4), 197–203.

Savickas, M. (1995). Constructivist counseling for career indecision. *The Career Development Quarterly, 43,* 363–373.

Savickas, M. (1998). Career style assessment and counseling. In T. Sweeney (Ed.), *Adlerian counseling: A practitioner's approach* (4th ed., pp. 329–359). Philadelphia, PA: Accelerated Development.

Savickas, M. (2012). Life design: A paradigm for career intervention in the 21st century. *Journal of Counseling and Development, 90,* 13–19.

Savickas, M., Nota, L., Rossier, J., Davwalder, J., Duarte, M., Guichard, J., . . . Vianon, A. (2009). Life designing: A paradigm for career construction in the 21st century. *Journal of Vocational Behavior, 75,* 239–250.

Sax, A. (1981). New VEWAA/Carf standards for work evaluation and adjustment. *Vocational Evaluation and Work Adjustment Bulletin, 14,* 141–142.

Sax, A. B., & Pell, K. C. (1985, Summer). A primer on tools of evaluation. *Vocational Evaluation and Work Adjustment Bulletin,* pp. 57–60.

Saxon, J. P., & Spitznagel, R. J. (1995, Fall). Transferable skills and abilities profile: An economical assessment approach in the vocational placement process. *Vocational Evaluation and Work Adjustment Bulletin,* pp. 61–67.

Schalock, R. C., & Karan, O. C. (1979). Relevant assessment: The interaction between evaluation and training. In G. T. Bellamy, G. O'Connor, & O. Karan (Eds.), *Vocational rehabilitation of severely handicapped persons* (pp. 33–54). Baltimore, MD: University Park Press.

Schlenoff, F. (1974). Considerations in administering intelligence tests to the physically disabled. *Rehabilitation Literature, 35,* 362–363.

Scherer, M., & Glueckauf, R. (2005). Assisting the benefits of assistive technologies for activities and participation. *Rehabilitation Psychology, 50*(2), 138–139.

Scherer, M., & Sax, C. (2010). Measures of assistive technology predisposition and use. In E. Mpofu & T. Oakland (Eds.). *Rehabilitation and health assessment* (pp. 229–254). New York, NY: Springer.

Schlossberg, N. (1984). *Counseling adults in transition.* New York, NY: Springer.

Schuster, D., & Smith, F. (1994). The Interdisciplinary Council on Vocational Evaluation and Assessment: Building consensus through communication, advocacy, and common goals. *Vocational Evaluation and Work Adjustment Bulletin, 27*(4), 111–114.

Scissions, E. H. (1993). *Counseling for results: Principles and practices of helping.* Pacific Grove, CA: Brooks/Cole.

Scott, K. (1998, May). The psychological emergency of new onset physical disability and deformity. *Jacksonville Medicine,* pp. 1–8.

Sedlacek, W. (1994). Issues in advancing diversity through assessment. *Journal of Counseling and Development, 72,* 549–553.

Seligman, L. (1994). *Developmental career counseling and assessment* (2nd ed.). Thousand Oaks, CA: Sage.

Shallcross, L. (2010). A voyage of self-discovery. *Counseling Today, 52,* 32–38.

Sharf, R. (2002). *Applying career development theory to counseling.* Pacific Grove, CA: Brooks/Cole.

Sherman, J. S., & Robinson, N. (Eds.). (1982). *Ability testing of handicapped people: Dilemma for government, science, and the public.* Washington, DC: National Academy Press.

Shertzer, B., & Linden, J. (1979). *Fundamentals of individual appraisal.* Boston: Houghton Mifflin.

Shipley, W., Gruber, G., Martin, T., & Klein, A. (2009). *Shipley Institute of Living scale–Second edition.* Los Angeles, CA: Western Psychological Services.

Siders, J., & Wharton, J. (1982). The relationship of individual ability and IEP goal statements. *Elementary School Guidance Counseling, 16,* 187–192.

Siefker, J. M. (1996). *Tests and test use in vocational evaluation and assessment.* Menomonie, WI: University of Wisconsin–Stout.

Sikula, L. (1994). *Changing careers: Steps to success.* Pacific Grove, CA: Brooks/Cole.

Simon, S. B., Howe, L. W., & Kirschenbaum, H. J. (1972). *Values clarification: A handbook of practical strategies for teachers and students.* New York, NY: Hart.

Simpson, R. G., & Umbach, B. T. (1989, July/August/September). Identifying and providing vocational services for adults with specific learning disabilities. *Journal of Rehabilitation,* pp. 49–54.

Sinick, D. (1969). Training, placement and follow-up. In D. Molikin & H. Rusalem (Eds.), *Vocational rehabilitation of the disabled* (pp. 185–199). New York, NY: New York University Press.

Sink, J., & Field, T. (1981). *Vocational assessment planning and jobs.* Athens, GA: Udare Service Bureau.

Sink, J., & King, W. (1978, July). The vocational specialists: Preparation for court testimony—Fact or fantasy? *Careers,* pp. 28–32.

Sitlington, P. L., Neubert, D. A., Bejun, W., Lombard, R. C., & Leconte, P. J. (1996). *Assess for success: Handbook on transition assessment.* Reston, VA: The Council for Exceptional Children.

Sitlington, P. L., Neubert, D. A., & Leconte, P. J. (1997). Transition assessment: The position paper of the Division on Career Development and Transition. *Career Development of Exceptional Individuals, 20*(2), 69–79.

Skiba, R. J., Knesting, K., & Bush, L. D. (2002). Culturally competent assessment: More than non-biased tests. *Journal of Child and Family Studies, 11*(1), 61–78.

Slosson, R. L., Nicholson, C. L., & Hibpshman, T. H. (1990). *Slosson intelligence test– Revised.* East Aurora, NY: Slosson Educational Publications.

Smart, J. (2005). The promise of the International Classification of Functioning, Disability and Health (ICF). *Rehabilitation Education, 19,* 191–199.

Smart, J., & Smart, D. (1992). Curriculum changes in multicultural rehabilitation. *Rehabilitation Education, 6,* 105–122.

Smith, F. G., Lombard, R., Neubert, D., Leconte, P., Rothenbacher, C., & Sitlington, P. (1995). Position statement of the Interdisciplinary Council on Vocational Evaluation and Assessment. *Journal for Vocational Special Needs Education, 17,* 41–42.

Spizlberger, C., Gorsuch, R., & Lushens, R. (1970). *Manual for the State-Trait Anxiety Inventory.* Palo Alto, CA: Counseling Psychologists Press.

Spokane, A. R. (1991). *Career intervention.* Englewood Cliffs, NJ: Prentice Hall.

Stano, J. F. (2004). Test review. *Rehabilitation Counseling Bulletin, 48*(1), 56–57.

Stensrud, R., Millington, M., & Gilbride, D. (1997). Professional practice: Placement. In D. Maki & T. Riggar (Eds.), *Rehabilitation counseling* (pp. 197–213). New York, NY: Springer.

Stewart, W. E., & Vander Kolk, C. J. (1989). Instructional model for assessment of injured persons. *Rehabilitation Education, 3,* 123–135.

St. George, D. (2010, July 25). Dealing with a double blow. *The Washington Post,* pp. C1–C4.

Strong, E. K., Hansen, J. C., & Campbell, D. P. (1994). *Strong interest inventory.* Palo Alto, CA: Consulting Psychologists Press.

Stuart, S. (2008). *Brighter outcomes: Getting started making connections.* Williamsburg, VA: Parent Resource Center, Williamsburg–James City County Public Schools.

Sue, D. W., & Sue, D. (1977). Barriers to effective cross-cultural counseling. *Journal of Counseling Psychology, 24*(5), 420–429.

Sue, D. W., & Sue, D. (1999). *Counseling the culturally different: Theory and practice* (3rd ed.). New York, NY: Wiley.

Sundberg, N. D. (1977). *Assessment of persons.* Englewood Cliffs, NJ: Prentice Hall.

Super, D. E. (1957). *The psychology of careers.* New York, NY: Harper & Row.

Super, D. E. (1990). A lifespan, life-space approach to career development. In D. Brown, L. Brooks, & Associates (Eds.), *Career choice and development: Applying contemporary theories to practice* (2nd ed., pp. 197–261). San Francisco, CA: Jossey-Bass.

Supported employment (Rehabilitation Research and Training Center Brief). (1988). Richmond, VA: Virginia Commonwealth University.

Sutton, J. (1985). The need for family involvement in client rehabilitation. *Journal of Applied Rehabilitation Counseling, 16,* 42–45.

Suzuki, L. A., & Kugler, J. G. (1995). Intelligence and personality assessment. In J. G. Ponterotto, J. M. Casas, L. A. Suzuki, & C. M. Alexander (Eds.), *Handbook of multicultural counseling* (pp. 493–515). Thousand Oaks, CA: Sage.

Taber, B., Hartung, P., Briddick, H., Briddick, W., & Rehfuss, M. (2011). Career style interview: A contextualized approach to career counseling. *The Career Development Quarterly, 59*(3), 274–287.

Talent Assessment, Inc. (1985). *Talent assessment program.* Jacksonville, FL: Author.

Tarvydas, V., Cattone, R., & Saunders, J. (2010). A new ethics code as a tool for innovations in ethical practice. *Rehabilitation Counseling Bulletin, 53*(4), 195–196.

Thirtieth Institute on Rehabilitation Issues. (2003). *A new paradigm for vocational evaluation.* Hot Springs, AR: University of Arkansas CURRENTS.

Thomas, S. (1991). *Vocational evaluation and traumatic brain injury: A procedural manual.* Menomonie, WI: Material Development Center.

Thomas, C., Curtis, R., & Shippen, M. (2011). Counselors', rehabilitation providers', and teachers' perceptions of mental and physical disabilities. *Journal of Counseling and Development, 89,* 182–188.

Thorndike, R. L., Hagen, E. P., & Sattler, J. M. (1986). *Stanford-Binet intelligence scale–Fourth edition.* Chicago, IL: Riverside.

Thorndike, R., & Thorndike-Christ, T. (2008). Reliability. In B. Bolton & R. Parker (Eds.). *Handbook of measurement and evaluation in rehabilitation* (pp. 33–55). Austin, TX: PRO-ED.

Tien, H. (2007). Practice and research in career counseling and development–20006. *Career Development Quarterly, 56,* 98–140.

Tracey, T. (2010). Interest assessment using new technology. *Journal of Career Assessment, 18*(9), 336–344.

Tyler, L. (1984). What tests don't measure. *Journal of Counseling and Development, 63,* 48–50.

Tymofienich, M., & Leroux, J. (2000). Counselors' competencies in using assessment. *Measurement and Evaluation in Counseling and Development, 33,* 50–59.

University of Phoenix Research Institute. (2011, July/August). *The Atlantic.*

U.S. Bureau of Statistics. (2004). *News.* Washington, DC: U.S. Government Printing Office.

U.S. Census Bureau (2010). U.S. projections. Retrieved from http://wwwquickfacts.censusgov/fd/states/00000.html

U.S. Congress, House. *Rehabilitation Act Amendments of 1986.* 99th Congress, 2nd Session, October 2, 1986. Report 99-955.

U.S. Department of Education, Rehabilitation Services Administration. (1985). *Program policy directive RSA-PPD-85-3,* January 24th.

U.S. Department of Labor. (1977). *Dictionary of occupational titles* (4th ed.). Washington, DC: U.S. Government Printing Office.

U.S. Department of Labor. (1981). *Selected characteristics of occupations defined in the Dictionary of Occupational Titles.* Washington, DC: U.S. Government Printing Office.

U.S. Department of Labor. (1991). *Dictionary of occupational titles* (4th ed., revised). Washington, DC: U.S. Government Printing Office.

U.S. Department of Labor. (2010–2011). *Occupational outlook handbook.* Washington, DC: U.S. Government Printing Office.

U.S. Technology-Related Assistance of Individuals with Disabilities Act of 1998. Pub. L. 100-407, 29 U.S.C. 2201 et seq.

Vandergoot, D. (1982, November). Work readiness assessment. *Rehabilitation Counseling Bulletin,* pp. 84–87.

Vandergoot, D., Swirsky, J., & Rice, K. (1982). Using occupational information in rehabilitation counseling. *Rehabilitation Counseling Bulletin, 26,* 94–100.

Vander Kolk, C. J. (1995). Future methods and practice in vocational assessment. *Journal of Applied Rehabilitation Counseling, 26*(2), 45–50.

Virginia Commonwealth University. (1989). *Return to work following traumatic brain injury.* Richmond, VA: Rehabilitation Research and Training Center on Supported Employment.

Vocational Evaluation and Work Adjustment Association. (1975). *Vocational evaluation project final report.* Washington, DC: Author.

Vocational Research Institute. (1989). *The APTICOM aptitude test battery.* Philadelphia, PA: Author.

Vocational Research Institute. (2010). *Career scope, version 10.* Philadelphia, PA: Author.

Vogel, S. A. (1989). Adults with language learning disabilities. *Rehabilitation Education, 3,* 77–90.

Wagner, C. C., & McMahon, B. T. (2004). Motivational interviewing and rehabilitation counseling practice. *Rehabilitation Counseling Bulletin, 47*(3), 152–161.

Walk, T. E. (1985, Spring). A review of commercial vocational evaluation systems and disability groups. *Vocational Evaluation and Work Adjustment Bulletin,* pp. 29–34.

Walls, R. T., Zane, T., & Werner, T. J. (1979). *The vocational behavior checklist* (Experimental ed.). Dunbar, WV: West Virginia Research and Training Center.

Walsh, W. B., & Betz, N. E. (1995). *Tests and assessment* (3rd ed.) Englewood Cliffs, NJ: Prentice Hall.

Wechsler, D. (1981). *Manual for the Wechsler Adult Intelligence Scale–Revised* (WAIS-R). San Antonio, TX: Psychological Corp.

Wechsler, D. (2008). *Wechsler adult intelligence scale–Fourth edition.* San Antonio, TX: Pearson.

Weinstein, H. (1983). Transferable skills analysis in the rehabilitation process. *Rehabilitation Forum, 9,* 25–27.

Welch, M., & Condon, D. (2011). *Ability to work assessment.* http://www.welchcondon.com

West-Olatunji, C. (2009, April). African Americans. In J. Christenson (Ed.), Cultural communications [Special issue]. *Counseling Today,* 32–33.

Whiston, S. C. (2000). *Principles and applications of assessment in counseling.* Belmont, CA: Brooks/Cole/Thomas.

Whitehead, D. (2003, December). *Rehabilitation counselors' perceived competence working with African Americans and other culturally diverse consumers with mental illness.* Unpublished doctoral dissertation, University of Maryland, College Park.

Wiger, D., & Huntley, D. (2002). *Essentials of interviewing.* New York, NY: Wiley.

Wilkinson, G., & Robertson, G. (2006). *Wide range achievement test–Fourth edition.* Lutz, FL: PAR.

Wintergreen-Orchard House. (1998). *Major decisions: A guide to technical, trade, and business schools.* Itasca, IL: Author.

Wollack, S., Goodale, J. G., Wijting, J. P., & Smith, P. C. (1976). *Survey of work values.* Bowling Green, OH: Bowling Green State University.

Workman, E. (1983). Vocational rehabilitation in the private, profit-making sector. In E. Pan, T. Backer, & C. Vash (Eds.), *Annual review of rehabilitation* (pp. 292–321). New York, NY: Springer.

World Health Organization. (1980). ICIDH: *International classification of impairments, disabilities and handicaps: A manual of classification relating to the consequences of disease.* Geneva, Switzerland: Author.

World Health Organization. (2001). *ICF: International Classification of Functioning, Disability and Health.* Geneva, Switzerland: Author.

Wright, G. (1980). *Total rehabilitation.* Boston, MA: Little, Brown.

Wright, G. N., & Fraser, R. T. (1976). *Improving manpower utilization: The Rehabilitation Task Performance Evaluation Scale.* Madison, WI: University of Wisconsin.

Zadny, J., & James, L. (1977). Time spent on placement. *Rehabilitation Counseling Bulletin, 321,* 31–35.

Zeigler, E. A. (1987, January/February/March). Spouses of persons who are brain injured: Overlooked victims. *Journal of Rehabilitation,* pp. 50–53.

Ziezula, F. R. (Ed.). (1986). *Assessment of hearing-impaired people: A guide for selecting psychological, educational, and vocational tests.* Washington, DC: Gallaudet University Press.

Zuniga, R., & Fischer, J. (2010). Emotional intelligence and attitudes toward people with disabilities: A comparison between two cultures. *Journal of Applied Rehabilitation Counseling, 41*(1), 12–15.

Zunker, V. (2006). *Career counseling: A holistic approach* (7th ed.). Pacific Grove, CA: Brooks/Cole.

Zytowski, D. G. (1965). Avoidance behavior in vocational motivation. *The Personnel and Guidance Journal, 43,* 746–750.

# Author Index

Subject Index